# THE AUTHOR OF LOVE

## Understanding a Misunderstood God

JOC ANDERSON, PsyD.

*Second Edition- August 13, 2013*



*Website contact: www.docjocanderson.com Email: docjoc316@aol.com*



*WestBow Press books may be ordered through booksellers or by contacting:*

*WestBow Press*
*A Division of Thomas Nelson*
*1663 Liberty Drive*
*Bloomington, IN 47403*
*www.westbowpress.com*
*1-(866) 928-1240*



*ISBN: 978-1-4497-0802-3 (sc)*
*ISBN: 978-1-4497-0804-7 (dj)*
*ISBN: 978-1-4497-0803-0 (e)*

*Library of Congress Control Number: 2011928112*

*Printed in the United States of America*

*WestBow Press rev. date: 8/13/2013*

# PREFACE

Just what the world needs….yet another devotional book. Ah, but this one is different. I'm sure you've heard that before. But, before I get into a discussion as what sets this devotional from so many others, allow please a moment's digression. (They'll be more than a few digressions call them, once we get going. Hopefully, they'll add interest.)

Perhaps ten or so years ago (my mother left us in 2007), my mother had just finished reading a devotional when she asked me to explain to her what she'd just read. What she was having difficulty grasping was the author's notion of a vengeful God. Back in the "Ozzie and Harriet/Father Knows Best:" days, when a kid stepped out of line, the most oft-repeated phrase he was apt to hear was: "God will punish you for that." It's a little wonder that many of us grew up with the perception that God is, if nothing else, sheriff, posse and lord (with a small "l", of course) high executioner.

I explained to Mother that what the author was saying was that even a loving God has boundaries and limits. The author contended that there would ultimately come a day when God would lose patience with humankind, much as had occurred in the days of Noah, just prior to the flood. Mother pondered my response for a brief moment and replied: "Hindi ganyan ang Dios," which is Filipino (Tagalog) for: "God is not that way." Without taking a breath, she added: "I wish someone would write a book which reflects the true essence of God." "The true nature of God," she insisted, "is one of love, NOT of vindictiveness."

And so I began to ponder the commonly-held notion of a judgmental God versus what I and a good many others are convinced is a more appropriate depiction, and that is of a God who is at once demanding and caring – whose demands are a reflection of His concern for those He created in His own image and whose caring is emblematic of His love for those same beings. This devotional, therefore, is the result of mother's determination that the truth be told, as well as MY OWN personal walk with God, that it is about time that someone present a more accurate depiction of God.

How well do we really know God? Some of these very questions are raised in the Book of Job. "After the Lord had said these things to Job, he said to Eliphaz the Temanite, "I am angry with you and your two friends because you have not spoken of me what is right, as my servant Job has." Job 42:7. Can you imagine a loving God being angry because His character was maligned? I think we all have had similar experiences: people misrepresenting our character. (More on this subject matter in the devotional).

Have the authors in the Old Testament spoken wrongly about God's character. Did He favor the Israelites over the other nations? If so, why? In the New Testament the first five authors shares with us a Savior who is called Immanuel (God with us). This God is named Jesus. We are introduced to Him in the innocence of His infancy. He matures into what those of His time might have regarded as a rather ordinary man. His style and method, however, puzzled His generation. He goes against the grain of conventional love. He rebukes hypocrisy and pharisaic love. He tells a perfect law abider to sell all his earthly possessions and follow Him. On the surface, certainly, this would appear to be a rather strange way in which to display love and affection.

Then comes the God in the book of Revelation who promises judgment and death to the unbelieving. Those condemned to damnation will be thrown in the "lake of fire" with the devil and his followers. It's a dire predicament for those who don't make the grade in God's kingdom. The notion of a God of this kind is, to say the least, unnerving. So, what are we to believe? How do we navigate our way through the religious doctrine of eras gone by? The answer is not as complex as it might appear. God knew the best way to express who He is and His love was through His Son. God actually gave us Himself disguised as an innocent, vulnerable and harmless baby.

Who is Jesus, the Son of God? Perhaps the single verse that best characterizes how God loves us in human language is found in I Corinthians 13: 1-13 "If I speak in the tongues of men and of angels, but have not love, I am only a resounding gong or a clanging cymbal(if you've ever heard a gong or cymbal played by itself, it's a rather irritating sound).

The fact is that we are not a faultless people, and there are likely none of us who can live up to this definition of love. Many have tried, and even the rich young man managed to keep all of the commandments. Anyone who can keep even one of the commandments should be commended. But was his keeping of the commandments strictly a clanging cymbal? On our own, we all fall a bit short with respect to the commandment of love. No human measures up to the commandment of love, but we have a Savior who can and did. He is the Author of Love. Jesus not only talked and walked love, but He lived it. He is, after all, the Author of Love.

God cannot govern His universe in any other way but through love. Love is the foundation of who He is. He was not nor will ever be a clanging cymbal. Whenever you read a verse that condemns a Sabbath breaker or an addict or a liar or an adulterer or a sinner or a homosexual to death then you have come across a resounding gong or clanging cymbal god. The list of what man condemns in the Bible is endless. Remember that is what man deems an abomination to God. We are all sinners but amazingly God never condemned a sinner. "**For God did not send His Son into the world to condemn the world, but to save the world through him**." John 3: 17. Can you be merciful to "those people?" Would you give up your life for them? I know this a hard thing to even say let alone do. God thought you were worth it. His whole essence is love. God said everything in your life is summed up in this one rule: "Love your neighbor as yourself." "Love does no harm to its neighbor. Therefore Love is the fulfillment of the law." Romans, 13:9 & 10. Whether we feel like it or not, God has commanded us to love our neighbor as ourselves. We can achieve that through His Spirit in us.

**God's first choice, after His Son, in revealing His love to you and me is through you and me. "Dear friends, let us love one another, for love comes from God. Everyone who loves has been born of God and knows God. Whoever does not love does not know God, because God is Love. This is how God showed his love among us; He sent his one and only Son into the world that we might live through him. This is love; not that we loved God, but that he loved us and sent his Son as an atoning sacrifice for our sins. Dear friends, since God so loved us, we also ought to love one another. No one has ever seen God; but if we love one another, God lives in us and his love is made complete in us. We know that we live in him and he in us, because he has given us of his Spirit. And we have seen and testify that the Father has sent his Son to be the Savior of the world. If anyone acknowledges that Jesus is the Son of God, God lives in him and he in God. And so we know and rely on the love God has for us. God is love. Whoever lives in love lives in God, and God in him. In this way, love is made complete among us so that we will have confidence on the day of judgment, because in this world we are like him. There is no fear in love. But perfect love drives out fear, because fear has to do with punishment. The one who fears is not made perfect in love. We love because he first loved us. If anyone says "I love God," yet hates his brother, he is a liar. For anyone who does not love his brother, whom he has seen, cannot love God, whom he has not seen. And he has given us this command: Whoever loves God must also love his brother."** I John 4: 7-21.

**Do you know God? Do you love God? Do you hate your neighbor but love God? You have read the answers to these questions. You want to follow God. Heed to His command: "Whoever loves God must also love his brother." That includes those you hate and despise as well as your enemy. Not any easy concept to hear, let alone follow. But even God provided a remedy for such thinking. He said He will send the Spirit to reside in you. That is how you will love like God. Isn't our God wonderful! God's love can only be complete when it is reciprocated. Whatever love you have, that love is not complete until that love is reciprocated.**

Remember, **Love is a person. It is not things, status or wealth. Love is God.** You may have faith, hope and love, "But **the greatest of these is…God (love)." I Corinthians 13:13**

# A FEW QUESTIONS IF YOU WILL

This book, not surprisingly, will deal with a good many issues that have to do with faith. Sadly, more and more of us seem to be giving up on faith and giving up on God. When asked why they have strayed, the most typical response is something to the effect that the faith of their fathers leaves too many important questions unanswered. We are a people who demand answers to the questions that most concern us, and, when the answers are not forthcoming, we tend to move on to something else. Some maintain that this is why church attendance (with some notable exceptions) is diminishing in our country.

Throughout this text, we will raise a good many questions. A number of them are somewhat controversial. It is NOT our intention to render judgment with respect to controversial matters. Rather, it is our hope that, in framing the questions and, objectively as possible, presenting both sides, we provide the reader with the foundation for further consideration of the issue. I feel ever so strongly, however, that treating the most difficult issues serves to sustain our faith, not undermine it. If you are to sustain your own beliefs, you would be ill-advised to pretend that these questions have not crossed your mind. Moreover, as you encounter others whose inability to deal with these issues has compromised their own belief system, you will be able to assist them in dealing with these important matters. These questions are not new. The sooner we confront them and deal with them to our satisfaction the greater your walk with God will be secured.

**We have a duty, call it, to spread God's love, and one way to do that is to help others understand the Author of Love. The personal time you spent with God is highly personal. These questions and issues you struggle with will be interspersed throughout the devotionals. At the conclusion of these devotionals, you will have an opportunity to take a "Love Quotient" (L.Q.) test to see how deep is your love. The questions, answers and key are all at the end of this book. I welcome your comments. "Come let us reason together."**

## **HAPPY NEW YEAR GOD** | JANUARY 1

*"In the beginning God created the heavens and the earth."* Genesis 1:1

---

Happy New Year! Are you ready to tackle another list of resolutions? Each year, newspapers across the land suggest New Year's resolutions. Typically, they deal with becoming physically fit, reducing stress, getting organized, gaining financial security, finding a new hobby, getting along better with co-workers, family or friends, learning to forgive, and the like. Have you made your resolution list?

In a recent "Dear Abby" column, a writer tells of her failure to adhere to her vow to lose weight by swearing off chocolate. She soon discovered, by evening, she would feel tired and depressed. One evening, she ate an entire chocolate bar with almonds. She felt disgusted and defeated. Abby suggested that she stop beating up on herself. If she slips up again, she should not concede defeat, and if she succeeds, she should praise herself? Does that sound familiar? Do you struggle to keep even one resolution before the year is up? You're not alone.

**The fact is that there is one all-encompassing resolution that we are all capable of achieving, and that is to KNOW GOD.** God tells us that His yoke is easy and His burden is light. Resolve not to strive for things and personal achievements, resolve instead to get to know God. He is the answer to all your resolutions. All your resolutions are in Him. For once in your life, try God, all that you've tried have ended in "clanging cymbals." **Won't you give God a chance this year? I guarantee you won't regret it.**

Remember, in the beginning, God created the heavens and the earth. Just as our world was dark and void, God created light and brought about a new earth verdant and lush with everything imaginable for your pleasure. God saw what He created and declared it good, beautiful and perfect. God can do the same for you beginning right now. It doesn't matter what your background or condition is. Whatever it is you are struggling to resolve, the answer can only be found in God. Trust God to help you right now. Allow this very same God to create a new you. He will create a new heart and spirit within you. Invite His Spirit to dwell in you right now.

To resolve to know God you must first trust in Him and His word. Second, walk in faith and not by sight. Third, be receptive to His Spirit. He also speaks through other godly people. **You may not feel open to His Spirit but you MUST have a RECEPTIVE heart. Without His Spirit in you, you cannot know God.** Thank God for this New Year and all of the promise He offers; for God, **the Author of Love is the ultimate grantor of New Year's and all other resolutions.** Wish God a Happy New Year and get ready to experience the greatest of these, His Love.

## A VERY GOOD GOD | JANUARY 2

*"God saw all that He had made and it was very good." Genesis: 1: 31*

In what was otherwise a void and a darkness; God's love was evident, even before He created light. The God of Love sees goodness in all of us. When we were created in His image, we were also void, empty and dark when He touched the dirt and dust with His hand. God then fashioned a body and a face, and He breathed into that face's nostrils the gift of life. You were right then and there declared made in God's image. All the fruit of the Spirit was imbued in your soul. Your characteristics and personality traits that God was were bestowed on you. Afterward, He declared His crowning achievement not only good but VERY good.

This is the only time in the last verse of Genesis chapter one when the Author of Love uses the word VERY before good. During the first five days of God's creation He would declare each day "good" but on the sixth day He declared it "VERY" good. The dictionary defines "very" as an adjective from the Latin root word verax meaning truthful. The dictionary further adds secondary meaning of exact, precise, and absolute used as an intensive. God was indeed excited by His creation of man – not unlike the emotions we experience when our first-born is delivered. Although the child is covered in blood and mucous, we immediately see beyond this; for we know that we are, at that moment, a party to our God's handiwork. God was overjoyed in creating us. He created us for His pleasure. We are a very great delight to Him. After all, He is our Father, our Parent.

Unfortunately, the image we inherited from God was marred by sin. Are you feeling void, empty, unloved, lifeless and discounted? Are you going through a crisis that appears insurmountable? Are things looking bleak and hopeless for you right now? Remember this verse and creation day. **Just as the spirit was hovering over the waters of the earth – empty, dark and formless, like maybe your life right now, God's Spirit is always near you. Even when you do not see evidences of His Spirit, do not lose faith. God is with you.** God sees beyond the emptiness of your life. He is a perfect and complete God. The Author of Love can make something out of nothing of your life today. You too can be complete in His love. You may not see it right now or in your life time but rest assured God will deliver.

Believe in Him. He wants you to trust Him no matter what your circumstances may be this moment. His love is what governs His actions for you. When He makes all things good in your life right now remember **He will also declare them VERY good. He is the "VERY EXTREMELY" good GOD.**

## A SPECIAL DAY TO REMEMBER | JANUARY 3

*"By the seventh day God had finished the work He had been doing; so on the seventh day He rested from all His work. And God blessed the seventh day and made it holy, because on it He rested from all the work of creating that He had done."* Genesis 2: 3

---

After a week of labor God decided to rest on the seventh day. It kind of makes you wonder: Does God need to rest? Does He get fatigued? After all, He is God. Why would God need to rest? Rest means a relief from work. God ended six days of work and declared the seventh day as a day of rest. God not only rested on the seventh day but pronounced it holy. God is Love and He is also holy. God says, "Remember the Sabbath Day to keep it Holy." The Creator of all things has set aside a day as Holy because He is Holy. In the Lord's Prayer, Jesus Himself said, "Hallowed be thy name." Something that is hallowed has been set aside to be venerated. This is a sacred day to honor. It is a true reflection of the character and nature of God, holy and pure.

It's astounding how marriages or relationships can be fractured by being remiss of an anniversary, Valentine's Day, Christmas or birthday. I remember the first year my brother celebrated Valentine's Day with his wife. He totally was negligence. He took for granted Valentine's Day and did nothing for her. His wife was so hurt because she didn't receive even a card or flowers. She said "just because we're married doesn't mean you stop expressing your "courtship moves." He felt remorseful. He learned a valuable lesson. He never forgot another Valentine's Day or a special occasion of theirs and he was pleased to show his love for her especially when it counted most. You too can treat God's day as incidental. God does not lose out as much as you do.

God loves and cares for you seven days-a-week. He doesn't stop loving us on the seventh day. **Your salvation is not mandated on Sabbath keeping.** He maintains His "courtship moves" to us every moment of our lives. **Everything God does or sanctioned is motivated by His desire to express His care and love for us.** He loves us whether we remember His day or not. We can reciprocate our love for Him by honoring the special day He chose for us to worship Him. We can show our love to Him any day of the week. But one day He has set aside and pronounced it special and holy, the seventh day. There is something very sacred that God wants to give you on the Sabbath day. He wants you to be happy. He desires for you to experience His love. Unless you worship Him on that day, you will miss out on the essence of who HE is. **When you truly KNOW GOD, you will know why He set aside a holy day just for you.** He sanctified a very special day for you to remember and experience not only the Author of the Sabbath but the Author of Love- love for you.

## A HELPMATE | JANUARY 4

*"So the man gave names to all the livestock, the birds of the air and all the beasts of the field. But for Adam no suitable helper was found. So the Lord God caused the man to fall into a deep sleep; and while he was sleeping, He took one of the man's ribs and closed up the place with flesh. The Lord God made a woman from the rib He had taken out of the man and He brought her to the man." Genesis 2: 20 & 21*

---

After creating Adam, the Lord God knew that Adam was alone. He said, "It is not good that the man should be alone; I will make him a help meet for him." Our perfect God provided a perfect partner for Adam. We as human beings were never made to be solitary creatures. We were made in the image of God. God is not alone. He is social. He made everything so wonderful and good so we could share it with one another. God is more than a sharer of good things, He is a giver. God's kingdom is not to be hoarded and enjoyed in solitary fashion. Without another person to share the Garden of Eden, its delights would have been created for naught.

It is noteworthy that, in creating Eve, God took, not of Adam's brain but of the side of his flesh. **Clearly, God never intended for man to be the head and woman to be subservient but rather for them to be equal partners. Just as the Father, the Son and Holy Spirit are all One in purpose, so did God want our relationship to mirror their relationship.** The derivative in Hebrew of help meet is "ezer" and "K'enegdo." Ezer means "strength and savior." K'enegdo means "exactly corresponding to," like when you look at a mirror. God knew what He was doing when He created Eve. She possessed the qualities, responsibilities and attributes that Adam lacked. Together they were a perfect fit. Women are "savior" to men. Eve played a significant role in the salvation of Adam and mankind. Just as love between two people is nothing without each other's reciprocity, we are nothing without Christ.

E.G. White in Patriarchs and Prophets p. 17 says "A part of man, bone of his bone, and flesh of his flesh, she was his second self, showing the close union and the affectionate attachment that should exist in this relation." The union between Adam and Eve reflected the oneness that was shared with God, His Father and the Spirit. God can provide you a helpmate. He knows your every need even before you ask. Ask Him. But be prepared to love that person as you love yourself.

**As women today demand equal rights, we need to remember that this was God's plan from the beginning. As God dealt with us in love, let your motives and actions become one with the mind of Christ when you express love for your helpmate or any other person for that matter.**

## I PROMISE | JANUARY 5

*"And I will put enmity between you and the woman, and between your offspring and hers; he will crush your head, and you will strike his heel." Genesis 3: 15*

---

At the wedding of my close friends, the bridal couple, as is the custom, exchanged vows of love and fidelity…'til death do them part – the latter, at least in theory. My friends were quick to start a family, and as the family grew and began to mature, it became apparent that the groom longed for the single life he had abandoned on his wedding day. At first, it was just one supposedly inadvertent tryst, but, before long, he was observing those wedding vows more in the breach than in the practice. Not surprisingly, his wife caught on and filed for divorce.

My friend broke his promise to be faithful to his wife. Adam and Eve broke their promise to be loyal to their Maker. They decided they would listen to the serpent in the tree and trust his word than rely on the God who was their creator. Even before Adam and Eve's downfall, even before they were created, God knew they would falter. God made a plan with His Son to redeem us back to Him. God would send His Son, Jesus to receive the punishment of their sin. Jesus took it upon himself to go through death for our sake that we might have not only eternal life but restore the relationship that was fractured by our infidelity.

You may be a recipient of a broken promise or you may be the one who broke a promise of fidelity, regardless of your situation, don't fret and fear for the God of faithful promises has come through. The Author of Love took the promise He made to all of us in Genesis 3: 15 and kept it. **This verse is the greatest hope and expression of love God has promised us.** Whether you are a recipient of a broken promise or the culprit of a broken promise, God has more than made up for all your failures. His Son paid the price for all of us. We were redeemed by the shedding of His blood on the cross. And He promised to eventually crush the serpent (Satan) forever. **You can have eternal life right now.**

**God may be the recipient of your broken promise to Him but you are the recipient of His kept promise to you.** Our God is faithful and has been since even before your creation. He has never failed you in any of His promises to you. The saying "promises were made to be broken" is not true with God. You can rest assured in His promises. He will never leave nor forsake you, even when death do you part He has promised to raise you up. He has delivered His promise to save you. Now wait in patience for Him to finish what He started in your life. You'll be amazed at the eternal love life He has in store for you.

**Look to Him for He is your Savior, your salvation, your eternal life. I promise.**

## STARING AT THE FACE OF GOD | JANUARY 6

*The man said, "Let me go, for it is day break." But Jacob replied, "I will not let you go unless you bless me." Genesis 36:26*

---

This story has a unique twist that begs illumination. Jacob wanted to be left alone prior to meeting his brother. He felt a need to contemplate and pray to God for repentance for the grievous sin he committed twenty years ago when he fraudulently stole the birthright of his older brother Esau. As Jacob was praying with earnest tears and supplication, he suddenly felt a strong hand laid on him. Sensing an enemy was seeking his life, he began to wrestle with his foe. This encounter went on for what appears to be from midnight on to the break of dawn. Finally with the break of day peering in the horizon, God said, "let me go for it is daybreak." Jacob replied, "I will not let you go unless you bless me." God then asked him "What is your name?" He answered "Jacob." God then conveyed to him that his "name will no longer be Jacob, but Israel, because you have struggled with God and with men and have overcome." Jacob then asked, "Please tell me your name." But God replied, "Why do you ask me my name?" Then He blessed him there. Jacob called the place Peniel, Saying, "It is because I saw God face to face, and yet my life was spared."

Many of us have one time or another have gone through a similar incident as Jacob. You may be experiencing a burden that you can't shrug off right now. You may have an issue that's eating you inside. Is there some pain that you've carried far too long? We tend to carry burdens that nag at the root of our inner-most being. We struggle with a horrendous guilt and shame that we can't seem to dissolve. The problem with guilt and shame is it originated from Satan. Such emotional feelings are not of God. God is peace, joy and kindness. He wants to bestow the Spirit of calm assurance in your soul right now. His face is nothing but blessings. God wants to relieve you of all your miseries. **Seeing the face of God is seeing goodness all around you.** Granted, there is still suffering and sorrow. But God has left an indelible expression of His grace in every good thing.

The Author of Love wants to touch you today. He wants to relieve you of that nagging burden. If you stop struggling and wrestling with Him you will not suffer any more. If you let Him take control of your life you will be blessed. The control you seemingly think is the solution is in vain if God doesn't control it. When you realize all God wants to do is save you, you will stop wrestling with Him and be at rest. When you finally grasp it is God alone who can quell the storms in your life you will proclaim Peniel, and you, too, will be staring at the face of God. **Want to see God? Then stop nurturing your past wounds and let God take care of them.**

# **NO REGRETS** | JANUARY 7

*"The Lord was grieved that he had made man on the earth, and His heart was filled with pain." Genesis 6: 6*

Have you ever looked back in your life and felt a sense of regret? Regret that you did not pursue a particular career path? Maybe it was someone you should have married, or one you did and shouldn't have. Have you ever asked yourself, "I wonder what my life would be like if I married so and so or dated so and so?" If only I did this or that, instead of this or that. These thoughts of what ifs and regrets can consume you to the point that it affects your ability to move forward in your present life.

I have a very dear close friend who was married for over 30 years. They were pillars in their community. They were well respected and looked up to. They were the ideal family and the envy of all. He had a medical practice and she owned a thriving business. Their children were well educated and accomplished as well. Yesterday he called me and said he and his wife were separating. Reflecting back in his life he felt he had failed in his personal life. He regretted the failures in his past life. What is your regret right now? Are you still carrying past regrets? When will you finally bury your past regrets? Living your past in the present is regretful.

No doubt, we've all experienced such regrets. It is particularly regrettable however, that God Himself was grieved that He had made man on the earth. God's heart was filled with pain but He never ever wanted to lose us. God has witnessed every atrocity and perversion that humankind has committed – senseless wars, destruction of our natural resources, abusive relationships, fractured households. Even to this day, acts of vengeance and cruelty are undertaken in the name of the God of life.

God is the Author of life. He is not a destroyer. **Only when we are NOT in the presence of God, death occurs**. God has never regretted creating us. He was saddened by our degradation. If anything, He loved us so much that He sent His Son to save us from sin's destruction. God's pain and grievance is that we did not trust Him and His word. When you truly know your Maker, you will understand His love for you.

Our trust in God and believing Him at His word is what will keep us from death's door. Yes, it's that simple. Stop fighting with His Spirit of peace and your regrets will dissipate. **If only we would stay connected with the Author of Love, we too, would have no regrets.**

## DON'T FALL FOR ANYTHING | JANUARY 8

*"When the woman saw that the fruit of the tree was good for food and pleasing to the eye, and also desirable for gaining wisdom, she took some and ate it. She also gave some to her husband, and he ate it." Genesis 3: 6*

---

This chapter in Genesis is the fall of man from Eden. So much was riding on their decision. The end result has become a reality. We not only reaped death but gained the knowledge of evil. Or have we? The adage "history repeats itself," has never been so true. To obtain a perspective on knowing evil, we must first look at the foundation of this "simple" act. After Adam and Eve were created, they were constantly forewarned of the one tree they could not eat of the fruit or touch. That tree was smacked in the middle of the garden. The angels also constantly reminded them of the wiles of Satan and to always be on guard, never leaving one another's sight, not even for a split second. The decision to pluck and eat of the fruit of this particular tree was not spontaneous. Rarely is a decision to commit an act of evil made right then and there. The act is the result of contemplating, entertaining and ruminating over the "what-ifs" and "why- not." It was not a snap decision but one which was weighed and considered throughout their waking lives. The key issue for them was who to believe – the admonitions of God and His angels or the temptations of a crafty serpent.

Some would argue that this seemingly minor indiscretion has been blown out of proportion. However, it is the so-called little things in life such as ignoring the homeless person who begs for a quarter, padding one's expense account, a furtive glance at another's spouse or not returning a book borrowed from the library or a friend. It is these "little" transgressions that are the seeds that ultimately lead to more heinous acts. We are confronted daily to choose of the tree of good or that of evil. These little things come in all shapes and sizes. They are relentless and crafty. It only takes this one little thing to repeat the Garden of Eden temptation.

If you are not connected with Him, you are apt to err in your selection. Do not for one second think you can make decisions that are noble or wise. You must depend on God in your thinking, your choices as well as your desires. Just as He reminded Adam and Eve of the consequences if they stray, so is He reminding you of Adam and Eve's "error of judgment". Be wise in your decision making by believing in God and not the wiles of the tempter. Sometimes, things you fall for seem harmless and trivial, especially when you get away with it the first time. **Don't fall for what tempts you; you have enough evidence to know it leads to death, instead fall for God.**

## **NEVER AGAIN** | JANUARY 9

*"Never again will I curse the ground because of man, even though every inclination of his heart is evil from childhood. And never again will I destroy all living creatures, as I have done." Genesis 8: 21*

---

After Noah and his family left the ark, Noah expressed his gratefulness to God by building an altar of sacrifice and, at the same time confirmed his faith in the coming of the Messiah, Jesus. Noah could have sacrificed their worldly possession or their personal treasures. Noah had been taught from birth of the coming messiah to redeem the world. Noah instead found the best animal and sacrificed it to God. God smelled the "sweet savor" and the Lord said in His heart that He would never again curse the ground even though man's heart is evil from his youth. And to seal this proclamation, the Lord set a rainbow in the clouds.

Does God need to remind Himself of His promise? I think not. We, however, do. God in His love and mercy wanted to allay any doubt in our mind. He said He would never allow any calamity of waters to cover the earth. God did not curse the ground of man. We left His holy presence, thus we cut ourselves from the giver of life. Our evil ways since childhood is what doomed us. God further declared there would always be "seedtime and harvest, cold and heat, summer and winter, day and night will never cease." God will always be faithful to us.

After World War II the Jewish community sang out in unison "Never again!" The eradication of over six million Jews took its toll on their community but their spirit could not be compromised. They vowed never again to go meekly to the slaughter house. There are some today who try to discount this event ever took place. These are men who turn a blind eye. Are you one of these men? Do you turn a blind eye to injustice around you? Or are you a champion of justice for all mankind? It's time to take a stand for truth, justice and God.

Historians and even some theologians have pondered the question: where was God throughout this ordeal? The more telling question of course, was: where was man? God did not fail man. Man failed God-both by virtue of sins of commission and, in the case of those who stood by and watched in silence-sins of omission.

Next time you are tempted to turn a blind eye to injustice, just look at the rainbow and tell yourself never again. **God, the Author of Love, did not forget His promise; it is we who forgot, and we must do so NEVER AGAIN!**

## DON'T BE AFRAID, I AM YOUR SHIELD | JANUARY 10

*"After this, the word of the LORD came to Abram in a vision: don't be afraid, Abram, I am your shield, your very great reward." Genesis 15: 1*

---

I have a co-worker who is going through some tough times. He can't remember what happened a few days before. He is going through medical tests to determine the cause of his illness. He is scared and anxious. He gets touchy, irritable and impatient. I have another friend who is presently incarcerated for a felony he claims he did not do. He is despondent and fears for his life while in jail. I have another friend who is still raising her 30-year-old son. He was recently terminated from his job. He refuses to seek work or even apply for unemployment benefits. He's purposely missed appointments. He's developed a fear of being rejected. I attended a relative's wedding. It was a beautiful ceremony. She was thrilled to get married but she married a non-believe. She wonders why God has not answered her prayer for his conversion. Most recently, I received a text message from a dear friend requesting everyone to leave her alone. She wants to wallow in her feeling of abandonment without the help of any of her friends.

What are you anxious for today? What is your story? What are you afraid of? Does it appear that your prayers have gone unanswered? Are you losing hope? Do you see no light at the end of the tunnel? Your fears are unfounded. When you trust God, you will rest assured that all will be well despite the obstacles you're facing.

Abraham, one of the pillars of faith, harbored similar feelings. He was no different. The God of Abraham is the same God today. And He still speaks with each of us. Listen. When God called Abram out of Haran, God said, "Leave your country, your people and your father's household and go to the land I will show you." God further made a promise, "I will make you into a great nation and I will bless you; I will make your name great and you will be a blessing. I will bless those who bless you, and whoever curses you I will curse; and all peoples on earth will be blessed through you."

God has made a plan in your life to make everything turn out in your favor because He is a good God. Whatever anxiety you are wrestling with, do not be dishearten. God has heard your plea even before you asked Him. He wants you to place your whole trust in Him. Just like Abraham, God is telling you He has control of your life. **Trust Him and you will be able to face any fear. Remember, He is your shield. That in itself is a reward, a very great reward.**

## HOPE AMIDST DESTRUCTION | JANUARY 11

*"Now the men of Sodom were wicked and were sinning greatly against the Lord." Genesis 14: 13*

---

This is the first recorded message regarding the city of Sodom. Lot chose to live near Sodom. He was attracted to the lush fertile green gardens and well watered plains of Jordan. It rivaled the Garden of Eden. But what was the real reason God destroyed Sodom and Gomorrah? Genesis 18 and 19 devotes two chapters to the condition of the people of that city. In Genesis 18: 20 the LORD says "The outcry against Sodom and Gomorrah is so great and their sin so grievous that I will go down and see if what they have done is as bad as the outcry that has reached me. If not, I will know." God came down and He saw for himself. Genesis 19: 13 read "because we are going to destroy this place. The outcry to the LORD against its people is so great that He has sent us to destroy it."

This text has been used to justify persecution of certain gay minority groups throughout the world. Just what was so wicked about this city that God warned them of their impending doom? The explanation of just exactly what God detest so much about Sodom's behavior is found from the prophet Ezekiel. He too witnessed Jerusalem falling lower than their idolatrous and pagan neighbors. Can you imagine Israel, God's chosen people falling to the depths of depravation even more despicable than Sodom and Gomorrah? Ezekiel 16: 47 "You not only walked in their way and copied their detestable practices, but in all your ways you soon became more depraved than they. As surely as I live, declares the Sovereign Lord, your sister Sodom and her daughters never did what you and your daughters have done."

This is serious stuff. Verse 49: "Now THIS was the sin of your sister Sodom: She and her daughters were arrogant, overfed and unconcerned; they did not help the poor and needy. They were haughty and did detestable things before me." It was not because of whom they were but what they did. **THEY LEFT GOD. When you leave God you become godless in thought and practice.** Anytime you depart from God's presence you are certainly inviting death. Without the presence of God in your life you are removing yourself from the safety of His arms.

Being in God's presence protects you from the destroyer of life. Don't stray from God's holy presence. To stray from God is to engage in self-destruction. That's what really happened to Sodom and Gomorrah. God did not destroy them. They removed themselves from His presence. **They chose to love themselves more than their Maker. In God is your only salvation and hope amidst any destruction that may befall you.**

## **SARAH'S LAUGHTER** | JANUARY 12

*"Then the LORD said to Abraham, 'why did Sarah laugh and say, 'Will I really have a child, now that I am old?' 'Is anything too hard for the LORD? I will return to you at the appointed time next year and Sarah will have a son.' Sarah was afraid, so she lied and said, I did not laugh. But He said 'Yes, you did laugh.'" Genesis 18: 13-15*

---

God invented laughter. Laugher is good medicine. There are many forms of laughter. You can tell a lot about a person's attitude, beliefs and disposition by what they laugh at or about. Sometimes, laughter at inappropriate times can conjure up quizzical looks of uncertainty about your mental health. Laughing too hard can also evoke tears, which is an irony. Then there is the gallows laughter. This is a sign of discomfort and fear: like Sarah's. Everyone enjoys a good laugh but hopefully not at your expense. In Sarah's case, her laughter was of unbelief.

Whether by today's standards or then, women past childbearing years just don't conceive. The interesting scenario here is the dialogue between God and Sarah. Sarah laughed when she was told she would have a child. God even memorialized her laugh by naming her son "Isaac." This means laughter. God wanted her to remember her doubting laughter. However, most people forget that not only Sarah laughed but Abraham too. Abraham actually laughed first.

Note the verse before this text. Genesis 17: 16 & 17 "I will bless her and will surely give you a son by her. I will bless her so that she will be the mother of nations; kings of peoples will come from her. Abraham fell facedown; he laughed and said to himself, "Will a son be born to a man a hundred years old? Will Sarah bear a child at age of ninety" Abraham's laughter was not doubt or unbelief. He was amused. It's like saying "you gotta be kidding." Sarah's laughter was unbelieving with no faith at all. She was skeptical but also afraid. When we're afraid we're prone to lie. The key difference is found in verse 14. "Is anything too hard for the LORD?"

**Faith in God is the real test**. ALL of God's promises will come true. Do you have the faith of Abraham or Sarah's laughter? You know the results of their faith in God. God has provided enough evidence for you to believe His word. Never forget, with God there is absolutely nothing that is impossible. Remember, God has promised you salvation. **This is not a laughing matter. Now go and claim God's faith for yourself and you'll understand the difference between Abraham and Sarah's laughter.**

## HAGAR'S CRY | JANUARY 13

*"God heard the boy crying, and the angel of God called to Hagar from heaven and said to her, 'What is the matter, Hagar? Do not be afraid; God has heard the boy crying as he lies there. I will make him a great nation.'" Genesis 21: 17 & 18*

---

When Sarah's impatience and controlling spirit took the better of her, she suggested to Abraham to take her maidservant, Hagar to produce the heir they thought God intended. The consequences of that decision reverberate even today. What is particularly moving about this story is how the Author of Love made something good out of a bad situation. God's love was shown to Hagar and her son Ishmael. God in His mercy and grace did not abandon them. In fact God stayed with them throughout their sojourn. Verse 20 says, "God was with the boy as he grew up." Do you see the love of God? He loves all regardless of their background or ethnicity. The heritage of Ishmael is seen throughout the world, especially in the Middle East. These are the descendants of Ishmael. They are a seed from Abraham. God did not forget nor neglect them. God cares and blesses everyone unconditionally and equality.

This story has an even deeper significance when you truly know the Author of Love. You and I are a story too. We live today as a result of someone's choice. Even when our choices are bad, God makes something beautiful out of them. Regardless of our past, it is God who cares for us. God is so good and gracious that He treats everyone without prejudice or favor. He treats them as only a loving father or mother can love. If you are unable to see that in your life, then you have forgotten your God. He will never leave nor abandon you.

Are you contemplating a decision that could affect the course of your life? Are you impatient and like Sarah feel a need to assist God's plan for you? Remember what happen to Sarah when she decided to take matters into her own hands. Her scheme backfired. Can you wait on the Lord's time? Don't rush matters and make things happen by your own accord. You need to wait patiently on the LORD. Do not be discouraged and restless. God in His right time will answer your prayer. Can you believe and trust Him? He's heard your cry.

Wait on the Lord and you will not need to cry Hagar's cry. In case you do make that mistake, God will still love and comfort you as He did Hagar and her son. That is how God evidences His love to us. God knows the end from the beginning of your life. **All you have to do is trust Him. Can you see that? If you can't, you will cry Hagar's cry. While you weep, He will see you through because He loves you despite the choices you make daily.**

## THE COST OF YOUR BIRTHRIGHT | JANUARY 14

*"'Look I am about to die,' Esau said. 'What good is the birthright to me? Swear to me first.' So he swore an oath to him, selling his birthright to Jacob." Genesis 25: 32 & 33*

Prior to this verse, God had told Rebekah that, "Two nations are in your womb, and two peoples from within you will be separated; one people will be stronger than the other, and the older will serve the younger." In other words, Jacob would be the heir to the birthright and not Esau.

This birthright was considered of great importance. Esau and Jacob were taught the plan of redemption at a very young age. They were told that this birthright was invaluable. Whoever received the birthright in the family would be the priest of his family and the line from which Christ would come. One son valued this privilege more than the other did. Esau lived for the moment. He indulged his passions. He wanted it now. He acquiesced to his every desire. Hebrews 12: 16 sums up the life of Esau; "See that no one is sexually immoral, or is godless like Esau, who for a single meal sold his inheritance rights as the oldest son."

Of great significance is the fact the Author of Love did not abandon or forsake Esau or his family. God also blessed him and his family. Esau lived a very comfortable and affluent life. He thrived and was blessed with many children, land and possessions. All these things were meaningless to him in the scope of the decision he made to sell his birthright. The lessons his parents taught him became even clearer in the light of the redeemer who sacrificed His life to save all of us.

When faced with a similar choice, Jesus sacrificed His birthright in order that we may inherit the eternal birthright. Do you have hunger pangs that may cost your "birthright?" Think about Esau's choice next time you are confronted with an "Esau moment." Is it worth it? We regularly confront choices that place our inherited eternal "birthright" at risk. You have an opportunity to choose a heavenly birthright or an earthly one. Choose the inheritance God has planned for you. God's plan for you is always good because He is a very good God. **No matter who you are or what you've done in the past, God NEVER stops treating you with His great love and kindness.** That's just the nature of God, to love even His erring children. Like Esau said "What good is the birthright to me?" What good is your salvation to you? Everything!

**Like Esau's negligence, God still saved him, but this time the wrong choice you make may cost you your eternal birthright.**

## **ONLY A FEW DAYS** | JANUARY 15

*"So Jacob served seven years to get Rachel, but they seemed like only a few days to him because of his love for her." Genesis 29: 20*

---

I love this story. If you've ever experience love, you will identify with this story. Can you imagine courting the woman you love for seven years? Now-a-days courting is measured in months or even weeks. The sad part of this story is that, after seven years of toiling for Rachel's hand in marriage, her father, Laban deceived Jacob on the night of his marriage. Instead of giving Rachel, he told Leah, Rachel's older sister, to go into the honeymoon suite. Jacob did not know it was Leah until the next morning. Jacob was furious for the deception that was heaped on him from Laban. Laban explained that it was their custom to have the older sister married first before the younger. Laban then requested that Jacob serve him another seven years for the hand of Rachel. After the one-week honeymoon with Leah, Jacob also received Rachel. But he had to serve Laban another seven years.

It is likely that Jacob felt duped. It is equally likely that Jacob reflected on the deception he perpetrated on his brother, Esau, when he captured his birthright. The good news for Jacob was that he was able to place these events in a proper perspective. Verse 20 says seven years "seemed like only a few days to him because of his love" for Rachel. Have you loved like Jacob? Or are you still waiting for your love?

Whatever issue you are going through is but a moment in comparison to the bigger picture God has planned. Our Father loves us more than Jacob's expression of love. To God a thousand years are but a day. He cannot wait another second to take His "bride" (us) home to be with Him. Someday, we, too, will look back at our struggles and our imperfect love life and conclude it was worth the wait. When you have the love of God, time truly flies. Whether you're waiting seven years plus seven or twenty years or a lifetime for Christ to return don't be disheartened because you will have eternity to fully realized God's love. When you finally return home with Him you too will say the wait "seemed like only a few days." Do you have the patience here on earth to wait for the" love of your life"? Are you willing to toil through another "seven years" to be with the one you love? Love waits in love. Believe me, in the end you'll find the wait worth it.

With love there is no time frame, there is only the moment, the here and now. Love makes you see the object of your affection in a totally different time frame. Each moment with your loved one is cherished. **With love there is no beginning, middle or end, love is more than eternal. Remember, love is not things or accolades. Love is a person. Love is God. How long will it take for you to really know God's love?**

## WORRYWART | JANUARY 16

*"Therefore do not worry about tomorrow, for tomorrow will worry about itself. Each day has enough trouble of its own." Matthew 25: 34*

---

Are you a worrywart? A worrywart is a person who excessively and needlessly worries about anything and everything that can and could go wrong. I have a close friend like that. His glass (as he sees it) is typically half-empty. He is a pessimist. When we had a small earthquake recently that registered 3.7 he ran under the table for protection. After a few seconds he remarked that's a prelude to the "big one."

Mahatma Gandhi had a lot to worry about. Born in India during British rule, He led peaceful marches, fasted and urged the mass defiance of many unfair British laws. Though jailed for civil disobedience he was later released and led his countrymen to fight political injustice through a non-violent manner. Gandhi had every right to worry about his country, his family and his life. He was in the spotlight and felt a calling to lead his people to freedom and independence. Gandhi's take on worry; "There is nothing that wastes the body like worry, and one who has any faith in God should be ashamed to worry anything whatsoever." Gandhi had faith. He was successful in obtaining India's independence from Britain on August 15, 1947. When asked his opinion of his oppressor, he said "I like your Christ; I do not like you Christians. Your Christians are so unlike your Christ." Gandhi was justified to worry because He carried a whole country on his shoulders. He deemed such matters of worrying and anxiousness as a waste of time.

Christ had much the same philosophy with respect to worry. Are you presently worrying about something that you can't let go? Listen to what God is telling you. Let tomorrow worry about itself. You have only today and God wants you to make the most of today by leaning on Him and following His guidance. There is no greater joy than for God to know you will trust Him with your anxieties and your life.

God is the Author of Life. In Him, you have no worries. The worrywart will respond "easier said than done." God is not discounting your feelings, He is trying to open your eyes and see beyond the portals of your fears because He has already conquered them. You must trust Him that He is greater than all your worries. Your life can be without any anxiety when you totally depend on Him. If you are still worrying and have no inner peace, then you do not have His Spirit in you. God's spirit is peace. Try Him today. As a famous humor magazine character once said: **"What me worry?" No need to when God is your Lord and Savior.**

## FAVORITE CHILD | JANUARY 17

*"Now Israel (Jacob) loved Joseph more than any of his other sons, because he had been born to him in his old age; and he made a richly ornamented robe for him. When his brothers saw that their father loved him more than any of them, they hated him and could not speak a kind word to him." Genesis 37: 3*

---

Jacob's beloved wife Rachel had two sons. The first was Joseph and, later, before she died, she gave birth to Benjamin. Joseph means "May he add." This was Rachel first child. It was a total surprise for both of them. Joseph was only seventeen years old when his brothers (including those from Jacob's other wives) plotted to kill him. Parents, as much as they wish to show impartiality toward their children, are oftentimes less than convincing. Jacob had such love for Rachel that he was especially joyful when she bore him this son (Joseph). The proverbial straw that broke the camel's back for Joseph's siblings was the robe that Jacob proudly bestowed upon Joseph. His brothers reaction? -They threw him in a pit and soon sold him into slavery.

Had Joseph's brothers been receptive to God's Spirit, they would not have treated their brother in a jealous manner. They would have shared in their father's joy of being blessed with another son at his old age. The root of jealousy comes from the father of lies, Satan. Do you have jealousy in your heart? Don't entertain that spirit of jealousy in your heart. Jealousy turns deadly.

How often do we as parents fail to treat each child equally as much as might we try? We rationalize we are attracted to a certain personality type that seem to complement our own personality. It's easier to cleave to the lovable personality amidst our family circle. The incorrigible child is someone we find hard to get along with. If we are to be true to ourselves, our favoritism should not be in things or, for that matter, in objects of the world. Our only favorite should be in Christ. Christ has shown us favor. When you favor Christ more than child, object or thing, you will be able to love even the unlovable child because you will see them through the eyes of God rather than your subjective bias. True un-bias love can only come from God's Spirit dwelling in you. Are you having difficulty dealing with a child, friend, co-worker or stranger? Don't focus on that person, focus on God. He will give you the Spirit and mind to handle any relationship you have in a godly manner.

God still has a job to complete and that is "to do the will of Him who sent me and to finish His work." (John 4: 34). **Whenever you are feeling un-favored, take heart, for the Author of Love has chosen you. You can say you are His favorite child.**

# HOW THEN COULD I SIN AGAINST GOD | JANUARY 18

*"'No one is greater in this house than I am. My master has withheld nothing from me except you, because you are his wife. How then could I do such a wicked thing and sin against God?' And though she spoke to Joseph day after day, he refused to go to bed with her or even be with her." Genesis 39: 9*

---

After Joseph's captors reach Egypt, he was sold into slavery and was bought by Potiphar. Potiphar was a captain in Pharaoh's army. One can only imagine what went through Joseph's mind as he was led to the house of his master? All the years he was growing up at his father's care, he was indulged, protected and favored. Joseph reflected on the lessons his father taught him early on his childhood. These lessons would sustain him through this trying ordeal.

Joseph's character shined through the ten years he was in service for his master. But Joseph's faith was once again tested. Potiphar's wife noted Joseph was a well-built, handsome man. Through the years of service she noticed Joseph's over-all attractiveness not only in body but also in spirit. Her passion took control of her senses and she tried to entice him to sleep with her. This was an idea that had been lurking in the back of Potiphar's wife for a long time. And she hunted Joseph with her lust day after day. Joseph felt totally uncomfortable and avoided her advances at all cost. However, Potiphar's wife desires were undiminished, until one day, she rather flagrantly endeavored to seduce him. Had Joseph yielded to this temptation, his life would not have had a "happy ending." Even with the right choice, Joseph still paid a miserable price. Joseph remembered his Father's God and said, "How then could I do such a wicked thing and sin against God?" He did not say how he could sin against Potiphar or his wife but against God.

The originator of evil constantly tempts us. Day after day he patiently plots for us to succumb to his wiles. He is like a roaring lion waiting to devour his prey. You may be contemplating giving in to such temptation right now. I don't claim to be a Joseph in character but I can identify with him. I treated a person kindly and she misinterpreted my kindness for interest. It was not easy to let her down gently. I did not succumb but the "day after day" torture was needless to say harrowing. Don't succumb to the wiles of a moment's pleasure. You will end up reaping a lifetime of sorrow and pain. Nothing good can ever come out of a loveless lust. **Just as Joseph trusted God, you, too, must learn to give in to one temptation, and that is the temptation of God's Love.**

## PRISONER OF LOVE | JANUARY 19

*"Joseph's master took him and put him in prison, the place where the king's prisoners were confined. But while Joseph was there in the prison, the Lord was with him; He showed him kindness and granted him favor in the eyes of the prison warden." Genesis 39: 20 & 21*

---

Potiphar threw Joseph in prison after Potiphar's wife accused Joseph of raping her. She bore false witness against Joseph, which, of course, is a violation of one of God's commandments. "Thou shalt not bear false witness." God was watching over Joseph during his incarceration, much the way He watches over us when we are distressed. Joseph's imprisonment served as a test, and Joseph proved equal to that test. God allows tests on us virtually every day – oftentimes, with what, on the surface, might appear to be little challenges. E.G. White, in Patriarchs & Prophets p. 224 & 225 says, "Nothing with which we have to do is really small. The varied circumstances that we meet day by day are designed to test our faithfulness and to qualify us for greater trusts. By adherence to principle in the transactions of ordinary life, the mind becomes accustomed to hold the claims of duty above those of pleasure and inclination. By faithfulness in that which is least they acquire strength to be faithful in greater matters. An upright character is not only success but is of greater worth than fame of riches. This noble character does not happen overnight in one's life. But it is the constant tests in one's life that produces the godly manner."

God wants us to realize that success should not be measured in terms of acquired riches, but rather in terms of our character development. As Joseph learned at a very young age, if we cling to God, follow His leading, He will be with us, even during our darkest days. As Joseph was in prison the Lord was with him. God is with us wherever our lot in life is. As God treated Joseph with kindness and favor you will also be treated in kind. That is the nature of our God. He treats us no other way than through His character of love and kindness.

You may be a prisoner in your mind, at home, work or school but when you are connected with Him, you will always be free. The Lord will be with you and will treat you with kindness and favor. Just like Joseph, you can rise above all earthly temptations. You will know the difference between man's love and God's love. You are never shackled and confined in Spirit when you are a prisoner of God's love. His love is freedom from all the cares and imprisonment of this world. **His love for us has already paid the price of freedom through His Son. Why not become a prisoner of God's love.** It is not only invigorating but a freedom worth living.

## INTERPRETATIONS BELONG TO GOD | JANUARY 20

*"We both had dreams, they answered, but there is no one to interpret them. Then Joseph said to them, do not interpretations belong to God? 'Tell me your dream.'" Genesis 40: 8*

---

Genesis Chapter 40 is devoted to interpretations of dreams that Joseph gave to two fellow prisoners. One was for a cupbearer, a person who tastes the king's food and drink to be sure it is safe to eat. The other was a baker. The significance of their story is in dreams they had simultaneously. The two were frustrated by the fact that nobody could interpret their dreams, and their dreams were indeed worrisome.

Once again Joseph testified on behalf of God saying, "Interpretations of dreams belongs to God." The cupbearer shared his dream. He saw a vine with three branches. Once they had budded, blossomed and the grapes ripened, he had Pharaoh's cup in his hand. He then took the grapes, squeezed them into the cup and handed the cup to Pharaoh. Joseph said his dream meant the three branches were three days. In three days the cupbearer would be restored to his original position as a cupbearer for the king. Joseph then added a request to the cupbearer. He asked the cupbearer to show him kindness by mentioning him to Pharaoh.

Hearing that the interpretation for the cupbearer was positive, the baker shared his dream. The baker said that he had three baskets of baked goods on his head for the Pharaoh. However, the birds were eating the baked goods out of the baskets on his head. Joseph interpreted his dream to signify that the three baskets were also three days. And in three days Pharaoh would lift off the baker's head and hang him on a tree. The birds would eat away at his flesh.

Joseph's interpretations came true. Here were two tales and two outcomes. These appear to be examples of our final outcome here on earth. The saved and unsaved. You can have God's freedom in your life right now. Are you uncertain about your future? Are you seeking answers or interpretations of your earthly dreams through fortune tellers or mediums? God has the answers to all your questions. God, who knows the end from the beginning and can interpret all your dreams. Pray to Him to give you His answer to all your questionings and dreams. The fact of the matter is, He has already shared with you His plan for your future. He wants you to know He has saved you and will reunite with you soon.

God is the Author of true freedom. **Accept His gift of freedom through His Son, Jesus and you will be free from whatever it is holding you back or that might otherwise imprison you.** After all, doesn't every good thing belong to God?

## BAD INTENTIONS TURNED TO GOOD INTENTIONS | JANUARY 21

*"But Joseph said to them, don't be afraid. Am I in the place of God? You intended to harm me, but God intended it for good to accomplish what is now being done, the saving of many lives." Genesis 50: 19 & 20*

---

Then Pharaoh felt burdened by a couple of unusual dreams. In the first dream he observed seven cows grazing. All were well nourished. Additionally, there were seven cows which were clearly gaunt and under-nourished. The cows that were under-nourished and gaunt devoured their fatter brethren. In his second dream, he observed seven heads of grain in a single stalk, and these were indeed healthy. However, seven additional heads of grain were thin, and they clearly suffered from exposure to the scorching east wind. The thin heads of grain swallowed up their healthier counterparts. Pharaoh awakened very troubled. He summoned all the wise men and magicians, but no one could interpret his dreams. Then the cupbearer recalled Joseph's ability to interpret his dream, and he relayed his experience to Pharaoh. Pharaoh summoned Joseph and said: "But I have heard it said of you that when you hear a dream you can interpret it." "I cannot do it" Joseph replied, "but God will give Pharaoh the interpretation." What a testament to God, Joseph always placed God first.

In performing these interpretations, Joseph relied on God's leading through the Holy Spirit. Joseph was honored and uplifted for his interpretation. His life changed for the better. He was promoted to become second in command only to Pharaoh. He was thirty years old when he ascended to the throne next to Pharaoh. Joseph's life ended happily for him and his family. His faithfulness to God made him revered by his peers, family and even Pharaoh and his kingdom. Joseph remained faithful to God and was blessed. His whole family was spared and they lived in abundance. His brothers did a disservice to Joseph years ago, but Joseph did not retaliate nor seek vengeance for their misdeed. Joseph was operating on his knowledge of God. He followed God's leading and also operated in Godly love only. In fact Joseph said, "You intended to harm me, but God intended it for good to accomplish what is now being done, the saving of many lives."

Joseph's good fortune is another example of the handiwork of God. You may be going through a similar fate. Things look bleak for the moment, but don't lose heart. **What seem like bad intentions right now will turn to good if you stay connected to the God who accomplishes only good in your life.** God is in the business of saving lives, especially your life.

# GOD HAS HEARD OUR GROANING | JANUARY 22

*"God heard their groaning and He remembered His covenant with Abraham, with Isaac and with Jacob. So God looked on the Israelites and was concerned about them." Exodus 2: 24 & 25*

---

Have you ever groaned -- the kind of groaning that is gut wrenching, the kind of groaning that emanates from your innermost soul? Groaning is another form of intense communication. It tells of a person in distress and needing immediate relief. This form of expression is a cry of helplessness and hopelessness.

Have you ever felt that intense groaning too? Now imagine, if you will, the groaning of the Hebrews, who were subjected to slavery during Joseph's time. Joseph's stellar reputation in Egypt was but a distant memory. A new king was at the helm, and the many wonderful deeds that Joseph had undertaken during seven years of famine were a very distant memory. This new king despised the Hebrew people. He arbitrarily subjected them to the most barbaric form of slavery.

We live in a land that once tolerated slavery, and while Lincoln may well have proclaimed the emancipation of America's slaves, we are somehow willing today to be subjected to slavery of a different kind. No, it is not the type of slavery that the children of Israel suffered; nor is it the type of slavery that African Americans experienced prior to the Civil War. What so many of our generations are a slave to is sin. In many respects, sin is indeed our master. This enslavement is called lust, pornography, fornication, substance abuse, child abuse, spousal abuse, diet abuse, greed, selfishness, recognition, competition, theft, cleanliness, perfection, thus said the lord, prejudice, love, the list could fill a good many pages. Which one are you a slave to? Are you struggling to free yourself from the chains that bind you? Are you indulging so much that you don't want to let go? Do you have no strength to control your vices? There's good news, God has heard your groaning and He will save you no matter what ails you. You must really turn it over to God. He is your only hope and answer.

Whichever sin that controls your life, God is listening to your cries. He remembered His covenant with us. He cares about us. He wants to relieve our slavery to sin. If we let Him serve as our master, we can escape the slavery of sin that enslaves us. I know the misery that your sin has brought you. It is not an easy task to break the years of hell you've been through. Sometimes you feel like giving up. But there is real hope. You really must trust God in your life. **Won't you place your trust in the God who cares and hears your groaning?**

## SPEAK FOR YOURSELF | JANUARY 23

*"The Lord said to him 'Who gave man his mouth? Who makes him deaf or mute? Who gives him sight or makes him blind? Is it not I, the Lord?' 'Now go; I will help you speak and will teach you what to say.' And Moses said, 'Oh Lord please send someone else to do it.'" Exodus 4: 11-13*

One of the greatest fears of humankind is speaking in public. It makes most of us feel as if we were under a microscope. The exposure can be more than a trifle frightening.

When God asked Moses to speak to Pharaoh, Moses felt terribly inadequate; for he was "slow of speech and tongue." (Exodus 4: 10). Some have speculated that Moses had a stutter or perhaps some type of speech impediment. He had an inferior complex when it came to speaking in public. It's arguably peculiar that a man who grew up in Egypt and was taught in the royal courts by the finest teachers, who spoke the language eloquently, could shun the Lord's calling? Moses, however, had departed from Egypt some 40 years earlier. He had forgotten the language. He was a shepherd. He had been the ways of his past and was expected to learn the ways of the Lord. This prospect frightened him.

God summoned Moses in as unique a way as might have been imaginable. Moses was tending his flock when he came upon a burning bush that somehow was not being consumed by the fire that engulfed it. As he approached the bush, the voice of God warned Moses not to come too close and to remove his shoes inasmuch as this was holy ground.

Over the centuries, God has revealed Himself in a wide array of manners. This was the first in a series of such revelations that God would communicate to Moses in behalf of the children of Israel. God called Moses to lead the people of Israel out of bondage in Egypt because God heard their cries.

The God of Moses has heard your cries and has called you to come out of your bondage as well. He has witnessed your wanderings aimlessly. He wants to bring you home with Him in the Promise Land. Your crying days are over right now. Listen to His voice telling you to trust Him and rely on Him. Will you accept His call or make an excuse and refuse? Will you tell God to send someone else to do the task? Whatever your doubt or fear may be, remember what God said: "I will help you speak and will teach you what to say." **The same God of Moses is speaking to you right now and assuring you He will never let you down. You don't have to speak for yourself.**

## OUR PURPOSE IN LIFE | JANUARY 24

*"But I have raised you up for this very purpose, that I might show you my power and that my name might be proclaimed in all the earth." Exodus 9: 16*

---

And then, there is the age-old question: "Why was I born? Do I have a purpose in the grand scheme of things?" I have an agnostic friend who debated the existence of God with me. He views the Bible as a collection of fables – mere fairy tales – albeit, he is quick to add, with underlying things that are oftentimes useful lessons. He insists on proof-historical and otherwise. Faith, he argues, is for the weak of mind. To believe in God, he stipulates, is to deny fact. The "fact" is that we exist only to the extent that we have faith and to the extent, very importantly, that we not only believe in God, but that we also believe in ourselves.

In my friend's scheme of things, we are placed on earth but for a season, and then we die. I asked my friend if he has any hope at all. His response: "Our only hope is now. We must make the most of the present. We have no future." This thinking does not give us much hope but relegates us to the here and now. We can sum up this philosophy with the old adage of "eat drink and be merry for tomorrow we die." What do you think is your purpose in life? Do you know why you were put here on earth? Do you believe there is a God? Do you believe in life after death? Do you have a purpose at all?

God, the Author of Love, did not create us for a moment in time, nor did He intend for us to be reincarnated into some other life form. Rick Warren, pastor of a so-called mega church in California and the author of the best-selling book, "The Purpose-Driven Life" devoted an entire chapter to the question of "What on earth am I here for?" He quotes from Proverbs 11: 28 (Msg): "a life devoted to things is a dead life, a stump; a God-shaped life is a flourishing tree. For everything, absolutely everything, above and below, visible and invisible…everything got started in Him and finds its' purpose in Him." Though this pastor recently experienced the death of his son through suicide, he is still focusing on God.

Our existence or creation is not about us but about God. God created us for His pleasure. His love for us, which is His character, is why He created us. Can't decide or understand what your purpose is in your lifetime? Learn from your Creator your purpose. To know God is to know your purpose. Your whole purpose starts and ends with God. When you accept that, then you would have lived your purpose in life. **The Author of Love revealed Himself entirely through His Son, Jesus Christ. He is our purpose in this lifetime and for all eternity. Really invest your time, purpose and life in getting to know Him.**

## A HARDENED HEART | JANUARY 25

*"But I will harden Pharaoh's heart, and though I multiply my miraculous signs and wonders in Egypt, he will not listen to you. Then I will lay my hand on Egypt and with mighty acts of judgment I will bring out my divisions, my people the Israelites. Yet Pharaoh's heart became hard and he would not listen to them, just as the Lord had said." Exodus 7: 3, 4 & 13*

---

The Story of Exodus tells of Moses and Aaron instructed by God to ask Pharaoh to let the Israelites go so they might worship God. The Lord told Moses you will be like a "god" to Pharaoh and Aaron a prophet. They would perform miraculous wonders in front of Pharaoh and all of his subjects. Pharaoh, however, was unwilling to hear Moses' plea to let the Israelites go. And it was not that God didn't endeavor to win Pharaoh's attention. The LORD sent plagues of death to their livestock, festering boils on their bodies; hail raining down locusts infesting the entire ground and houses. He brought darkness upon the land for three days. He inflicted the plague of death on every first-born in Egypt as well as livestock. Only those who dabbed blood from the Passover lamb on the sides and tops of their door jambs were spared this death sentence. It was, of course, this final plague that ultimately compelled Pharaoh to let the Israelites depart from Egypt. These plagues were not sent by God, God warned them of the impending plagues if they did not turn away from their evil doings. Satan was behind all these maladies. Pharaoh could have avoided this doom had he listened to God. Instead he depended on his own will. He believed the ungodly spirit that catered to his ego. He deceived himself and was delusional in his thinking. His strong will persuaded himself to go against the God who loves and protects.

This story repeats itself in each of our lives. Anything that opposes the call to worship and serve the Almighty God is subject to the plagues of this world, whether it is wealth, or image, or pride, or competitiveness, or our most secret sin. God sends us warnings and signs each step of the way to focus on Him, for He is our only answer, our true salvation. Failure to heed to His admonition will be a matter of life and death.

With God is life. Without God is death. Is your heart hardened by your quest for the material or the self? Are you unwilling to give your heart to God? God "strengthened" Pharaoh's heart, and so shall He yours-whatever lies within – be it the hardness of pride or a passion to serve. Some people believe God manipulated Pharaoh's heart to make him stubborn. If so, then that would contradict God's character of love and giving us freedom of choice. God did not, nor can He ever manipulate Pharaoh's or anyone's will. It was Pharaoh's own stubborn will that brought about his down fall. **Don't wait until life plagues you. Don't assert your obstinate will when God leads you. Won't you heed to the Passover and live?**

## TO THE VERY DAY | JANUARY 26

*"Now the length of time the Israelite people lived in Egypt was 430 years. At the end of the 430 years, to the very day, all the Lord's divisions left Egypt. Because the Lord kept vigil that night to bring them out of Egypt, on this night all the Israelites are to keep vigil to honor the Lord for the generations to come." Exodus 12: 40 & 41*

---

How long have you waited to fulfill an important dream? Was it for the man or woman of your dreams? For a freedom promised but not delivered? Though God's promises may sometimes seem long in their realization, you can be sure they will arrive on "the very day." I remember, in our church a single lady who never married. She was 66 years old when she finally accepted a suitor. When he died ten years later, she went on to marry another widower. Her life was amazing. She waited on the Lord for her life partner.

Whatever our wait may be, when the event that is the subject of our prayers and dreams occurs, what seemed like an eternity will be like a moment in time. God promised Abraham hundreds of years before his dream was realized that his seed would be a great nation and as numerous as the sands in the shore. The Israelites lived in Egypt for 430 years before they left. They waited for the Lord's promise made to Abraham. Generations died (including Abraham) and never witnessed the fulfillment the Lord's promise to Abraham. But God's promise is, as they say, bankable. Moreover, His timing is never just close; it is precise, "to the very day" (verse 41), perfect to the microsecond.

Have you ever been the victim of a broken promise? Mr. or Ms. Right turned out not to be quite so perfect, or the so-called opportunity of a lifetime turned out to be a dud. Have you been waiting for your "ship to come in?" Are you groaning like the Israelites to God asking Him when will all this misery end? Are you thinking if only …? You may not see Christ's return in your lifetime or you may. What is important is that you believe His promise. That is God's "Good News" for you and me. His promise is clothed in hope, faith and love. He is telling us we need not despair because His timing is perfect, and our day, our moment will eventually come.

God knows His timetable perfectly. The same God who watched over the Israelites is watching over you in your journey to the "heavenly" Promised Land He has prepared for you and me. **That day will happen to the "very day" He said it would. Can you wait? Can you trust Him? You must. He is your salvation.**

## YOU NEED ONLY BE STILL | JANUARY 27

*"By the day the Lord went ahead of them in a pillar of cloud to guide them on their way and by night in a pillar of fire to give them light, so that they could travel by day or night." Exodus 13: 21*

---

What a loving and thoughtful God. The Author of Love was not only with the Israelites in their journey to the Promise Land, but He was there guiding their every step. He provided all their needs. God was with them in a pillar of fire to give them light so that they could travel in warmth and light at night. In the daytime they had a pillar of cloud to keep them shaded from the burning desert sun. God thought of everything for His children.

Can you imagine that in your life today? The truth is that God is with us each and every moment. The seasons we experience here on earth are from God. The sun, rain and the air we breathe all come from the Author of Love. He thinks of everything to care for us. Like a doting Parent there is nothing He hasn't thought of.

The Israelites were encamped near the sea when on the horizon they saw a cloud of dust swirling towards them. Suddenly they realized its Pharaoh and his men, bent on revenge and destruction. You sense the terror in their voices of as they cried out to Moses. "Was it because there were no graves in Egypt that you brought us to the desert to die?" Some thought it would have been better to be a slave to the Egyptians than to die in the desert. They had forgotten how God had rescued them.

Isn't that how we are with God when things don't seem to be going our way? We complain and blame God. But Moses knew that the God of Love would provide. Just as He provided the pillar of cloud and fire by day and night, He was going to provide a way out for them. He was going to protect them from any harm from their enemies. God told Moses to tell his people "Don't be afraid. Stand firm and you will see the deliverance the LORD will bring you today. The Egyptians you see today you will never see again. The LORD will fight for you; you need only be still." Exodus 14: 13 & 14.

What a magnificent display of love and care! The same God of yesterday is the God today. He still cares and loves each of us as He did then. All you need to do is be still. Do you understand what it means to be still? Being still means accepting God's will in faith. You have nothing to do but believe Him. **Are you ready to be still and trust Him? Then, cancel everything that is hindering you from seeing God and be still for once in your life.**

## TRUSTING IN HIS MIGHTY LOVE | JANUARY 28

*"And when the Israelites saw the great power the LORD displayed against the Egyptian, the people feared the LORD and put their trust in Him and in Moses His servant." Exodus 14: 31*

---

The Israelites were on the brink of annihilation at the hands of the Egyptians. They were crying to Moses in fear. The army of Pharaoh was only a stone's throw from overtaking them right on the edge of the Red Sea where they were encamped. The Egyptian Army could hear their cries but they can't seem to locate them. The armies of Egypt could not see through the darkness in front of them. But that same cloud that darkened the Egyptian's sight was light on the other side of the Israelites. And one lone angel that was leading them in front went back to the rear to protect God's chosen people. Can you believe that it only takes one angel to repel an entire throng of God's enemies? And yet, despite abundant evidence of God's watchfulness, the Israelites evidenced a lack of faith in God. Quite evidently, they had failed to learn their lessons from the previous miracles that God had performed. (Does this sound familiar?)

While all this was going on God instructed Moses to raise his staff and stretch his hand over the sea to divide the water. The people passed through dry land. The walls of water stood on either side. The passage took all night. And just when they reached the opposite shore, the cloud behind them was lifted and the Egyptians saw the sea was divided. They could see the last few Israelites climbing on to the other side of the shore. The Egyptian army pursued them. But midway through their pursuit, their chariot wheels jammed or fell off. They tried to abandon their pursuit. They realized that the God of Israel was fighting them and discovered they were no match for God. But it was too late. God instructed Moses to stretch his hands again to return the waters back to normal. Had the Egyptians not pursued the Israelites, they would have lived. But in their stubborn will, they went against the character of God's protection and they were met with a deadly fate.

The Author of Love wants to express that care and love He displayed with the Israelites with you today as well. God does not want you to lift a finger for your salvation. Can you distinguish between His control and your control? Are you afraid to let go of your control in your life? You must **Wait on the LORD and trust Him. He will lead you to a safe journey. He says, "Be still and know that I AM GOD."** The Israelites were convinced, at least that day. Are you convinced in God? What would it take for you to believe in God's mighty love for you?

## **DO NOT BE DISCOURAGED** | JANUARY 29

*"The LORD himself goes before you and will be with you; he will never leave you nor forsake you. Do not be afraid; do not be discouraged." Deuteronomy 31: 8*

What are you afraid of? Do you have a phobia? What is your greatest fear? Fear of death, fear of failure, fear of the unknown, fear of abandonment, fear of being alone or fear itself? I remember as child being chosen by my parents to live with my aunt for a short while. She had just arrived from the Philippines and she too was alone here. She left her family back home in order to pave the way for them to follow. Living with a woman I never knew at the ripe old age of six years was daunting for me. I was afraid to be in the presence of a stranger. No amount of coaxing or bribing could have allayed my fears. But I was the dutiful son who obeyed his parents' requests. I trusted them.

In order to conquer one's fears, -- be they of matters real or imagined – one must face those fears, head-on. Prior to knowing her, I had conjured up images that would have made the Wicked Witch of the East appear angelical. Once I met my aunt, she became a source of comfort for me while away from home. She was a kind and generous woman. I was the envy of my siblings for all the toys and candies she gift me. My trust in my parents' decision to choose me to live with my aunt was an unexpected great reward for me.

How many times have we imagined something that's really not there? How often do we punish ourselves needlessly because of our all-too-vivid imaginations? We live in fear every day. We carry fears that have been with us since childhood. Would you believe that such fear is oftentimes not based in reality? It's real only when we believe it's real to us. Whether it's real or not, it's still scary and daunting to face those fears. How do we overcome such trepidation?

God knows all about fears because He shares all our experiences. If we truly know God, then we know that His love for us will overshadow even the utmost dire of our fears. The Author of Love casts our fear. Mind you, this is not to say that God will paint a rosy picture when gloom is in the air. He said He would go before us and be with us as we journey through our fears and trials. He promised too, that He would NEVER leave nor abandon us.

What a wonderful promise. What a wonderful Savior. He, who reminds us never be afraid or discouraged can undoubtedly be trusted. **Even if you're uncertain or don't "feel it," give God a chance to reveal Himself to you. You'll be amazed at His goodness.**

## THE LORD WHO HEALS YOU | JANUARY 30

*"He said, 'If you listen carefully to the voice of the LORD your God and do what is right in His eyes, if you pay attention to His commands and keep all His decrees, I will not bring on you any of the disease I brought on the Egyptians, for I am the LORD who heals you'" Exodus 15: 26*

---

I can vividly recall the doctor telling our family as we were gathered near mother's bedside in the hospital that she had probably three months to live. She was diagnosed with cancer of the colon. The doctor further stated there was no use operating on her because the cancer had spread throughout her body. Word soon spread of mother's prognosis. People everywhere came to pay their respects. Even the elders of the church came to anoint her. One pastor said it was the "Lord's will" and mother must accept her fate with the Lord's blessing. He further added God knows best. Although this pastor meant well, I refused to accept so ominous a prediction as if it were a final verdict. Needless to say, this was a most trying time for all of us. Even my father who was also ill and bedridden because of diabetes suddenly exclaimed to mother that it was a surprise to him that mother would go before him. Amidst all the weeping, gloom and commotion, it was mother who was comforting and reassuring that this was NOT God's will. God is NOT the Author of death.

She felt that God knew the length of life she'd been allotted and that the doctors were not privy to this information. She informed the pastor that he might believe it is God's will that her remaining days should be few, but she knew that it was God's will that she continue to live. And, so at mother's prodding a second medical opinion was sought, and it was learned that the root of mother's problems was significant but localized to her colon. Surgery and chemotherapy followed, and mother survived another 12 years.

God's will is always life for He is the Author of life. Whenever we hear it is God's will that one's life is taken, that is NOT from God. God never intended death for us. He is Life eternal. But we live in an imperfect diseased-ridden world. Cures abound but all is temporary. You will witness some miracle cures as well as passing of loved ones. Don't despair or lose faith. The God who heals wants to give you not just temporary healing but eternal good life. **Do you want healing right now? A healing that is greater and eternal than the temporal healing here on earth? Then trust in the LORD your God and do what He says for He is the "Great Physician."**

## **WHAT IS IT?** | JANUARY 31

*"When the Israelites saw it, they said to each other 'What is it?' for they did not know what it was, Moses said to them 'It is the bread the LORD has given you to eat.'" Exodus 16: 15*

---

During a missionary trip to Thailand, we stayed at a hotel in Chiangmai. In the lobby of the hotel, in the elevator and on each floor was a sign permanently affixed which read, "No durian allowed in this hotel." Many of the young kids and some of the adults as well never heard of durian, so they asked, "What is it?" Durian is a tropical fruit indigenous to Asia. Once opened, it emits an offensive aroma. Some have likened its smell to rotten garbage. The texture and taste, however, is velvety and smooth, close to the texture of honeydew or peach. It melts in your mouth and the flavor is indescribable. The smell however, depending on your distinguishable smell may be offensive or aromatic.

The Israelites were hungry. They had begun their journey to the Promise Land but had run out of the food they had taken with them from Egypt. They once again began complaining to Moses. The Lord told Moses that He would supply them bread in the morning and quail in the evening. Early each morning the Israelites noticed there was dew on the ground. When the dew dissipated it turned into thin flakes like frost. The Israelites asked Moses "What is it?" He said it was food. The people of Israel called it manna which means "what is it?" in Hebrew. It was like coriander seed and tasted like wafers made with honey. They were instructed to gather just enough for the day and to gather a double portion on the sixth day, for they were to do no gathering on the Sabbath. As might be expected, the non-believers among them gathered more than they could eat. The results were maggots and a rotten smell, probably like durian.

For 40 years the Israelites traveled in the desert toward the Promised Land and for 40 years the Lord rained manna and quail for their daily meals. It ended when they reached the Promised Land. God wanted to teach the Israelites as well as you and me that the true source of life is He alone. He wants you to depend on Him daily. You can eat of the earthly manna but the food that will sustain you eternally is God Himself. Rely on the true source of your daily bread, God.

**You ask what is it? Two thousand years later, Jesus came and reminded us, "I am the bread of life."** Our life, our sustenance, our every good thing is in His Son.

## **TESTING GOD** | FEBRUARY 1

*"So they quarreled with Moses and said, 'Give us water to drink.' Moses replied, 'Why do you quarrel with me? Why do you put the Lord to the test?'" Exodus 17: 2*

---

As the Israelites were traveling through the Desert of Sin, they discovered one day that the area in which they were camped was without water. They took their gripe to Moses, who knew, of course, that, just as the Lord had provided them with sustenance, so, too, would He quench their thirst. God instructed Moses to take some of the elders, along with his staff, and strike the rock at Horeb. Moses did as the Lord commanded, and water gushed out of the rock.

When was the last time you had your prayer answered only to turn around and complain when another need arose for which you saw no remedy? When the chips are down, when things appear hopeless and no clear answer is in sight, we end up putting God to the test. We complain, we bargain and then make promises that we can't keep. "If He would answer my plea for good health, I would serve Him faithfully." "If He would let me win the lottery, I would double my tithing and offerings." "If He would let my team win, I'd vote Him MVP." Does the Author of Love expect us to barter with our health, our finances and other matters important to us? The fact is that He knows our needs even before we ask. God's track record is, to say the least, rather impressive. We tend to forget that He has led us this far, and He will lead us to the eternal Promised Land. The fact is that, despite our shortcomings, He still cares and provides.

Test yourself. Test your loyalty to God, who watches out for our well-being every day. The faithful among us are keenly aware that God has already passed the test. They are the ones who talk to the rock rather than strike it because they know God does not need to prove His faithfulness to them. Which one are you? Which faith do you have? Why do you quarrel with God? Are your issues too enormous for God to handle? You lack faith.

The Author of Love demonstrates His love for us each and every day. Granted there are times when life here may not be rosy and clear. He has said to be faithful to the end and you will receive a reward greater than anything this world can offer. Do you wonder what could that reward could be?

**That reward is really His Son. Can you believe that? You can continue to test God's faithfulness. He will deliver. It is we who must demonstrate that we are grateful for His love. That is one test we must not fail.**

## NO OTHER LOVE | FEBRUARY 2

*"And God spoke all these words: 'You shall have no other gods before (besides) me.'" Exodus: 20: 3*

The first commandment: Satan tempted Eve by suggesting that, if she partook of the fruit from the forbidden tree, she would be as gods with the knowledge of good and evil. What does it mean to be a god? Well, there was no dictionary back in Eve's time, but, in most of the nations of the world, a god came to be understood to be one possessing extraordinary power, but rather ordinary with respect to morals and righteousness. Of course, by that definition, we would, collectively at least, all be gods; for we have the power or, better said, the ability to destroy not only the lives of others, but the very planet we inhabit. (Some would argue we are well on our way to carry it out).

In one of the many movie versions of the tale of Robin Hood, Maid Marian purports to demonstrate her love for Robin by proclaiming: "I love you more than God." God understands our love for one another. He is, in reality, the source of that love. When our love for another exceeds the boundaries of what might best be termed "earthy love," then we are beginning to scratch the surface of how God loves us. Fortunately, for us, God has a different point-of-view. Our God of mercy, righteousness, and forgiveness is in fact the only true God, and He is, therefore, the one God who is worthy of our reverence, our hearts, our minds, our bodies and spirits. To place anything before the Lord is idolatry.

It is not unusual today to observe a batter in a baseball game or a kicker in a football contest make the sign of the cross to seek God's intervention for victory. Some have gone as far as kneeling after scoring a touchdown. They have coined the phrase "Teabowing;" named after the man who started the gesture himself, Tim Teabow. He even trademarked the term. Truly, if God is first among your priorities, the gestures on the baseball diamond, the football gridiron, or whatever your field of play might be are superfluous.

God will know that you have placed Him first. No one of us can lay claim to such a privilege; we ALL can – that is, if our behavior – not just our gestures – evidences the fact that God is indeed our number-one priority.

How you treat your neighbor or stranger will evidence God's love in your life. You cannot be choosy or selective on whom you bestow God's goodness. If that's a difficult behavior for you to extend to your neighbor, then let God help you first. God proclaims there is no other love that will satisfy than His. **When you have His Spirit of love dwelling in you, you can love anyone. That's what the first commandment means.**

## THE OBJECT OF OUR AFFECTION | FEBRUARY 3

*"Thou shalt not make for yourself an idol in the form of anything in heaven above or on the earth beneath or in the waters below. You shall not bow down to them or worship them; for I, the LORD your God, am a jealous God, punishing the children for the sin of the fathers to the third and fourth generation of those who hate me, but showing love to a thousand generations of those who love me and keep my commandments." Exodus 20: 4*

---

The second commandment: It was a picture perfect wedding held in a perfect setting in the Napa country of Northern California. Old and new friends gathered together to celebrate the most ideal couple they ever witnessed. It was an unbelievable wedding. It seemed as though the characters of the fairy tale story of Cinderella came to life on that blissful summer day. Everyone who was there that witnessed this wedding came away assured that Sarah and John's love story would be a "happily ever after" ending story. Three years later she born a handsome child they named Trent. They continued to follow the storybook script, until last year when Sarah called me out of the blue confessing, John was leaving her. He cheated on her.

Unfortunately, fairy tale stories are fairly tales. The real life story is here on earth. During the Israelites journey in to the promise land they encountered many nations with varying forms of idol worship. God wanted the Israelites to know that there is only one true God, and it was their God. To substitute God with material objects lowers man's concept of God. The focus becomes the creature rather than the Creator.

History has repeated itself. Israel began to adopt the way of their heathen neighbors. The infamous gold calf was only the beginning of a rebellious and hard-necked society which was every bit as wicked as their neighbor. You become who you focus on. Generations later they sacrificed their children to the "god, Molech." How could this have happened to the chosen people of God? The chosen nation that God wanted the world to see as a representation of the true God ended up in the vilest pit of degradation and sin. Unless you are connected to God, you will be lured into having affairs with other gods. You will leave your first true love and become embroiled into ungodly practices that will lead to ruin. And along the way you will affect love ones into your lair. It's not only you that is affected with your scandalous choice but many others as well. The error reverberates throughout not only this world but God's entire the universe.

**Remember, God is our true love. We will be safe and secure with Him. Be faithful to our "eternal husband" because we are the object of His affection.**

## DO NOT MISUSE THE NAME OF THE LORD | FEBRUARY 4

*"You shall not misuse the name of the Lord your God, for the Lord will not hold anyone guiltless who misuses his name." Exodus 20: 7*

---

The third commandment: Perhaps the most popular book series of our times and certainly one of the highest-grossing film series has been the Harry Potter series. I do not ascribe to this fantasy nor do I advocate it. However, in that series, the wizards are warned never to evoke the name of "He Who Must Not be Named". The "he" in this instance is Harry's arch rival, Lord Voldermort. Harry is one of the very few who would dare to call out that name. Is it because Harry is aware that there is only one being worthy of such treatment, and this is the One to which the book you are now reading pays tribute, God, The Author of love? It would be nice to think so, but the Potter series gives us nothing that would support such a premise. In fact, the Potter series (both the books and the movies) have generally been panned by Christian clergy for this and a host of other reasons.

In the Jewish religion, Hebrew references to God (except in actual prayer) typically use one of two words: "Hashem", which means "the name" or "Adoshem", which is a combination of "Hashem" and the Hebrew name for God, "Adonai". Oftentimes, when a rabbi is depicted in the act of reciting a prayer in a movie or television show, "Adoshem" will be substituted for "Adonai" – this, inasmuch as this is theater, and it would be inappropriate to use God's name in vain. Many American Jews follow the practice of spelling God without the "o", that is, "G-d". This, too, is so as not to take the name of God in vain.

The Jewish people before us and we of the various Christian sects have come to realize that it is disrespectful and irreverent to misuse the name of our Lord. Certainly, God's name is NOT to be uttered when we stub a toe or find ourselves in bumper-to-bumper traffic on a highway; nor should we utter His name on happy occasions, such as when we win a major prize, "Oh My God" (OMG). When you misuse the name of God it is a reflection on your knowledge and relationship of Him. This has led some Christian pundits to point out that this is a misuse of the name of God. When you love someone you will not speak ill of them or disrespect them.

When you truly know your Maker, and you practice living a holy life in word and deed, you will always be on guard to revere even His name. **Every word spoken** reveals the true character of not only what's inside you but your relationship and knowledge of God. **You must speak the name of the Lord with reverence for He alone is worthy. Reverencing His name is not only in words but your way of living.**

## REMEMBER ME | FEBRUARY 5

*"Remember the Sabbath Day by keeping it holy. Six day you shall labor and do all your work, but the seventh day is a Sabbath to the LORD your God. On it you shall not do any work, neither you, nor your son or daughter, nor your manservant or maidservant, nor your animals, nor the alien within your gates. For in six days the LORD made the heavens and the earth, the sea, and all that is in them, but he rested on the seventh day. Therefore the LORD blessed the Sabbath day and made it holy." Exodus 20: 8-11*

---

The fourth commandment: Jesus said, "The Sabbath was made for man and not man for the Sabbath." Man was God's focal point when He instituted the Sabbath. It is a day of remembrance, faith and hope as we celebrate His love for us as shown by His concern for every detail of our lives. To keep the Sabbath holy is to rest from our own works and enter into His.

There have been numerous debates on how to keep the Sabbath holy. Most ardent adherents in keeping the Sabbath holy won't do even the most menial of tasks such as riding in a car or washing the dishes after a meal. Some will confine themselves to church quarters all day until Sundown. Some are prone to keeping the Sabbath by taking a nature walk after church service. I remember disliking the summer months because sunset was later which in turn impinged on our sundown social activities. Is that what God intended when He said to rest on the Sabbath from all our labors? Just what constitute work and rest? How did God instruct us to rest on the Sabbath? What are the works of God?

On this, both the Old Testament and New Testaments are very clear. They are works of mercy, of giving to those who cannot give back, of defending those who cannot defend themselves – the poor, the powerless, the orphans, the widows, the prisoners, and the "strangers" in our midst. As a nation, we do right by all of those except for the last two groups. "Strangers" are those from another country, another culture, another belief system than ours. They are the legal and the illegal together. Regardless of our politics, we are to love and care for them as if they were our own, for they too are God's.

Prisoners are a bit more problematic. We typically have less sympathy for murderers, thieves, rapists, and the like. We must remember, however, that those we classify as sinners are no less loved by the Almighty. How does one keep the Sabbath? **If we are to keep the Sabbath holy, we must do more than merely refrain from work. We must (for instance) care for the orphans, feed the hungry, shelter the homeless, visit the imprisoned, keep company with the widow, etc., these are indeed the works of God and not only on the Sabbath but every day of our lives.** These are true acts of love. These acts will help us to: "Remember the Sabbath Day to keep it holy."

## HONOR YOUR FATHER AND MOTHER | FEBRUARY 6

*"Honor your father and your mother, so that you may live long in the land the Lord your God is giving you." Exodus 20: 12*

---

The fifth commandment focuses on your earthly parents. Why would God place a priority on honoring one's parents? because God expects parents to communicate His character, His commandments, and His love to their progeny.

Honor encompasses more than respect, it also requires us to give them love and care, especially in their old age. As a society, our care these days for our elderly parents has limitations. We hire others, if we are financially able, to free us of what we perceive to be a burden. Christ reminds us to honor them and guard their reputation, to comfort them regardless of their character. To honor our parents is far more than speaking well of them, but to love them. And sometimes love must confront sin. We do not care for the ones we love by ignoring their abusiveness, their infidelity, their addictions, but neither do we withdraw from them. To treat them as God treats all of us requires that we essentially be lock-step with God.

Some psychologists today say parents need to also earn respect. They have to prove themselves worthy. If that be the case, how many of us will prove "worthy" when the time comes? God has cared for us over the years, despite our disrespectfulness, despite our abusive nature, despite our hypocrisies. Christ even took the matter further; it's not only our parents we should honor but parents in the household of faith, in other words everyone.

Do you remember when the disciples informed Him that His mother and brothers were outside a house waiting to see Him? He replied "who is my mother?" They were astonished at the apparent tepid treatment He showed them. They concluded that Christ was being disrespectful to His family. They did not know their Maker. Jesus was operating on a higher level than their thinking. Christ was making a point. He was saying there are no blood lines drawn with God. He set the example. He wanted us to treat each other with honor and dignity, regardless of our personal lineage. If you're struggling with a disrespectful parent in your life pray for them, love them nevertheless as God loves the errant child, then go cleave to the person who demonstrates God's love toward you; that is your mother, your father. You must rise above earthly parents to truly accept this commandment. When you see God's love in all people, then you have honored your parents.

In God's kingdom, we are all family. **To honor your parents or ANY PERSON is an expression of honoring God.** After all, that's how God honors us. Can you follow God's example?

## KILLER INSTINCTS | FEBRUARY 7

*"You shall not murder." Exodus 20: 13*

The Sixth Commandment prohibits us from killing one another. Not many years after the fall of Adam and Eve, the first act of murder occurred. Cain, in a jealous rage, killed his brother Abel. (That's where we got the term "raising Cain"). Today, murder is so commonplace that we often take such acts for granted. We read of murders by street gangs, murders of passion, Mafia wipeouts, homicides, the tolls of war, suicide bombings, and even so-called mercy killings.

Jesus said in Matthew 5: 21 that the sin of hatred was the same as murder. "Anyone who is angry with his brother (without cause) will be subject to judgment." Hatred is the seed of murder. This goes even deeper. All acts of injustice, revenge, or any passion that injures someone else, whether physical or emotional, has violated this commandment. There are few of us, who, at one time or another, have been guilty of such sins. And then there is what some would term the sins of omission.

When we fail to care for those who are not fully capable of taking care of themselves – the needy, the sick, the physically-deformed, is our sin any the less? When we consciously disparage or, in some instances, physically injure because of our prejudice, are we any the less sinners? When we fail to take a stand against the prejudicial acts of others, when we fail to stand up to the world's bullies, is our sin any the less? When we feel indifferent or callous to the panhandler or beggar in the street, is that considered an ungodly behavior? Yes, all of these are part of the Sixth Commandment.

The good news is that the Author of Love can change your heart. Whatever seed of contempt or disdain you are holding on to God can melt it away. Even the thought of contemplating an affair, God can help you. He can free your soul of any malice, evil or aversion, if you allow Him to do so. Nothing is hopeless with God. He can change the heart of the most hardened killer. Give your heart to Him right now and you will be set free from your heavy burden. Giving heart means being receptive of His Spirit dwelling in you.

Remember not even death can separate us from the love of God. Why not let Him love that killer instinct out of you today. God deals only within the parameters of His character, love. Killing is against His nature. God does not kill. **Are you struggling with anger or hatred for a fellow person? Is it eating you alive inside out? It's time to give it to God. When you allow His Spirit to control the killer in you, you'll not only be relieved but you will have His inner peace.**

## JUST ONE LOOK | FEBRUARY 8

*"You shall not commit adultery." Exodus 20: 14*

The seventh commandment is placed right where God wanted it to be. The number seven symbolizes perfection. His relationship with us was perfect. Earthly marriage is a shadow of our relationship with God-not the other way around. We had such openness with Him that there were no boundaries to consider, no need for privacy, no baggage or secrets. It was total freedom and disclosure with no limitations to His Love. We communicated with no reservations or inhibitions. We were naked without shame. It was an ideal marriage.

Then came the fall, and with it came blame, suspicion, mistrust, infidelity and clothing. Marriages today are oftentimes lacking in fidelity and trust. Divorce is fast becoming the rule. Statistically speaking, 50% of marriages today end in divorce. The divorce rate for second marriage is 70%. While third marriages divorce rate is 80%. Somehow there seems to be a pattern of "history repeating itself." The so-called "nuclear family" (mother, father, and the offspring they produced together) is a minority household. We are no longer shocked when we learn that a couple in our midst is calling it quits. Yet for those directly involved, the wound never truly heals. Cheating by partners in marriages is also fast becoming the rule. A term that is commonly used these days is "open relationships." Partners in a marriage agree in advance that they will take their business, so to speak, elsewhere. By agreeing to this in advance, it theoretically removes the sting from the act. This is certainly NOT what God intended; nor did He intend divorce. As always, God relents but the effects of our choices we reap.

Since the fall, of course, we have lived in a flawed world. Does this give us license to be adulterers? Hardly, in fact God has made it clear that His definition of adultery goes beyond the physical. He has proclaimed that lust and desire outside our committed relationship defiles the seventh commandment. The fruits of adultery are rooted in our unfaithful hearts. Out of the heart flow the secret thoughts, desires as well as inclinations. God considers just one look or thought of sensual consideration as the act of adultery. Are you guilty of such thoughts? Are you tempted to look at porn in the privacy of your bedroom? Does your mind wander about with your fantasies? I must confess I have. But, God knows your heart and He can keep you faithful. You must turn away from such urges. It's a daily, moment to moment commitment of yielding your thoughts to Him. I read recently of a dentist who went as far as firing his dental assistance for fear of a potential future affair with her because he was attracted to her. That is not how God intended us to treat our neighbor or any person.

**There is a difference between looking with the eyes and looking with heart. Guard your thoughts and actions lest you falter, because just one look is all it takes for the heart to succumb.**

## YOU SHALL NOT STEAL | FEBRUARY 9

*"You shall not steal." Exodus 20: 15*

The eighth commandment: It's easy to steal. We do it daily without blinking an eye, yet we don't realize the seriousness of what we do. Stealing began with Satan when he stole a third of the angels in heaven from God. Then he stole our parents' (Adam & Eve) hearts by convincing them that they knew better than God.

Stealing can take on more subtle than plucking the fruit from a tree. You take an extra box of clips or pens from the supply room at work. You fib "just a little" on your tax returns or employee time cards. What about leaving work early? How about skimming a little off the top of an expense account; a little here and there no one will miss. Oftentimes, the justification is: everyone's doing it; it's the norm. But it's not God's norm.

This commandment, however, goes deeper than stealing. God knows our motives. He reads each heart. The act of stealing begins with a thought. The thought instigates the act of stealing. Have you ever said to yourself, "a one night stand won't hurt anyone?" Yes, maybe not for that very moment. But why seek the pleasure for a moment and then reap the misery of a lifetime? More than the misery is the fact you betrayed a loved one.

Whether it's a covert personal affair, a business transaction that's unfair, such acts or thoughts of such acts violates our allegiance to God. Stealing compromises the core of your soul. When Lucifer captured the angels' allegiance, in so doing, he stole their hearts from God. Satan does that with each of us every chance he can. The motive is theft. Whatever he says is built on lies and deceptions. Anything he does is untrue.

Jesus said "I am not a thief." God sent His Son Jesus to redeem us from Satan's thievery. Satan accused God of stealing our hopes, our dreams, our lover, our children, our home or whatever else you have lost in your life. Satan is the accuser and father of thieves. Don't allow him to steal your life. Don't steal from others because it will lead to ruin. Whatever you're harboring and resenting because someone stole from you, let it go. Most of our disappointments are stolen hearts. Someone stole your heart or you stole someone's heart. Nothing in this world hurts more than a broken heart. **God is the restorer of broken hearts, dreams and promises. His Son came and restored all that was stolen from you and me.** He restored your freedom, He restored your salvation, and He restored your relationship with Him that was fractured.

Above all He restored His Son to us and vowed to fellowship with us eternally. What a blessed hope to live by.

# TRUE OR FALSE | FEBRUARY 10

*"You shall not give false testimony against your neighbor." Exodus 20: 16*

---

The ninth commandment: In the Garden of Eden, Lucifer, the father of lies, deceived Adam and Eve by violating the ninth commandment. He lied to them. He convinced them that if they partook of the fruits from the tree of good and evil, they would be like gods and would not die. The proof is in the inevitable death of each of us. God warned them and told them the outcome of their choice, but they did not listen. Instead they believed the lie.

The face of lying takes on many forms. Even withholding truth is defilement of this commandment. What about slander, evil surmising, gossip or spreading rumors? They are all forms of lying. Oftentimes, the difference between truth and deception is subtle. Our choices are not always black or white. Over the years, scholars, theologians and clergy have disagreed with respect to the notion of a so-called "good lie." One example would be not telling someone something hurtful so as not to hurt their feelings. As an example, an overweight person asks how she looks in a new dress. The truth is that, unless she loses some weight, the look will not be becoming. However, to tell her that she looks terrific in order to save her feelings ultimately does her a disservice. When you are weak in Godly Spirit it becomes a challenge to distinguish truth from untruth. Stay true and connected to the Author of Truth and you will be able to know the real Truth.

On the other hand, what would you have done if, during WW II, you were harboring Jews and the Nazis came knocking on your door? What would God wish us to do under such circumstances? Would our loving God wish us to tell the truth, if, in the end, it supports the cause of evil? Truth is more than just a statement of fact. God is well aware of our inner thoughts and our motives. Certainly, when in doubt, it's always preferable to tell the truth. However, when it is clear that our motives are pure and that the outcome will be a good one in God's eyes, then we must do what is right – this, with the recognitions and beliefs that God is both a loving God and a just God. Truth sometimes does hurt but when it is conveyed in the attitude of love, you cannot fail.

You are challenged daily with true or false issues; who will you believe? When you are connected with God, you will know the way, the truth and the life. God saved you from the lies of the deceiver. You can have the wisdom of God to know what's true or what's false. **Always remember God stands for truth, Satan for false testimony. The choice is yours. Are you able to discern the difference?**

## COVERT COVET | FEBRUARY 11

*"You shall not covet your neighbor's house. You shall not covet your neighbor's wife, or his manservant or maidservant his ox or donkey, or anything that belongs to your neighbor." Exodus 20:17*

---

The tenth commandment: There is a famous proverb that says "Be careful what you wish for, it might come true." More often than not, when we covet something, we discover that along with the object we covet, there are so-called "unintended consequences." We have designs on the much larger house in which our neighbor resides. If we achieve that goal, we will likely find that our utility bills increase, property taxes skyrocket, maintenance bills become more burdensome, and our kids are not fighting over who gets the largest room.

The fact is that, any time we covet someone else's possessions, we place ourselves in the shoes of the originator of covetousness, Lucifer. Lucifer felt slighted and jealous that he was not included with God, Jesus and the Holy Spirit during the council which planned mankind's redemption. He felt slighted whenever the Father, Son and Spirit convened and He was not privy to their meeting. He began to covet their position of ranking. There was a time when Lucifer had his ranking in the hierarchy of heaven, but he wanted to be "...like the Most High." Eventually, of course, Lucifer let his ambition get the better of him, and in doing so, he violated the tenth Commandment, which admonishes us in detail as to what we are not to covet.

Over the years, our own violation of this commandment has led to war, murders, thefts, divorces, and the like. Most importantly, when we covet the possessions of others, we are being disrespectful to the God who loves us. What is it that you covet in your heart today? Are you longing for your neighbor's wealth, spouse, child or status? I have a dear friend who coveted her lover to the point of giving up everything for him. When she finally got him she said to me "Now that I have him, I'm not that thrilled." Be careful what you ask for. Free yourself from your covert covetousness; for there is truly nothing in this world worth coveting, save for the desire to know God.

The Author of Love wants us to live a happy and fulfilling life. **When you discover God's commandments of love and apply them in your life, you are fulfilling all His commandments.** His commandments are all about His love. Keeping them will come naturally for you. When you love someone, you will not disgrace them, speak unkindly about them, dishonor them, cheat, lie, steal or kill them, nor will you covet what's theirs. **The Ten Commandments is a reminder of God's faithfulness and love for us.**

# EVERYONE, EVERYWHERE, EVERY TIME | FEBRUARY 12

*"For if, by the trespass of the one man, death reigned through that one man, how much more will those who receive God's abundant provision of grace and of the gift of righteousness reign in life through the one man, Jesus Christ." Romans 5: 17*

---

Grace has been called the "Last best word." Though we are undeserving, God renders grace to us, nevertheless, and He does so without reservation. Our church's creed is: grace for everyone, everywhere, every time.

We are all familiar with the song "Amazing Grace," believers and non-believers alike. But have you practiced grace in your life? When you see a homeless person with a sign asking for a handout, how do you respond? When the obese person sitting next to you takes up a portion of your seat, do you become annoyed? Someone cuts you off on the freeway; how do you react? Your child or friend confesses to you they're gay, do you shun them? A refrain we hear so often these days, often without the appropriate religion intonation is: WWJD…What would Jesus do? Well, clearly He would have handled each and every one of these situations with kindness, dignity and, very importantly, grace. The same way He has given grace to us unreservedly, we are to do likewise with our neighbor. Can you give grace to your neighbor even when he or she slights you? Can you wave your hand with grace to a person who cuts you off on the freeway? Can you extend grace to the person who abused or murdered your loved one senselessly? God did and so can you.

God came to dwell with us. He dressed in the garb of humankind like us and mingled with harlots, wealthy opportunists, a demon-possessed woman, a Roman soldier, a Samaritan with sores, a leper and a woman with numerous husbands. In fact, He gained the reputation of hanging around sinners. He even publicly declared that He had come for the sinner and the unrighteous. Are you one of the sinners or unrighteous? Regardless of what you think or do, God has already "graced us" through His Son. Whether you are a sinner or saint, He deemed you worthy of His grace. Whether you accept His grace or not, it will always be there for you. **Grace is God's love revealed through His Son.**

Has our church failed to show grace to everyone, everywhere and every time? You are the church. Have you shown grace to your neighbor? Grace is God's gift for every one of us. In his book "What's So Amazing About Grace," Philip Yancey says "Grace does not excuse sin, but it treasures the sinner." **Grace is not only the last best word but it will lead us to our final home with the Author of Grace.**

## I KNOW YOU | FEBRUARY 13

*"For you created my inmost being; you knit me together in my mother's womb. I praise you because I am fearfully and wonderfully made; your works are wonderful, I know that full well. My frame was not hidden from you when I was made in the secret place. When I was woven together in the depths of the earth, your eyes saw my unformed body. All the days ordained for me were written in your book before one of them came to be." Psalms 139: 13-16*

---

Today's text is a moving picture of how God is totally absorbed and focused on our well-being and delicate care. Can you imagine the God of the universe intricately weaving you into a babe while still inside your mother's womb? Knitting takes a lot of patience, methodical planning and creativity to complete. God did not decide to put together a hodgepodge of blood vessels, sinews, derma and follicles to create a monster but a beautiful and masterful work of a human being. The Author of all artists was at work painstakingly creating a masterpiece. You were not an afterthought. Yet, the question begs to be answer, did God create the Down syndrome child or conjoined twins? How can He allow a hermaphrodite baby or a child born with no arms or legs? How can this happen? God has never created chaos or imperfection. Love dictates freedom to choose. Yet, God did not stop loving our imperfect world. God's love is constant and sure regardless of who we are and our condition. God also promised all these maladies are temporary. He promised to make ALL things new again.

Since the fall, the world has descended into chaos. Our genes are no longer perfect. Copying mistakes have crept in. Anything apart from God's way leads to an imperfect life and world. However, God can only operate in nothing less than His character of love. He exists and behaves in a character of love. God cannot force love or manipulate allegiance. God can only act in a manner that is holy, pure, just and true. That is His nature.

The world in which we live is indeed imperfect, but that is because, early on, mankind chose to live apart from God. Even in our upside-down and inside-out state that we live in, God can make good out of chaos. It's as if God is saying; "I can't remember a time when I wasn't in love with you." Despite our imperfections and disorders He loves us. In other words He knows all about you and loves you still. No one in this earth will love and accept you more than God. He proved that by giving His Son to us to redeem us. Isn't it a great feeling to know you were wanted? Isn't it wonderful to be known?

**Make the time to KNOW the One who loves and knows you. When you truly understand His love for you, you too will praise Him as the Psalmist did.**

## HE IS FAITHFUL | FEBRUARY 14

*"Let us hold unswervingly to the hope we profess, for He who promised is faithful." Hebrews 10: 23*

Today is Valentines' Day. The history of Valentine's Day is shrouded in mystery. The Catholic Church recognized at least three different Saint Valentine, all of whom were martyred. Each has a different story of their noble deeds. In 498 A.D. Pope Gelasius officially declared February 14 Saint Valentine's Day. Although the practice of Valentine's Day is not a tradition we sanction as a sacred day, yet we tend to be caught up with the occasion and we remember the one we love. We evidence our love in a good many ways. Some will dine in a fine restaurant. Others will celebrate over a candle-lit dinner in the privacy of their home. More flowers are exchanged during Valentine's Day than on any other occasion, and for the chocolate purveyors, it is a veritable field day. Sometimes, I wish it was Valentine's Day every day. What a different world this would be. We would cherish our neighbor and treat them in kind because the Spirit of love is in our hearts daily. Unfortunately, that is unrealistic.

Today I read some posting on Facebook by some who dislike this occasion because they are single and feel left out. If you do not have a mate to share this special day with, all is not lost. Don't sit around pitying yourself and feeling unloved. Love is not an act of receiving but of giving. Be the lover and give of yourself today. Consider sharing this special day or a portion of it with someone who needs some special attention. Perhaps it is the elderly widow next door. It may be a disabled person, living alone. Maybe it's the person who slighted you or you hurt. Today, give the gift of hope and faith to the person God leads you to. When you do, you will see how much God loves you. This is truly "caring enough to send – or in this instance give – the very best."

The Author of Love is, by the very definition of the term "Author," the originator of love. God promised to love us, honor us and cherish us, regardless of our fallen state. God was indeed faithful in His promise to us. (So let us not lose hope or grow weary of His promise to finally take us home to be with Him eternally).

He has, of course, evidenced His love for us in the nature with which we are surrounded, but perhaps more importantly, His love is demonstrated by the fact that He shed His blood so that we might experience the love that was lost in Eden. God loves us beyond any measure of love we shall ever experience on Earth. Even if this particular Valentine's Day came up a trifle short in the (earthly) love department, **rest assured that God will forever be faithful to you, for He has already sent you the greatest Valentine's Day gift of all, His Son.**

## A FULL LIFE SPAN | FEBRUARY 15

*"Worship the Lord your God and his blessing will be on your food and water. I will take away sickness from among you and none will miscarry or be barren in your land. I will give you a full life span." Exodus 23: 25 & 26*

---

What a promise! Yet disease, famine, miscarriage and barren land abound today. How can this be? Does God really bless those who worship Him and punish those who do not worship Him? Are we being punished for not truly worshipping Him? Although God sees all the miseries you experience here on earth, the Author of Love is not the author of heartaches, misery or barrenness. Only goodness flows from Him. Then why do we still have all this woe? There are laws in our land which if broken will send you to jail. God has warned us, if we go astray from Him it will not be pleasant -- not because He will actively punish us, but because of how the universe itself functions. It is the laws of cause and effect. God is a God of law and order, and even the minutest stray from His perfect knowledge brings on imperfections and thus woes.

Some 30 years ago, Rabbi Harold Kushner wrote what became a best-selling book entitled: "When Bad Things Happen to Good People". Kushner and his wife had recently lost a young son, and this caused the Rabbi to ponder a question that many had contemplated but few theologians had been willing to pose out loud. Many reacted by proclaiming that Kushner was indeed asking the less important question. Instead, they argued, the more compelling question was: Why do good things happen to bad people? Truly, they are the same question. Kushner's hypothesis in a single paragraph: "I no longer hold God responsible for illnesses, accidents, and natural disasters because I realize that I gain little and lose so much when I blame God for those things."

Tragedy is not God's will; we need not feel hurt or betrayed by God. It is NOT "GOD'S WILL" that anyone's life should perish. Never accept or say those words. **GOD' S WILL IS LIFE ETERNAL.** There are times when we suffer even when we have done right, but God still says "trust me." You may not see it yet, but I assure you God's promises are sure. Someday He will make all things new again. You will never suffer again.

Can you hold on and stay faithful to Him? You must believe Him. He is your hope and salvation. **His promises will not only cover your full life span here on earth but all eternity.**

## A DETAILED GOD | FEBRUARY 16

*"Make the tabernacle with ten curtains of finely twisted linen and blue, purple and scarlet yarn, with cherubim worked into them by a skilled craftsman." Exodus 26: 1*

---

Today's Bible verse is another favorite of mine. It reveals in a much deeper sense the love of God. Have you ever planned a wedding? Was it your own? The work that goes into planning a wedding or any party requires thoroughness and organization. No details are spared. You want the affair to be perfect. After all, this is a once in a lifetime experience that will never be duplicated again. Unfortunately the best laid plans sometimes go awry.

During the Israelites' journey in the wilderness, the LORD instructed them to make a sanctuary so He could dwell among them. Read the details of these instructions in Exodus chapters 25-31. I've heard it said that God created the universe in six days, but it took Him 40 days to tell Moses how to make a tent. Yet the tent was the place where the Creator God would meet with His children. As such, it had to be perfect in every detail, for every item was filled with meaning, from the silver loops binding each board together-speaking of our many member unity in the Redeemer-to the outer covering of skin-even as we, as the temple of the Most High, have an outer covering of skin. Scholars have spent a lifetime studying the significance of the details of the tabernacle, and the richness of the revelation of God's love is well beyond the scope of this devotional. God is intimately concerned with the most minute and boring detail of your life. Those are the things He cherishes.

Have you ever loved someone so much that there was no detail of his or her life that was beyond your interest? How far would you go to really know your lover? Are you interested in the number of hairs he or she has? Do you know his or her favorite things? Are you interested in his or her enemies as well? How deep and detailed is your love for your lover? This is how God loves us but ever greater. He is so detailed that He even knows the number of hairs you have on your head. He knows every line in the palm of your hand. Every wrinkle on your face has piqued His interest. Every segment and phase in your entire life He eagerly observed with the utmost pleasure. From your waking hours to your slumber God has never missed a micro second of your breathing in or breathing out. "What manner of love is this!"

A character of God's love is details. God is the Author of details in your life. After all, He created you. Since His love is perfect, you were created perfect. Yea! But you say you're not happy with you. That's your problem. There will never be a duplicate of you. You need to learn to love yourself as He does. Do you want to know the details of why He loves you? **You will have all of eternity to understand His detailed love for you.**

## A RELENTING GOD | FEBRUARY 17

*"Then the LORD relented and did not bring on His people the disaster He had threatened." Exodus 32: 14*

This is a very revealing text of God's love. We never fail to blame God whenever disaster strikes. After all, if God is all-knowing, all-powerful and in control, He can prevent any calamities that engulf us. He can shield us from any fatality. Even our verse conveys that God is responsible or is able to control disasters. But is this what God is really saying? When you read the verses prior to verse 14, you will understand the context in which this text was written. The Israelites grew restless waiting for Moses to come down from the mountain where he was communing with God. The people who instigated creating the golden calf were accustomed to seeing and touching a representation of their deity. They still wanted something tangible to worship.

Haven't we all experienced enough of God's tangibles that we don't need a graven image of tangibles to trust Him? Some people go to great lengths to seek guidance in their lives. There are tarot readers and sales of Ouija boards to help you know your future. Many people depend on these "tangibles" to govern their lives. Even prominent statesmen have admitted to consulting with card readers for their daily guidance.

The Israelites felt the golden calf was their answer to their immediate longings. We are physical and focus on the seen rather than the unseen. It is difficult for us to accept in faith the unseen. God is spiritual though, during the Israelites journey in the wilderness He was constantly a relenting God. He gave in to the people's desires. If you choose anything else other than Him, He graciously steps aside and relents sadly. He knows a life without Him will reap the consequences of your choices. That is all part of God's law and order. Despite our occasional stubbornness and our apparent predilection for poor choices, God relents.

He is a loving God who relents. Relent means to become softened or gentler in attitude. That's how God loves us. Not only does God relent but He does NOT bring disasters to His people. Then why do we have disasters? Anything apart from God is chaos. When we choose to remove ourselves from God we succumb to the author of disasters. God has provided you with ample warning signs to protect you from harms' way. God is also patient and longsuffering. His love gives way to your insistence. God is a relenting God who respects your freedom of choice. If it is tangibles you seek, look at everything about you. They are...you are...evidence of His majesty abounds. **Whether you are innocent or guilty of your choices the key to all this is to TRUST Him and He will not need to relent.**

## **MY PRESENCE** | FEBRUARY 18

*"And the Lord said to Moses, 'My presence will go with you, and I will give you rest.'" Exodus 33: 14*

---

Have you ever been sued? Have you been fired from a job? Have you ever been summoned to appear before the IRS or court? Have you ever gone for a job interview where it was narrowed down to two candidates, only to be rejected as the last? Have you ever been jilted or stood up? Have you ever gone through a divorce? Have you lost a loved through death? These are frightening and overwhelming situations. I wish them upon no one. But we have some times or another encountered unpleasant situations in our lifetime. I am sure you have your own story to tell. I have been through all of the situations mentioned above and I'm still alive to share it with you. I could not have survived any of these ordeals without God's presence. Yes, God was always with me amidst my turmoil and trials.

Yet God has said amidst your trials and unrest, He will give us inner rest. I did a lot of praying during those times. There were times I felt God's presence and there were times when I felt no presence. Whether I feel His presence or not was not the issue. I must take Him at His word and believe Him that His presence will go with me every day of my life. When the judge ruled in my favor I knew God's presence was there. But sometimes you may not see it or feel God's presence while you are going through your situations. Sometimes rulings may not go in your favor. Rest assured that He is there.

You remember the story of Daniel and his companions "Shadrach, Mishak and Abednego." When they refused to bow to the king's image, they were thrown in the fiery furnace but did not burn. The king observed the three milling inside the furnace with another person whom he called "one like the Son of Man." Yes, Jesus was in their midst as He promised in today's verse. Even the King recognized Jesus. Why? because He had been in the presence of Daniel and his companions. They reflected God in their lives to the king and his kingdom. God's presence is in you. Just as He was in Daniel and his companions, He is with you and me.

The Author of Love is the only one who can instill peace in you. He said "My peace I leave with you, Let not your heart be troubled." You can claim God's peace and assurance by letting Him into your heart right now. When you let God's presence reign in your life you will know His Spirit of peace and you will find rest. Others will see "His Presence" in you. **He says, "My presence is all you need." You can now rest.**

## **SILENT FAITH** | FEBRUARY 19

*"And he passed in front of Moses, proclaiming. 'The Lord, the Lord, the compassionate and gracious God, slow to anger, abounding in love and faithfulness, maintaining love to thousands, and forgiving wickedness, rebellion and sin. Yet he does not leave the guilty unpunished; he punishes the children and their children for the sin of the fathers to the third and fourth generation.'" Exodus 34: 6 & 7*

---

Sometimes when my faith wanes, I get into a questionable mood about God's existence. I ask God, just once, if you show me a sign, I will never need to doubt again. But all I get is silence. Silence so still that it almost seems as though He's up there screening my call. Job went through a similar experience. In Chapter 23 verses 8 & 9 Job says, "But if I go to the east He is not there, if I go to the west I do not find Him. When He is at work in the north, I do not see Him; when He turns to the south; I catch no glimpse of Him." For the first 37 chapters of Job all he does is question God and His silence.

We all go through a questioning period with God. There are some who question less and accept more of the silent God through faith. But faith is not a feeling. It requires no evidence, just trust at His word. It is called a child-like faith. Faith, like the Centurion that Jesus complimented. There's also the woman who touched the garment of Jesus as He walked by her. She was healed through that touch. But what about the faith like Job who saw no evidence or answer? What about your faith today? Do you trust God whether you see evidence or not? Does your faith waver according to the "climate." Do you know what this silent faith means?

There appears to be two types of faith in our world, those with child-like faith and those with adult-like faith. Where are you with your faith with God? Can you walk blindly in faith or do you need evidence? Children during their early childhood have a tendency to believe their parents. While the adult–type faith sees no evidence, hears no voice and receives no answer but still trusts. One faith has proof while the other has no proof. Which faith do you have? You must exercise the faith that God gives unreservedly whether you see evidence or not. You must be steadfast like Job. Silent faith is trusting God in the hope He gives you whether you see evidence or not. Don't think for one moment that you are being punished by God. God never punishes us. No. Our punishment is the result of our choices, when we are guilty. Don't let others convince you that God is behind all your calamities. That's a false assumption of God. If you can't accept this then you need to invest for more of your time and energy in getting to know God in a deeper level.

**When you realize and accept God's love for you, then you will never waver when the storms comes your way because you have His silent faith.**

## A RADIANT FACE | FEBRUARY 20

*"When Moses came down from Mount Sinai with the two tables of the Testimony in his hands, he was not aware that his face was radiant because he had spoken with the Lord." Exodus 34: 20*

---

When a survey was conducted on what's the first attraction that a woman notices in a man, the majority of women stated it was the eyes, then the face. Every culture summarizes the meaning behind a person's face. In our culture, a large forehead connotes an intellectual. Beady eyes as oppose to round eyes warns you a person's veracity may be questionable. The color of a person's gums or lips makes a statement of one's largess or miserliness. The list is endless, yet these myths have no reliability. We persist in using the face as a gauge to a person's character trait. Pop psychologists have produced books on how to read a person's face or how to read body language. Does the face really reveal the character of a person? Have you ever waited for a parking space in a busy parking lot only to be cut off by someone? "If looks could kill," the stare you give that obnoxious person would be deadly.

Only God can know the heart and motive of a person. Sometimes you cannot hide your emotions and feelings. It shows in your face whether darkness or light. I remember when I passed my oral exam for my Master's degree. I came out of that room beaming from ear to ear. My friends waiting outside didn't have to ask. They saw it on my face. I remember counseling a client who was in denial whenever I confronted him about his feeling for his ex-wife. He denied He was still in love with her but gave himself away just by the look in his face whenever he talked about her. His face had that certain glow of undeniable desire to reconcile with her. Have you ever notice a person in love cannot hide it? Their face, countenance and behavior give them away.

What type of person do you reflect? Do you start your day glowing or are you a "sour puss." Do you begin your waking moment each day as Moses did? He spent time alone with God. As you go about your daily life will people witness externally on your face a reflection of what is deeply rooted internally, God? Although the face does reveal a lot about a person, today's verse talks about a face that was with God.

When Moses came down from Mount Sinai his face was radiant. Radiant means he was reflecting the presence of God. God wants you to reflect a radiant face of His love so people will know you too have been with God. **A radiant face is more than a look; it's an attitude of the Spirit of God. Begin each day alone with God and you too will reflect a radiant face of God's love.**

## SPIRIT FILLED SKILL | FEBRUARY 21

*"and he has filled him with the Spirit of God, with skill, ability and knowledge in all kinds of crafts." Exodus 35: 31*

There are advocates today that promote positive thinking and believing in yourself, teaching that if you put your mind to any dream or goal you can achieve it. From the youngest to the eldest, we're encouraged to dream big and "go for it." Nike's "Just do it" emboldens athletic pursuits of greatness. These are all inspiring and motivating. We envy the skills of these exceptional athletes. Does that mean God favors these people over me? Or is it merely the "luck of the genes?" Why wasn't I blest with the gift and skill of playing tennis, or singing, or playing the piano? Have you ever had talent envy? When you watch great sports figures or talented singers or political statesmen do you wish you could be like them? Regardless of the answer, God has given every person a degree of "talent."

It isn't the talent that matter, but what we do with that talent. Is it a sprit filled talent? Today's verse talks of men named Bezalel and Oholiab who were not only talented and skilled in many crafts but were filled with the Spirit of God. They used their skills to help design the tabernacle and sanctuary in which God would dwell. They followed God's command. What's important is our life is a Spirit filled life. When God's spirit fills you, then you too will have a "filled skill, ability and knowledge in all kinds of crafts."

Our society uplifts "number one." Whether in sports, business, politics, religion or even family and relationships, someone will win and someone will lose. Second place in our culture is another word for "loser." Have you ever watched the Olympics? Did you notice those who came in second? Some of them were undoubtedly disappointed and dejected. Some have even gone as far as rejecting the silver medal. Yet for us, the only race that seems to count is whether we get into the kingdom. Win or lose, God values more a Spirit- filled life. Do you possess that?

God is the author of good gifts. He treats everyone equally insofar as His love for us is concerned. If you have a test, call it, it is to love others, much as God has loved you. Notwithstanding our differences with respect to various measurable talents and abilities, what God looks for is in the heart of the individual. His Spirit resides in the heart that loves. Do you love in His Spirit?

**A Spirit-filled with the Spirit of God in your life is what truly matters in this world and His kingdom.**

## PROMISE KEEPER | FEBRUARY 22

*"But with thee will I establish my covenant; and thou shalt come into the ark, thou, and thy sons, and thy wife, and thy sons' wives with thee." Genesis 6: 18*

Do you remember when you first heard about Santa Claus? I did. I was five years old. We were getting ready for bed when my father said to place my stockings at the foot of my bed and in the morning, Santa Claus would fill it with "goodies." I asked father who was Santa Claus. He said it was a jolly man dressed in a red suit that traveled around midnight on Christmas Eve with a sleigh and reindeers giving presents to boys and girls who have been good all year. Well, needless to say, I believed my father and placed a couple of socks at the foot of my bed and went to sleep. The next morning I found the stockings on the floor empty. I concluded that Santa Claus was a myth.

As I reflect on my father's story, I am reminded of our heavenly Father who made a promise to Noah that He would save them from annihilation. This is the first time that the word "covenant" appears in the Bible. Covenant is more than a promise. It comes from the Hebrew term grace. This connotes divine favor. There can be no covenant of relationship without Yahweh. God initiated the covenant as a relationship with Noah and his family. Why would God make such a covenant with Noah? God remembered His covenant with Adam and Eve, with Abraham, Isaac and Jacob. He made a covenant with Noah because He wanted to express His grace. God knew that if He did not destroy sin, it would engulf Noah and his family as well. The world had rejected God. an Just as in the days of Noah, today we witness so much senseless violence and deaths around us each day, if left to our own accord God knows we would self-destruct.

God is making the same covenant with you too. Trust His promise. Without God the end result is death. With God, there is eternal life. Sometimes it is hard for us to reconcile the injustice, the insanity and chaos the world is in with a loving God. We long for a day where there will no longer be chaos, wars and death. That day is about to happen. Trust in His promise. He keeps ALL His promises.

As we journey in earth's final chapter there is only hope in God's promise that He will return to take us home. That is why God must keep His promise. If God does not intervene, we will self-destruct. He will not let that happen because He made a covenant with us. **His promise is as sure as His existence. His covenant for us is His way of expressing His divine grace**.

Be ready to meet your promise keeper.

## THE GIVER OR THE GIFT | FEBRUARY 23

*"All who were willing, men and women alike, came and brought gold jewelry of all kinds; brooches, earrings, rings and ornaments. They all presented their gold as a wave offering to the LORD." Exodus 35: 22*

---

This is an interesting text. It talks about the Israelites giving of their gold for the work the LORD Moses commanded them to do. You will note the Israelites had in their possession brooches, rings, earrings and ornaments of every conceivable type. What were the Israelites doing with these jewelries? Remember they had "plundered" the Egyptians. Gold was just as precious then. The LORD commanded Moses to build a tabernacle, constructed with the finest materials. From gold, silver and bronze to blue, purple and scarlet yarn and fine linen to spices, for anointing oil and fragrant incense; and onyx stones to the choice acacia wood. All these items were to be artistically designed by those chosen artists filled with the Holy Spirit. What does this say about our God?

I am reminded of a story I heard a pastor share when he was growing up in church. His mother had very few possession of any value. One thing she treasured was a hat that she wore to church. However, one Sabbath day a lady in church made a comment about her hat as being an adornment and inappropriate to wear in church. The lady further added that it was an offense to God to focus attention on her as oppose to God. She was shocked and embarrassed and did not want to offend anyone. She never wore that hat to church ever again. The pastor's mother thought she was giving her best by dressing her best for the Lord. The lady questioned her "gift" to God. What is more important – the giver or the gift?

Where is our focus? Where is our heart? Does God need our Gold? God doesn't need our jewelry, our gold or our money. God created those precious gems. God owns this world and the universe. These are things to Him. They are not as valuable to Him as you are. He paid the ultimate price with His life in order to redeem you and me. God wants your heart. When you give is it from your heart? **The greatest test of love is in giving. You can give without loving but you cannot love without giving.** What have you given to your Maker? Remember, He does not need your gold. All He wants is your acceptance of His gift to you.

God did not hold back anything in His treasure trove. **God gave us the perfect gift, He GAVE us His Son.**

## **TO LIVE OR TO DIE?** | FEBRUARY 24

*"Altogether, Methuselah lived 969 years, and then he died." Genesis 5: 27*

---

Aging is inevitable. I don't know of any person who ever said, "I can't wait to grow old," which of course is different than "growing up." Eternal youth is the desire of our society. Everywhere around us the media expounds on the virtues of being youthful. Today our average lifespan is between 70-80 years. Ninety is old! However, our early ancestors were just starting a family at that age. Adam's first son was born when he was 130 years old; his son Seth had his first son at 105 years. Can you imagine having a child at 100 years old? It obviously was different then. However, you will also note that by the time Sarah and Abraham reached 90 to 100 years old they were by then considered old. And having a child at 99 years old was unbelievable, just as it would be today.

If you could live 969 years old today, would you want to? Looking at the early history of man, even God was discouraged. After Methuselah had lived 187 years he became the father of Lamech. Lamech was the father of Noah. Noah's grandfather was Methuselah. By the time Noah appeared, God said "My spirit will not contend with man forever, for he is mortal; his days will be hundred and twenty years." The word contends here means "my spirit will not remain in" and the word mortal means "corrupt." When God's Spirit is withdrawn here on earth, those who are sealed in His love will witness the full effect of sin. The Author of Love was striving with man only through His Spirit. Whenever God's spirit is withdrawn, corruption occurs. God saw that man was headed on a course of self-destruction. "The Lord saw how great man's wickedness on earth had become, and that every inclination of the thoughts of his heart was only evil all the time." Genesis 6: 5.

What do you think you'd witness if the earth were to exist another 900 years? I doubt if it would be a pretty sight. We have much evil now. And it doesn't appear to be getting any better. The U.S. is again at war. There are tensions among nations ruled by self-serving dictators in the Middle East and around the world as well. Most of the evil acts we witness in our own community make no sense or reason. The killings we recently heard in the news in Colorado, Wisconsin and Pennsylvania, critics declared as senseless. We are unable to find a reason for such events. We are witnessing a foretaste of a world without the Spirit of God. Don't let the Spirit of God leave your presence. **Stay connected with Him and you will live a godly life.**

As in the days of Noah, you will face a choice to live or die? Choose God.

## **TOMORROW** | FEBRUARY 25

*"Why, you do not even know what will happen tomorrow. What is your life? You are a mist that appears for a little while and then vanishes. Instead, you ought to say, 'If it is the Lord's will we will live and do this or that.'" James 4: 14 & 15*

---

Ralph Waldo Emerson said "Finish each day and be done with it. You have done what you could. Some blunders and absurdities no doubt crept in; forget them as soon as you can. Tomorrow is a new day; you shall begin it well and serenely." Why do we worry? One of my best friends had notice puffing in his right and left temples. He did not know what was going on. He thought the worst. Maybe he has a tumor or cancer. He called his doctor for an appointment and they could not see him for a week. He panicked. He could not wait a week to find out what was wrong with him. He asked the clerk at his doctor's office to call him if there was a cancelation. In the meantime he went to the internet to check some of the causes of his symptoms. He read the gamut from a cyst that's nonthreatening to a deadly disease which can be a tumor or cancer of the gland. As he read further he started to conjure up his life history and resigned to the inevitable that he might die soon. He even checked the calendar date and noted in a couple of days the number eight would be coming up. That was an ominous sign because his father died on the eighth. I met with him to console him. I took him out to dinner to talk things in a logical and rational manner. Just as we pulled out of his driveway a black cat dashed in front of us and he concluded back luck. Does his story sound familiar? Do you worry about your future? If you knew what your future would be like would you do things differently today?

God said it plainly and clearly in Matthew 6: 25-27 "Therefore I tell you, do not worry about your life, what you will eat or drink; or about your body, what you will wear. Is not life more important than food, and the body more important than clothes? Look at the birds of the air; they do not sow or reap or store away in barns, and yet your heavenly Father feeds them. Are you not much more valuable than they? **Who do you by worrying can add a single hour to his life?"** Can you trust God and say "If it is the Lord's will we will live and do this or that."

**Leave your worry for tomorrow. You have no control for tomorrow.** Tomorrow is neither here nor there. Live for today and leave tomorrow alone. **All your tomorrows are in God's care. Trust God. He is the Author of your life right now and all your tomorrows.**

## **A YES GOD** | FEBRUARY 26

*"Anyone who curses his father or mother must be put to death." Exodus 21: 17*

---

This is an interesting verse in the Bible that warrants scrutiny. Can you imagine children that cursed their mother or father during that period were put to death? Aside from the Ten Commandments, God gave Moses specific laws pertaining to servants, personal injuries, protection of property, social responsibility and laws of justice and mercy. Breaking these laws brought severe punishments. Death sentences were those act such as: cursing your mother or father, anyone who strikes a man and kills him; anyone who kidnaps; anyone who attacks his mother or father; practice of sorcery; sexual relations with an animal; sacrifices to any god other than the LORD; whoever does work on the Sabbath; A man who sleeps with another man; anyone who practices medium or spirits, anyone who commits adultery or incestuous relations. These are deadly sins. Isn't it interesting that our society selectively choose which commandments to follow? We condemn those whose life choices differ from our own, but neglect to see the other activities we have done in our own lives that warrant the most severe of punishments.

There were international headlines several years ago in Africa. A woman was convicted of having an adulterous affair. The tribal council condemned her to death. She was pregnant at the time of sentencing so they waited until she gave birth before carrying out the verdict. The emotional outrage and support she received worldwide required re-evaluating the verdict. The cries of injustice were heard loud and clear but just like the story in John 8, why wasn't the man punished? They relied on a man-made law called Sharia. It's obvious that the law is bias and chauvinistic. Such treatment and subjugation of women is enough to make you want to curse at them. Then there's the famous road rage, when an "idiot" behind the wheel cuts you off in the freeway without regard for your safety. What's the first thought that enters your mind… and suddenly you end up vocalizing a curse word.

The Author of Love was justified in cursing our behavior for swearing allegiance to the "evil one." But He didn't. **God in His mercy and grace decided to say Yes to His Father and take the curse that was for us**. Meditate on this; Matthew 5: 36 & 37, "And do not swear by your head, for you cannot make even one hair white or black, Simply let your Yes be Yes and your No, No," If you've ever felt like cursing learn to substitute each curse word with "YES." Better yet, let the Spirit of God dictate your mind, body and soul. **Don't you love to hear the word Yes? Can you say Yes to God? After all He is a Yes God. You can if you are connected to Him.**

## GOD'S WARNING SIGNS | FEBRUARY 27

*"Aaron's sons Nadab and Abihu took their censer, put fire in them and added incense; and they offered unauthorized fire before the Lord, contrary to His command. So fire came out from the presence of the Lord and consumed them, and they died before the Lord." Leviticus 10: 1 & 2*

---

Next to Moses and Aaron, Aaron's sons Nadab and Abihu were next in line in order of leadership and respect in Israel. They presided over the sacrificial services in the tabernacle. Each service they conducted was of great importance in the sight of all Israel and God. The people witnessed the services had great joy that God accepted their sacrificial offerings. God had shown the people He must be approached with awe and reverence. Anything short of this was unacceptable. For God is holy, pure and true. Any slight variation from the prescribed commandment had dire consequences. Sin and self-righteousness cannot intermingle. God's presence is a consuming fire.

Nadab and Abihu took that commandment from God lightly. They decided they had a better recipe for the incense. Perhaps even their senses and judgment had become hazy by indulging in drinking wine prior to their service. Aaron and his sons were admonished: "Do not drink wine nor strong drink you, nor your sons with you, when you go into the tabernacle of the congregation, lest you die:"

Reading this story can be puzzling in light of a God of Love destroying two people who thought they knew what God wanted. But there is a deeper significance in all this. God did not destroy Nadab and Abihu. His presence of Holiness and purity cannot be in the same room as disobedience. God is a "consuming fire" and anyone caught contrary to His Holiness will be consumed. Nadab and Abihu lost sight of God's holiness in their arrogance and lax obedience. Their judgment was marred.

Don't let a careless moment mar your senses. Be ever so vigilant in your walk with God. No matter how trivial the situation may be, always be on guard. Everything God has given us from His laws to His warning signs are not meant to prevent you from living an abundant life, they were given in love and care. God wants you to live life to the fullest. He knows best. When you follow His guidance your life will be filled.

**Remember Nadab and Abihu but never forget God's warning "love" signs.**

## EATING HEALTHY | FEBRUARY 28

*"The LORD said to Moses and Aaron, 'Say to the Israelites: Of all the animals that live on land, these are the ones you may eat;'" Leviticus 11: 1 & 2*

---

A whole chapter is devoted to dietary laws that God instructed Moses to convey to the Israelites. Why would God go through the trouble of explaining in details certain animals that can be consumed and animals that cannot? God begins Chapter 11 by stating animals that have a split hoof and chews the cud are clean. However, those that only have one or the other we must not eat. The creatures living in the water of the seas and streams, those with fins and scales are edible. Any sea creatures without these attributes God declared unclean and not to be eaten. Flying insects that walk on all fours are detestable, except those that have jointed legs for hopping on the ground. God named the locust, katydid, cricket or grasshopper as clean. God said the weasel, rat, any kind of great lizard, the gecko, the monitor lizard, the wall lizard, the skink and the chameleon were unclean. God further included any creature that moves about on its belly or walks on all fours or on many feet; it is detestable.

Why? Though we may not fully understand the nutritional reasons, we do know that Israel was to live differently than the surrounding nations-even to their diet. I am intrigued at a food cable network that glamorizes the travels of the host in foreign lands where he feasts on just about every creature mentioned in Exodus 11. He appears healthy and makes each meal rather curious and inviting. The people indigenous to the culture have a way of preparing those creatures in a palatable manner. Nevertheless, God knows His creatures and what is healthy and what is unhealthy. The illnesses and diseases we encounter today can, to a large degree, be attributed to our diet. You can rationalize and ignore these warning signs but our patient God once again relents and allows you to choose what you wish to indulge in. Your salvation will not be based on your taste buds or what you eat. Our taste buds have been adulterated. Our taste is cultural and conditional. The food you choose may taste good to you but God's way is best.

God is holy. He wants you to be holy too. In every law that God has ordained, there is a greater law that one needs to focus on. That is the GIVER of the law. God has given us ample guidelines to live a healthy life. To truly appreciate the laws, one must know the Lawgiver. His laws are a reflection of His character, love. There's a reason God said what to eat and what not to eat; to give you not only a healthy life but to know the source of all life, God. **What you eat is a reflection on the God you know and serve. Follow God's guidance, eat healthy and live an abundant life.**

## **LOVE YOUR HAIR** | MARCH 1

*"When a man has lost his hair and is bald, he is clean. If he has lost his hair from the front of his scalp and has a bald forehead, he is clean." Leviticus 13: 40 & 41*

---

It's a great feeling to be clean. It's even more appealing when you are pronounced clean. This text confirms that. The context is the ceremonial laws that God instructed Moses to follow in order to be clean. Though male-pattern baldness is extremely rare in middle-eastern people, it is common among Europeans. In ancient Israel, to be bald was to be thought ill. This verse tells us that is not the case. Hair is the crowning glory of one's overall appearance. For some, baldness renders one subject to discrimination. Some miss out on job opportunities or are shun by potential partners because of their baldness. Our culture places a premium on a full head of hair.

When my mother went through chemotherapy she lost all her hair. We shopped around to find just the right hair wig. Matching her skin tone was a challenge, but she wanted black since that was her true color. Today most people can identify a person wearing a wig or toupee. However, the cover-up can be uplifting to the wearer's self-image. When mother's hair was restored, she no longer needed to wear the wig; but a new dilemma occurred, her gray hairs began to appear. She immediately decided to color her gray hair black. As I age, I too am noticing the gray hairs and find it difficult to maintain the youthful appearance. I started to dye my hair. But to maintain the dye hair look can be burdensome. The grey roots start appearing every four weeks. Thus, the process of needing to dye starts all over again. At least I have a full head of grey hairs.

Many of us value our outward appearance more than anything. However, the Author of Love regards us for who we are, that is, what is in our hearts. Accordingly, for us to slight someone because of his or her hair, skin tone, height or weight, gender, facial features, educational background or socioeconomic status is both shallow and, more significantly, ungodly. God did not enter into our midst in order to die for our image, but rather to transform us to His image. God is not interested in a whole restoration of our appearance, but the restoration of the trust, love and relationship that were lost is His priority. To God it's the person and their character that's behind the hair that is more important. Stop loving your hair and start loving your God. He is your source for everything in your life. **God knows that outer beauty in this lifetime is fleeting but inner beauty, character, is eternal. Thank God your appearance is not your ticket to heaven.** God has promised to make all things new again. We must keep that hope alive in our heart and not in our appearance.

## CHOOSING RIGHT | MARCH 2

*"Do not give any of your children to be sacrificed to Molech, for you must not profane the name of your God. I am the Lord." Leviticus 18: 21*

---

We ask ourselves how loving parents could allow their children to be given to such abominable idolatry. The children didn't know any better. Tales of child sacrifice are virtually unheard of today. However, each of us can probably relate a story or two about modern-day parents who sacrifice their children's well-being, their very future, at the proverbial altar of Mammon, the god of money.

Whether we realize it or not, many of us have chosen career over our family. Too often a late night at the office seems more important than a sons' soccer game. Moreover, it is rather easy to rationalize such deeds…We are, we convince ourselves, investing in our family's future by sacrificing now for brighter days tomorrow. When tomorrow arrives, we discover that the children have become independent and, very often, disrespectful of their parents. A common refrain is: "If you had been around when I was growing up, I wouldn't be this way. It's all your fault."

"A child arrived just the other day. He came to the world in the usual way. But there were planes to catch and bills to pay. He learned to walk while I was away. And he was talking 'fore I knew it, and as he grew, he'd say, 'I'm gonna be like you, dad. You know I'm gonna be like you.'"

The Harry Chapin lyrics continue: "When you coming home, dad? I don't know when, but we'll get together then. You know we'll have a good time then." Was Chapin singing about you? What is it that our children want? An I-Phone, maybe an I-Pad or an I-something-or-other? Or is it our time, our love, our attention? Do they feel as if they are at the top of our priority list, or do they feel more like an annoying distraction?

The good news is that, if we are indeed looking for role models, there is none better than God. The earlier in our kids' lives that we evidence our love for God the greater the likelihood that our children and ultimately, their children will follow in our footsteps; you must set the example of choosing God to your child. Your children mimic your behavior, your likes and dislikes and above all your God. You are, to a very significant degree a representation of how they see and relate to God. Yes, you are the God they will know and trust.

"Train a child in the way he should go and when he is old he will not turn from it." Proverbs 22: 6. **Choose God foremost in your life and you will bring up godly children.**

## **HANDICAPPED** | MARCH 3

*"Do not curse the deaf or put a stumbling block in front of the blind, but fear your God. I am the LORD." Leviticus 19: 14*

When was the last time you felt really good about yourself? Was it when you finally graduated high school or college? Or was it when you received a well-deserved promotion? Maybe it was finding the love of your life. Or the day you shot your best game in golf, tennis or baseball. Sometimes, unfortunately, our elation is at the expense of others. One person is happy and the other is not. People possess varying degrees of mental and physical prowess, not to mention differences in emotional makeup. Some even use their handicap to their advantage; while others abuse the handicapped for their advantage.

It is particularly easy to ignore the un-or less-lovable amongst us. We are prone to rationalize: "I have enough of my own problems and challenges." The truth of the matter is we are all handicapped and in need of compassion and acceptance. Whether a person's handicap be visible or invisible, that person deserves to be treated as God treats us. God understand how much it hurts to be ridiculed, to be discriminated against, to be rejected. God has shouldered every handicap this world has ever produced and has redeemed us. Without the Author of Love dwelling in our heart we will "curse the deaf and put a stumbling block in front of the blind."

At the heart of man's law is the need to protect the vulnerable amongst us. Oftentimes, unfortunately, man's law misses the mark. God, on the other hand, turns His back on no man or woman, for He knows that we are indeed all handicapped in one way or another. He knows we are all in need of a Savior to save us.

Who are the undesirables in your world? What handicaps or flaws-seen or unseen-describe either you or those you reject? Whether fat or skinny, old or young, immigrant or native-born, Jew or gentile, male or female, black or white, gay or straight, handicapped or normal, all are eligible to receive the healing attention of the Author of Love. No one's handicap is excluded. In other words, God has excluded no one in His kingdom. We are all welcome and wanted. But most of all He really loves us not just as we are. Your handicap here on earth is still desirable. He knows your imperfections but sees beyond those flaws. That's because He knows He will create a new you someday. Are you feeling handicapped? Forget it! You are whole and desired in God's kingdom.

**Just as God has shown you acceptance and mercy so are you to do likewise.**

## REJOICE, PRAY AND GIVE THANKS | MARCH 4

*"Rejoice always, pray without ceasing, and in everything give thanks for this is the will of God in Christ Jesus for you." IThessalonians 4: 16-18*

I received an earnest plea from a dear friend of mine requesting I pray for her and her boyfriend. She was forlorn and anxious the day she called me. She was struggling with a dilemma that needed a prayer intervention. They had been having a long-distance relationship that was not working out. She lived in Southern California and he lived in Northern California. But neither one wants to give up their established job and livelihood in their respective place of residence. I pondered why doesn't she pray? Why ask me?

What is your idea of prayer? Do you pray to God only when the need arises? Do you pray only when there's a huge problem you need resolution? Do you pray for your health your school, your job or your future spouse? Do you pray for safety in time of danger? Do you pray for wealth when you're in dire financial straits? Do you pray to "win" when you are about to compete in sports as some athlete do before a game. There is a huge fan base that follow Tim Teabow, a quarterback for the New York Jets who poses to kneel when he is about to start a game or when he completes a touchdown pass. What about those who pray but yet perform acts contrary to their prayer. Like, knowing full well, drugs are deleterious to your health but you continue to engage in them. Or you are involved in a secret "love affair" when suddenly you are diagnosed with cancer. Does that sound hypocritical? Will God hear your prayer?

There are so many ways and reasons to pray. Prayer is all of the above mentioned but so much more. As Andy Rooney once said "I've learned…that I can always pray for someone when I don't have the strength to help him or her in some other way."

Paul recommends "pray without ceasing," why? because he learned the secret to a **PRAYERFUL LIFE**. Do you pray five times a day as the Muslims do? Prayer is more than the act of pausing to kneel and bowing one's head to pray. Prayer is all about living a **PRAYERFUL LIFE with Christ**. You breathe prayer in and out as well as each heartbeat. "Let this mind be in you, which was also in Christ Jesus: Philippians 2: 5 Christ's mind, body and spirit were all in tune with His Father.

You can have the **PRAYERFUL LIFE** that Christ has with His Father, too. And you too will give thanks to God for the joy of being one with Jesus Christ.

## A SURE CURE FOR THE ADDICT'S DEPENDENCY | MARCH 5

*"Do not defile yourselves in any of these ways, because this is how the nations that I am going to drive out before you became defiled. Even the land was defiled; so I punished it for its sin, and the land vomited out its inhabitants." Leviticus 18: 24 & 25*

---

Do you love to eat chocolate? I know some people do and some even to the point of being addicted to it. Any type of addiction produces conflict in your life. Patrick Carnes wrote a book "Out of the Shadows: Understanding Sexual Addiction." According to Carnes addictions are driven by feelings of loneliness, depression, anxiety and unworthiness which are temporarily relieved through a high similar to that achieved through mood-altering chemicals such as alcohol or cocaine.

We live in a world full of all types of addictions. Bottom line, we are addicted to sin. Each of us is struggling to overcome our own personal "high." You "remedy" your addiction by joining Alcoholics Anonymous, Weight Watchers, Sex Anonymous, hypnosis, psychotherapy, etc. These all have their merits and are positive methods of arresting your addiction. And I encourage you to seek help for your addiction. The first step for any healing to begin, when a person is struggling with an addiction, is to come to a realization and acceptance that he or she is powerless in healing themselves and must surrender their will to God.

God is your best, truly, your only source of hope. Perhaps it sounds easier said than done. It's not. Addiction is a real disease. In my counseling sessions, when a person is in denial or rationalizes his or her addictive disorder, the end result is predictable; they will either go to jail, an institution or die. I've witnessed all these dire consequences time and again. The disease is deadly. The sooner the person surrenders their addiction to God's power, the sooner their healing will begin. Any addictive disorder God can arrest. He knows your vulnerability and your proclivity to sin. He gave us the answer to sin, and that's only through His Son. His Son took all those addictions upon himself that we can be free and made whole again. Clinging to His promise of healing is a daily process. As A.A. motto is, "one day at a time." God can overcome your addiction. With God nothing is impossible. The term "dependency" has, in recent years, taken on a very negative connotation.

**There is however, one dependency that is without penalty, and that is our dependency on God. He is your "Higher Power."**

## WHO'S YOUR HERO? | MARCH 6

*"Do not pervert justice; do not show partiality to the poor or favoritism to the great, but judge your neighbor fairly." Leviticus 19: 15*

---

I'm sure you've heard of the television program "American Idol." Contestants appear before four judges. Their fate, depending on the judge's critique can either make them or break them. The contestants are often criticized. Occasionally they are vigorously applauded. Thousands from each venue perform, and out of thousands of hopefuls, only 30 make it to the first round. The high and lows experienced by these contestants makes you wonder why anyone would want to subject him- or herself to such an ordeal. Many leave the audition in tears and humiliation. Eventually 10 finalists are chosen to compete for a record contract.

This is our culture. We are partial to the rich and famous and indifferent to the undesirable, poor, homeless or indigent. God cautions us not to show favoritism to the great but judge all fairly. Many of us are guilty of such discrimination. After all, the poor, we are wont to say are just so…unpleasant to be around. We feel vaguely guilty around the homeless and ignore them to the extent that we are able to do so. We shun the obese, those of foreign tongue, different skin color, the derelict, the aged. It's not easy or comfortable to love everyone.

I have a friend who occasionally dines with me. Her favorite restaurant is Home Town Buffet. They offer large quantities of food at reasonable prices. It is all you can eat for one price. Every time we go there, she comments that a disproportionate number of the patrons are overweight. She concluded that obese people tend to visit a place like this because of the unlimited portions. Clearly, she is being judgmental. I'm sure such thought enters our minds.

Do you often feel as if others are judging you, whether they speak their feelings or they keep their thoughts to themselves? Are you guilty of such discrimination whether knowingly or unknowingly? It's so much easier to look down than look up at your neighbor. There is a reality show that allows their characters to speak their mind. One such person commented "I don't like being around ugly people." She got a shocking laughter from the viewers. They tweeted, "you're my hero."

You can change your attitude and focus to the perfect hero when you are connected to God's Spirit. You should know that your God is NON-judgmental. He accepts you for who you are. **In God's eyes, there are no losers. Moreover, you have a hero and fan in His Son.**

## RUMORS AND GOSSIPS | MARCH 7

*"Do not go about spreading slander among your people. Do not do anything that endangers your neighbor's life. I am the LORD." Leviticus 19: 16*

---

Everyone has heard gossip at one time or another. Somehow, it feels as if you have power over someone by knowing some secret, even more by repeating it. That may be true, but God understands just how destructive gossip can be. Even before we were created, Lucifer began a campaign to spread rumors about God's character. Lucifer slandered God's name and character and told anyone who would listen that God was not the merciful and longsuffering God He claimed to be. Lucifer further announced God was judgmental, demanding, unloving and would make life miserable for all of us by virtue of impossible rules and regulations that would take all the fun out of life.

God is truth. Look around you today and you will see the difference between truth, which is of God, and lies which are Satan. Lucifer falsely accused God and spread lies that convinced even a third of the angels in heaven. His slanderous gossip continues to this day. Much of the misery we now suffer is because of a slander that was uttered thousands of years ago. Spreading rumors about God is a heinous act. To this day, we suffer the consequences of such gossip. Are you the recipient of some "juicy" gossip? Maybe you can't wait to spread a gossip you heard recently. I know the temptation is strong and trusting a close friend would be safe. If you do so, you are repeating the author of such malicious rumors, Satan.

You'll recall that God told the Israelites not to be bearers of slander? It can, He warned them, come to no good. The end result is always deadly. One of the ways in which God negated the slanders of Lucifer was to send His Son among us. Jesus dwelt with us. We saw His holy character. He was humble, meek and benevolent. Jesus made it clear that the malicious gossip spread by Satan was false, misleading, and thoroughly out of character of a loving God. The Bible further shares with us that Jesus had no guile. He was blameless, innocent and righteous.

Ever feel like being the first to share a juicy gossip to a trust worthy close friend? It's so tantalizing isn't it? The more you're the first to spread gossip or rumor the more you tread on Satan's ground. It's an arrogant and haughty feeling to be the bearer of the "latest news" because you feel uplifted. It's all false superiority and destructive thinking to talk unkindly about another person, whether the information is fact or fiction, true or false.

**The next time you have an opportunity to spread a rumor, spread only the Good News of a loving and truthful God.**

## SHOW RESPECT FOR THE ELDERLY | MARCH 8

*"Rise in the presence of the aged, show respect for the elderly and revere your God, I am the Lord." Leviticus 19: 32*

---

If you have reached that golden age of 65 years old, our society has deemed you a senior citizen. There are more than 36 million people in the United States over 65. This age group is expected to rise by 20% in population by the year 2030.

Geropsychology is a relatively new field in psychology which started 25 years ago, and is concerned with the mental health of the elderly. Elderly people face two issues: (1) disorders of mood, anxiety and substance-related disorders, and (2) delirium and dementia (including Alzheimer's disease). When you witness these traits in the elderly, it's time to take them under your care. They cannot thrive on their own with this condition.

The elderly today are a neglected minority in our society. For whatever reason, our society does not look kindly upon aging. Just go to any nursing home, and you may, in many instances, find yourself a witness to what, for lack of better term, has been described as the warehousing of the elderly. Once youthful and aspiring, the most senior of our citizens oftentimes sit in stupor, waiting for the "grim reaper" to knock on their door. It is estimated that over 35 percent of elderly singles live alone. The majority are women. We spend billions of dollars pursuing youth, but spend on the elderly in a most begrudging manner.

A fact of life is that all of us will eventually wither and fade."A voice says 'cry out,' And I said, 'what shall I cry?' 'All men are like grass, and their glory is like the flowers of the field. The grass withers and the flowers fall, because the breath of the Lord blows on them. Surely the people are grass. The grass withers and the flowers fall, but the word of our God stands forever.'" Isaiah 40: 6-8

God knew the ruthlessness of growing old, balanced only by the love of family and community. God has promised to eradicate all aging and dying someday. He does not want you to feel discouraged and loose hope. This aging process of our body is only temporary. Do you believe God's word? "The grass withers and the flowers fall, but the word of our God stands forever."(v8). That is a promise you can bank on for eternity.

Next time you come upon an elderly person, hug them, kiss them and show them reverence and respect, for God has commanded us to do so. **How we treat the elderly is a reflection of our relationship with God.**

## MEDIUMS AND SPIRITS | MARCH 9

*"Do not turn to mediums or seek out spiritists, for you will be defiled by them. I am the LORD your God." Leviticus 19: 31*

---

Mediums and spiritists have been in existence since the beginning of recorded history. Lucifer used the serpent as a medium to attract Eve. Saul sought out the witch of Endora for counsel. The Israelites ventured into this practice through the influence of their idolatrous neighbors. Today there are talk shows that promote this practice. It's quite popular, literally a billion-dollar business. The "Psychic Hotline" is inundated with calls wanting advice about their love life, wealth, or health. Many wish to make contact with their loved ones who have passed beyond the grave.

Why would a person want to know their future? You can pick up any local or national newspaper and you'll find a daily horoscope that purports to provide information about your future. I have friends who say they don't believe in this practice but read their horoscope daily "just for fun." Some have even gone as far as paying a fortuneteller. Yet they deny believing in this practice. One of my best friends consults a fortuneteller regarding her marriage and love life. She shares with me what the fortuneteller told her and how his ability to read her past is uncannily accurate. She now depends on him for all her personal and business matters. She confessed to me that she knows it's wrong but because many of what he said came true she can't help but believe. When I last spoke with her, she informed me the psychic told her she should have come to him sooner. He would have been able to save her break-up from her boyfriend. He then said, I can make him love you for an additional $3,000.

God instructed Moses to tell the Israelites to avoid all such practices. God even said in Chapter 20 verse 27 "a man or woman who is a medium or spiritist among you must be put to death. You are to stone them; their blood will be on their own head." Why such strong language from a loving God? God knows that such practices emanate from Lucifer and that, absent mankind's adherence to God's rules, the outcome for man will be nothing short of death. Are you depending on anyone other than God for your guidance? Think again.

God, the Author of Love, continues to remind us that He is: "The Way, the Truth and the Life." Depending on any medium or spirit other than God will defile you says our Lord. If you want answers, go straight to God. He knows everything about you. He created you. He will reveal to you the answers to all your questions. He will point you to His Son. **Depend on the Author of Creation and know it ALL. And He won't charge you.**

## A VERY GREAT REWARD | MARCH 10

*"After this, the word of the LORD came to Abram in a vision: 'don't be afraid, Abram. I am your shield, your very great reward. 'But Abram said, 'O sovereign Lord, what can you give me since I remain childless and the one who will inherit my estate is Eliezer of Damascus?' And Abram said, 'You have given me no children; so a servant in my household will be my heir.' Then the word of the LORD came to him. 'This man will not be your heir, but a son coming from your own body will be your heir. He took him outside and said, 'look up at the heavens and count the stars-if indeed you can count them.' Then he said to him, 'So shall your offspring be.'" Genesis 15: 1-5*

---

This was God's covenant with Abram. When God appeared to him with a promise of an heir he and his wife were past the years of having children. He was 75 years old. It would be another 25 years before he witnessed the promised birth. Many will go to their graves never seeing their prayer answered.

Have you ever prayed for something and did not see the answer until 25 years later? Regardless of your wait, God hears and answers prayers. He will bring to fruition His promises. Abram saw the fulfillment of God's promise and named his son Isaac, which means laughter. Throughout history, Sarah and Abraham and others who have heard this story laughed because to us it's impossible to give birth at the ripe old age of 90 years old.

God said, "I am your shield and your very great reward." The word shield here means more than physical protection it means you will be protected from the failures or even the failure of our own hope and faith. Anyone who comes to God in faith will be a part of the promise He gave to Abraham. Anyone, whoever you may be and regardless what your fate has been in life is loved by God unconditionally. The hopes and dreams you have been praying for, waiting patiently all these years, have been answered... even before time entered this world.

You must believe in God's word. ALL of His promises will come true. God's word is as sure as His existence. A true confirmation of His word is found in this verse. God told Abram his heir would come from his own body. He took him outside and told him to look up at the heavens and count the stars-if indeed he could count them. God said his offspring with be as numerous as the stars. There are billions of stars in God's universe. All this came true. We see Abrams offspring today and they number in the billions. This lesson reverberates even today with you. He has promised to save you and restore you anew. You must believe that promise.

**Can you believe God now? If you still are uncertain then the truth of God's promises will pass you by and you will miss out on His reward, Jesus. He is also your very great reward.**

## DO NOT TAKE ADVANTAGE | MARCH 11

*"Do not take advantage of each other, but fear your God. I am the LORD your God." Leviticus 25: 17*

---

At one time or another, each of us has been taken advantage of. It happens every day, and, typically, we don't realize what has occurred until it's too late. From the very start, Satan has endeavored, and, on a good many occasions, succeeded in taking advantage of us.

I have a vivid recollection of one such incident. My father was sitting in his car, waiting for my mother to return from shopping, when a stranger approached him. The man was peddling video playback units, what we used to refer to, back what seems like forever ago, as VCR's. The stranger offered to sell my father a brand new unit for what was then the rather mind-boggling price of $50. The typical VCR was selling back then for over $200. My father was thoroughly shocked by the price. The man showed my father an actual unit, and said that, if my father accepted the offer, he would come back with a brand-new unit in a sealed box. My father inspected the VCR and noted that it bore the name of a top-notch manufacturer. He agreed with the sale. The man returned to his van to fetch my father what appeared to be a new box with the brand and item he had held in his hands only minutes before pictured right on the box. When my mother returned to the car, she noted how happy my father appeared. He told her about his sensational deal, and his pride as a shrew bargainer was very evident. My mother inquired of my father whether he had inspected the box's content before he handed the stranger the $50. Of course, he responded that he had not. After all, he had inspected a unit only a moment earlier. My mother proceeded to inform my father that he'd been duped. Much to his chagrin, when he opened the box, he discovered several bricks taped together.

The Author of Love has, over the years, observed all of man's foibles. He has listened to her cries of woe. Your failures, your disappointments and your deceptions He has witnessed. There is nothing new that God has not seen or heard. God knows the answer to your foibles. The fact is God bore the weight of our failed undertakings on the cross. You need not ever feel taken advantage of again. We have a God who is our LORD and Savior. He will never dupe us. All duping and being taken advantage of comes from the father of deception, Satan.

**You MUST TRUST GOD regardless of your past experience or lot in life. The beginning of this wisdom is to "fear" Him, your God. Fear does not mean being afraid of God, it means trusting and believing Him.**

## **FROM RAGS TO RICHES** | MARCH 12

*"If one of your countrymen becomes poor and is unable to support himself among you, help him as you would an alien or a temporary resident, so he can continue to live among you. Do not take interest of any kind from him, but fear your God, so that your countryman may continue to live among you. You must not lend him money at interest or sell him food at a profit." Leviticus 25: 35-37*

We have all heard a fair number of so-called rag-to-riches stories. Someone "makes good," either through hard work, through inheritance, perhaps by virtue of luck. Oftentimes, those of us who have not enjoyed such experiences feel more than a twinge of envy when we hear such tales.

My own tale is one of rages to riches and back to rags (figuratively speaking, of course). There was a period in my life when, due to business success, I had everything -- or should I say, every material thing – I wanted. There was the home in the city and another in the country. I changed cars the way most people change their sox. (Forgive a minor exaggeration). One day (actually, one year), it all came crashing down. Turns out I was better at spending than at managing my financial assets, and there I was, all of a sudden, in the poor house. Oh yes, the writing on the wall was very evident, but I was wearing blinders. Very importantly, my prosperity and my extravagant ways were very much apart from God. I could have easily blamed God for cursing me. I could have strayed away from God and never wanted to have anything to do with Him. But I was fooling no one but myself. God was with me through my riches as well as my poverty. I did not listen to His still small voice. I am grateful He did not abandon me the way my business associates did. I finally learned the truth about God's saving grace. As I reflect in my own personal life and saw how God rescued me in my despair, I am not ashamed to disclose this personal event. I know God and I know He is able to see me through anything this world takes or offers. He can do the same for you too. God is not adverse to anyone being wealthy. The problem is; can you distinguish what is earthly riches and heavenly wealth? Remember, where your treasure lies is where your heart is.

The Son of the Author of Love knew true richness as well as the depths of poverty. He forsook all of His universal goods and wealth for our sake. He knew His greatest treasure trove was in saving us. He valued us more than His life. He bore our spiritual and physical poverty so that we might receive His spiritual richness. True richness is in knowing God. Ultimately, I learned, perhaps the hard way, that He is indeed my answer.

**Knowing God is worth giving up all the rags and riches you will ever own.**

## MANKIND AND WOMANKIND | MARCH 13

*"Thou shalt not lie with mankind, as with womankind: it is abomination." Leviticus 18: 22, KJV*

Other than the story of Sodom and Gomorrah, this text appears to be the first explicit law that God gives to the Israelites addressing homosexuality. At least until recently, the vast majority of theologians have taken this verse quite literally... end of discussion. Well...maybe. Apparently, the original language, according to certain Orthodox rabbis, spoke more to manipulation and taking advantage of another. There is in the Old Testament specific language to the effect that each of the following would be what we today refer to as capital punishment. These include cursing one's parent, working on the Sabbath, adultery, prostitution, and the list goes on. The fact is that there are few of us who would be spared the proverbial electric chair or lethal injection.

And then there is the New Testament, wherein Jesus is said to have mingled with the very ones whose crimes, so-called, were considered abominations and worthy of the death penalty in the Old Testament. What would Jesus do?

Today, of course, many argue that we need an even "Newer Testament." There are numerous references in the Bible to slavery and bigamy and a host of other behaviors that were deemed acceptable at one time but are clearly forbidden today. And, conversely, there are once-forbidden behaviors that are tolerated, if not sanctioned, by modern-day jurists. Only a decade or two ago, some states specifically outlawed the marriage between adults of different races. Today, we've witness even in our own church inter-racial couple being married. Even President Obama has made a stance on same-sex marriage. What would Jesus stance be about such a divisive issue? Would He condemn same sex marriage?

In the Jewish religion, on Yom Kippur, the so-called Day of Atonement, every worshiper in the sanctuary begs God's forgiveness for a long list of sins, even though he or she might not have committed that sin during the past year. It may be a bit of a contrivance, but the English word "atonement" is, when you add a couple of spaces, "At one ment." The Jewish people were taught to think as one in their responsibility to each other and, more importantly, to be at one with their God. "For God did not send his Son into the world to condemn the world, but to save the world through Him." John 3: 17. **God did not condemn mankind or womankind.**

**When you use "God said" or Biblical verses of condemnation, you are not of God for that is ungodly behavior. Remember, whoever has shown love knows God for God is love.**

## FIRST BORN | MARCH 14

*"Reuben, you are my first born, my might, the first sign of my strength, excelling in honor, excelling in power. Turbulent as the waters, you will no longer excel, for you went up onto your father's bed, onto my couch and defiled it." Genesis 49: 3*

For the next 12 days, I will venture into human personality traits based on the twelve children of Jacob. Psychologists have noted where you are situated in the order of birth shapes your personality traits. However, given the nature of our imperfect world, there are of course exceptions to this rule.

Usually the first-born is responsible, a natural leader and independent. Reuben. Which means "see" was the first born of Jacob's children. Jacob considered him his right-hand man. He was strong and mighty, honored above his other siblings and treated with respect by his siblings. However, given his uncontrolled passions, Reuben faltered and slept with Bilah (Genesis 3: 21) his father's concubine. It is not easy to take on the responsibility of being the eldest in a large family. Many responsibilities fall on their shoulders. Parents are too busy working and the raising of the younger children falls to the eldest.

We have a heavenly Father who cares for us. He is a friend, father, brother or sister you do not have to worry about. He's honored, mighty and powerful but also dependable. He will never disappoint you. If you've been disappointed with an older brother or sister don't hold a grudge. Even if they acquired Reuben's personality trait and hurt you forgive them. You can only forgive if you believe God. You must trust Him and give Him all your inabilities to forgive. He alone can give you that new heart, new patience and new love.

If you are the eldest in your family and failed to live up to your role, stop berating yourself. God understands and still loves you. In our family, I have six siblings. I am the third oldest. However, the responsibility and care for my elderly parents was a choice I made. I gladly volunteered to care for them. I could have reasoned the eldest should take on the responsibility but I wanted to take on that role. Don't try to live up to other people's expectations, you can't. Live up to God's expectations. His way is peaceful.

The Author of Love knew the deficiencies we would encounter here on earth. God knew there would be a "Rueben" in your life. Some would carry out their role with distinction while other will disappoint. **Whatever our own birth order, we must all recognize that the ultimate "First Born" is our LORD's Son, Jesus Christ.**

## **HOT TEMPERED PERSONALITY** | MARCH 15

*"Simeon and Levi are brothers-their swords are weapons of violence. Let me not enter their council, let me not join their assembly, for they have killed men in their anger and hamstrung oxen as they please. Cursed be their anger, so fierce, and their fury so cruel! I will scatter them in Jacob and disperse them in Israel." Genesis 49: 5-7*

---

Have you ever encountered a hot-tempered, uncontrollable person who "goes ballistic" at the slightest provocation? I have and it's not a pleasant sight to be around. My fathered was temperamental, especially if he hadn't eaten. When he went on a rampage, you stayed clear away from his path. I suppose given the right stimulus we all have our breaking point. In fact, you want to stay clear of that type of person.

The first ever-recorded anger from the Bible is found in the story of Cain and Abel. Through a fit of rage and envy, Cain lost his composure and killed his brother. The story of Simeon and Levi was in the same vein. Simeon, the second child of Jacob means hearing. Levi, the third son means attached. Their sister Dinah was raped by a Hivite neighbor named Shechem. In order to avenge their family's disgrace, Simeon and Levi plotted a vengeful act by agreeing to let their sister intermarry as long as all the men subjected themselves to the rite of circumcision. The Hivites agreed and all the men were circumcised. Three days after all the men were circumcised; Simeon and Levi went into the city and slew every male. Those helpless men recovering from circumcisions, unable to defend themselves, died a merciless death.

The act of aggression and violence are still prevalent in our society even today. Psychologists believe that violence is instinctual. Konrad Lorenz, a Nobel prize-winning scientist (1966, 1974) proposed that aggression springs mainly from the inherited "fighting instinct" that is in our genes. (In addiction treatment, anger is considered a hidden form of depression.) However, I would call this fighting instinct, "sin." But even the most hot-tempered and volatile person can change to a mild manner and peaceful person through God's Spirit.

Inherited or otherwise, God gave us the ability to decipher right from wrong, and to commit such wrongs is clearly sinful. God is peace. He stands for patience rather than impulsiveness, for kindness rather than hatred. God saw the results of sin and He decided to show us the way to live truly godly lives.

**He can take away that Simeon/Levi temperament if you listen to His counsel, trust Him and follow His way**. Give God a chance.

## A JUDAH PERSONALITY | MARCH 16

*"Judah, your brothers will praise you; your hand will be on the neck of your enemies; your father's sons will bow down to you. You are a lion's cub, O Judah; you return from the prey, my son. Like a lion he crouches and lies down, like a lioness-who dares to rouse him? The scepter will not depart from Judah, nor the ruler's staff from between his feet, until he comes to whom it belongs and the obedience of the nations is his. He will tether his donkey to a vine, his colt to the choicest branch; he will wash his garments in wine, his robes in the blood of grapes. His eyes will be darker than wine, his teeth whiter than milk."* Genesis 49: 8-12

---

The fourth son of Jacob is described as "Yahweh be praised." The middle child is supposed to be the healthiest and perhaps the strongest child. Through Judah lineage, God's son Jesus Christ would come to be. This verse speaks of a leader whose "brothers" would praise him but his "hand will be on the neck of your enemies." In other words, this is a foreshadowing of Christ, the leader, the healthy one that would go through perilous times to save His people. How is it that a God so majestic and awesome in power, that at the sound of His voice, the universe would bow down in adoration...how is it that He would stoop to our depths? At the sound of His voice stars and planets are born. At the sound of His voice nature trembles and obeys. Yet He would stoop so low as to be born as a humble baby. From there, He would subject himself to the life of a human being, just like one of us, exposed to the wants and needs of an earthly body. He was dependent on a teenage mother's inexperienced guidance and care.

Whatever your birth order, whatever your personality, you should feel neither inferior nor superior. With God there is no superior or inferior personality. With God there is no first or last. With God there is no male or female. With God there is no black, yellow, white, brown or red. With God there is no number one. With God as your role model, you will not only be praised, but you will praise God. A Judah personality is desirable and honored. You are a born leader. There are born leaders and made leaders. Between the two, you will most likely be drawn to the born leader. This type of personality is certainly a gift from God. However, how you use your leadership gift will affect many other people for better or worst. How you lead or follow God will be dependent on your personal relationship with Him. **To live a truly godly life follow God's leading and prompting in your heart.** His leading will lead you to still waters and peaceful shores.

Indeed, we have a Savior who personifies who and what we are. He says: "Fear not; I have already overcome." **Our God is our king, our true Judah.**

## JUSTICE FROM GOD | MARCH 17

*"Dan will provide justice for his people as one of the tribes of Israel. Dan will be a serpent by the roadside, a viper along the path that bites the horse's heels so that its rider tumbles backward. I look for your deliverance, O Lord." Genesis 49: 16-19*

---

Each of us encounters injustice one or more times in his or her life. For me personally, there is no greater injustice than when someone takes advantage of me. One such incident that comes to mind concerns a tenant of a property we were leasing who, without warning, abandoned his lease obligation. As if to add insult to injury, he inflicted considerable damage to our property. The repairs proved costly. His lease prohibited pets; yet the property had become flea ridden. As I attempted to restore the property, my feet were bitten by fleas, even though I wore socks. Each flea bite intensified my anger. I was enraged. For a moment or two, I fantasized about capturing all of those fleas in a jar and hurling the jar's contents at my ex-tenant. At that moment, it seemed like perfect justice. Not exactly what you would call turning the other check, however. But would it have been "perfect justice?" How do you treat someone who has done you wrong? Do you sue them or just let it go?

The fifth son of Jacob evokes justice in his personality trait. His name means judge. What type of justice does Dan display? He is a crusader who fights for your right. He will not allow anyone to take advantage of the helpless, the poor, the widow or the indigent. He is your champion for justice. Wouldn't you prefer to have a judge like that on your side? That's how God deals with us. Justice from God comes from above.

We had a famous Gospel singer come to our church for a concert. The advertisement stated those who purchased a "Gold seat ticket" would be allowed at a reception to meet this celebrity. At the day of the concert, management changed the rules and allowed anyone who purchased a CD to take part in the reception. Well, needless to say, this didn't sit well with gold ticket holders. Their cry of injustice was heard. Considered to be the greatest philosopher, Plato said: "Justice in the life and conduct of the State is possible only as first it resides in the hearts and souls of the citizens." There is man-made justice and there is God's justice. Which would you prefer?

The Author of Love has demonstrated that justice is more than merely having right on your side. **The only "perfect justice" in this world is Godly justice; and that justice is wrapped in mercy, kindness and charity.**

## A DOE SET FREE | MARCH 18

*"Naphtali is a doe set free that bears beautiful fawns." Genesis 49: 21*

---

Napthali is the sixth son of Jacob. His mother was not Rachel but their maidservant Bilhah. Jacob describes his son as a "running deer." In the Song of Deborah (Judges 5: 18) the Napthali tribe is described as brave soldiers. His name was given by Rachel because she said "with great wrestling have I wrestled my sister." Genesis 30: 8. The struggle Rachel had with her sister Leah was the fact she could not bear Jacob children. So, she recommended to Jacob to sleep with their servant Bilhah and he did. Thus, Napthali is considered a brave warrior and also recognized as a fast runner. What a complementary combination to have as a soldier.

People with these characteristics typically believe that the cause for which they are fighting is worthy and just. Others, on the other hand, may argue that there is no such thing as a just war; that a so-called "just cause" is very much in the mind of the beholder. If we examine one of this nation's most recent wars (or is it a skirmish?) some argue that, absent weapons of mass destruction, we had no business upending the Hussein regime and undertaking nation building, regardless of the purity of our intentions. Others, as you know, argue that, when innocent people are being oppressed and, in many instances, annihilated, it is our duty to insert ourselves. They would argue that the U.S. (and other nations) were too slow to react to the tyranny of Hitler and that we were indeed guilty of a very serious sin of omission by sitting on the sidelines as millions of innocents were mercilessly slaughtered. That is happening today in Syria. Thousands of innocent civilians are been slaughtered while the rest of the world ponders on what sanctions to impose on this country.

Through this text we had shied away from political positions. It is important to note, however, that we are all a party to an on-going struggle or war between evil or sin, as personified by Lucifer, and the goodness of our God. God wants us to experience this freedom as aforementioned in the doe running freely in the fields. To have the true freedom, we must be one with God. Paul tells us in Galatians 5: 13 that we have been set free to "serve one another in love."

Can you imagine a country where we treat one another in kindness and with respect regardless of who we are or what we are? That is God's manner. **The service we do to one another must always be done in love. That is the freedom that is truly fruitful-and bears "beautiful fawns."**

## BAND OF ATTACKERS | MARCH 19

*"Gad will be attacked by a band of raiders, but he will attack them at their heels." Genesis 49: 19*

---

Gad means "good fortune" because he was the first born of Zilpah, the maid servant of Leah. He was the seventh son of Jacob. Have you ever felt paranoid? People with this type of personality tend to approach relationships with caution and skepticism. They can be highly critical of others and may go on the offensive before you can offend them. They are unable to recognize their own shortcomings and may be hypersensitive to criticism. Often argumentative, rigid and suspicious of others, they will verbally attack others about everything that goes on in their lives. They bear grudges. Have you ever experienced such behavior? Are you sometimes guilty of it yourself? Maybe you have inherited the personality of Gad. Though his name meant good fortune yet he was constantly attacked by bands of raiders.

According to the American Psychiatric Association, 1994, between 0.5 to 2.5 percent of the adult population often feel paranoid, apparently more men than women. Certainly, we all exhibit some paranoia at one time or another, but some of us operate under the cloak of virtually full-time paranoia, and, in that sense, they seem to have inherited the Gad trait. The important question for each of us is: "Whom do we trust?" The unfortunate fact-of-life is that we live in a rather untrusting world. A Pew Research study of a few years ago revealed that only 41 percent of us claim that they generally trust people. Not surprisingly, trust begins with family. Children trust their parents almost intrinsically. However, when that trust is shattered as the result of lies, broken promises, abuse and the like, these same children often lose their ability to trust anyone. When trust is lost, children become attackers rather than peacemakers. Be careful you don't fall into the same trap.

The Author of Love, knowing just how far man had fallen, cautioned us: "Trust in the Lord with all your heart, and lean not to your own understanding." Whenever we rely on our judgment and forget to depend on the Author of "good fortune" we will live a paranoid life. With paranoia come misfortunes and fears.

**The Good News is that, if we trust in the Lord, we need not burden ourselves with paranoia and bands of raiders.**

# RICH GLORIOUS FOOD | MARCH 20

*"Asher's food will be rich; he will provide delicacies fit for a king." Genesis 49:20*

Asher, the eighth son of Jacob means "Happy. " His mother Leah named him. Does eating give you pleasure? Most of us do. What and how we eat can tell us much about one another. There's something about eating food that tames the beast in each of us. We feel happy. Matthew 15: 11 say "What goes into a man's mouth does not make him 'unclean', but what comes out of his mouth, that is what makes him 'unclean.'" Food in our culture has become an intrinsic part of who we are. Food is part of almost any social setting. Some cultures find it insulting not to offer food to guests even when uninvited. Food was the medium Lucifer used to tempt our first parents in the Garden of Eden. Food is both alluring and can be addicting.

Obesity is a ballooning problem in the U.S. (to risk a pun), especially among children. With food obsessions comes a myriad of health problems and personality disorders. Anorexia nervosa is people who starve themselves to death. People with bulimia nervosa go on frequent eating binges and then force themselves to vomit to keep from gaining weight. Some obese people should not be looked upon as weak and out of control. There is mounting evidence that their obesity is a result of multiple biological and social factors. Some blame God for their corpulence. "If God wanted us to all look alike, he'd have populated the world that way."

The fact is that, whatever one's shape, it is the result of either our own doing or genetic make-up. Our body shapes is a result of our imperfect world. We will never enjoy a world of perfect shapes no matter how much we emphasize all the health messages this world has to offer. You can spend millions of dollars working out and getting in great shape or succumb to the short cut method of gastric bypass surgery but all will be in vain if God is not your motivating factor.

Rather than advocate healthful eating practices, which is important, greater yet is our acceptance of the body shapes we shun. We need to show them Godly love and genuine acceptance. Be aware that God has promised that, for those who take Him into their hearts, He will create a new heart, mind, and Spirit in you.

**The "true food" you need to consume can only be God. True happiness is accepting God's invitation: "Oh taste and see how good God is."**

## EFFORTLESS | MARCH 21

*"Issachar is a rawboned donkey lying down between two saddlebags. When he sees how good is his resting place and how pleasant is his land, he will bend his shoulder to the burden and submit to forced labor." Genesis 49: 14 & 15*

---

Have you ever been accused of having a "Messianic Complex?" I have. This is a need to help or rescue people. Whenever a problem occurs; whether at school, church or home, people will turn to you because they know you are always willing to help. They can depend on you. Some people go so far as to carry the blame or burden of the other person and feel weighed down in their burden. They have a "woe is me attitude."

Issachar, the ninth son of Jacob is noted for being the man of hire. The donkey is symbolized as the hard working "beast of burden." They're always there to carry your burdens. I have noticed that whenever our church calls for a Sunday work bee event, less ten percent will show up. These are the "Issachar" of our church. Whether it's clean-up work, working in an office, or supplying a last –minute substitute, the Issachar person is willing to take up the slack.

Are you this type of person? Are you a person who can't say "No?" These character traits can also spread to other areas of their life. Ever heard of the term "enabler" or co-dependent?" These are people who rescue, make excuses or cover up other people from their dilemmas or vices. This type of personality often affects addictive personality behaviors. What makes these people want to carry other people's burdens? The reasons are varied and depending on which school of thought you ascribe to; the explanation for such behaviors range from intrinsic, cognitive, social, genetic, environment and psychological.

Regardless of the reason, the Author of Love knew that man would need a Messiah to help us not only carry our burden but to relieve us from this trait. Haven't you notice there are people who dislike depending on anyone. They would rather starve than ask for a handout. Then there are people who take advantage of the system. They feel they deserve to be taken care of. Regardless of your thinking, God sent His Son Jesus to carry our burden and our warp thinking for us. You can let go and stop worrying, people will like you or not even if you say "no" to them. You don't have to carry the Messianic complex anymore. God sent His Son Jesus to do that for us.

**All God's ways are totally effortless when His love overtakes you.**

## AN OCEAN OF FEARS | MARCH 22

*"Zebulun will live by the seashore and become a haven for ships; his border will extend toward Sidon." Genesis 49: 13*

Zebulun, the tenth son born to Jacob, means to "dwell". He resided by the seashore. There are people who not only love living near the ocean but they are water lovers as well. I have met some of these people. I inquired of one of these friends just what it was that so attracted him to the ocean. His response: It is another unique and peaceful world down there… a world where one can forget one's earthly problems and just take in the serenity and beauty of it all.

Serene? Perhaps…but there was a time when I harbored a deep-seated fear of the sea. I set out to conquer that fear by confronting it head-on; I enrolled in a scuba-diving class. My friends graduated with flying colors after three months of intensive training. However, I was detained. My instructor felt I needed another three months of mainly ocean diving before he could grant me my certificate. He saw in my eyes I was not yet comfortable with the ocean. Then, one day, a group of us went diving in the seas of Phuket, Thailand. It was a thrill unlike anything I had ever experienced. The corals and sea life under water was a thrill I have never experienced in my life. It was a different world down there. I even noticed blue starfish everywhere which I've never seen before. I was not conscious of it at the time, but from that moment on, my fear of diving disappeared.

One fear that some many people have is the fear of God. In fact, we frequently hear or even use the term "god-fearing." With all of the fire and brimstone we observe on televised, so-called religious programs these days, it is no wonder that many have a notion of a judgmental God, who is ready to punish us whenever we falter.

Truthfully, I must confess I felt the same way, too, until I came to know God. God cares for your happiness. He is not the God we were brought up to believe. Knowing Him brings an inward peace that leaves you content and not wanting. You must experience Him in your life right now. I truly believe you will have no fear or regrets when you allow Him to dwell in your heart. Having Him dwell in your heart is a daily surrender of your will to Him. That's how you develop a relationship with God. That's how you also develop a stronger faith in Him.

**When you truly get to know Him, you will be able to confront any and all of your fears – even if you are burdened by a veritable ocean of fears.**

# JOSEPH/JESUS | MARCH 23

*"Joseph is a fruitful vine, near a spring, whose branches climb over a wall. With bitterness archers attacked him; they shot at him with hostility. But his bow remained steady, his strong arms stayed limber, because of the hand of the Mighty One of Jacob, because of the Shepherd, the Rock of Israel, because of your father's God, who helps you, because of the Almighty, who blesses you with blessing of the heavens above, blessing of the deep that lies below, blessing of the breast and womb." Genesis 49: 22*

---

The eleventh son of Jacob, Joseph, means "the Lord will add a son." This godly man was a figure type of Jesus Christ (Immanuel, means God with us). The coat that his father Jacob gifted to him was of many colors. This was a precept of how Jesus had his vesture dipped in blood as Savior to all colors and races of humankind. Joseph was the first son of Rachel. She had been barren for seven years until she finally gave Jacob a son. The story of Joseph is quite fascinating. His brothers hated him for being their father's favorite son. It was these very same brothers who, for the sum of 20 shekels of sliver sold Joseph into slavery. While enslaved in Egypt, he was falsely accused of sexual assault by the wife of his master. He was then thrown in jail for a good many years, yet he thrived despite his unjust punishment.

There are several parallels between the life of Joseph and the life of Jesus. Both were relentlessly pursued and attacked by visible as well as invisible forces of evil. Each was falsely accused of crimes, and each was the victim of betrayal. Both, despite their ordeals, remained steadfast, focused and reliant on God for strength as well as guidance. For each, their respective upbringings played significant roles in their character development. In Joseph's case, Jacob and Rachel served as excellent role models. Joseph learned at a very early age from his parents that he could depend upon God, regardless of how dire his circumstances seemed. Jesus' character was at least in some measure a reflection of his mother's character. Jesus, of course, is topmost in all of our minds, but we should remember that Joseph, too, was brought up to respect, honor and rely on God.

The early foundation given to Joseph by his parents paved the way for a better future for him and all of his descendants. All of Joseph siblings were also given the same upbringing of reliance on their Maker. However, none was more receptive and ready for the task that was given than Joseph. Joseph was very receptive to the promptings of God's Spirit. **Joseph's character was very much a reflection of his unwavering desire to enrich his relationship with God, the Author of Love.** You too can have the same relationship with God.

## ON BEING THE YOUNGEST CHILD | MARCH 24

*"Benjamin is a ravenous wolf; in the morning he devours the prey, in the evening he divides the plunder." Genesis 49: 27*

---

Benjamin was the youngest of the twelve sons of Jacob and Rachel. His name means "Son of the right hand." This was the second child she gave birth to before she passed away. Next to Joseph, Benjamin became the second favorite son of Jacob. When Jacob later blessed Benjamin he said he was "a vicious wolf, devouring the prey in the morning, and dividing the spoil at night." A wolf is typically regarded as a cunning, fierce and audacious spirit. Oftentimes, the youngest child was portrayed as an attention seeker and something of a "spoiled brat." Benjamin, with his cunning, might have turned out to be the proverbial wolf in sheep's clothing. Over the years, however, he grew to know God and became a credit to his upbringing and to his community.

I think of a modern-day Benjamin, a former colleague of mine, whose circumstances were a good deal less favorable than Benjamin's. Jonathan, an only child, lost his father at a young age, and, soon thereafter, his mother went to prison. He was the product, therefore, of foster homes and was abused and neglected. Jonathan, like so many others in situations like his, might have played the "victim" card, but he decided early in life that he would excel, despite the hand he'd been dealt. He was already hard at work by age 16, and he put himself through high school and college. He went on to secure a doctoral degree in education and is today a prominent and highly-regarded educator and member of his community. I vividly recall a lecture of his in which he told of others who ultimately became victims of the system and wound up in prison.

He related that, from an early age, he conversed daily (in his mind) with two wolves. One was the voice of evil, the voice of shortcuts and unconcern for others. This voice was easier to listen to because you didn't have to work hard to get what you wanted. The voice was always tempting him to take advantage of the system because no one will ever find out.

The other small but, for him, more compelling voice was the wolf who introduced him to the Spirit of God. The more compelling of the pair of wolves taught Jonathan that he would never be lacking, if he continued to develop his relationship with the voice of God. The end result for Jonathan is proof of his own life.

**The Spirit of God speaks to every heart. Those that listen to God's Spirit will always end up with a blessed life.**

## ON BEING A SLAVE | MARCH 25

*"Your male and female slaves are to come from the nations around you; from them you may buy slaves." Leviticus 25: 44*

---

This is an unusual Biblical text. The Lord, it would certainly appear, is condoning slavery. Does a God of love condone slavery? What gives? The practice of slavery was well known among all nations on earth at that time. And who would know better about slavery than the Israelites themselves? After all they had been enslaved in Egypt.

God is a loving and forgiving Father that puts up with our poor choices without sanctioning them. But again, we must ask whether God specifically condones slavery, as the above passage might suggest. God never condoned slavery but He relented to the choices people made. God is a very patient and relenting God. In an earlier section, we referred the fact that the Old Testament tended to be rather rigid in its interpretations while the New Testament tends to be more nuanced. Slavery, we now understand, can take on more than one form. Its most common meaning, of course, is physical servitude. One person becomes the property of another. Today, however, there is yet another form of slavery, and that is what might most appropriately be termed "virtual slavery." (Certainly, our lives these days seem to be filled with "virtual" everything else).

We are not as conscious of this type of slavery, even when we are the enslaved. Some of us are virtual slaves to various addictions – drugs (illicit and over-the-counter), alcohol, sex, etc. Others of us are slaves to foods, to credit cards, to television, to computers, to cell phones, and, very importantly in modern-day America, to work. What are you enslaved to? Whatever that may be, don't be dismayed. Look at them in its proper perspective.

It is when these things or objects, call them, become more important to us than our loved ones and even more important to us than God Himself that we discover that our master is indeed Lucifer and we have become his slaves. Once again, however, there is Good News on the horizon for all of us. We can take comfort in the fact that, whatever our shortcomings, God still loves us. He accepts us, just as we are.

**Wouldn't you rather be a slave to the One who loves you most, and that is God, the Author of Love.**

## LOVE YOUR NEIGHBOR | MARCH 26

*"Do not seek revenge or bear a grudge against one of your people but love your neighbor as yourself. I am the LORD." Leviticus 19: 18*

Jesus talked about loving your neighbor as yourself as one of the two great commandments. The first, of course, was to love God. The second commandment begs a question as to the definition of neighbor. Typically, we think of neighbors as being the people whose properties abut our own. Jesus, however, used the term in a more all–encompassing way -- meaning all those with whom we come in contact.

I think back to a family that lived next-door to my family for over thirty years. Our property was several acres, and theirs was a small fraction of that. Our association with them was quite cordial; so, when their son asked us if he could park his newly acquired motor home in our driveway, we did not hesitate to oblige. There was a clear understanding -- clear, at least in our minds -- that this was to be a temporary arrangement. At about the 12-year point, it had become abundantly clear that, not only wasn't this arrangement temporary, but, clearly, we were being taken advantage of. And so we told the son that it was time to move his motor home. With that you'll not be surprised to learn, our decades-long relationship turned very sour. He did not take kindly to our request. He hemmed and stalled, almost defiant of our request. A mutual friend of ours had to talk him in to relenting. Needless to say our relationship has never been the same.

This, I suspect, is where you expect me to inform you that we ultimately realized that we must love God first, and He will help us love the otherwise unlovable. The Holy Spirit will prompt us and show us how to love our neighbor. Unfortunately this was not a happily-ever-after ending. We encounter people throughout our lives who will either be a blessing or a curse. Guess what! They are your neighbor. God loves them just the same. Selective feelings aside, unless we are connected to God Spirit, we will love selectively.

While man's injustice was likely on our side throughout this little ordeal, had we been closer to God, I suspect that we and our neighbors could have found some common ground. In that sense, I must admit, we not only failed our neighbor, but we failed God.

**Clearly, God evidences His love for us every day, and, had we given God the chance, He would have demonstrated to us how to express love for our neighbor. I would have loved my neighbor as myself, for the LORD has commanded me.**

## **STRANGE FIRE** | MARCH 27

*"Whenever the tabernacle is to move, the Levites are to take it down, and whenever the tabernacle is to be set up, the Levites shall do it. Anyone else who goes near it shall be put to death." Numbers 1: 51*

Do you remember the story of Aaron's sons, Nadab and Abihu? (Leviticus 10: 1-3). The two were next in line (after Moses and Aaron) to lead the Israelites. Their tale is a sad one, and it is one that has had some among us suggesting that the Author of Love was not evidencing His love when He killed them for what, on the surface, might have appeared to have been a minor offense – the use of unauthorized fire – in this instance, incense. We might relate this incident to a minor infraction in terms of man's justice system – something that might have been worthy of a warning or the proverbial slap on the wrist – certainly, not a capital offense.

The truth is, however that the pair deliberately disobeyed God. Early in their youth, they had indulged in uncontrolled passions. Their father was aware of their transgressions but failed to disciple them. They evidenced no respect for their father, and they exhibited the same brand of disrespect for their Heavenly Father. Had they listened to the promptings of the Spirit of God, their lives would not have ended so tragically. God did not kill them. It was their defiance of God's admonition that brought their fate to a sad ending. It is against God's plan or nature that anyone should perish.

We are taught that our God is not vengeful God, that His essence is one of purity – that He is thoroughly without guile. Yet some of us would liken this incident to capital punishment of jay walking. The fact is that anyone who would suggest that this be the case has given God a very bad wrap. God recognizes that, whenever purity and impurity merge, the end result is nothing short of catastrophic. While God takes absolutely no delights in the death of any of His subjects, He recognizes that the very survival of His throne depends on maintenance of that purity. There are some among us who take God's commandments with a grain of salt. They feel as if they can "get away" with a minor infraction of God's laws here and there. That type of thinking is self-destructive. Be ever vigilant of God's "smoke signals". They are His "love signals". Follow His lead for His way saves lives.

**God sends us warning signs through His commandments and His Holy Spirit – this, so that we do not subject ourselves to the punishment of strange fire. God is on our side...are we on His?**

## IS THE LORD'S ARM TOO SHORT? | MARCH 28

*"The Lord answered Moses, 'Is the Lord's arm too short? You will now see whether or not what I say will come true for you.' " Numbers 11: 23*

There was an amusing movie a few years ago entitled, "Shallow Hal." Hal got the nickname because he was only interested in skin-deep beauty, never seeing the beauty beneath. One day, however, he was unknowingly hypnotized into being blind to anything but inner beauty. Of course, he fell madly in love with a very fat girl. To Hal's friends, she was unworthy not only of his affections, but of their attention. Hal couldn't understand why his friends couldn't see how charming, how witty and how thoroughly lovely she was.

We live in a society obsessed with the shallowness of outward appearance. People will often say: "Certainly, I care about what's in a person's heart and mind, but it is just human nature to be attracted first to another person's outer appearance." There have been a number of surveys which demonstrate that great-looking people outperform the unseemly by a wide margin. In some measure, this is because one's good looks are apt to give a person a good helping of self-confidence. Surveys have also demonstrated that, all things equal, tall people outperform short people. The lion's share of our country's Presidents, have been taller than the average of their fellows. Beauty and height are not, of course, our only prejudices. We tend to be dismissive of obese people, of people whose skin color is not of the majority, or people with various physical handicaps or of those with other (in our eyes) shortcomings. As we age some of us will consider cosmetic surgery to arrest the inevitable aging process. Others will succumb under the knife to reduce that waistline or buttocks. We are enamored by our desire to be desirable. And we will go to great expenditures to arrest father time. I too have been guilty of conditional love. I'm embarrassed to admit some reasoning for my conditions have been pretty shallow.

The Good News is that God's love and regard for us is NOT skin-deep. In His eyes, we are all perfect; for we are a reflection of God, and His is, in every sense of the term, perfect. If you find yourself lacking and seek wholeness, you will not find it in a person, a place or things, you will find it in God's Word. For whatever He has said will come true. God is never lacking. Remember His Word was made flesh and dwelt among us. **Friend, God's arms are not too short to accomplish His promises. God will deliver. He has proven that in our past, He will today, and your future as well. Our completeness, He assures us, is in His Son, Jesus**. Let Him embrace you with His arms right now.

## **HUMBLE ME LORD** | MARCH 29

*"Miriam and Aaron began to talk against Moses because of his Cushite wife, for he had married a Cushite. 'Has the Lord spoken only through Moses?' They asked. 'Hasn't he also spoken through us?' And the Lord heard this." Numbers 12: 1 & 2*

---

I remembered years ago, when one of my relatives had married an African-American man. Her parents were shocked and disappointed with her. It took them a long time to accept their son-in-law. With the birth of their grandson, the hurt diminished, but interracial marriage is still often frowned upon in today's society, just as in Moses' time. Moses married a Cushite. She was a woman from the upper Nile River. Today we call "Cush" the Sudan, Ethiopia, Somalia and Uganda. Moses married an African. Moses' sister Miriam spoke as if Moses had affronted his God and his people, but, truth be told, Miriam was envious of Moses' access to God. She went so far as to reason with her brother Aaron that God also spoke to them. God, however, knew each sibling's heart and motive, and Miriam's was not pure. Moses' humility was not something he was born with. In fact, it took Moses some 40 years of tutelage under God to gain a true sense of humility.

Surprisingly, even to this day, interracial marriage raises eyebrows and whispers of disapproval. I suppose prejudice of a certain race can now be said to have its root in Moses ear? Or does it go deeper than that?

To be humble is to put aside one's ego in the service of God. It means to not lust for power or control. God actually declared that Moses was indeed the most humble man on the face of the earth. God knew, on the other hand, that Miriam had a good deal to learn. She was indeed humbled when she strayed from God's presence, she was inflicted with leprosy. Her brother Aaron was horrified by the course of events, and he begged Moses to intervene. Moses was moved with compassion for his sister. He pleaded with God to heal her. God loved Miriam so much that He was willing to teach her a painful lesson. He restored her health after seven days. She learned humility the hard way.

Our God acts without prejudice. His concern is only for us, and He acts with equanimity. There is a place for all of us in His world, if only we find a place in our hearts for Him. Whatever your issue in life is, healing begins the moment you are humbled. **Humility of self is the first step in learning to be like God. That humbleness is derived only from God.** Start by being more humble in all your dealings with your neighbor. You can pray "Humble me, Lord, to be like you." This is the secret of how God loves us.

## TWO OUT OF TWELVE | MARCH 30

*"So the men Moses had sent to explore the land, who returned and made the whole community grumble against him by spreading a bad report about it---these men responsible for spreading the bad report about the land were struck down and died of a plague before the LORD. Of the men who went to explore the land, only Joshua son of Nun and Caleb son of Jephunneh survived. " Number 14: 36-38*

---

This is a strange and intriguing story of 12 men who set out, in today's jargon, on a surveillance mission. Their objective was to gain intelligence with reference to the land God was planning to give the Israelites. Ten of the twelve falsely reported that the land was occupied with giants -- the suggestion being that to enter into the land would lead to the certain demise of the Israelites. Very importantly, the clear implication was that God was about to perpetrate a deceit on the Israelites. The ten mistrusted God. Two members of the group, Joshua and Caleb, issued a very different report. They said: "The land we passed through and explored is exceedingly good. If the Lord is pleased with us, He will lead us into that land, a land flowing with milk and honey, and will give it to us."

As you now know, the fate of the ten who spoke untruthfully about God was their demise. They chose that verdict for themselves when they decided to turn their backs on the very One who had delivered them from bondage and guided them to freedom after all these years. God did not destroy them. They made the choice to remove themselves from the giver of life. How do you see your life before you? Are part of the "ten" that see "giants" in every corner you turn? Is your life a mistrust of the One who gives you life? Or can you humbly say; my life is a "land flowing with milk and honey?" How you view your lot in life is really how you view God in your life. Don't give God a bad report.

Oftentimes, in our modern-day lives, we observe giants of despair – sometimes, to the point of resignation. God reminds us that He sent us His Son in order that we might rejoice in His salvation. If we have faith in Him, our fears will dissipate. In Him, we are truly secure, and we ought not, therefore, heed the false testimony of the unfaithful. Remember that there were only two out of twelve who believed in the saving grace of God, ultimately, it was the conviction and faith of these two that prevailed.

**Do you want to live a life just like the two out of twelve? Know your Maker and trust His word, and you will live not only a fearless life, but you will inherit a land flowing with milk and honey.**

## YOU WILL SUCCEED WITH GOD | MARCH 31

*"But Moses said, 'Why are you disobeying the Lords' command? This will not succeed! Do not go up, because the Lord is not with you. You will be defeated by your enemies.'" Numbers 12: 41& 42*

---

Were you ever told by your parents when you were a child not to go to movie theaters, bars, nightclub or dens of iniquity because the angel of the Lord will not be there? I was. A preacher related a story about a young man that was struggling over whether or not to enter a movie theater and as he got closer to the entrance of the theater door he decided to reprimand the devil and said, "Get thee behind me Satan." The devil got behind him and pushed him through the doors.

Is it true God is not with you when you enter "sinful" places? Look at this world, is there any place on this earth that is not affected by sin? Does the edifice of the church protect you from sin? God is right in the thick of things in His entire universe, especially our own world. In the verse today, Moses warned the Israelites that if they disobey the Lord's command, they would not succeed. "Your enemy will defeat you," He proclaimed. The Israelites did not listen, and they were defeated in battle. God warned our parents in the Garden of Eden that if they disobeyed His command they would surely die. They chose to go against God admonition, and we bear, to this day, the consequences of their actions.

When we were teenagers growing up in Los Angeles, we had a church friend who was the life of the party. He was also entertaining and quite intelligent. We looked up to him because he was so accomplished. We eventually grew up and went our separate ways. Twenty years later we heard that he succumbed to drugs. His affliction affected his ability to think, reason and function. He paid the price.

We are not exempt from the woes of this world. Everywhere around us is the enticement of a better you, a better life or a better world. How we obtain that "Shangri-La" can either be through your wisdom or God's wisdom. Your decision to a great extent is how you make your world. Regardless of how bleakly things are turning out in your life, due to self-sufficient choices, you can still have peace because God promised to be with you.

There is no place in this world that God is not there. Why not wait on the Lord and listen to His command before pursuing your "own thing." You will see your success from God's point of view and not earth's definition of success. **Place your trust in Him and He promised you will succeed.**

## CHILDREN OF GOD'S KINGDOM | APRIL 1

*"People were bringing little children to Jesus to have him touch them, but the disciples rebuked them. When Jesus saw this, he was indignant. He said to them, 'Let the little children come to me, and do not hinder them, for the kingdom of God belongs to such as these. I tell you the truth; anyone who will not receive the kingdom of God like a little child will never enter it.' And he took the children in his arms, put his hands on them and blessed them." Mark 10: 13-16*

---

Do you remember your childhood? In childhood, you develop characteristics that mold your persona throughout your life. It reminded me of a story I read in Reader's Digest about a church school teacher who asked her students, "If I sold my house and my car, had a big garage sale and gave all my money to the church, would I get into heaven?" "No!" the children all answered. "If I cleaned the church every day, mowed the yard, and kept everything neat and tidy, would I get into heaven?" Again, the answer was "No!" "Well," she continued, "then how do I get to heaven?" A five year-old boy shouted out, "You gotta be dead!"

To our dismay, children imitate their parents' actions far more effectively than they respond to their words. Children who are considerate, kind and compassionate towards others generally received those from their parents. And contrary to this are those children who have had little regard from their parents. They tend to have low self-esteem and are not as sociable or outgoing. Which child are you? The disciples were adults who seem to have had low self-esteem. This is based on the attitude they displayed towards the parents who brought their children to Jesus. They reprimanded the parents. They seem to have an attitude of "god can't be bothered with such trivial matters such as kids." Jesus was dismayed.

In Christ's circle we are ALL embraced. We are welcomed. In God's kingdom He welcomes child-like spirits. To be childlike is to be Christ like, not childish necessarily, but rather playful, trusting and innocent. Jesus not only welcomed the children in His kingdom but also placed His arms around them and blessed them "for the kingdom of God belongs to such as these." Sadly the disciples had to learn another lesson the hard way. God was teaching His disciples and us that His kingdom was made up of people that were childlike in His Spirit regardless of age, gender, status, color or creed. Isn't it time you started acting like a child of God?

As children are trusting and receptive so are God's children. God said if you do not receive His kingdom as a little child, you will not enter it. **Can you imagine entering God's kingdom and finding everyone in a child-like Spirit? That would be fun and free. That is what God's kingdom is all about.**

## STONED ON THE SABBATH | APRIL 2

*"While the Israelites were in the desert, a man was found gathering wood on the Sabbath day. Those who found him gathering wood brought him to Moses and Aaron and the whole assembly, and they kept him in custody, because it was not clear what should be done to him. Then the Lord said to Moses, the man must die. The whole assembly must stone him outside the camp. So the assembly took him outside the camp and stoned him to death, as the lord commanded Moses."* Numbers 15: 32-36

---

There are sins of commission and sins of omission. In other words there are sins that are a consequence of our actions as well as those that result from our inactions. This decree from God to put to death a person gathering wood on the Sabbath goes against the character God. The Sabbath was given for three purposes: First, it is to remember the Creator of the creation, in six days the Almighty God created the heavens and the earth and then rested on the seventh day; second, our observant of the Sabbath is a demonstration of our faith and trust in God and our acknowledgment of the fact that all that is good in our world is a reflection of His love for us. Third, under the New Covenant, the Sabbath serves to remind us to look forward to the day when we shall leave behind all that is earthly and enter into the eternal goodness which God ultimately seeks to bestow upon us.

During the Israelites' journey in the wilderness, they were totally dependent on the LORD for their day-to-day provision – their sustenance, their garments, and their shelter from the elements. By his actions, the man who gathered up the wood on the Sabbath gave a clear signal that a pile of wood took precedence over love for God and His weekly holy day. It was as if he had thumbed his nose at the Lord most high and announced: "I know better than you." The fact is, of course, that none of us knows better than God. To suggest otherwise is not only a betrayal of His love for us, it is a major affront. In essence, this man cut himself off from the Giver of Life, and, in so doing, he called out his own imposition of the only penalty that befitted such total disregard for God, he paid with his life. God relented to man's corporal punishment of that time. Was this man out of his mind? When I ponder and think whether this man lost His eternal salvation, I can only look to God. I will place my trust in Him that He is just and righteous. God is the only one who judges fairly.

Whenever we decide to choose to be god and flaunt our independence that we know better than God, our Creator, we place our lives in the hands of the original transgressor, Satan. Satan equates death, God life. God does not kill. His nature, character and being are life eternal. God always seem to relent on our foibles.

**Don't go against the giver of Life. He knows better than you. After all, He is the true God.**

## TALK TO THE ROCK | APRIL 3

*"But the Lord said to Moses and Aaron, Because you did not trust in me enough to honor me as holy in the sight of the Israelites, you will not bring this community into the land I give them." Numbers 20: 12*

---

After all the trials and tribulations Moses and Aaron went through for over 40 years in the wilderness, they were denied the opportunity to enter the Promised Land. They had disobeyed God's commandment to speak to the rock, and, as a consequence, their dream was denied them.

The people entered the land of Kadesh. There they continued their rant, their virtually non-stop complaining. They complained about the lack of grain, the paucity of figs, the absence of grapevines and pomegranates. They complained often about the lack of water. Moses and Aaron promised to serve as go-betweens, and they took these complaints right to the Top. God in turn instructed them to speak to the rock. Instead, however, Moses took his rod and struck the rock twice. It isn't altogether clear why it was that Moses seemed to have disobeyed a direct order from God. Obviously, in God's eyes this was more than a minor infraction. I can identify with Moses' moment of poor judgment. He succumbed to the evil one's influence. He lost sight for a brief moment of Christ. It's a very painful lesson to learn. I know, I've been there too. Just how serious was this? Well, Paul, in 1 Corinthians 10: 4, tells us that the rock which followed Israel in the wilderness was indeed Christ and that He was stricken but once from the foundation of the world (Hebrews 9: 12). We are also taught that "all things happened to them as examples" to us. We can learn from Moses but even more so from Jesus.

For Moses' to strike the rock a second and then a third time was a foreshadowing of the crucifixion of the Messiah, through which we as the people of promise in the midst of the wilderness receive the water of life. After the crucifixion, we needed only speak to the Rock to receive life, to be washed in the water of the word, to be forgiven. Moses' disobedience deprived him entrance to the Promised Land.

Whom do you most trust in your life? Nothing quenches your thirst or satisfies your palette more than Jesus. But you will never know or understand the magnitude of this point unless you fully place your whole trust in Him. You must believe that with ALL your heart, mind and might. When you come to that realization, you will not only trust Him but honor Him as the Holy One. Then will you experience Him personally ushering you into the Promised Land prepared for you.

**Learn to talk to the Rock (God); for He is your salvation.**

## OPHIDIOPHOBIA | APRIL 4

*"The Lord said to Moses, 'Make a snake and put it on a pole; anyone who is bitten can look at it and live.' So Moses made a bronze snake and put it up on a pole. Then when anyone was bitten by a snake and looked at the bronze snake, he lived." Numbers 21: 8*

---

I have Ophidiophobia, a fear of snakes. Any type of snake terrifies me. Snakes are quite intriguing and mysterious. There is something about these creepy, slithering and scaly reptiles that appalls me. Can my fear of snakes be attributed to environment or genetics? Whatever the reason, I set out to conquer my fear through desensitization. The process was slow and methodical. It took a while but I can face and handle a snake today.

In today's verse, the snake was used to save lives. As had so often been the case, the Israelites were once again complaining about being in the desert, about the lack of water, and about "this miserable food." Talk about ungratefulness! It seemed as though they would have preferred the foods they enjoyed in Egypt, notwithstanding their status as slaves, rather than the miraculous provision of God.

In this story, the serpents represent the original tempter and the seductions of the world. In essence, the LORD said, "Fine, if you still chose what the serpent offers and reject my provision, you may have it. But the consequences of that choice will lead to death." Clearly Israel understood the choice they had made. "We sinned when we spoke against the LORD and against you" (the vessel through whom the LORD spoke). In response, the LORD said, "Make a snake (representing the temptation of the sinful nature) and put (literary impale) it upon a pole; anyone who is bitten can look on it and live." Bronze was the material used. Moses did what God instructed Him to do. Everyone who looked up to the snake after they were bitten lived.

Jesus said "Just as Moses lifted up the snake in the desert, so the Son of Man must be lifted up, that everyone who believes in Him may have eternal life." (John 3: 14). Salvation is really quite simple yet it is the greatest gift God can give us. You don't have to go through any rigorous steps to prove your worthiness. Jesus has done it all for us. There is absolutely nothing in this world you can do or give to God to earn your salvation. The only exercise required of you is your trust/faith in God. The essence of this story is our God says to never fear. Your salvation is in Him. What are you afraid of?

**What a wonderful Savior we have. The Author of Love has lifted Him up for you. We need no longer fear the serpents in our lives.**

## BLESSING YOUR ENEMY | APRIL 5

*"Balak said to Balaam, 'what have you done to me?' I brought you to curse my enemies, but you have done nothing but bless them!' He answered, 'Must I not speak what the Lord puts in my mouth?'" Numbers 23: 11 & 12*

---

Have you ever felt such contempt for someone that you cursed them in your heart? Sadly such thoughts have entered my mind, especially when an injustice has been done and I wish revenge. Have you ever been wrongfully accused of a grievous sin? Ever been betrayed by a loved one? Recently a woman caught her husband having an affair with his secretary. She followed him to work one day and ran her vehicle over him, killing him. She was so enraged that she lost control.

Most of us one time or another has ruminated on inflicting harm upon someone who has wronged or harmed us. It happens every day – at work, in school, perhaps even in church. Balak, the son of the King of the Moabites, asked Balaam to curse the Israelites because they were more numerous and powerful than he. In return, he would reward Balaam enough to make him very wealthy. Balaam was tempted to the point that he prayed to God five times, and each time God said do not curse His people but instead bless them. And each time Balaam reluctantly obeyed. Can you imagine, asking God the same question five times? One would imagine that after two or three times receiving a no answer one would accept the answer. Balaam entertained the temptation of "living the good life." Balaam struggled for the prize of wealth and prosperity because it was very alluring. He tried but he could not curse the Israelites; instead words of blessing came out of his mouth.

Balaam was smart not go against the LORD. If he had he would have received the curse he would have given. The Author of Love seeks to bless rather than curse. He wants to teach us how He loves us and how we should deal with our enemies. However unjust the circumstances may, at first blush appear, God urges us to bless our enemies. That's an awfully hard thing to accept or demonstrate. It is. But God is not asking you to go meekly to the "slaughter house" in order to bless your enemy. He is telling you to focus ALL of yourself on Him first.

Next time you contemplate getting even with someone who has wronged you or someone acting in a vengeful way towards you, consider instead praying for them the same. **The prayer you pray for your enemy will give you the serenity to accept them in the same way God blesses your enemies**. Remember God died for them too. You also ought to treat them as God treats you.

## MAN'S BEST FRIEND | APRIL 6

*"Then the Lord opened the donkey's mouth, and she said to Balaam, 'what have I done to you to make you beat me these three times?' Balaam answered the donkey, 'you have made a fool of me! If I had a sword in my hand, I would kill you right now.'" Numbers 22: 28 & 29*

---

Do you like animals? They say a man's best friend is his dog. I didn't particularly care much for animals when I was growing up. I remember playing with some of my friends on the street where I lived in San Francisco. I was about six years old when a group of marauding dogs came through our street. One of the dogs bit me on the side of my stomach. The incident left a lasting impression but not enough to develop a phobia. Our traumas often color our actions much as Balaam's did.

Donkeys are stubborn animals. A horse will run himself to death for you. A donkey, however, will reach a point where nothing you can do will get him to move any further. In this situation, Balaam's ass suddenly stopped, and no angry shouting or furious beating would convince him to take another step. Balaam did not know that the donkey could not pass through because there was an angel blocking the way. The donkey could see the angel but Balaam could not. Balaam was focused on only one thing, obtaining a reward of gold and riches. He could not see the angel or hear the voice of the Lord. He got so angry with the donkey's unwillingness to move forward that he beat the Donkey again and again. Finally the donkey spoke. Balaam was so narrowed minded that he didn't even realize he had conversed and argued with a donkey. There are countless stories of animals coming to the rescue of a person in distress. God knew something about us and our needs. One of those needs he fulfilled through His creation of animals. These creatures are undoubtedly a testament to how much God loves us.

Do you have a "Balaam complex?" Are you going through life unaware of your surroundings? You may come across a road block that impedes your goal. Unaware to you that road block could save your life. Don't stubbornly insist on moving forward. An angel is in your path and you do not see him. If you're saved by a road block, an animal or an angel, give thanks to God. Sometimes God has allowed these road blocks to care for you. How we treat these creatures or circumstances in our life is a reflection of our relationship with God. Balaam's stubborn donkey likely saved his life. Everything God created was given for our pleasure and well-being. Animals may not have the verbal ability to communicate in like manner with us but their ability to love us unconditionally is from God.

**Man's true best friend is God.**

## THE SPIRIT IN THE PERSON | APRIL 7

*"So the Lord said to Moses, 'Take Joshua son of Nun, a man in whom is the Spirit, and lay your hand on him.'" Numbers 27: 18*

---

Have you ever been in love? Most of us have been. What is it that we see in a potential date (and, ultimately, a potential mate) that stirs the romantic juices? It seems that men are more concerned about female attractiveness than females about male attractiveness. Of course, the definition of attractiveness differs between cultures and even between times or eras. The women depicted during the Baroque period were often on the plump side. During the mid1960's, the look that appeared in a good many magazines was perhaps best personified by Twiggy. A model by today's standards would appear emaciated. It was, according to some, an androgynous look. Beauty is indeed in the eyes of the beholder, it would seem.

What we as a society are oftentimes prone to forget is that physical attractiveness is just that. The Bible says "man looks on the outward appearance." We have a tendency to rely on the outward appearance or the shell of a person and ignore the inner person. A dear friend of mine is single again and is excited to be involved in the dating scene. One thing she observed is that after a few dates, she becomes bored with her suitor and decides they're not the one. I asked her what is it that makes her conclude such findings. She said they have no staying power. In other words, it's not clicking and the "love spirit" is just not there. I suppose she knows what she's looking for.

"God looks at the heart." God told Moses that Joshua had the Spirit, and he was to lay his hand on him and anoint him as his successor. What do we mean by the term spirit? The spirit is what makes the person who he or she is. That is the whole entity of a person. Without the spirit, the person is merely a shell. There are good spirits and evil spirits that influence your being. God saw in Joshua a Godly spirit. Joshua had the privilege of leading Israel into the Promised Land; Moses did not. Joshua and Caleb were the only two of the 12 spies that entered the Promised Land. A whole generation of people died before the next generation entered the Promised Land.

It is your Godly spirit that will ultimately lead you to your Maker. There is no one like you. There will never be another like you. What makes you unique is the Spirit in you. **How you respond to the Holy Spirit is what will seal your salvation.** Listen to the Spirit's wooing of your heart. Joshua did. **The Spirit is God**. Invite Him to dwell in you. May you also be anointed by God today because He sees the Spirit in you.

## **EVEN OUR FAITH** | APRIL 8

*"This is the victory that has overcome the world, even our faith." I John 5: 4*

What exactly do we mean by "Faith?" I am relegating two pages to our devotion today because of the subject matter. I believe this is very important to know and understand. Faith typically refers to beliefs based not on verifiable fact, material evidence of logic. Does this mean that, when we speak of faith in God, what we are describing is hocus-pocus? God speaks from burning bushes, and He parts seas, but those events are purported to have occurred so long ago that their verifiability is, arguably, tenuous. Some have quipped that, when they see God as a guest on Oprah, only then will they have faith.

Paul in Hebrews 11:1 says this about faith: "Now faith is the substance of things hoped for, the evidence of things not seen." (KJV) In verse 6 Paul further states "And without faith it is impossible to please God, because anyone who comes to Him must believe that He exists and that He rewards those who earnestly seek Him." Wow. Sure sounds as if Paul is urging us to have "blind faith" in God. Not terribly reassuring? Why then should we have faith? This would be apt subject for a book in itself, but here are a few reasons, just for starters.

First, even the fiercest skeptics among us must marvel every day at what we commonly refer to as "nature" but what is really the handiwork of God – the majesty of all that surrounds us. It is all so vast and yet so terribly intricate. Recently, on the popular show, "Jeopardy," a computer dubbed "Watson" defeated the two biggest money-winners in the game's history. Some would regard that as the defeat of man and a victory for so-called science. Well, it was man who built Watson and God who breathed the spark of life into man. If someone snips any of Watson wires, he becomes a heap of nuts, bolts, wires and chips. Shoot a bullet through the brain of a human, and miraculously (as in of a Godly nature), the brain, over time, will re-wire itself and ultimately recover most or all of its functions.

Many today believe that the universe came to be as the result of a so-called "Big Bang." The fact is, however, that the Big Bang fails to explain how and why we are here. It fails, for instance, to explain how something came from nothing (often referred to as the "the uncaused cause"). It fails to explain what there was, the moment before the Big Bang. Some scientists, of course, would raise similar questions about God. Where did He come from? Who begat Him? We have difficulty enough conceiving of infinite time on a go-forward basis. When we contemplate the notion of infinite time on a go-backward basis, most of us find the concept mind-boggling. However, our own logic tells us that in fact a forever past has to have been. And, so even if we were, ONLY for discussion's sake, to forsake the Biblical notion of creation, it is thoroughly UN-reasonable to cast aside the notion of a Creator who has existed forever in the past and will, presumably, live forever in the future, a Creator who knows no spatial boundaries.

Remember science is NOT antithetical to our faith. There is however, the science that is willing to allow for the inexplicable, and then there is, not blind faith, but rather "blind science." Some have argued that the Bible predisposes us toward blind faith, particularly among those for whom the Bible is either the word of God or is perceived to be divinely-inspired. They want to know, for instance, who recorded the events that occurred in the Garden of Eden. For the sake of discussion, it almost doesn't matter whether you regard the Bible as God-inspired or merely a collection of allegories. The fact is God Himself is NOT an allegory. He is very real. There can be NO reasonable debate however, with regard to one all-encompassing fact, and that is: we, the planet we inhabit and the universe that surrounds that planet are compliments of a Divine One, who was here before there was a Big Bang (If ever there was one) who will be here long after the next scientific notion of a creation becomes ancient history.

Therefore, when we speak of faith, we are NOT, as some would have it, speaking of chicanery. We are clearly NOT saying, as some in the scientific community may suggest, **that faith is what we have when all logic and reason fail us. To the contrary, "even our faith" in God is more reasonable and more logical than any concept with which science has provided us over the centuries. Want to have faith in God and His word? Now is the time to fully invest your all in knowing the Author of your faith. It's not so much our faith but God's faithfulness in us. That's the faith God wants from us.**

## WAR, WHAT IS IT GOOD FOR? | APRIL 9

*"Then I said to you, 'do not be terrified; do not be afraid of them. The LORD your God, who is going before you, will fight for you, as he did for you in Egypt, before your very eyes, and in the desert. There you saw how the Lord your God carried you, as a father carries his son, all the way you went until you reached this place.'" Deuteronomy 1: 29-31*

---

Our troops had been occupying Iraq for more than ten years and just recently left that country. The war in Afghanistan appears equally unpromising for us. There are talks our troops with leave that country by 2014. These efforts have divided us as a nation. It is, of course, rather easy to judge these wars when we are doing so from the comfort of our living rooms. We can even voice a strong opinion and exercise our right to vote. But we are not directly involved in the war zone. We can talk all we want and demonstrate too, as some "occupy" demonstrators have done in many parts of our country but we are not engaged personally in that particular war.

I have never experienced war first hand. During the Viet Nam era my three brothers and I had high lottery numbers and were spared active service. My mother, on the other hand, knew firsthand just how brutal war can be. She recalled for us the Japanese occupation of the Philippines during World War II. One story that stands out in my mind was how she smeared her hair, face, and garments with chicken blood in order that she would be able to walk the streets. There were enemy soldiers occupying her village, and they would select attractive women and rape them for their amusement. Her little ruse with the chicken blood enabled her to keep a step ahead of them. She shared stories of friends and family who were less fortunate. Nothing good can come out of war. My mother learned to despise war.

God never sanctioned war. War is hell, it has been said. The first war Biblically recorded took place, not on earth, but in Heaven, when Lucifer rebelled and convinced a third of the angels to join forces with him. The Bible does not suggest there was a nuclear war in God's universe as we know about weapons of war today. As a consequence of that "war" in heaven, our worlds' history has been marked with such caliber of weapons.

There is, however, another type of war. It is fought, not with guns, rifles, mortars, and bombs; it is the war that is fought in so many of our hearts when we choose for or against God. Each day you are confronted with a decision that may have a detriment to your salvation. Paul refers to a war that is not against flesh and blood, but rather against spirits, not of the visible world. What is our recourse amidst all these wars? **If we choose the Lord as our general, we will always be victorious**.

# THAT'S ENOUGH | APRIL 10

*"But because of you the LORD was angry with me and would not listen to me. 'That is enough,' the Lord said. 'Do not speak to me anymore about this matter.'" Deuteronomy 3: 26*

Moses was pleading with God to allow him to cross the Jordan with his people. But God told him enough is enough and not to ask Him about the matter ever again. I like our LORD's response. He allows us to communicate freely with Him, yet He knows what is best for us. When it becomes crystal clear that He has a better plan for you and me you better obey Him. Argue and plea with God all you want but you better listen to His call because once you understand what God's purpose is in your life , you too will say that's enough for me. There was no mistaking the fact that Moses received an answer from God. Yet, many of us wonder, sometimes out loud: "Where is the answer? Where is God when I need Him most?"

In our walk with God, when we witness a miracle, such as healing we praise and welcome God with open arms. However, when our prayers don't appear to be answered, when there is apparent silence from God, we are typically less forthcoming with praise.

C.S. Lewis' book entitled, "A Grief Observed," discussed this issue. His wife was diagnosed with cancer and he prayed that she be healed. When his wife succumbed to the illness, he became something of a skeptic. Lewis' experience is not unusual, of course, and he reacted much the way many of us either would have reacted or in fact have reacted when confronted with similar life challenges.

The Bible tells us of any number of characters who had experiences not unlike Lewis'. Certainly, there were circumstances in Jesus' life that might have caused Him to lose trust in His Father. Yet He said: "Nevertheless, not my will but yours be done." We must take comfort in the fact that God has a plan for us. We must have faith in the unseen, much as we do in the seen. God's answer to us (or, in some instances, His apparent lack of an answer) may seem to run contrary to what we perceive to be our best interests, but the fact is that we can't grasp the larger picture the way He can. Your faith does not require a faith like Jesus. It can start as small as a "mustard seed." When that type of faith is nurtured it will become a Christ-like faith.

**The true test of our faith is not in the applause we render unto God when our most heartfelt prayers appear to be answered, but in our continued devotion to Him** when events may not, on the surface, appear to be what we might have wished for. **Have faith in God until you too can affirm "that's enough."**

## THE OBJECT OF YOUR AFFECTION | APRIL 11

*"You saw no form of any kind the day the Lord spoke to you at Horeb out of the fire. Therefore watch yourselves very carefully, so that you do not become corrupt and make for yourselves an idol, an image of any shape, whether formed like a man or a woman, or like any animal on earth or any bird that flies in the air, or like any creature that moves along the ground or any fish in the waters below. And when you look up to the sky and see the sun, the moon and the stars-all heavenly array-do not be enticed into bowing down to them and worshiping things the Lord your God has apportioned to all the nations under heaven."* Deuteronomy 4: 15-19

---

God gives us a detailed list of what we should look for when creating an object of our affection. He admonishes us not to participate in idol worship. He is rather specific as to the prohibitions, which include: an image of any shape, whether formed like a man or woman' any animal on earth, any bird that flies in the air, or any creature that moves along the ground as well as any fish in the water below. He further stipulates that, when we sit on a meadow and look up to the sky and notice the sun, moon, stars or any heavenly object, we should not be enticed to make them as an idol to worship. In other words, God does not want you to focus on the things He created but rather on the Creator. It's that simple.

It has been said that God is a jealous God. The sound of that may, on the surface, appear to be just a little difficult to comprehend. After all, He is God. What could God possibly be jealous of? He's the One who put us here, and He's the one calling the play-by-play. Some modern-day dissidents have gone so far as to portray God as something of a "drama queen." These skeptics and non-believers have so totally missed the bigger picture. The emotion of jealousy can be detrimental to your health or affirming to your doubts about someone's love for you. Unless you have loved and experienced the unfaithfulness of a loved one, you will not understand the meaning of a righteous jealousy.

God looks at His relationship with us as something of a marital partnership. He knows that, if you allow anything in your life to take precedence over this relationship, you are not only short-changing Him, but you are definitely short-changing yourself. It is easy to fall in love, so to speak, with the things that God created to the exclusion of the Creator Himself. Things of this earth can also mean your lover, spouse or partner.

Remember your complete happiness cannot be dependent on another person. If you do, you will be disappointed. Why, because they are fallible. Everything in this world is temporary. Focus on things above. Those above are eternal. **Make certain that the true object of your affection is God. You are His.**

## IT IS WRITTEN | APRIL 12

*"He humbled you, causing you to hunger and then feeding you with manna, which neither you nor your fathers had known, to teach that man does not live on bread alone but on every word that comes from the mouth of the Lord." Deuteronomy 8: 3*

---

Jesus was tempted by Satan to turn the stones into bread after He had fasted for 40 days and 40 nights in the wilderness. The devil (tempter) came to him and said, "If you are the Son of God, tell these stones to become bread." Jesus answered "It is written: Man does not live on bread alone, but on every word that comes from the mouth of God." Jesus must have known the scriptures since He quoted from the Old Testament.

Have you ever been hungry? I mean REALLY hungry that anything you ate tasted really good. I have never known real starvation, not eating for days. The longest I've ever gone without eating was 24 hours. That was a challenge, and I began to feel the hunger pangs in my stomach. However, to go without eating for 40 days and nights, now that is unfathomable. Man needs food to live. Water is even more critical. You cannot survive 40 days without water. Yet, Christ survived. And there have been others who starved themselves just as long for the sake of their convictions.

Most people in our culture can't seem to get enough food. The U.S. is known as the world's bread basket. Food is plentiful, and we have the waist lines to prove it. The first temptation our parents were subjected to was to eat from the forbidden tree of the fruit of the knowledge of good and evil. To this day, we constantly crave those foods which are the least healthy. We are a fallen people, and our diets mirror this fact. God has warned us that filling our stomachs with food will satiate our hunger only temporarily, but food itself will never satisfy our deeper hunger. There have been times when I ate until I was full but I was not satisfied. Have you ever felt that way too? I felt something missing. I was craving for something but did not know what to eat to quell that desire.

Partaking of the " Bread of Life" will provide you with the true sustenance-eternal sustenance. **God is the Bread of Life.** God said that we will not live by the bread we eat but because of Him. You really need to KNOW the sustainer of life and giver of all good things. When you place your faith in Him, your hunger will be satiated. Your hunger will be made complete in Him because you have tasted your ETERNAL BREAD.

**Get to KNOW GOD and when you receive Him in your life you will hunger no more.**

## REMEMBER GOD | APRIL 13

*"**Remember how the Lord your God led you** all the way in the desert these forty years; to humble you and to test you in order to know what was in your heart, whether or not you would keep his commands." Deuteronomy 8: 2*

---

For me turning 40 was a trifle depressing. As a child, 40 years of age was borderline-ancient. Today, of course, when I speak of my youth, I include my 40's. I realize now that I must relish each and every year as it comes, and I realize, too, that age is indeed little more than a number. Some are truly old at age 30, and others are youthful, at least in spirit, well into their 80's. During my most recent 40 years, there is perhaps one event that served for me as a turning point in my relationship with God. Back in 1989, my business partner and I were engaged in the second year of what promised to be a prosperous business. We had recently doubled our revenues, and our staff numbered 12. God had blessed us, and I recall how thrilled I was to purchase the Steinway baby grand piano that had been forever in my dreams. I lived in a beachfront home overlooking the Pacific Ocean. Life was indeed good. I lacked nothing – well, almost nothing. God had become an afterthought.

As I reflect back on those days, the true meaning of today's verse becomes painfully apparent. The fact is that I failed to pay heed to the true source of my wealth, health and affluent lifestyle. I paid God no more than lip service tribute. What is worse, I knew better. Regrettably, it was not until I lost it all that I again turned to God. Lest this be yet another of those "money isn't everything" lectures, let me tell you that, on most days of the week, all things equal, possessing earthly riches beats abject poverty.

I thought I knew where my heart was, but God knew better. Since being keen to God's presence, I am more grateful for the little things in life I took for granted. By that I mean, feeling physically well, able to enjoy a meal prepared by loved ones. I am able to walk in the cool of the evening or play social tennis with vigor and reckless abandonment and come out of it feeling good. To enjoy the company of family and friends is gratifying. To play with grand nephews and nieces and reminisce about your childhood brings a nostalgic of my youth and how God cared for me all these years.

God wants us to have the abundant life. Be sure He is always with you through your journey of success and failures. True wealth, peace and completeness are of no consequence, if you don't know the source of all good things, God. **In the end, though we may forget and forsake Him, REMEMBER the Author of Love will never give up on us.**

## VERONICA'S SONG | APRIL 14

*"They are the ones the Lord has sent to go throughout the earth." Zechariah 1:10*

At approximately 7:00 a.m. Veronica gasped her last breath. This was a total shock to her husband, family and friends who knew her. She was young, just 52 years old. She was the mother of four grown daughters and grandmother of three.

I had met Veronica three years earlier. We were members of the social committee at our church. She loved music and had a beautiful soprano voice. The week before she passed away, she was the designated soprano soloist for "Handel's Messiah." I had heard her sing before but this rendition was very special. Her notes were quite distinct, her voice voluminous and poignant. It was almost as if an angel was among us. I greeted her after the program to say how much I enjoyed her singing. And as usual she gave me a hug and a kiss and said, "I love you honey." Those were her last words to me.

No doubt, each of us has had a Veronica or two in our lives. I even know Veronica's dearest friend, Norma who also has the Spirit of God. There are Veronicas in our churches, our homes, our schools, our work places, the stores in which we shop, and yes, even in our prisons. God knows where the need is. Oftentimes, we take the Veronica's in our lives for granted and, sometimes we are even skeptical of their motives. How can it be, we wonder, that someone can give of him – or herself so freely and with such a kindly spirit? The fact is that the Veronicas of this world are possessed of the infinite love that can only be in God. Were it not for the Veronicas amongst us, our world would be a bleak place indeed. All of us are a Veronica. All of us were made in God's image. All of us carry the Godly Spirit that touches lives like God touches us. God wants us to extend that Spirit to everyone you come in contact with. You are given an opportunity every day to share God's Spirit. How you treat that stranger, acquaintance, friend, child, family member or spouse will determine whether you have a Veronica Spirit.

There are people in your life whom the Author of Love has sent to touch you, to demonstrate His infinite love for you and to render your life a bit brighter and good deal more joyful. We all have the potential to be one of these people. All we need do is take the Lord to heart and share His love to all.

I miss Veronica and her hugs as well as her affirming words of "I love you honey." Somehow, when she demonstrates her love to me, I feel God's presence. **God sends the Veronicas in our lives to express His love to each of us.** Won't you express your love to your neighbor today?

## POOR PEOPLE IN THE LAND | APRIL 15

*"There will always be poor people in the land. Therefore I command you to be openhanded toward your brothers and toward the poor and needy in your land." Deuteronomy 15: 11*

---

As I was driving on a heavily congested freeway, practically crawling to get to work, my mind began to fantasize what it would be like to be rich. I would never have to get up at the crack of dawn to beat the traffic. They used to refer to such a job as working "bankers' hours." There was a time (those of us older than 40 will recall) when banks operated from 9 a.m. until 3 p.m., five days-a-week. It was a commonly-held perception, albeit an erroneous one, that the most successful business people worked such hours. Essentially, or so the myth went, they could come to work when they chose and leave when they felt like doing so. Rush-hour, it was commonly believed was for the "little people."

One morning, as my car inched ever-so-close to the vehicle ahead of me, I spotted a bumper sticker which read: "Poverty Sucks!" In truth, relatively-few of us have ever experienced true poverty. However, most of us would concur with the bumper sticker's sentiments. Why is there so much poverty in our world? We have enough to eradicate poverty throughout the world but we still have the poor dwelling among us.

The fact is, too, that most of us look with disdain upon the poor. They are, we think to ourselves, lazy, ignorant, and careless in their ways. Their poverty is their own doing, we might assert, were it politically correct to express such thoughts. As we ponder the impact of the current recession, we think of the oft-voiced slogan: "It's a recession when the other guy is unemployed." On the other hand, "It's a depression when you are unemployed." When it's you or a friend or relative collecting unemployment our level of disdain for the less fortunate diminishes. Can we look at others in the same light? After all, doesn't God treat us in the same manner? Whether we are rich, poor, disabled, dependent or independent, no one is exempted for the openhandedness of God's care towards us.

Those of us who have taken God into our hearts know that helping the poor, is what the Kingdom of God is about. God knew we would have the poor among us that is why He commanded us to open our hands and feed them, care for them. We all fail to measure up to God's glory, some perhaps a little bit more than others. None of us is exempt from sin. **When you help the poor, you not only come to the aid of someone less fortunate than you, you honor God and His Kingdom.**

## **TEN PERCENT** | APRIL 16

*"Be sure to set aside a tenth of all that your fields produce each year." Deuteronomy 13: 22*

---

Do you tithe? Do you give 10 percent of your wages for tithe? It is not easy to give away a tenth of your wages when you are struggling to put food on the table, a roof over your head, school payments for the kids and monthly mortgage payments. Why would God want our money when He owns everything? What is the purpose of tithing anyway? The first mention of tithing in the Bible is in Genesis 14. The story is told of Lot taken prisoner in a regional war. Abraham gathered together a band of his own men and in a surprise attack defeated Lot's captors and regained all the stolen booty. Abraham returned triumphant. He met and gave a tenth of everything he garnered to Melchizedek, the king and high priest.

God knew that giving a tenth is the reflection of what's truly from the heart. In Matthew 23: 23, Jesus would address tithing in the context of the whole law. He said, "You give a tenth of your spices-mint, dill and cumin. But you have neglected the more important matters of the law-justice, mercy and faithfulness. You should have practiced the latter without neglecting the former." Jesus plainly indicates that He is not rejecting tithing, but its practice is no substitute for justice and mercy. When you follow His command in tithing you trust Him no matter where you are financially, emotionally, psychologically or spiritually. This practice will allow you to carry that trust in Him in all matters of your life.

God wants to restore you to the wholeness you were before the fall. The first step in loving God with ALL your heart and with ALL your soul may be in the first tenth. How can you give all without first giving the first tenth? God does not need our tenth. He wants our tenth because He is a giver and He gave ALL to redeem us. He gave His Son.

**Tithing is not just giving ten percent but it's all about faith and trust in the Author of Love**. Are you still in doubt? I challenge you today to start giving your tithe for just one month and if God does not bless you, you never have to do it again. The truth of the matter even the tenth that you give God has a way of returning that to you. If you're still uncertain about giving, God will still bless you. He loves you regardless of who you are or what you do or don't do. God just wants to give you a more abundant life.

**He holds nothing back for you. Just look at His Son. He gave ALL.**

## TRADE INSULT WITH BLESSING | APRIL 17

*"Finally, all of you, live in harmony with one another; be sympathetic, love as brothers, be compassionate and humble. Do not repay evil with evil or insult with insult, but with blessing, because to this you were called so that you may inherit a blessing." I Peter 3: 8 & 9*

---

It is easy to exchange kind with kind. I have played tennis with a player who has the reputation of making bad calls. I know he doesn't purposely do it because off court he is one of the kindest people I know. He is generous and kind hearted. I was watching him play a person who was out of his league. This person had beautiful classic tennis strokes and could easily control the point. During the course of the match my friend called his opponent's ball out and his opponent gave that glare of "are you sure you made the right call?" They continued play, and, before long, my friend made a dubious call. The score was tied at three all when his opponent gave up and walked off the court, murmuring something to the effect that he refused to play with someone who made so many bad calls. The two have not played together since.

I had a similar experience playing tennis with a friend who has a temper and on rare occasion loses it. On this particular day I gave him that look of incredulity after a questionable call. He stormed off the court and smashed his racket. This was followed with a tirade on court etiquette, after which he demanded that I replace his racket. My initial instinct was to tell him what he could do with his racket. Instead, however, I asked him how much would it cost. He was stunned. It broke the "ice."

Today's text urges us not to trade evil for evil, insult for insult, but rather respond with blessing – this, with the knowledge that you reap what you sow. If you give a blessing, ultimately (not always immediately, mind you) you will receive a blessing. God would have been justified to have repaid our mistakes and insults in kind. Some of us have been con or duped by unscrupulous people. We believe "karma" will play out in our desire to get revenge. Our desire to seek vengeance is tops on our-to-do list. If you place God first in your to do list, you would have traded that insult to a blessing because that is how God treats us, even when we have insulted Him.

Remember, He evidenced His love and care for us by returning our insult with redemptive blessing. **He gave us this blessing in the person of His Son, Jesus.** He set an example for us. Try returning an insult with kindness and you'll inherit God's blessing.

## A CURSE VS. A BLESSING | APRIL 18

*"See, I am setting before you a blessing and a curse-the blessing if you obey the commands of the LORD your God that I am giving you today; the curse if you disobey the commands of the LORD your God and turn from the way that I command you today by following other gods, which you have not known." Deuteronomy 11: 26-28*

---

"Shhh, God does not like children who misbehave. He will punish you if you're too noisy in church." Those words still echoes in my ears whenever I see children misbehaving and their parents scolding them. Did you ever hear that as a child? I did, and it colored my impression of God. The God I thought I knew as a child was tyrant, waiting to pounce on us for any infraction or mistake. I obeyed God because I literary was afraid of the wrath He might impose on me. In Jesus' time, whenever the blind or the disabled came to Jesus to be healed, the gossip mill had it that their maladies were a curse resulting from their own sins or the sins of their parents.

I wonder how many of us still carry that cultural or religious mentality of curses? My friend's nieces were killed in a car accident at the tender age of 14 and 16. Their grandmother concluded that God took them early so they would not suffer in their adult age. I hate to admit it but I was raised with that notion and once in a while when I experience "bad karma" or fail to give tithe, I think of my past sins or the sins of my forefathers and become dejected for having such an hex in my life. I can remember my elders telling me that so and so got married and will also inherit that family's legacy of curses. Ouch!

This notion of a God who seeks retribution for the commitment of evil deeds begs an important question: what about the innocent? – the children caught in the crossfire of war, victims of childhood abuse, or victims of natural disasters. Is God punishing them? Absolutely not! Hopefully, if there is a single point that comes across loud-and-clear in these writings, it is that God is a God of Love, NOT a God of retribution. The evil that exists in this world is NOT God's doing. Suffering is NOT from God. However, caring and loving are. That there is evil in the world is an unfortunate fact. God is NOT the author of evil. To the contrary, He said **"For I know the plans I have for you," declares the LORD, "plans to prosper you and not harm you, plans to give you hope and a future."** Jeremiah 29: 11.

God sent us His Son to give us hope and a better future. If you obey this command of the Lord you will be blessed. Above all though, never think for one minute God is the author of curses or calamities. There is an evil force that is like a roaring lion waiting to devour and curse you. **Never forget that God only blesses.**

## THE VICTORY IS YOURS | APRIL 19

*"For the Lord your God is the one who goes with you to fight for you against your enemies to give you victory." Deuteronomy 20: 4*

---

Can war ever be justified? There are numerous accounts in the Bible about children of God going to war with neighboring people and conquering them. God condoned such activity because His children were indeed striking down those who practiced evil. The Israelites, however, had forsaken their Godly ways and were becoming very much like their evil, corrupt foes. This, not surprisingly, was detestable to God.

War, it should be pointed out, began way before man entered the scene. War had its roots in heaven. That war continues even to this day; for the devil continues in his efforts to lure us into his camp. God has committed to be with us as we encounter Lucifer's evil ways. In fact, He will not only be with us; He will defend us against the evil in the world. What a remarkable promise, particularly in view of the fact that, when it comes to God versus the devil, God continues to pitch a no-hitter -- a perfect game, moreover.

Each of us can be a trifle pig-headed, and we are prone to fight our own battles. We don't need God's help, or so we think. Be aware that the most important wars in our lives are not the North Korean threats of nuclear bombings, Iraq or Afghanistan conflicts or the war on terror; the most important wars are the wars of good against evil, and each of us is a soldier in that war every single day of our lives. There has been no armistice, so to speak, in that war, and the leader of the opposition, Lucifer, is not one to wave a white flag. Over the centuries, he has proven to be more than a little resilient.

Don't be discouraged if things look bleak for the moment, it is only temporary. God has promised the victory is yours. He will fight your battles. Can you see the victory now? If you are to prevail in your own skirmishes with yourself or the evil one, you will only succeed if you look to God as your General. If you allow God in your heart, then you will certainly prevail, regardless of the evil forces' strength around you.

Remember, God will give you the victory. You don't have to lift a finger or a weapon to fight your battle. You must believe He is on your side. You must trust Him regardless of the evidences to the contrary. Can you place your dependency on Him. He's been waiting for your reception. Trust His plans for you. **He never loses and you won't either if you let Him fight the battle for you**.

## WHY ARE YOU CRYING? | APRIL 20

*"Finally the other disciple, who had reached the tomb, first, also went inside. He saw and believed." John 20: 8*

---

Do you ever doubt the Bible's authenticity? How can you be sure? Do you believe in the resurrection of Jesus? Many today do and many today still doubt. Mary was the first person to arrive at the tomb. She was saddened that the body of Christ was not there when she arrived. She was crying when she went into the tomb and noticed two angels in white seated where Jesus' body had been laid. One of them was at the head and the other at the foot. They asked her, "Woman, why are you crying," 'they have taken my Lord away,' she said, 'and I don't know where they have put him.'" (John 20: 10-14) At this, she turned around and Jesus was standing there, but she did not realize that it was Jesus.

Many Christians around the world celebrate Easter to commemorate our risen Savior. However, there are many who regard this as a story or yarn with relatively-little significance for them. Easter for them is about jelly beans and egg coloring. How does Christ's resurrection from the grave over two centuries ago impact their lives today? The fact is that Jesus is beside us, even closer today than when He was here on earth. In John 20: 15 & 16, He said: "woman, why are you crying? Who is it that you are looking for?" Thinking that he was the gardener, she said: "Sire, if you have carried Him away, tell me where you have put Him, and I will get Him." Jesus then called to her: "Mary." She finally recognized Him.

Why are you crying? Are you saddened by the cares of this world? Are you afraid this story of Jesus is all a fairy tale and your faith will all be in vain? Do you sometimes feel your faith waning and ready to throw in the towel? Is your life marred by the distractions of this world that you cannot see Him or hear Him call you? Do you struggle to believe, too? As Jesus told Thomas (John 20: 20): "because you have seen me, you have believed; blessed are those who have not seen and yet have believed." Are you a so-called doubting Thomas, a skeptic?

There are those who have NOT seen Jesus first hand yet have believed, they must know something or have a faith that you don't have. Believe me, when you SEE Jesus you will know and you will be the ones who are truly blessed. Just as He said "Mary," **God is calling your name right now. Do you recognize His voice?** When that happens, your tears will be tears of joy.

## TRUE FRIENDSHIP | APRIL 21

*"A man that hath friends must show himself friendly: and there is a friend that sticketh closer than a brother." Proverbs 18: 24 KJV*

Whose name would you immediately say if I were to ask you who is your best friend? I have a number of good friends. However, I always welcome new ones.

I met Jack in the summer of 1996. He was a handsome young man with a personable appearance and a likeable and sociable personality. Jack had a voracious appetite for people. He enjoyed meeting them and engaging them whenever the opportunity arose. Jack had Tourette Syndrome, an involuntary and uncontrollable muscle spasm occurring anytime. His "tics" could be terribly distracting. But his vivacious personality covered all his idiosyncrasies. Jack also valued my friendship and acceptance. He introduced me to his friend, Gerri and from her I have learned the value of friendship that "sticketh closer than a brother." Gerri has gone beyond friendship and considered me family. She has been an invaluable friend to me and my family and friends.

Today's text proves that, to have friends, you must show yourself friendly. Sounds like a statement of the obvious, doesn't it? However, it is a point that many of us forget from time to time. Fortunately, we have a role model when it comes to friendship, and that is the Author of Love. He was the first friend we ever had, and, although the list of people we call friends will no doubt change over the years, His friendship is steadfast. In John 15: 15, Jesus says: "I no longer call you servants, because a servant does not know his master's business. Instead, I have called you friends, for everything that I learned from my Father I have made known to you."

God invites us to be His friend. He is your best friend. The friendships I have with Jack and with Gerri are because of the friendship Jesus has shown us. Jack and Gerri are a reflection of God's friendship towards me. Granted, human friendships have its flaws and can sometimes disappoint, but the Spirit of love can only be derived from God.

When you are receptive to God's Spirit of friendship, then you are friends with God. Jesus knows what it means to have a best friend. He has extended His friendship to everyone.

**You may have good friends here on earth, but your true best friend is the ONE who comes from heaven.**

## GOD SAVES A PROSTITUTE | APRIL 22

*"Then Joshua son of Nun secretly sent two spies from Shittim. 'Go; look over the land,' he said, 'especially Jericho.' So they went and entered the house of a prostitute named Rahab and stayed there." Joshua 1: 1*

---

The entire chapter of Joshua 2 tells of two spies that went to spy on Jericho. The spies entered the city undetected because of the help of a woman named Rahab. The names of the spies are never mentioned. Only the prostitute Rahab is named. Rahab risked her own life by harboring the two spies. She hid them in her house and protected them from the king's men. She heard stories about the God who cared for Israel. She beseeched the two spies "Now then, please swear to me by the LORD that you will show kindness to my family, because I have shown kindness to you. Give me a sure sign that you will spare the lives of my father and mother, my brothers, and sisters, and all who belong to them, and that you will save us from death." The spies assured her that her family would be spared.

The lives of Rahab and her family were indeed spared, and, after the conquest of Jericho, she and her family lived with the Israelites and intermarried, and she became a part of the lineage of Jesus Christ. Who would have imagined that the Promised One would have a prostitute in His ancestry? What a heartwarming and fascinating story. Here was a prostitute that was receptive to God's calling by carrying out His purpose. God calls each of us daily. He wants to reveal Himself to you and me. His whole purpose for us was to reconcile us back to Him. Can you hear His call? Are you willing to accept His invitation?

All are called for His purposes, but few respond to the Spirit's calling. Rahab responded. Have you ever wondered why God chose a woman to save and on top of that a prostitute? Consider the fact that Rahab represented God. She was chosen and not a man because God knows the end from the beginning and He knew His Son would come through a woman. In "Patriarchs and Prophets," (P. 54, by Ellen G. White), she says: "All these events were known to the inhabitants of Jericho, and there were many who shared Rahab's conviction, though they refused to obey it, that Jehovah, the God of Israel, is God in heaven above, and upon the earth beneath." It was not God who rejected even the inhabitants of Jericho but the people who rejected God. Don't remove yourself from the life giver. He is the God of your salvation. There's still hope for you and me, no matter what our background, regardless of how sordid our reputation.

**Respond to His Spirit and you too, will be saved, just as He saved a prostitute.**

## GOD WILL BE WITH YOU | APRIL 23

*"Have I not commanded you? Be strong and courageous. Do not be terrified; do not be discouraged, for the LORD your God will be with you wherever you go." Joshua 1: 9*

---

The Iraqi war invasion was over. Victory had been declared. The city of Baghdad was slowly returning to its normal state. However, the price of war had taken its toll on the lives of the people as well as the soldiers fighting the battle. Being a soldier requires always being on guard with every sense on full alert. What must it feel like to be a soldier in a foreign land? You are unfamiliar with the people, their culture, or the environment. Do you ever fully acclimate yourself? It's not your home. You are there temporarily. You are just passing through and you pray that victory be swift so that lives, including your own, may be spared,

I recall vividly the saga of a friend who shared his war experience with me. One thought, he told me, that was always top-of-mind was: will I get out of this place alive? When you are watching your comrades fall right by your side, there is that moment of ambivalence – feeling at once gratefulness that it was "the other guy" and guilt that perhaps it should have been me instead. What an awfully feeling to entertain such thoughts, yet it is all part of war. Is God in the midst of the fighting during conflict? YES, God said He is with us wherever we go, even to the gates of hell. And God promised us He will be victorious in the final chapter of our history.

Most of us will never experience war, first-hand. However, we are all soldiers of a different kind. Our struggle is the battle between good and evil. On the one side is the enemy, the soldier of darkness, and, on the other is the light. Do you know the difference? The choice seems obvious, but it's typically a bit more complicated than that. You see, Satan doesn't play with a rule book. Jesus warned Peter: "I prayed for you that you would not be snared by Satan." Just as Jesus prayed for Peter, would you believe He is praying for your strength and courage? Yes, God is ever watching over you wherever you go.

The good news is that, whatever your path or dilemmas you will encounter in your journey, God will soldier on with you. He never slumbers nor sleeps. He is constantly on guard. God is ever watching for your safety so that you are not snared into Satan's wiles.

If God is in your heart, you will ultimately prevail: for **the Author of Love is an undeterred, ever-vigilant, forever dependable ally.**

## OUT OF DARKNESS LIGHT | APRIL 24

*"He who says he is in the light and hates his brother is in darkness until now. He who loves his brother abides in the light, and there is no cause for stumbling in him." I John 2: 9 & 10*

---

Yesterday I saw on the news another astonishing moment in the war against terrorism: Two women blew themselves up in a market place in Baghdad, Iraq. Hundreds perished. A city block was utterly destroyed. It is apparent that these terrorists are blinded by a cause that is shrouded in darkness. They believe that the havoc, carnage and devastation they wreak serve as testimony of their love of God, and yet, whether they realize it or not, they are soldiers of Satan. Satan is the father of lies and chaos. All our maladies in this world did NOT come from God. There are an evil forces perpetrated by Satan's legions, just as there are godly angels.

You ask then, where was God? Many of us no doubt questioned. Has He abandoned us? God is a God of free will. Were God to control every evil deed before it was perpetrated, we would no longer have the ability to choose between good and evil. We would be automatons. God has NOT abdicated His role as overseer of our world. He is, however patient and long-suffering. He does not want anyone to perish. He knows that, ultimately, we must choose between good and evil. He recognizes, too, that, while war may represent the darkest among man's acts, it is the hidden prejudice that so many of us harbor that ultimately leads to war. So often, we look to perform good deeds in God's name and for His sake but fail to see His light.

Two football teams enter the playing field, and the captain of each team leads his team in prayer, seeking God's help in achieving victory. Obviously, God can't please both teams. The captains are not wrong in asking for God's help, but, to the extent that the points on the score board at the end of the game are what matters, God will, it might seem, be leaving one team disappointed. Does this scenario sound familiar? Have you ever asked God's help during a game you were in or observed? I must admit I'm guilty of such thinking and behavior. God's answer to me is it's not about winning or losing but your character during and after the game. The fact is, God is not calling the plays; the team members are. He has given us the free will to make the right choices, but that isn't to say that He is not there with us every step along the way. It's really your call. But be sure it's done in God's spirit.

**The most important play in our play book is to remain faithful to Him who is our light out of darkness.**

## THE LORD'S GOOD PROMISES | APRIL 25

*"Not one of all the LORD'S good promises to the house of Israel failed; everyone was fulfilled." Joshua 21: 45*

There is something powerful about a promise made even more about one kept. Promises are made during wedding vows. Promises are made to children by parents if they behave or do well in school. Promises are made to friends to keep secrets forever. Promissory notes are made in business transactions. A promise is a pledge that is meant to instill confidence and good will. There is, on the other hand, an adage that says: "Promises were made to be broken." A promised unfulfilled is, of course, more heart-wrenching than one never made. The child who is promised a new bike by the Christmas tree and left wanting is more hurt than the child never promised one at all.

Couples make vows to love, honor and cherish each other, but those vows are often observed more in the breach than in the practice, and our growing divorce rate bears testimony to that unfortunate fact.

Today's text reminds us that, while mankind may have a less-than-stellar track record when it comes to honoring promises, God's record is unblemished. All of God's promises are intended for our benefit, and each and every one of those promises will be met.

What has God promised? He has promised us sunshine and rain, both to the righteous and the un- and marginally-righteous. He has promised never to leave nor forsake us. He promised us a Savior for our sin. He promised to build each of us a mansion in Heaven, where we shall live with Him throughout eternity. He promised us a "Promised Land," where there will be no more sorrow, pain, tears or death. He promised us a land devoid of darkness, a land with eternal sunshine. Can you imagine a heavenly place where we will live with the Author of true promises for all eternity? Can you believe in Him?

Since man's fall from grace, every promise God made has come true. You can bank on that from now until His return that every GOOD promises of God you will see come to fruition. Not one of His promises will fail. He said every single one of His promises will be fulfilled. Yes, every one. Have you seen them yet?

**GOD'S WORD IS AS SURE AS HIS EXISTENCE**. Trust in God; for His promises are TRUE and GOOD.

## A WOMAN IS CALLED | APRIL 26

*"Deborah, a prophetess, the wife of Lappidoth, was leading (judging) Israel at that time." Judges 4: 4*

---

Quickly! how many women can you name that are authors of the Bible? Rarely in ancient times did women play leading roles in society. One in particular who led Israel was Deborah. She was a prophetess used by God to conquer the Israelites' enemies. In this particular instance, the Israelites came to her to settle their disputes. She sent for Barak and said to him, (verse 6 & 7) "The LORD, the God of Israel, commands you; Go, take with you ten thousand men of Naphtali and Zebulun and lead the way to Mount Tabor. I will lure Sisera, the commander of Jabin's army, with his chariots and his troop to the Kishon River and give him into your hands." Sisera was an enemy and oppressor of the Israelites. Barak replied that he would go on condition that Deborah would go with him. If she did not go with him then he would not go. Deborah agreed, but she also said because he did not go alone, the glory of conquering Sisera would go to a woman and not to him. Her prediction came true. Barak did not receive the glory for defeating Sisera; it went to Jael, a woman who killed Sisera while asleep in her tent.

Women have played a significant role in the salvation of man. Today's text shows that, when you are called by God to accomplish a task, God will honor those who obey His calling regardless of their gender, socioeconomic status, educational accomplishments or religious affiliation. God knew women would experience special challenges. Nevertheless He paved the way and called Deborah to lead a nation. Throughout earth's history, many women have played a significant role in the salvation of humankind. God chose a woman as a helpmate from Adam. He chose a woman to conceive our Savior. God is really saying He calls everyone but whoever will receive Him will be saved.

Women's subjugated role in the Bible and in our world did not come from God. Man created that subservient role for women. But the all-inclusive God knows that a woman is an embodiment of the true nature of God. We were all created in God's image. The closest character and love that personifies the image of God is a woman. Her nature is similar to how God cares and nurtures us. The most influential person in the family household is the mother. God chose the woman to represent His love for us here on earth. Man is not discounted but a woman is the closest reflection of God's true nature. You may agree or not, but remember wherever love is there is God. Whether you are male or female and called to lead at home, your church, community or nation, **your faith and trust in God will determine the success or failure.**

## NOT WILLINGLY | APRIL 27

*"For He does not willingly bring affliction or grief to the children of men." Lamentations 3: 33*

What was the worst physical pain you have ever experienced in your life? No doubt, each of us has his or her tale of woe.... a root canal, a sports injury, a traffic accident, a fall, a surgery. Some of us have endured the pain of cancer or a coronary event and survived to tell the story. I've had my own share of physical pain, although I consider myself fortunate in that regard. I'll spare you the gruesome details. Suffice it to say that, in each instance, it seemed like the worst possible hurt at the time. In each instance, when the pain ebbed, I was left with little more than a vague memory of the incident.

There is one type of pain, however, whose impact is far more enduring. It lingers not for a week or a month but rather for the rest of one's earthly days, and that, of course, is the pain associated with the loss of a loved one. Who have you grieved for? Which loved one did you lose? Are you still grieving? God knows a thing or two about grieving. He experienced the loss of His Son.

For me, none was more grievous than the loss of my mother. I recall visiting her in a nursing home. She was on feeding tube. She was as frail as could be. Her once-lithe body had become nearly rigid, and she was virtually immobilized. She could no longer feed herself, nor could she tend to her bodily functions. Her mind could not recognize loved ones. In reality, she was already gone but her body stayed. "This is no life," I said to myself. At once, I prayed that she be relieved of her affliction and that God take her, and at the same time, I, perhaps selfishly, wished that she not be taken from me. In a weird sense, I wanted her alive even with all her frailties. Letting go is very hard to do. Just like God, I was not willingly accepting mother's imminent fate.

Could it be, I wondered, that the Author of Love is, at the same time, the author of grief and suffering? He is not but He gave the gift of grieving to comfort our cries of agony. I know today that mother's suffering was not because of God. I am reminded of how God grieved for His own Son when He lay unjustly crucified on the cross. The fact is that God loved us enough to allow His only Son to experience the agony of torture and a hideous death – this, in order that we might never suffer that final death. God sees the complete picture. I only see what's immediate.

We wait with Him for that final salvation; eventually our story will have a happy ever after ending. For **God is NOT the bearer of grief and affliction**, but rather the Author of life eternal.

## ATTITUDE CHECK | APRIL 28

*"Your attitude should be the same as that of Christ Jesus." Philippians 2: 5*

---

Early during my career, I participated in a multi-level marketing program. My goal was to discover the path to success and riches. Like so many others, I was searching for a shortcut. We all crave success, and we typically grow impatient and seek a quicker route to fame and fortune.

This particular program focused specifically on attitude and behavior change. Techniques that are often employed include modeling. Besides the boundless tapes, books and meetings I attended to reinforce my psyche to think and grow rich, one aspect of our exercise required us to change our attitude. Whenever my "up-line" (my sponsor and mentor) asked us "attitude check?" Our programmed response was always "I FEEL GREAT!" Whether we felt great or not, our response was always the same answer. We were constantly bombarded with positive slogans, positive people and positive thinking.

Behavioral psychologists use the technique of attitude change to remedy unwanted behavior, thinking, and psyche. Albert Bandura, a social learning theorist, founded a therapy technique known as "Modeling." This method of therapy was based on the therapists demonstrating appropriate behavior for the client to imitate. Through the process of imitation and rehearsal the client eventually performs the desired behavior. Obviously there are pros and cons to any method of therapy. Whether we want to admit it or not, children imitate their parents' behaviors. Kids today will either have their parents as heroes or a celebrity of their generation. Which one would you rather be? In our text today, Paul counsels us to be like Christ. What was Christ like?

Jesus was the incarnate God. To be like Christ is to have the very nature of God dwelling within us. One of Christ's disciples urged Him to "show us the Father." Christ's response was: "Have I been with you this long and you still don't know the Father?" Imitating Christ comes from within our heart, soul and mind. It is more than behavioral. Jesus was indeed our role model, and His is the behavior we must emulate every day of our lives. To be like Christ is not only a life time process but process for all eternity. The end result is more than imitation. You can do all things externally as Christ did, just like the rich young ruler did. The greater attitude is what comes naturally and effortlessly because God's Spirit dwells in you. Remember, there are NO shortcuts.

**Attitude Check: "Your attitude should be the same as Christ Jesus."**

## **A VOW OF REGRETS** | APRIL 29

*"And Jephthah made a vow to the Lord: 'If you give the Ammonites into my hands, whatever comes out of the door of my house to meet me when I return in triumph from the Ammonites will be the Lord's, and I will sacrifice it as a burnt offering.'" Judges 11: 30 & 31*

---

Have you ever made a vow to God and kept it? I did. I can recall one such instance in my life. My mother was enduring the nightmare that is colon cancer, and my pain was almost the equal of hers. I vowed to God that, if He healed my mother from this wretched disease, I would be faithful to Him and would attend church faithfully. God answered my prayer and mother was able to return to a more normal life. Here cancer was in remission for the next twelve years. I thanked God.

In today's verse, Jephthah was asked by the Israelites to lead them into battle with their enemy, the Ammonites. Jephthah's father was Gilead; his mother was a prostitute. As the son of a whore, Jephthah was spurred by both of his half-brothers and the local community. Yet Jephthah was a mighty warrior, and when the Israelites went to war with the Ammonites they requested Jephthah to lead them. Eventually Jephthah agreed making a vow to God that if he would gain the victory over his enemy he would sacrifice a burnt offering to God whatever came out of the door of his house to meet him when he returned in triumph. When he returned home after a victorious battle who should come out of his house to greet him but his daughter. The end result was a deadly vow. What was he thinking? Couldn't he have back tracked and said "I made a mistake. I will make an exception." No, instead he kept his vow and executed his own daughter. Have you entertained similar thinking or behavior? Do you make statements that you wish you could take back but because of pride you stubbornly "stick to your guns."

God does not need our vows. What we owe God is not our promises, but rather our worship. We cannot trust our heart but we can trust God's heart. One of the ceremonies of the Day of Atonement is to renounce all vows you have made for the previous year which you have been unable to fulfill, then asking God for both forgiveness and the wisdom not to make such foolish promises in the year to come.

**Our ways and thinking are foolish if God is not the center.** He does not ask for your vows or promises; He merely asks that we accept His love of us. In truth, there is but one vow you need make, and that is to keep God always in your heart. If you do, you will undoubtedly have no regrets.

## **DRINK NO WINE** | APRIL 30

*"The angel of the Lord appeared to her and said, "You are sterile and childless, but you are going to conceive and have a son. Now see to it that you drink no wine or other fermented drink and that you do not eat anything unclean." Judges 13: 3 & 4*

---

Studies have shown that there is deleterious effect from the consumption of alcohol or drugs especially if taken by a pregnant woman. Other studies indicate that a glass of wine drunk in moderation results in a longer life span. What do you believe? Why would God admonish the wife of Manoah to drink no wine or fermented drink, or eat anything unclean? Who would you believe? Current studies made by man or God's wisdom?

All alcoholic beverages contain "ethyl alcohol." This is a chemical compound that is rapidly absorbed into the blood and it takes immediate effect to the entire nervous system, where it acts to "depress," or slow its functioning by binding to a variety of neurons. The person loses inhibition and one's judgment is impaired. The person becomes either talkative or relaxed. They feel safe, confident and happy. Their motor skills become impaired, they're sensitive to light and their face and neck becomes flushed. The more they drink the more their judgments declines, their speech becomes less guarded, their memory falters, their vision is affected and they lose control of themselves. Ever been around a person that has been drinking? They can say and do the most obnoxious things. The life of an alcoholic is quite self-absorbing and depressing. I have been around inebriated people, alcoholics and addicts and treated them as well. It is a sad case to witness such behaviors.

God must have known the seriousness of this malady when the Angel of the Lord instructed the wife of Manoah not to eat unclean foods or drink fermented drink of any type. God was preparing a child for them that would lead Israel out of bondage from the Philistines. That future leader would be named Samson. Manoah's wife did conceive as God prophesized and had a son who was filled with the Holy Spirit. The child was consecrated to God as a Nazarite from birth. God instructed Samson's parents that the child was to be taught the lessons of temperance, self-denial, and self-control from babyhood. Samson grew in wisdom, strength and stature. He was filled with the Spirit of God. However, as he entered upon manhood, the time when he was about to fulfill his calling in leading the Israelites from the Philistines, he allowed his unsanctified passions to control his heart. **His use of alcohol betrayed his faith in God.**

## THE SECOND MIRACLE OF JESUS | MAY 1

*"This was the second miraculous sign that Jesus performed, having come from Judea to Galilee." John 4: 54*

John chapter 4 recorded the first miracle Jesus performed in turning water into wine at a wedding feast in Cana at Galilee. His "second miracle" is recorded in Chapter 4: 43-54. This was a story of a royal official whose son lay sick at Capernaum. This official heard Jesus had arrived in Galilee from Judea. He went to Jesus and begged Him to heal his son who was close to death. Verses 48-53 Jesus responded: "Unless you people see miraculous signs and wonders, you will not believe." Does it take a miraculous healing for you to believe in Jesus as your salvation, great physician, sustainer of life and friend? Do you first need a miracle of such magnitude to believe in Him? We all want something tangible to taste, smell, feel, see or hear that would make us believe. It's "human nature" to want physical evidence as proof before we exercise faith. What's sad is that God has given us more than enough evidence to prove Himself as our LORD and GOD.

In his book entitled "Lord, I Have a Question." P. 132, Dr. Daniel G. Smith, concludes that: "Inductive logic and observation of modern-day miracles leads to the conclusion today, God's work seems to be primarily internal than external, spiritual rather than physical." Back in Jesus' days, man virtually demanded physical proof of God's handiwork. Thus, the official again begged Jesus to "…come down before my child dies." Jesus replied, 'You must go, your son will live.' The man took Jesus at his word and departed. While he was still on the way, his servants met him with news his boy was living. When he inquired as to the time when his son got better, they said to him, 'The fever left him yesterday at the seventh hour.' Then the father realized this was the exact time Jesus had said to him, 'Your son will live.'

The second miracle may have been healing the royal official's son but **the TRUE miracle is recognizing who the source of all miracles is: Jesus.** The Author of Love is no different today. "For the one whom God has sent speaks the words of God, for God gives the Spirit without limit. The Father loves the Son and has placed everything in His hands. Whoever believes in the Son has eternal life."

Miracles never ceases even to this day. When we witness healing we are moved and attribute such miracles to God's goodness. To us it may be a miracle but to God it's a matter of faith. Your faith in God is the greater miracle. (Today's devotional is dedicated to Pastor Dan and Hilda Smith)

# THEY HAVE NOT HURT ME | MAY 2

*"My God sent his angel and he shut the mouths of the lions. They have not hurt me, because I was found innocent in his sight. Nor have I ever done any wrong before you, O King." Daniel 6: 22*

---

The lion is one of the most powerful and intimidating animals in God's creation. Yet even the lion is subjected to the power of the Almighty God. Daniel was respected and beloved by King Darius. The king had appointed 120 satraps (princes) to rule his kingdom. Three administrators were also appointed to rule over the 120 satraps. One of them was Daniel. Daniel's position and status with the king provoked jealousy among administrators and princes. They plotted to do away with Daniel. They spied on his daily habits and noted he prayed to God every day. They persuaded the king to issue an edict of anyone who prayed to any god or man, except, of course, to the king himself, be thrown in the lions' den. Given the king's ego and pride, his edicts could not be altered or repealed. There were no exceptions.

Daniel remained undaunted in his love for God, and he continued to, pray three times each day. Spies told the king of Daniel's disregard of the edict. The king favored Daniel, but he had no choice but to throw him in the lions' den. The king's final words to Daniel before he threw him in the den was, "May your God, whom you serve continually, rescue you!" Even the king must have known something of Daniel's God to say such confident words. He had a stone brought and placed over the mouth of the den and the king sealed it with his own signet ring, so that Daniel's situation could not be overturned.

The evening brought the king turmoil because he reflected on what he had done. He knew something was not right. He could not sleep. At the break of dawn, the king returned to the den and in an anguished voice called to Daniel, "Daniel, servant of the living God, has your God, whom you serve continually, been able to rescue you from the lions?" And Daniel answered with today's text. The king was overjoyed and gave orders to lift Daniel, who was unscathed, out of the den.

Are you experiencing a "den of lions" like Daniel in your life? Do you feel suffocated by those that bring you down? Are you discouraged and feeling helpless? Don't despair. Stay faithful to God, even the myriads of turmoil and trials you are going through will not snuff you from God's care. As He cared for Daniel, He will do the same for you. **Faith in God can render your enemies mute and harmless.** You too will say "they have not hurt me."

## CREATION OF THE SABBATH | MAY 3

*"And God saw everything that He had made, and behold it was very good." Genesis 1: 31*

When God created this world, He specifically had in mind only the best for us. In six days, He completed his great plan and was very pleased with the outcome. He instituted the seventh day Sabbath to commemorate the marvelous results of the prior six days' effort. He wanted, too, that this Sabbath He created be a joy, not just for Him, but for His beloved subjects as well.

A subject of considerable debate over the centuries has been the question of precisely what constitutes rest. Orthodox Jews, for example, will forsake their cars on the Sabbath in favor of walking to the synagogue. Their reform brethren, on the other hand, would argue that such practices made sense during the age of the horse-and-buggy, when hitching up the horses was very real work. They maintained that driving a car exerts less energy than walking.

Our pastor once described two groups of Sabbath keepers. They are the "A" keepers and the "B" keepers. The "A" keepers may do a nature walk on the beach, allowing the waves to coddle their feet only, while the "B" keepers go knee deep. I suppose you can add a "C" group that jumps in the ocean to swim. Does all this sound amusing to you? What type of Sabbath keeper are you? Do you know how to keep the Sabbath holy? What was the purpose of the Sabbath anyway? To debate on the water level one engages in? I don't think God had that in mind.

When Christ was here on earth, the same type of question arose. However, instead of "A" keepers versus "B" keepers, He compared God keepers with man keepers. Jesus asked: if one of you had an animal stuck in a ravine, injured and in pain, would you not go and rescue that pet, even on the Sabbath? He underscored that the Sabbath was made for man and NOT man for the Sabbath. The practice of Sabbath keeping has been a "thorn in the flesh" for many Christians. The debate of its relevancy today is personal. However, you will understand its relevancy when you get to know the Author of the Sabbath. Remember, God is love.

God made His priorities clear when He created man before He created the Sabbath. Do you see it? God's love for man created the Sabbath for Man. This was just one of many creations that God gave to us. All motivated by God's love for us. **When you know the Author of the Sabbath and love Him as your LORD and Savior, then you would have learned to rest in His Sabbath.** He gave you this holy day as a revelation of who He really is. What more cogent way could there be for God to express His love for humankind.

## NEVER EVER FEAR AGAIN | MAY 4

*"Fear not for I bring good tidings of great joy. For unto you this day in the city of David is born a Savior." Luke 2: 10 & 11*

What is your fear? What are you afraid of? We all have fears. Not all fears, of course, are bad. Studies have indicated that babies placed on a table will crawl only so far then hesitate to crawl to the edge for fear of falling. However, when fears are based on the irrational, we label them phobias. The fear of black cats, or stepping on sidewalk cracks are clearly irrational fears. Some fears are so prevalent that society at large makes accommodations for them. An example would be fear of the number 13. It costs no more to omit the 13th floor and proceed immediately to the 14th (except in places like Japan, where is a superstition respecting the number four, which is perceived to have an ominous connection).

While fears begin at a young age, they appear to multiply and intensify as we mature. When fear becomes so overwhelming as to be debilitating, it is often referred to as an anxiety disorder. As an example, one of the most common phobias is agoraphobia, which signifies fear of open spaces. A person finds going out of the comfort of his or her own home agonizing. They are not able to function of cope properly in open spaces. Other phobias: People who have qualms interacting with others or talking or performing in front of others. Specific phobias; these fears are intense fears such as animals, insects, heights, enclosed spaces or thunderstorms. And it is normal for some things to upset us more than other things. Sometimes fears affect us more so in certain times of our life than others. One survey showed of crowds, death, injury, illness, and separation were more common among people in their 60s than in other age groups.

Once again, there is good news. With every imaginable fear that one might encounter, God is telling us not to fear because He has sent a Savior, His Son to face all fears on our behalf. Jesus met the foe with "Thus saith the Lord." His word alone made all the enemies flee. The angels knew the truth about God when they proclaimed: "FEAR NOT" for they brought good tidings of great joy for unto us a Savior was given to save us from all these fears. Not only did He conquer all fears but He brought "GREAT JOY." Do you see that?

With joy all fears are gone. That joy came from our LORD, Jesus Christ. **Our Savior came to bring us salvation, a salvation that is devoid of fear**. Come what may, you never ever fear again.

## MOTHER-IN-LAW | MAY 5

*"Look," said Naomi, "your sister-in-law is going back to her people and her gods. Go back with her." But Ruth replied, "don't urge me to leave you or to turn back from you. Where you go I will go, and where you stay I will stay. Your people will be my people and you God my God. Where you die I will die, and there I will be buried. May the Lord deal with me, be it ever so severely, if anything but death separates you and me." Ruth 1: 15 & 16*

---

"The worst person I know. Mother-in-law. Mother-in-law. She worries me so. Mother-in-law. Mother-in-law. If she'd leave us alone, we would have a happy home. Sent from down below. Mother-in-law. Mother-in-law." {Written by Allen Toussaint, copyright EMI Music Publishing}.

The butt of so many jokes was an early 60's hit. This lyric says how many feel but few will say out loud about their mother-in-law. A poll taken by NBC's iVillage showed that 51% of respondents would rather stay home and clean than spend the day with their mothers-in-law. If there is any solace in the study, it is that only 28% would prefer a root canal to a day with dear, old mother-in-law. All jokes aside, the fact is that many of us actually like our mother-in-law. Such was the relationship of Ruth and Naomi. However, each of us, has, at one time or another, felt slighted by a relative.

In our story today, Naomi entreats her daughters-in-law to leave her so they could continue with their lives while still at that desirable age. The women have become widows. One daughter-in-law, Orpah, listened and left while the other, Ruth, refused to depart. She felt an affinity to her mother-in-law that can only come from the Spirit of God. Ruth knew God because of the love and influence her mother-in-law gave her. In the end, her loyalty proved a blessing for out of her lineage the Christ Jesus would eventually come.

God has told us that He will never leave nor forsake us. He has told us, too, that our in-law family will be His people, and nothing will ever separate us from His love. **God is not only loyal to us but faithful in His word and His promises.** He will never let you go, even if you go to the grave. In fact, He promised to wake you up from your sleep. God has promised to come back soon and take us home to be with Him eternally.

God is saying, where you go I will go, where you stay I will stay. God is really demonstrating His love to us in a way that He will never depart from us. What an unbelievable God we have! Don't you wish your mother-in-law was like that?

## CREATED IN GOD'S IMAGE | MAY 6

*"Then God said, 'Let us make man in our image, in our likeness, (27) so God created man in his own image, in the image of God He created him; male and female He created them." Genesis 1: 26-27*

---

Have you ever heard the phrase, "He's the spitting image of his father?" We all resemble someone, most notably our father or mother. Extended families may all share distinctive traits. No matter who we resemble, our original maker is God. Does this mean we look like God? Are we a spitting image of God? What does God look like? Does He even have a face like us?

Moses asked God to reveal himself so he may gaze upon the face of God. God acquiesced. He passed by Moses but placed His hand as a covering to prevent Moses from dying. We all probably have a different notion as to God's physical appearance. However, we have essentially reached a consensus as to His character, and it is indeed God's character that sets Him apart from all others. God is infinite love, and grace. When you long for a physical manifestation of God, look at your neighbor, a child, your mother, your father, that stranger on the street, your co-worker, the transient, the preacher, a teacher, your friend, a politician, an actor, an alien, or any of the nearly seven-billion people who populate our planet.

All of us were created in God's image. We are an integral part of God. God has embodied us with the Godhead. He wants us to be a part of the body of Christ and the Holy Spirit. He wants you to know that, when He created male and female in His likeness, you became one with Him in body and spirit. When you treat anyone you come in contact with in the image of God, you, too, are reflecting God's image. When you show compassion, patience, kindness, understanding to even the very least of these people, when you have embraced one of these and when you have kissed one of them, you have seen and touched the image of God.

Wherever love abounds, you will see God. You will know and see God in your daily walk with Him. You will encounter people of all faiths and walk in life, how you relate to them and treat them will be a reflection on your love for God. God's image is all about love.

I see God everywhere I go. He touches me whenever I gaze at my neighbor; for he or she, too, was created in the image of God. **Want to know what God looks like? Look in the mirror, look at your neighbor, look at Jesus**.

## WALKING WITH GOD | MAY 7

*"And after he became the father of Methuselah, Enoch walked with God 300 years and had other sons and daughters." Genesis 5: 22*

---

What does it mean to walk with God? Enoch walked with God for 300 years and had sons and daughters and was taken to heaven. He never experienced death. Does that mean Enoch never sinned and was exempted from God's redemption? No. All have sinned and all have fallen short of God's glory. Christ died for all.

God chose to take Enoch to be with Him. But what does it really mean to walk with God? Enoch had a strong abiding trust and dependence in God. He did not waver in his faith in God. Whether he saw evidence or not he stayed the course; for he loved God. He would have sacrificed his life for God's sake, if God asked Him. You could say Enoch was joined at the hip with God. God was moved by Enoch's loyalty and abiding faith. He was pleased with Enoch and was drawn to his Spirit of tenderness, compassion and love. Enoch sought God's wisdom in all of his endeavors. Accordingly, Enoch knew when to go and when to stay, when to speak and when to remain silent. Enoch sought nothing more than to please his Maker. He was a son of God in the truest sense.

Have you met any Enoch in your walk with God? There are many "Enochs" in our midst who have a faith in God just like Enoch. Wherever love has been shown to you, there is God. What is your walk with God like today? When you pray to God, do you always end with "not my will but yours be done." When you converse with God, who does most of the talking, and who does the listening? Walking with God is receiving His Spirit in you every moment of your life. When you truly walk with God, you experience His Love.

Very importantly, would you say that you are at peace with God? Do you harbor uncertainties about God's love for you? How much of your being are you willing to dedicate to God? Does your degree of faith in God permit you to trust Him with your choices such as those involving family, career and life in general? What is your present walk with God like today? Are you satisfied like Enoch? I know, you're thinking there's always room for improvement. It's not about growth daily but more about trusting Him daily. Whatever your walk with God here on earth may be, someday soon we will meet our Maker and walk with Him just as Enoch did. This time our walk will take eternity.

Above all this, **it is not our walk with God that matters most, but God's walk with us.**

## SUCCESS COMES FROM GOD | MAY 8

*"In everything he did he had great success, because the LORD was with him." I Samuel 18: 14*

---

Everyone loves to hear success stories. How many stories have you heard or read in which the main character fall in the end? We all want to see the happily-ever-after ending story. What would you say was the most successful campaign or endeavor you ever witnessed or were involved in? Was it building your church, graduating from high school or college, raising a family of which you are proud? Might it have been a church baptism or bringing souls to Christ? Arguably, any one of these and, of course, a whole lot of other such endeavors reflects our success.

Our so-called successes are a reflection, however, of not our efforts alone; for, without God, we could boast of no achievements. It is He who set the stage for us. It is He who breathed life into us and set our hearts beating. When we think about God, we seldom think in terms of His success. We take it for granted that He succeeds in everything He does. He is, after all, the Almighty, and failure is not part of His lexicon. God never wants us to fail. Sometimes our choosing or unforeseen circumstance places us in the realm of failure. God has a way to turning those failures into something good. **For God is a good God.** He wants to show that goodness to us. Though God rules His universe and all the complexities of this world, He will always have time for you. When it comes to you and me, we are His priority in the scheme of all things. When we stumble, we need look no further than to God for insight with respect to how we might do better next time; for His track record is devoid of failure. Want success? Pursue and really get to know the Author of success, God.

It would be presumptuous for us to attempt to place God's various successes in some rank order. That would be to judge the Ultimate Judge. However, our fall and His demonstrations of His unceasing love for us by sending His Son to redeem us from darkness and sin…that one has to be right up there. God's reign over us and our planet is a work that is yet incomplete. It would be premature to label it a success story. But the greater point here is, each day you have the opportunity to exercise your faith in Him. However, as we wait on the LORD, everything we do we will be successful because our LORD will always be with us. That is comforting to know.

God has, however, promised us an eternity with Him and, given His impressive track record, **you would do well to stick with the ultimate winner…God**.

## SPEAK LORD | MAY 9

*"So Eli told Samuel, 'Go and lie down, and if he calls you say, Speak LORD, for your servant is listening.' So Samuel went and lay down in his place. The LORD came and stood there, calling as at the other times, "Samuel! Samuel!" Then Samuel said, 'Speak, for your servant is listening.'" Samuel 3: 9 & 10*

---

With each new electronic device, we wonder how we ever lived without laptops and desktops, without cell phones, without iPods and iPads. These devices have, it is said, opened up an entire world to us. There was a time when people went to the library to search for an answer to a particular question. Now, at our very fingertips, we have thousands, perhaps millions of times the information that one traditional library contained. Where once we used maps to plot our travels, today, voices speak to us from a little box, and they guide our every turn. Why…even a church service can be beamed to you in the comfort of your home. Surely, this veritable explosion of information is a good thing. Are our lives not better for these wonders that man has created?

Well…yes and no. Indeed we have more information than ever before, but we are so caught up in the accumulation of data that we often fail to analyze it and render it useful. We can watch a service that is at least nominally dedicated to God on our televisions, but sometimes fail to understand that we are not to control God with a remote control. We do not serve God from an easy chair any more than we share our love for others by way of instant messaging or forward e-mails. And, it is wonderful that a little voice can now guide us from point A to point B, but through all of this, we may be denying the one voice that is with us, regardless of the technology of the moment, and that voice, of course, is God's voice. Do you hear God speaking to you? Maybe you are in the midst of a cacophony of distractions and voices that it's difficult to decipher the voice of God. God is calling your name right now.

Today's verse deals with Samuel, son of Hannah. One day, the Lord called: "Samuel, Samuel, Samuel," and, it was on the third pronouncement of his name that Samuel recognized the voice of his God. Can you hear Him calling you? Will He also need to call you three times? **Don't be caught up in the service of things (technology and the like) that you fail to recognize His voice at all.**

Stop! Whatever you're doing this very moment, be still and listen. Do you hear Him speaking to you? Then you can be sure to be there for His call. When that happens be ready to say "speak LORD."

# LONG LIVE THE KING | MAY 10

*"But the people refused to listen to Samuel. 'No! We want a king over us. Then we will be like all the other nations, with a king to lead us and to go out before us and fight our battles.' When Samuel heard all that the people said, he repeated it before the LORD. The LORD answered, 'Listen to them and give them a king.'" I Samuel 8: 19-21*

---

During Samuel's time, every nation had a king that ruled over the citizenry. The Israelites wanted a king, too, and they beseeched Samuel to ask the Lord for a King. God knew that these kings were typically false kings. Oftentimes, the king sought to be treated as a deity. God, of course, knew better and advised Samuel that the only king that Israel needed was God Himself and not a king who was of the earth. Nevertheless, God relented and told Samuel to give the people what they wanted. God must have winked when He condoned this course. Even though God knows better, He does not interfere with the choices we make. God knows that, sometimes, the only way we will learn is when He allows us to make the less-appropriate choice.

Each of us has, at one time or another requested of God something that ultimately may prove to have been an unwise choice. We can get so caught up in our quest for something – some end result – that we fail to consider the consequences. All too often, the end simply does not justify the means. We may want something so badly that our ambition or craving blinds us to the unintended consequences of our actions. Or we fail to account for the fact that our own success takes a heavy toll on others. You may want things your way and because God is gracious, He relents but don't blame Him when things go awry in your life. You made the choice and God respected your choice.

Saul seemed the perfect candidate for king. He was handsome, distinguished-looking and literally stood head and shoulders above all others. The Israelites were thrilled with Samuel's selection and shouted: "Long live the king!" Their king, however, was of the earth. Saul reigned for 42 years, but his reign was marked with a good deal of upset and turmoil. Are you depending too much on the things of this earth? You know where your loyalty and security lies. Whatever it is that seems to be hindering you from knowing God, your true King, there's still time to make an about face and claim Him as your true leader. Don't ask for earthly things that don't live up to the "Long Live the King" hype.

**Stick with God. He is your true and Eternal King.** By deferring to an earthly king, the Israelites had, of course, neglected the King of All Kings, the Author of Love.

## CAN A MOTHER FORGET HER BABY | MAY 11

*"Can a mother forget the baby at her breast and have no compassion on the child she has borne? Though she may forget, I will not forget you!" Isaiah 49: 15*

---

There was an interesting story in the news a few years back. A 10-day-old girl had been kidnapped from her home. The perpetrator covered her tracks by setting fire to the infant's room. The devastation was so thorough that fire officials had no choice but to assume that the infant had perished. This mother went back to the ruins and charred bedroom and saw the crib where her baby laid. But she did not see her baby in there. The firemen concluded the baby was burned and presented her with a burnt unrecognizable object wrapped in a blanket.

Half a dozen years later, the mother was attending a birthday party given by a friend in her neighborhood, and she spotted a little girl appeared to be the age her girl would have been, had she not been taken so tragically. While, clearly, the mother had no idea what her little girl might have looked like, had she survived the fire, her motherly instincts told her that her dimples looked familiar. In order to verify her suspicion, she told the little girl that she had gum in her hair and proceeded to take a few strands of hair for DNA testing. Tests revealed that the little girl was indeed hers. Somehow, mothers seem to have extraordinary instincts when it comes to their children. God also had a hand in returning the little girl to her true mother.

There is, of course, one other who knows His children equally well – likely, even better – and that is God. He knows our every nook and cranny – physically, psychologically, spiritually and emotionally. He has "…engraved you on the palms of my hands; " (verse 16). Not unlike the little story we just related, you were taken from Him by an unscrupulous demon. Satan deceived you and snared you into his web of lies. The devil has endeavored to brainwash you and to distance you from your Heavenly Mother, but God has never given up on you. God gave mothers the privilege of raising children. The intimacy a mother and child experience is the intimacy God has with each or us. **A mother is an earthly representation of God on earth**. You are the center of His joy. Wish God a happy mother's day, after all, God created you. **God is your mother.**

Today is Mother's Day. We honor our mothers, who are steadfast in their love for us. **Just as God keeps us in His heart this day and every day of the year we are to treat our Mothers in like fashion.**

## GOD LOOKS AT THE HEART | MAY 12

*"But the LORD said to Samuel, 'Do not consider his appearance or his height, for I have rejected him. The LORD does not look at the things man looks at. Man looks at the outward appearance, but the LORD looks at the heart.'" I Samuel 16: 7*

---

We as a culture tend to look at the surface beauty of things. We view billboards promoting products by associating with the body of an attractive male or female model. Studies in psychology indicate that the taller or more handsome the man the better their chances of getting the job over a shorter man but will also earn more money than an unsightly person. It is a fact of life; we appreciate and desire outward appearance. Ever seen a particularly healthy person and thought, 'Wow what a liver they must have!" God is correct in saying we look at the outward appearance to fulfill our choices.

Israel wanted a king to rule over them just like their neighboring nations. God told them that an earthly king would oppress them and tax them. But the people would not listen. God was already their King. God relented and allowed them to crown Saul king. But Saul was human and full of frailties and not in tune with following God's leading. Saul failed God.

God told Samuel to meet with the family of Jesse and there he would find the next king. Jesse asked all his sons to pass by Samuel and each time a son appeared to Samuel to be the chosen king, God said, "No that is not the one." Jesse had seven sons pass before Samuel and each son was rejected. Can you imagine Samuel's dismay when each time he thought he made the right choice the Lord told him that's not the one? He too relied on the outward appearance. Jesse sent someone to fetch David. When Samuel saw David he noted his healthy "ruddy" appearance. He was handsome and pleasing to behold. The Bible described David as a man after God's own heart. What's amazing about this story is that the people did not learn from their first "king Saul syndrome," instead they asked for another king. If they had listened to God in the first place, they would have said, **"We will keep God as our King."** But even David failed them with his surreptitious ways. You want a king to govern your life?

**Just like David, everyone is called upon and given equal opportunity to be anointed by God but only those with a receptive heart of God's Spirit will be chosen. Make God your King.**

## BETTER TO OBEY | MAY 13

*"Does the LORD delight in burnt offerings and sacrifices as much as in obeying the voice of the LORD? To obey is better than sacrifices, and to heed is better than the fat of rams." I Samuel 15: 22*

---

I remember my father urging us to study hard because my parents were making sacrifices to send us to college. I am not sure that, during my youth, I fully comprehended those sacrifices, but I am, to this day, grateful, nonetheless.

Our family owned a fish factory, and during production, my parents would work virtually around-the-clock in order to process the fish so it would not spoil. When I was barely old enough, I worked alongside my parents, and I recall day after day of no work breaks and little if any sleep. There was a time when we had to gut each sardine or mackerel one by one by hand. The work was so overwhelming that it provided my siblings and me ample motivation to go to school so that we might prosper on our own. We learned to listen to our parents commands and obey their instructions. It was not until later in life, when we had our own families, that we realized their true motivation was for our happiness and well-being.

Most of us have made sacrifices in order to obtain some end result. The Biblical sacrifices, however, were of a different nature. The Israelites, who perfected the art of sacrifice, were known to sacrifice a lamb as a token of their belief in the coming Messiah. On the surface, these appeared to be Godly acts, but, in truth, they sometimes merely paid lip service tribute to God. Without the corresponding faith and obedience, theses sacrifices were without merit. God does not want us to go through the motions of evidencing fealty to Him. God made it known that obedience was more important to Him than such ceremonial acts.

**When God speaks of obedience, He is referring to a relationship, and that relationship is characterized by faith, honor, respect, and, very importantly, love.** God makes it very clear that it is far better to obey than to make sacrifices, but He counsels us that this obedience must be of the heart.

God, as we know, governs in love. He will always be there to lead us, but our obedience should never be blind obedience, but rather obedience that is predicated on the type of love that emanates from God Himself.

## SAVED BY AN ACT OF KINDNESS | MAY 14

*"One of the servants told Nabal's wife Abigail: 'David sent messengers from the desert to give our master his greetings, but he hurled insults at them.'" I Samuel 25: 14*

---

Have you ever been dealt evil as a recompense for your good deeds? Have you ever treated someone with loyalty only to have that person betray you?

The above verse relates such a story from the life of David. David and his men protected Nabal's property when they were within the borders of his land. David made certain that no harm came to Nabal from his rivals. Realizing that his supplies and rations were running low, David sent 10 men to ask Nabal if he could assist them with replenishments. Nabal replied: "Who is David? Why should I take my bread and water and the meat I have slaughtered for my shearers and give it to men coming from who knows where?" The 10 men returned to David to relay Nabal's insults. David responded by taking 400 of his men to do battle with Nabal's household.

However, a wise and vigilant servant told Abigail, Nabal's wife, what had occurred and, being an "intelligent and beautiful wife" she quickly took 200 loaves of bread, two skins of wine, five dressed sheep, five seahs (bushel or 37 liters) of roasted grain, 100 cakes of raisins and 200 cakes of pressed figs, and loaded them on donkeys. David met Abigail, and she immediately got off her donkey, bowed before David with her face to the ground and said: "My lord, let the blame be on me alone. Please let your servant speak to you; May my lord pay no attention to that wicked man Nabal. He is just like his name. His name is fool and folly goes with him. But as for me, your servant, I did not see the men my master sent." The story in this chapter ends with David sparing Nabal's household. Let's also not forget the servant who warned Abigail. She too was attuned to God's Spirit. **Her act of kindness saved her life and her household**. The Bible never mentions that servant's name. Anytime you trade insult with kindness, no matter how small an act of kindness it may be, you have displayed a Godly character. That is the way God treats us. Never neglect to show kindness in all your dealings. You will be amazed how it can save your life. You cannot live a life of kindness if you are not connected to God's Spirit.

We have a Savior who watches and cares for us. He sacrificed Himself for our shameful deeds. His act of kindness was the ultimate act of love; **you were saved by an act of kindness; and His name is Jesus.**

## A LOVE MORE WONDERFUL THAN THAT OF WOMEN | MAY 15

*"I grieve for you, Jonathan my brother; you were very dear to me. Your love for me was wonderful, more wonderful than that of women." II Samuel 1: 26*

---

Today's text sums up friendship at its highest point. Who would you say is your best friend? Someone you've known for many years? Someone who you can trust and rely on? What constitutes friendship? Who would you call in the middle of the night if you were stuck on the freeway?

According to psychologists, friendship usually evolves when two people have something in common and can encourage and reinforce each other's goal, character and priorities. Whether that commonality is race, gender, sports, money, education, family, religion, food, hobbies or community, there must be some kind of element that intertwines two individuals to establish some kind of friendship. How many friends would you say you have? Are you one too slow to extend your hand in friendship? Being shy and timid can certainly limit your circle of friends, after all Proverbs says, "He that has friends has shown himself friendly." Proverbs 18: 24.

David and Jonathan had a special kind of bond. Most scholars concur that their love for one another was platonic. It was generally held that, when such camaraderie between two men had for its basis some selfish end that friendship would not endure. However, when such a bond was not for selfish ends, it would likely endure and thrive. Such was the bond between David and Jonathan.

God extended such a friendship to us. God is sensitive, caring, and unwavering in His concern for us. He is a friend who is even closer than the most intimate relationship you will ever experience here on earth. This is truly a Godly friendship. God demonstrated His love for us by sacrificing His Son in order that His friendship with us – forfeited by us in Eden – might be restored. Our earthly loves and friendships are flawed. People will disappoint us. We cannot depend on friendships or marriages to save us. There is only one true friend you can count on. And He will not disappoint or fail you either.

There is no greater friendship than for a man or a woman to lay down his or her life for their friend. God's Son, Jesus, did precisely that for us. **He is the greatest friend you will ever know or have.**

## UZZAH'S IRREVERENT ACT | MAY 16

*"When they came to the threshing floor of Nacon, Uzzah reach out and took hold of the ark of God, because the oxen stumbled. (7) The Lord's anger burned against Uzzah because of his irreverent act; therefore God struck him down and he died there beside the ark of God." II Samuel 6: 6 & 7*

---

David, along with 30,000 of his men, journeyed to the land of the Philistines to bring back the Ark of God. During the procession, one of the oxen stumbled, and the ark appeared to be unstable. Uzzah, who was walking alongside of the ark, reach over to steady it, and his single touch of the sacred ark resulted in his instant demise. Scholars have debated over the years why God would destroy the life of a man who was merely trying to be helpful. E. G. White (Patriarch & Prophets, p. 797) says: "Upon Uzzah rested the great guilt of presumption. Transgression of God's law had lessened his sense of its sacredness, and with un-confessed sins upon him he had, in face of divine prohibition, presumed to touch the symbol of God's presence. God can accept no partial obedience. The judgment upon Uzzah, He designed to impress upon all Israel the importance of giving strict heed to His requirements. Thus the death of that one man, by leading the people to repentance, might prevent the necessity of inflicting judgments upon thousands."

There are at least two very important lessons to be gleaned from this event. The first, of course, is that our obedience to God's law cannot be nuanced; it must be precise. Scholars and theologians have debated whether there is a second point – to wit, that God is quite capable of fending for Himself insofar as the protection of His laws, His kingdom, and His very being are concerned. God is just and true. Uzzah's fate was a tragedy. Sometimes, a sacrifice of one person is made to save a multitude of people. God's Son did that for us. **Just as Uzzah's death seems unfathomable, we will never fully realize the extent of Jesus' sacrifice for us**. But regardless of what we've witnessed, we will all confess, God is just, fair and true. Uzzah's demise was his choice but his eternal life is in God.

We have all acted presumptuously toward God at one time or another, yet none of us has suffered Uzzah's fate. How come? God does not want any of us to perish. He has demonstrated His own willingness to carry the burden for us by sacrificing His own life. He gave it up so that we might enjoy eternal salvation.

**You must trust God. Just and true are the ways of the Lord**. You can accept this only if you know Him.

## DANCING WITH DAVID | MAY 17

*"David, wearing a linen ephod, danced before the LORD with all his might, while he and the entire house of Israel brought up the ark of the LORD with shouts and the sound of trumpets. As the ark of the Lord was entering the City of David, Michal daughter of Saul watched from a window. And when she saw King David leaping and dancing before the LORD, she despised him in her heart." II Samuel 6: 14-16*

---

I remember sitting in our weekly pastoral staff meeting discussing the drama the youth were planning to perform Sabbath morning. The five-minute drama would depict God's grace in the form of body movements. There would be no singing, only accompanying music. There would be no leaping or jumping, and the performers were instructed not to even lift their feet off of the floor. They were merely to slide about. The performance turned out to be inspirational, notwithstanding what, on the surface, might have appeared to have been overly-strict rules. A few among the congregation thought that the rules were not sufficiently strict. They argued that any form of dancing in God's house was an affront to the Lord.

This is not the first time such an issue has been debated in our church nor will it be the last. Recently, my church has decided to implement two church services; one in the morning for the "traditional" second service and one at noon for the young adults. Anyone can choose their time of worship, but the noon service has the guitars and drums as part of their service. The question that begs to be answered, which of these services will God be in? Regardless if it is dancing, lifting of hands in praise or shouting "amen" during church service, no one can deny the fact that when the Spirit of God fills you, you cannot keep still or silent. Have you ever been moved by a sermon or a music that you could not help but praise God by lifting your hands or saying "amen?"

Was David's dancing, as told in the above verse, inappropriate? Truly, the answer would depend on David's motive. If the dance were sensuous in its intent, then it would be deemed inappropriate. If, on the other hand, as was presumably the case with David's dance, the dance was a celebration of our Lord, then the dance would be deemed to be quite appropriate. **David, quite clearly, danced and leaped for joy because he was unable to contain his gratitude for how God had demonstrated His love, mercy, and blessing for His people.**

Clearly, his dance was in service of his God and in no way a sacrilege. Does that describe your dancing?

## CAN I BRING HIM BACK AGAIN? | MAY 18

*"He answered, 'While the child was still alive, I fasted and wept. I thought, who knows? The LORD may be gracious to me and let the child live. But now that he is dead, why should I fast? Can I bring him back again? I will go to him, but he will not return to me.'" II Samuel 12: 22& 23*

---

One evening, while David was walking around the rooftop of his palace, he spied a woman below bathing. He inquired about her and learned she was the wife of Uriah the Hittite. Knowing full well that she was married, he nevertheless summoned his staff to fetch her. David had allowed his arrogance, selfishness, and lust to out-duel his sense of decency and his duty to his God's commandments. He sent messengers to bring her to him. Their liaison produced a child. David attempted to cover up his indiscretion by offering Uriah time off from the battlefield so that he might sleep with his wife and thereby give the appearance that the child was his. Uriah, however, was a dutiful soldier, and he chose to sleep instead with his confederates at the entrance to the palace.

David then proceeded to devise yet another scheme in order to cover his tracks. He directed Joab, the general in charge of his armed forces, (II Samuel 8: 16) to assign Uriah a front-line position where, or course, the battle would be the fiercest. Uriah met his demise, much as David had planned. In due time, David sent for Bathsheba, Uriah's wife, and made her his own wife. Bathsheba bore him a son.

The prophet Nathan informed David that the son born to him would soon die. For six days, he fasted, wept, and prayed to God to spare his son, but, on the seventh day, his son perished. David proceeded to get up, clean himself and eat, much to the surprise of his servants. His response was todays verse. God did not take David's son. God merely showed David the result of his sin. David, in a contrite spirit accepted the consequences of his choices. He learned a very valuable lesson. Sin cannot be compromised.

YES, God can "bring him back again" and all the loved ones we've lost. Let us not forget where the source of life originates, God. But let us equally not forget that when we stray from the God of Life, we venture into the valley of death.

God has promised a day when there will no longer be tears, death, sorrow or pain. For **"God does not take away life," but is the Author of life.**

# ENOUGH IS ENOUGH | MAY 19

*"When the angel stretched out his hand to destroy Jerusalem, the LORD was grieved because of the calamity and said to the angel who was afflicting the people, 'Enough! Withdraw your hand.' The angel of the LORD was then at the threshing floor of Aranunah the Jebusite." II Samuel 24: 16*

---

This is a rather interesting Bible passage. David requested his armed forces general, Joab and commanders to conduct a census of their fighting men so that David might know the exact troop strength. Joab questioned the need for such a count, but King David overruled him. Joab performed as ordered and reported back to David that the troops numbered 1.3 million.

The act of taking a census was not sinful in and of itself. After all, God had Himself encouraged a more general census of Israel's population. What grieved God was David's motivation to conduct the census. David saw the census' outcome as a bragging right. He was in essence holding himself up to the citizenry as the glorified ruler of so large an army. David had apparently forgotten that glory comes from God, not from the people.

God responded to David by offering him three options. The first was three years of famine in his land. The second was three months of fleeing from his enemies. The third option was three days of plague. David replied: I am in deep distress. Let us fall into the hands of the Lord, for His mercy is great; but do not let me fall into the hands of men." David chose God's mercy, and one angel stretched out his hand as 70,000 of David's subject suddenly perished.

An oft-used phrase to describe a particular management style is: "My way or the highway," which means, of course: "I'm the boss. I really don't need your input: I'm doing just fine without it." That type of arrogance is a formula for ruin. Don't think for one minute you are self-sufficient and in control of your life. All it takes is a moment's lapse of self-sufficiency.

David had an apparent lapse of judgment and forgot that, ultimately, it was not his way that counted, but rather God's way. David learned that lesson, but at a very dear price. You can glean a valuable lesson from David's arrogance. Never trust in yourself. Always lean to God's counsel and you will know when enough is enough.

**When you trust God; that will be enough for you.**

## RAVENS TO FEED YOU | MAY 20

*"Then the word of the LORD came to Elijah: 'Leave here, turn eastward and hide in the Kerith Ravine, east of Jordan. You will drink from the brook, and I have ordered the ravens to feed you there.'" I Kings 17: 2-4*

---

The Story of Elijah is one of pure active trust and belief in the word of the Lord. Elijah had just finished telling Ahab, King of Israel that there would be neither rain, nor even dew for the next few years in all the land. God in his mercy and patience instructed Elijah to leave and hide in the Kerith Ravine east of Jordan. The people of Israel under the reign of Ahab did evil in God's eyes. Of all the kings of Israel none was more evil than Ahab. He set up altars for Baal worship. He even intermarried and took a woman named Jezebel, daughter of Ethaball king of the Sidonins to be his wife. Together they served and worshiped Baal. Their practices were an abomination to God. No other king had so incensed God. It was as though Ahab were slapping God's face with his irreverent practices. Our degradation is not a result of God's punishment; it is because of our delineation from God presence.

To serve as something of a wake-up call to the people of Israel, to remind them that their allegiance should be to the One who created their world, He cast a devastating dry spell upon the region. The dry spell was not given by God; the dry spell was a result of the people's refusal to listen to God's servant prophetic doom. Ahab refused to heed Elijah's admonition, and his nation met its downfall.

The God of Elijah is again attempting to turn us from our evil ways, back to His loving hands. He welcomes all of us, whether we are drug addicts, atheists, agnostics, sex offenders, murderers, thieves or just ordinary folks. He will wait for us, however, long it takes, but to delay is only to spite ourselves; for there is no greater love than that which emanates from the Author of Love. God is faithful to see you through your ordeal. Just as He cared for Elijah and sent ravens to feed him during his run, He will do the same for you and me. God is more than your friend. He is also your Savior. He is willing to wait for you to return to Him, but don't wait a lifetime. You will miss out in the abundant life He wants you to have immediately.

**There is nothing on this earth worth clinging to other than the God who sends ravens to feed you.**

## INTERMARRIAGE | MAY 21

*"They were from nations about which the Lord had told the Israelites, "You must not intermarry with them, because they will surely turn your hearts after their gods." Nevertheless, Solomon held fast to them in love." I Kings 11: 2*

---

Marriage is a sacred commitment to your spouse and God. God knows that, if a person who holds God in his or her heart commits to another whose heart is devoid of God, the resultant marriage is doomed to failure, regardless of how deeply the two believe they are in love with one another; for if both hearts do not have the love of God within them, their earthly love cannot be complete love.

God admonished Solomon not to marry outside his faith because God knows that any such marriage would seriously compromise Solomon's relationship with God. Ultimately, Solomon took literally hundreds of wives and additionally engaged in hundreds of affairs. He even practiced the idolatry that was customary among a good many of his wives. The ever gracious God relented. Solomon forsook the God who had given him the wisdom to rule, and it led to the downfall of his kingdom.

This all begs an important question: How do we define intermarriage? There was a time, for example, not long ago, when some states specifically prohibited the marriage of blacks and whites. Today that might seem preposterous. When a Baptist marries an Episcopalian, does that qualify as inter-marriage? How about a Lutheran and a Catholic? or a Presbyterian and a Jew? Each faith has a slightly different notion as to what constitutes inter-marriage, and in some instances, different branches within each of these may have nuanced beliefs. What did God have in mind about inter-marriage? Well, at the time, there was only one monotheistic religion, and so there were no nuances; a person who held the One God in his or her heart could have done no less than marry one of the same belief. To have done otherwise would have been to have denied the most important relationship in their lives, their relationship with the Author of Love.

Are you contemplating an inter-marriage? Have you shared your decision with God? God loves all peoples and faiths but He knows the world's thinking on this matter. He knows the heartaches you will encounter.

**Trust God to lead you to the right person in your life.** Be patient and wait for His guidance. Rely on God in all matters of your life and you'll be surprised on what He's planned for you.

## TROUBLEMAKERS | MAY 22

*"So Obadiah went to meet Ahab and told him, and Ahab went to meet Elijah. When he saw Elijah, he said to him, 'is that you, you troubler of Israel?' 'I have not made trouble for Israel,' Elijah replied. 'But you and your father's family have. You have abandoned the Lord's commands and followed the Baals.'" I Kings 18: 16-18*

---

Have you ever been accused of being a troublemaker? Elijah was thusly labeled. You'll recall that Elijah foretold of a dry spell throughout the land. His very appropriate response was that he was not the troublemaker; Ahab and his followers were the troublemakers inasmuch as they had worshipped false gods. God had intoned without equivocation: "You shall have no other gods before me." He named no exceptions. Today, Elijah might have advised his detractors: "Don't shoot the messenger."

Who are the modern-day troublemakers, and what, if anything, do they have in common? If you ask a dozen people who the biggest troublemakers of our time are, you'd likely come up with a dozen very different lists. Ask a Republican, and he'll respond "Barak Obama." Ask a Laker fan, and he'll reply: "LeBron James." As a Mac user, and he'll say: "Bill Gates." Yes, trouble making is, arguably, in the eyes of the beholder. Have you ever been viewed as a troublemaker?

All jesting aside, however, when we think of the real troublemakers of the world, they are typically people who are either Godless or people who invoke the name of God as a cover for their Godless, nefarious acts. The first group, typically have no moral compass. The second group is perhaps the more interesting one. They perform atrocities, unspeakable acts, in the name of God, and, in doing so, they violate everything that we hold sacred. Many genocides of certain ethnic and religious groups of people have been persecuted in the name of God. Sadly, they have maligned His character and are deceived. God is not a destroyer of lives.

Which group do you fall under? God's children are peacemakers, they are not troublemakers. His kingdom is strictly the Spirit of peace and harmony. There is no dissension or conflict in His nature. God has commanded us not to take His name in vain, and those who would invoke His name for purposes that are clearly ungodly have done precisely that. They are the true troublemakers of this world, **but our God is stronger than they are and, if we trust Him, we need not fear the troublemakers of this world.**

## **NO GOD LIKE YOU LORD** | MAY 23

*"There is no one like you, O LORD, and there is no God but you, as we have heard with our own ears." I Chronicles 17: 20*

---

David became the ruler of all the tribes of Israel when Saul died. David was, at once, God's ultimate spokesman and promoter and, at the same time, one who proved he was capable of straying. Many have asked why God tolerated David's uneven behavior and ask whether He will tolerate our own shortcomings.

In our times, we have witnessed the fall from grace of some of the most highly-respected religious personalities. More than a score of televangelist have been implicated in various scandals involving misappropriation of funds, sexual affairs, and the like. Several of the best-known alleged perpetrators include Jim Bakker, Ted Haggard, Jimmy Swaggart, Robert Tilton, and Bill James Hargis. Most acknowledged their sins. Others denied them. Virtually all saw their public images destroyed. It has been argued by some that what most if not all of these had in common is that they let their personal quests for fame eclipse their service to the One whom they were supposed to be serving. They undoubtedly did not practice what they preached. They became the servants of greed and lust. Their master became Satan. Several of these so-called televangelists have claimed to have seen the light, repented and returned to God's fold. Regardless of their "sin" anyone can return to God and be forgiven. "All have sinned."

And so the question becomes whether, as was the case with David, God will provide these high-profile sinners a second chance? David knew his weaknesses, but he trusted in God and repented for his sins of his own volition. Arguably, the sins of these televangelists, these false prophets, were that, in virtually every instance, it was not until they were caught in the act that they sought repentance. We'll not pass judgment on the televangelists. That is God's job. God knows each heart. He knows the heart of the person who is genuinely contrite, and He knows the heart of the person who is sorry he was caught.

**God is more than a God of a second chance. He is a God of forgiveness and grace**. Just as David was a man after God's own heart, so is there a place in God's heart for each of us, and yes, that includes the fallen televangelists. God is amazingly awesome. He is full of grace and mercy. **In truth, there is no GOD like our LORD.**

## YOU ALONE KNOW MY HEART | MAY 24

*"Then hear from heaven, your dwelling place. Forgive, and deal with each man according to all he does, since you know his heart (for you alone know the hearts of men)." II Chronicles 6: 30*

---

Do you think you know your closest friends? Every time I want to answer yes to that question, they surprise me. A case in point… some years back, I attended the 25th anniversary party of my close friends. The 200 or so guests, including their two beautiful children, witnessed the couple's renewal of their wedding vows in a church ceremony. It was very touching, particularly in view of the fact that a good many of those in attendance were less fortunate in marriage. Less than a year later, divorce papers were filed. It seemed that one of them had strayed. I have witnessed enough of these true stories in my life that one wonders "who knew?" Obviously, only God knows the heart of each of us.

So often, we are fooled by appearances. We think we know our friends, but we don't fully comprehend their inner dimensions. We do business with people every day, and we think we know those people, and all of a sudden, one of them goes to jail, and it turns out that he defrauded thousands of people and squandered many billions of their dollars. We vote for candidates who vow to safeguard our tax dollars and end up diverting those funds for their personal enjoyment. It would seem that our collective and individual judgment are lacking. Who can know the real you? Do you think your spouse knows you better than anyone? How about your therapist? Maybe it's your neighbor. I would venture to guess that most of us don't really know who we are. Most of us aren't enamored with what we see in the mirror. Each of us would like others to see us in the best light, so, we put forth an appearance of goodness. Paul however, says even our best is "filthy rags."

God, on the other hand, knows what is in our hearts. No one knows our hearts better than God. God even knew each of us before our date of birth. He knows our motives. He knows what makes you who you are. Even before you act out what is in your heart, God has found a way to save you. **God knows that we will never live up to His standard, but He loves us nonetheless.** God in His grace and mercy, found a way to love and accept you. It was through His Son, who has invited us to be one with Him. **For God alone know the hearts of each and every one of us.**

## DOES GOD PUNISH? | MAY 25

*"For the wages of sin is death, but the gift of God is eternal life in Christ Jesus our Lord." Romans 6: 23*

---

An oft-voice refrain which many of us heard growing up, especially when we were perceived to have erred, was: "God will punish you!" Some believe that the failure to tithe will affect their financial success. Earthquakes, some are certain, are God's retribution for the profligate ways of Californians. Some view the AIDS epidemic as payback for what they perceive as the sin of homosexuality. Today's verse might seem to underscore such notions. Does God punish us for our mistakes? Are we reaping the punishments of our forefathers? Does God ever punish? There are scriptures that purport such a notion, especially today's text.

Today is the birthday of my dear friend Lani. She passed away about a year ago because of breast cancer. She certainly was taken before her time. When I visited her a month before her passing, she confessed to me she knew God and believed in Him but could not obtain inner peace because she remembered her past life. She was not clear in her thinking of whether she was being punished for her past sins. I shared with her my own similar doubts at one time in my life, but relayed to her my own personal convictions that God has never punished us nor will He ever punish us. It is contrary to the nature of His loving character.

Let's review how God handled the first known act of disobedience. Adam and Eve failed to trust God. They sinned. How did God deal with them? First, He went looking for them. He asked them: "where are you?" That's love in action. Secondly, He fashioned clothing made of skin from a sacrificed animal to clothe them. The pair was not knowledgeable of the consequences of their mistake as well as the seasons they would encounter. They would need warm clothing for the winter months. Finally, God gave them a promised hope that someday someone would take the punishment of their sin. That someone would be their Savior. Would you believe that's how God treats every one of us whenever we err? But we do reap our own punishment.

Then why do we experience heartaches, guilt, shame and punishments on this earth? The answer is quite simple. Whenever we disobey God's law of love or mistrust Him, we reap the consequences of that separation. God's laws are all about His love and His character. Apart from Him is the punishment. God has "dementia" when it comes to our past sins. He remembers our sin no more and forgives us without conditions. He even said He buries our sins to the depths of the ocean floor. My friend was humbled and felt a great relief, her countenance radiated with inner peace. **We both rejoiced in knowing that God does not punish but instead took our punishment. What is also so amazing is the gift of eternal life through our Savior, Jesus Christ our Lord.**

## NEVER GIVE UP | MAY 26

*"But as for you, be strong and do not give up, for your work will be rewarded." II Chronicles 15: 7*

Have you ever felt like giving up everything you've worked for because of one incident that devastated you? I have, many times. During a moment of fear and helplessness you feel like "throwing in the towel."

I witnessed a championship fight between two boxers when one of the boxers became so dominant that the other boxer could not even defend himself. His ringside trainer threw in the towel indicating they surrender the match. When I was running cross country in high school and college, there were moments when I was tempted to stop and quit because the pain of going on was excruciating.

What is eating you up today to make you want to quit? Is it your family, school, work, relationship, health, a friend or lover? Winston Churchill, the prime minister of England, was the commencement speaker for a graduating class during the height of World War II. He rose from his seat and said these words "Never! Never! Never! Give up." He sat down to a thunderous standing ovation. Those five words were his entire commencement address. His attitude of never surrendering carried his nation to victory during WW II. It's so much easier to walk away from a marriage, quit that boring job, or drop out of school or even life than to tackle what appears to be a daunting task. Regardless what issues you are facing right now, never give up on God.

Granted, walking away or giving up when you know you are outclassed maybe a better option than possibly humiliating yourself. However, before you throw in the proverbial towel, pause for a moment and ask yourself: "Is quitting the best solution?" "Have I given my all before calling it quits?" Picture for a moment what might have happened if Jesus' prayer to His Father at that crucial moment as He lay on the cross had been: "Father, I cannot endure this a second longer. I give up." We would have been forever lost. Fortunately for us, He did not give up. He gave His life so that we might live forever.

Our text today reminds us to be strong and not to give up; for God will never give up on us. Whatever it is you are going through, nothing compares to what God has in store for you and me. You must continue to walk in faith and hold on to His promises. **God will finish what He started.** He will deliver the salvation He promised us. He can't wait to bestow His great reward for us.

## MANASSEH'S PRAYER | MAY 27

*"And when he prayed to him, the Lord was moved by his entreaty and listened to his plea; so he brought him back to Jerusalem and to his Kingdom. Then Manasseh knew that the Lord is God." II Chronicles 33: 13*

---

Manasseh was a mere 12 years old when he became king of Israel. His father was Hezekiah. Can you imagine being 12 years old and running a nation? Our president today is one of the youngest at 47 years old. Manasseh, however, did evil in the sight of God. He built altars to the gods of Baal and made Asherah poles. He totally abandoned the true God.

Our modern-day culture can virtually tap all five of a child's senses simultaneously. Manasseh had no iPad or X-Box, no texting or e-mail, but he likely had his share of distractions, and it is clear that he was distracted away from God. The distractions our children encounter today are, arguably, many times greater. We read almost every day that these distractions detract from their studies. It is ironic, too, that, in an age in which a myriad of information is right at our fingertips, our children have little knowledge of the goings-on in our world. These distractions have caused our children to give God short shrift.

How could a people whom God had chosen descend so low as the people of Israel under Manasseh? It is not difficult to understand. When you leave God, you are doomed to self-destruct. But no matter how pathetic Manasseh and his people had become, the Author of Love would neither ignore nor give up on them. When the king of Assyria defeated Manasseh, his soldiers took him prisoner to Babylon. There, in his distress, he prayed to the true God of his forefathers. God heard his plea.

This same God will also hear your prayer today. It doesn't matter how low the descent in your life or how sinister your deed, God is willing to forgive and heal you today, much as He did for Manasseh centuries ago. Manasseh had the good sense to realize who the true God is and was smart enough to return to Him. **You can always come back to God. He never leaves you or gives up on you. He waits patiently and with open arms for your return. Come home to Him right now.** You will be glad.

Reacquaint yourself with God today. He is a wonderful SAVIOR, LORD and GOD. Don't wait until you have your back against the wall. Are you willing to believe God's forgiving grace? Then do it now! Pray Manasseh's prayer right now.

## THE SPIRIT OF VENGEANCE | MAY 28

*"For the LORD has a day of vengeance, a year of retribution, to uphold Zion's cause." Isaiah 34: 8*

Have you ever wanted to seek revenge on someone who offended you? Forgive me for disclosing to you an awful pet peeve of mine but I hate injustice. I ask your forgiveness first before sharing with you my own personal experience regarding vengeance. I need you to know I am far from perfect and attempt to "die daily" in the Lord. Sometimes my guard is lifted and I am overwhelmed by an ungodly spirit.

It was the holidays and people everywhere were busy trying to do last minute Christmas shopping. The malls were full of shoppers and it's during this time of year that a parking space is quite a premium. Cars were moving at a snail's pace from aisle to aisle in order to spy on a vehicle moving out of their parking space. I happen to notice a couple go into their car before anyone could see them and I inched slowly behind them. I then turned on my signal light to let anyone else who happen to see the same space know I was waiting for that particular space. I waited for the couple to exit. Unfortunately, depending on how the person maneuvered his car out of his space, would determine who can drive to that space first. As I waited, another vehicle suddenly came from the opposite side of me. He saw me waiting. The car that exited came out with its rear lights facing me. I could not enter his parking space until he drove off. The other car, who came after me, drove straight through in front of the car exiting and took my parking space. I was livid. We came out of our cars. I cried foul play and injustice. The other guy claimed he was there first. We were literally face to face and ready to come to blows. It was a stare down contest that seem to last forever. As I was embroiled throughout this ordeal, a still small voice inside me said to "walk away." But another spirit inside me said "don't give in, you are in the right." I was now caught up in a dilemma, a struggle and conflict. Who would bow out first? Or who would throw the first blow? (Until this day, I am still remorseful to share this incident with you).

I ended up relenting. But my nerves were shot. I lost all interest in shopping. My day was totally ruined. I wanted vengeance. I was thinking horrendous things I could do to his car while he was shopping. What an irony? Here I am writing about love but am not practicing what I am "preaching." I realized in that moment, I forgot God. My heart was softened and I was humbled. Contrition overwhelmed me. I wanted to find the guy who slighted me and ask his forgiveness. **The spirit of God's vengeance is kind, patient, compassionate and longsuffering. You want revenge? Leave it to God, His retribution is Godly**.

## WHAT IS IT YOU WANT? | MAY 29

*"The king said to me, 'What is it you want?' Then I prayed to the God of heaven, and I answered the king, 'If it pleases the king and if your servant was found favor in his sight, let him send me to the city in Judah where my fathers are buried so that I can rebuild it.'" Nehemiah 2: 4*

---

Nehemiah was a cupbearer to the king. He had a rather precarious job in the King's court that risked his own life. I recently took a seven-day cruise in one of the largest cruise liners ever built. This ship held over 2,850 people. Since this writing new ships have been built to carry more than 6,000 people. There are two seating times for dinner: 6: p.m. and 8: 30 p.m. We chose the early seating. There is a waiter for every course served, starting with drinks. The waiter's uniforms distinguished their role. The waiter requesting what we wished to drink wore a faux gold chain with a four-inch medallion hanging in the center that was shiny and attractive. I asked the waiter what the medallion symbolized and he replied, "I am a wine taster."

I was immediately reminded of the text today. Nehemiah was also a wine taster for king Artaxerxes. Before any drink could be offered to the king, Nehemiah must first taste the wine. It was not uncommon in those days for people to attempt to assassinate the king through poisoning. This is why every king had a cupbearer. Should anyone attempt to poison the king, Nehemiah would be the first one to experience the deadly sting.

What a sacrifice the cupbearer had to make to protect his king. Nehemiah's job did not define him. He was also a godly man. He walked with God and wanted to please God. He placed His life and job in God's care. He trusted His Maker.

He felt a calling to restore the walls of Jerusalem that had earlier been destroyed. He wanted to pay homage to his God. The king asked what he wanted. The first thing Nehemiah did was pray to God. The key here is not the prayer but the prayerful life he led. It's the prayerful demeanor you project each moment of your life that is the essence of living a life in God. Just like Christ lived a prayerful life, Nehemiah, asked God for guidance in all his dealings.

God is also asking you, "What is it you want?" Think very carefully what you are asking God. Your answer will depend on your knowledge of Him. **Whatever it may be, may you find His will in your life today. To know and trust you Lord is my prayer today.**

## A GRACIOUS AND MERCIFUL GOD | MAY 30

*"For many years you were patient with them. By your Spirit you admonished them through your prophets. Yet they paid no attention, so you handed them over to the neighboring peoples. But in your great mercy you did not put an end to them or abandon them, for you are a gracious and merciful God." Nehemiah 9: 30 & 31*

---

Do you ever wonder if God is with you when trouble confronts you? In your frustration and despair, do you begin to doubt if there is a God? Do you feel abandoned and totally lost? What do you do? There are days when doubts enter your mind and you feel alone. Uncertainty creeps in and takes a hold of your very being. You feel helpless. You want to give up. You have nowhere to turn to and no one to lean on. Whenever you feel this way, don't fret or lose faith.

The same God who watched over the Israelites during their journey in the desert and provided all their necessities is the God watching over you today. Nehemiah 9: 21, 25 Says "For forty years you sustained them in the desert; they lacked nothing, their clothes did not wear out nor did their feet become swollen. (25) They ate to the full and were well-nourished; they reveled in your great goodness."

What a wonderful God we have! Each year just before school starts merchants have a "back to school" sale of clothing and school supplies. Once a year we purchase the latest fashions for our children before they return back to school. Can you imagine today if all your life you never needed to change your clothes because God was watching over you and allowed you to grow into your clothing? For the next 40 years the clothing looked as new as the first day you wore it. That's how God cares and provides for all your daily needs.

Have you reflected on the blessings of your past year and noted that instead of losing weight from starvation you have actually gained a few more pounds than the year before? God again has provided you with the abundance in food. In His great mercy He has not stop caring for you. He has not abandoned you nor neglected your needs. He is the same God that was with Nehemiah. Not only does He provide for you daily but He made provisions for your salvation long before you entered this world. God has you covered long before you ask.

**His love for us changes not. He tells us; " I'm your God I change not," Malachi 3:6.** That sure helps to know we can totally rely on Him. He will never surprise you. His love for us is steadfast and constant. He doesn't go through mood swings like your spouse, friend or lover. **He is ever faithful to you and me. He is truly a gracious and merciful God. Can do you likewise?**

## WHOM YOU LOVE | MAY 31

*"Then God said, 'Take your son, your only son, Isaac, whom you love, and go to the region of Moriah. Sacrifice him there as a burnt offering on one of the mountains I will tell you about.'" Genesis 22: 2*

---

Why would God want to test Abraham's faith at this stage of his life? He was old and feeble. He had been through much suffering and was tested every way during his journeys. Finally the promised son is born, and he was Abraham's pride and joy. He is beginning to grow to be a wonderful, obedient and spiritual young man. Suddenly, as if out of nowhere, Abraham is asked by God to sacrifice his only son. What a test of Faith! Abraham had to be conflicted of mind; he was after all only human. Some writers attest that the trial Abraham was put through was more severe than that which had been brought upon Adam. What a contrast. Adam was forewarned early on not to eat or touch the fruit from the tree of good and evil. He was not asked to sacrifice his wife Eve or even his first-born. His test of faith did not require any agonizing or suffering. Nevertheless, Abraham obeyed.

There was more at stake here. The entire universe and Satan were witnessing the foreshadowing of the promise made by God to Adam in Genesis 3: 15. "I will put enmity between you and the woman, between her seed and your offspring, and he will crush your head, and you will strike his heel." What made Abraham so obedient and unwavering? Can you imagine three days journey to the place God called him to make this sacrifice? He could have reasoned in his mind to turn back. How did he know for sure the voice he was listening to was God and not Satan's? After all, did not God say "Thou Shall not kill?" What an agonizing tug-of-war there must have been in Abraham's mind and heart. Yet he continued his task. Abraham knew God. After all the trials and temptations he had been through with God, he was steadfast in his knowledge that this was indeed the voice, not of Satan, but of God. He followed God's request, virtually without hesitation. What's even more amazing is the faith of Isaac.

Are you having an Isaac moment in your life today? Do you feel insecure and uncertain about what lies ahead? Are you hearing voices that you can't distinguish? You ask, why is God testing me at this stage in my life? God knows your plight and will save you. You needn't feel discouraged. Talk to God right now and tell Him what's on your mind. He will listen and He will answer you.

All you need is to exercise the faith of Isaac. **God wants you to have faith in Him; after all you are whom God loves. Trust Him. Your future has a very happy ending.**

## PRAYING FOR YOUR ENEMIES | JUNE 1

*"But I tell you: Love your enemies and pray for those who persecute you." Matthew 5: 44*

I remember walking into the attorney's office Friday morning right after Thanksgiving Day. The applicant's attorney subpoenaed me for a deposition. The attorney was noted for being ruthless. If you were a member of his opposition, he was aiming for you, and he wasn't shooting blanks. He had purposely chosen the Friday after Thanksgiving, knowing that most non-retail businesses were closed that day, and this, he likely felt, would further antagonize me. I have never been deposed before; so this was a new experience. I responded to his questions as truthfully as I was able. Afterward, our defense attorney commended me for my restraint. She had no idea how close I'd come to lashing out at the accusatory and insulting tone of the attorney's questions.

The opposing attorney set himself up immediately as my foe, and I almost immediately developed a thirst for vengeance. That was more than a dozen years ago, and I vowed to distance myself from this attorney to the extent possible in the future. My profession (worker's compensation) exposed me to numerous doctors, attorneys and insurance claims adjusters, and the working relationships are not always the most collegial.

I thought I would never see this attorney again; wishful thinking. Would you believe it, I had another meeting with this attorney. You might expect that the passing of so many years would have dulled my recollection of the experience, but it is as vivid as the day I entered his office. That attorney had pulled every trick in the book to demean and frustrate me, and, while I know better, it didn't occur to me at the time to pray. Do you have a similar situation – perhaps an individual who enjoys belittling you, an individual you do your utmost to avoid? Come on, if you're truly honest haven't we all experienced one of these people?

The thought of praying for someone who is persecuting you is, on the surface, anathema to us. Loving your enemy is even bizarre. Nevertheless, I would urge you to try it. You'll discover, perhaps to your surprise, that when you pray for your enemy, it gives you the upper hand. **The upper hand means inner peace, that you have placed your whole situation in God's trust.** With God you will be victorious. I did precisely that before my recent meeting, and this time I viewed him through the eyes of God. This takes total trust in God. My inner soul felt compassion for a man who seemed personally desperate for inner peace.

## TALKING BACK TO GOD | JUNE 2

*"But who are you, O man, to talk back to God? Shall what is formed say to him who formed it, 'Why did you make me like this?'" Romans 9: 20*

---

Have you ever talked back to your parents? Who among us can honestly respond: "no?" Very likely, these were not your finest moments. Today, it almost seems as if parents expect this kind of exchange. It wasn't that way for me, growing up. Anything bordering on disrespect met with swift and sometimes rather severe repercussions. I recall rather vividly my elder sister's complaining to my mother that her troubles in life were the result of our parents' strict upbringing. She specifically blamed my mother, and the conversation became heated. Mother would always end with "wait until you have your own kids." No doubt, afterward, both regretted things they'd said. There is merit to the oft-voiced advice that we should count to ten before we express our anger. It makes sense, too, to rehearse your expressions of anger. This will likely remove some of the edge.

At one time or another, each of us has probably hurled some of the same type of invective at God. In fact, we are prone to blame God for the way we turned out. "You made me this way. It's not my fault." To tell God that He messed up in His creating us is both presumptuous and arrogant. Moreover, it's just simply wrong. We must remember that it is we who chose to ignore His wisdom and counsel in the Garden of Eden.

Growing up had its awkward moments for all of us, and I was no exception. I was tall and gangly, and I was nicknamed "toothpick" and "string bean." I detest my body, and who was the handiest scapegoat? Well, I couldn't blame my parents or my siblings or my friends, so I blamed God. "Why did you make me this way?" Certainly, we are arrogant to think we know better than the Almighty, but in His love for us, He puts up with our talking back to Him. Someday, we will not talk back and blame Him but praise Him when He makes all things new again.

God is pleased to announce to the universe that He has made us in His image. Fortunately for us, He is open to discourse. Like a doting parent, He spoils us. **We could say and do anything to God and in return He just listens, waits patiently, relents and loves us unconditionally.** He treats us with kindness. He is a gracious God who condescends to our level of bratty behavior. How could we act this way towards God? Those of us who truly know God, we would expect no less, of course, from the Author of Love.

## SEEK HIS FACE ALWAYS | JUNE 3

*"Look to the LORD and His strengths, seek His face always." Psalms 7: 17*

How close are you to God? Do you start your day with a prayer to Him and end your day the same way? Certainly, your prayers to God upon your waking and your retiring at night and before you partake of each meal are important. The daily repetition adds discipline to our lives, but if this be the extent of our communication with God, then we may not be doing much more than going through the paces. Moreover, words that emanate from our hearts are so much more cogent than those that are to be found in a book of prayers. This is to say that, to the extent that our prayers and supplications become routine, they do not have nearly as much meaning as our unscripted dialogue with God at times other than those that are traditional.

It might be argued that, inasmuch as God knows our every act and more importantly, our every motive, it matters not how we express ourselves as we converse with God. True, it may not matter to God, but we are the better for having sought God out.

An important aspect of the Catholic Rosary is the Hail Mary. Over the years, some theologians have maintained that the repetition of that prayer (a prayer which asks for the intercession of the Virgin Mary) has served to trivialize the prayer, particularly when a supplicant who goes for confession is required, as a means of penance, to repeat that prayer and/or the "Our Father" five or ten times.

These same theologians have argued that God would be better served by an unscripted prayer that would emanate from the heart of the confessor. We'll not take a position respecting the practices of a particular religious sect. Suffice it to say, however, that, while God welcomes all of our prayers and communications, communications that are spontaneous and of the heart are the most meaningful. God sent His Son to show us His Father and to lead by example. Jesus' communion with His Father was virtually without interruption.

**Seeking His face means developing a deeper relationship with God. It means placing Him priority in your life.** Unless you build your relationship with God as your foundation, everything else you pursue or do will be in vain. God will show you Himself and will lead you closer to Him. You must be willing. Keep an open mind, heart, body and spirit. **You will really know God when you let Him love you. His life should serve as a lesson to always seek His face.**

## LIFE AND DEATH MATTER | JUNE 4

*"See I set before you today life and prosperity, death and destruction. For I command you today to love the LORD your God, to walk in his ways, and to keep his commands, decrees and laws; then you will live and increase, and the LORD your God will bless you in the land you are entering to possess." Deuteronomy 30: 15*

---

Today's text appears simple enough to follow. God has set before us life or death, blessings or curses. All we need to do is listen to Him, walk in His ways, and keep His commandments, decrees and laws. What's so difficult about that? From day one, Lucifer has contended that God's commandments are impossible to keep. It's too exacting, overbearing and unfair. Do you sometimes feel confined by God's laws? Do they take all of the fun out of life? Is there any person who can say he has never strayed from God's commandments? The scriptures tell us that: "There is none that does good, no not one."

David has a slightly different take on the issues. He writes in Psalms 26: 1, "Judge me O LORD, for I have walked perfectly before you…?" The next phrase explains what it means to "walk perfectly before the LORD," "for I have trusted in the LORD without wavering." Clearly, David was not one to boast of living a life devoid of sin. His life story is replete with sins, both common and grievous. If David was indeed a man of God, it was due to the fact that he fully comprehended the power of repentance and forgiveness. Though he strayed from time to time, his faith and trust in God were unwavering. He knew God. He loved God. He found the answer to all his insecurities, doubts and questionings; that God was ALWAYS accepting and FORGIVING of him. God feels the same for you. He loves you just as much as He loves David. When you see that and accept Him, you will experience the love David had for God.

God accepts us for who we are. He knows of every misstep we have taken; yet He still urges us to choose Him. The more I understand and know the nature of God, the more I am ashamed at my behavior towards Him. Reading these verses and seeing how God relates to us, I can see why He communicates to us in a child-like manner. We are spoiled and haven't matured enough to relate to Him as adults.

A young child was asked if she understood the difference between God and Santa Claus. "Santa Claus," she intoned, "knows when you've been naughty and nice, and, when you're naughty, he doesn't come down your chimney. **God also knows when you've been naughty or nice, but He loves you unconditionally** (sic). from the mouth of babes…

## GRACE IS MORE THAN EQUAL | JUNE 5

*"The law was added so that the trespass might increase. But where sin increased, grace increase all the more, so that, just as sin reigned in death, so also grace might reign through righteousness to bring eternal life through Jesus Christ our Lord." Romans 5: 20 & 21*

---

The Bible is explicit in Romans 5 verse 12-14, "Therefore, just as sin entered the world through one man, and death through sin, and in his way death came to all men, because all sinned-for before the law was given, sin was in the world. But sin is not taken into account when there is no law. Nevertheless, death reigned from the time of Adam to the time of Moses, even over those who did not sin by breaking a command, as did Adam, who was a pattern of the one to come."

If you were the first Adam would you have made a different choice than he? Would you not have sinned? Would you have been more circumspect and said no to temptation, thus avoiding that fatal sin? Scholars and theologians have debated over the years whether it be fair that many millions have paid the price for the failure of one man. Some have labeled it "equal justice run amuck." There are other Biblical examples in which many have paid for the sins of the few -- for example, the tens of thousands who perished by plague due to David's indiscretions.

Paul offers a contrary perspective (Verses 15-17): "But the gift is not like the trespass. For if the many died by the trespass for the one man, how much more did God's grace and the gift that came by grace of the one man, Jesus Christ, overflow to the many!" Adam may have cursed us with his choice, but God sent His Son to reconcile us and bless us through our individual choice for Him. That is grace. God's "enoughness" means God is enough for you and me no matter what situation we encounter. That grace can only be found in His Son, Jesus Christ our LORD.

Do you understand what this means? Do you understand God's grace for you? Can you accept these things God is offering you in your life? You are given the opportunity to be the Adam that failed and decide to live the life God has chosen for you or depart from it as your first father Adam did. He gave us a choice of His grace or Satan's condemnation. **His grace is not only sufficient for you; it is more than equal.** What a Savior we have in Jesus Christ our LORD!

## GOING INTO DEBT FOR LOVE | JUNE 6

*"Let no debt remain outstanding except the continuing debt to love one another." Romans 13: 8*

---

Have you ever done someone a big favor, and he or she responded: "I owe you big time." Or have you been the one who owes? Of course, not all of these debts are financial in nature, but it seems that a good many of them are.

Spending beyond our means has become a national pastime. Individually, a good many of us hopped on the housing bandwagon. It seemed that prices knew only one direction, and that was up. We were willing to leverage our futures because it was a sure thing, or so we thought. Now, we are experiencing the highest level of foreclosures and short sales most of us have ever seen. Out track record as a nation is not much better. At the time of the writing, our national debt exceeds $14-trillion. That's "trillion" with a "T." That's equal to nearly $46,000 per American citizen and approximately $128,000 per taxpayer. We have mortgaged, not only our children's futures, but, very likely, their children's futures.

There was a time in my own life when I became a slave to plastic (credit cards). I recall my mother's counsel: "If you don't need it, don't buy it." I suppose I was operating under the misapprehension that, at life's end, he or she who has the most toys wins. He or she who sets out to collect and accumulate the most "toys" will never have enough, will never be satisfied. And your possessions won't likely fit in your coffin. Are you accumulating stuff in your closets, basements or garages that's gathering dust, moths or deterioration? We have a rule of thumb in our household, if you haven't used it in five years, dump it or donate it.

Paul suggested that there was one form of debt that was worth the accumulation, and that was love. True love, he stipulated, has as its basis acts which are selfless in nature. It is not about being fed, he maintained, but rather about feeding others. Jesus said: "If you love me, feed my sheep." True wealth is not one's accumulated bounty, but rather one's accumulation of selfless deeds.

Our Savior, in truth, paid our debts with His own life. Moreover, He did so without ever uttering the words: "You owe me." **You want to hoard and accumulate debt... do it by loving one another.** That's a debt worth accumulating.

## LAUGHTER IS THE BEST MEDICINE | JUNE 7

*"He who sits in the heavens laughs; the LORD has them in derision." Psalms 2: 4 RSV*

We are all familiar with the phrase "laughter is the best medicine." It is now widely held that there is at least some modicum of literal truth to that notion. Back in the '70's, the late George Burns portrayed a God who was unlike any who'd ever come to the silver screen – certainly a marked contrast to the God depicted (but not seen) in Cecil B. DeMille's '50's version of the "Ten Commandments." Some critics have argued that Burn's depiction, as well as the more recent Morgan Freeman depiction in "Bruce Almighty" were sacrilegious. The very notion of a God who was not only funny, but self-deprecating was, to say the least, ground-breaking. Some argued that it was ground that might more appropriately not have been broken. While it can certainly be argued that the two films took a few liberties in their depictions of God, it must also be said that they portrayed a God who endeavors to relate to us. The films don't remove God from His pedestal; they in no way denigrate the Almighty. Instead, they portray a God who is approachable, a depiction very much in synch with the notion that God is indeed the Author of Love.

Dr. Norman Cousins noticed that laughing for at least ten minutes a day resulted in pain free rest for his inflamed joints and spine. He called laughter "inner jogging." He has implemented this in his medical practice. The term used is gelotology, from the Greek "gelos" meaning laughter. Conversely being morose, gloomy and despondent can create all kinds of problems in our lives. There is even a religious group that practice laughter as a spiritual exercise. I have seen people rolling in the aisles and floor in derision and laughter whether it's funny or not. They forced themselves to laugh. They have concluded it's healthy for the soul.

The founder of "Gusundheit! Institute," Dr. Hunter Doherty "Patch" Adams demonstrates that, when all else fails, laughter can in fact be the best medicine. Conversely, those who suffer from depression and anxiety set themselves up for a host of maladies. Solomon understood the virtues of laughter. He said "A merry heart does good like medicine." Spend time with family, friends and social groups and share a laugh with them. Your spirit will be not only uplifted but your burdens will be lighter.

**God's gift to us of laughter is further evidence of His love for us.** God loves to see us laugh. He delights in our joys and laughter. **God is the Author of our happiness and laughter.**

# THE TRUTH ABOUT TITHING | JUNE 8

*"You give a tenth of your spices-mint, dill and cumin. But you have neglected the more important matters of the law-justice, mercy and faithfulness. You should have practiced the latter, without neglecting the former." Matthew 23: 23*

---

Tithing is first mentioned in the Old Testament in chapter 14 verse 20 of Genesis, where Abraham gave "a tithe of everything to Mechizedek." Abraham obviously practiced tithing because he knew it was used for the work of the ministry as well to teach us to trust a faithful God. There are discussion today about the validity of tithing and how much to give. Some people say tithing was nailed at the cross and is no longer necessary. Others say you should give from the gross while others promote the net of your gain. Tithing is a privilege that allows us to return back to God a portion of the blessing He has bestowed on us.

We all want to express our opinion on how the tithe money should be used, but if the money does not produce a spirit of justice, mercy and faithfulness in our personal lives and in our community, then we need to take a second look at our hearts and ponder on Jesus' admonition. Do you give tithe because God commanded you? Do you give tithe because you do not want to be accused of robbing God? Do you give tithe because you are testing His promise that He will pour out a blessing in your life? What about giving your tithe while your family is starving or in dire economic consequences? Where do you draw the line in giving?

Jesus is saying the giving is secondary to your relationship with Him. God freely gave because He loved us. His giving of His only Son was motivated by the love He has for us so we may be treated with justice, mercy and faithfulness. God took upon Himself to treat the abuse and injustice that abounds in our world so that our lives might be blessed with justice. He did this for no other reason than His love for us. He was not given mercy when He pleaded for mercy at the cross, yet He stayed faithful to the end in order that we might know His love and faithfulness to us.

The true measure of giving is not in the sum that is offered but rather in the spirit with which it is rendered. Remember the woman at the temple? She was so embarrassed that she was giving only a few pennies that she was inconspicuous but Christ noticed and said she gave all. In contrast, the rich man gave so much money he made sure everyone saw him giving such an amount by being loud and pompous about it. Jesus compared the two givers and said the woman gave more than the rich man.

You can give to appease your guilt, but when you give in love you have given in His Spirit. **Tithing is truly about Love.**

## ENCOURAGE ONE ANOTHER DAILY | JUNE 9

*"But encourage one another daily, as long as it is called today, so that none of you may be hardened by sin's deceitfulness." Hebrews 3: 13*

---

Do you know people who are so willing to help others that they tend to set themselves up as targets for those who would take advantage? We may look at those people as being naïve. We like to think that we know better. However, we may know better to the point of being cynical. That is to say that one way to avoid the scammers and the unscrupulous is to assume that all people on this planet are schemers and to deal with all as if that were the case. Certainly, a case can be made that it is best to be somewhere near the middle of the continuum that goes from naïve to cynic. Most of us, however, tend to lean toward one extreme or the other on that continuum.

My friend Paul is a case in point. He is, some would say, trusting to a fault. He has a very giving and forgiving heart, and, at times, this sets him up as a target for those whose intentions are less than pure. A number of years back, Paul took in an unemployed person in order to help him get back on his feet. The visitor stayed with Paul for over two years. Not only did he not contribute toward Paul's expenses, but he failed to contribute in kind by helping out with chores and other such. He apparently saw himself more as a hotel guess. There are two ways that we might regard Paul. Some, perhaps most of us would consider him be a patsy, perhaps even something of a fool for allowing himself to be hoodwinked, so to speak, by an individual whose character was that of a leach. Others of us – likely a minority – would praise Paul for his giving spirit and his willingness to give of his heart unconditionally.

Then there are those who give of their time and service freely and without conditions to the helpless and needy. One individual I know took it to mean I was interested in her. Soon she was living a fantasy she imagined. Sometimes even our good intentions are misread. There are so many hungering for more than attention.

The fact is that God is that way with us. We have, over the centuries, taken considerable advantage of Him. When He came to live amongst us, He accepted the most downtrodden in our midst and loved them without reservation. **The same God who reached out to these people is reaching out to you today. You would do well to follow His example and reach out and encourage someone, even if that person be 100% taker.** When you do, you will be encouraged.

## PRAY IN THE SPIRIT | JUNE 10

*"And pray in the Spirit on all occasions with all kinds of prayers and requests. With this in mind, be alert and always keep on praying for all the saints." Ephesians 6: 18*

---

Have you ever wondered why God answers certain prayers and not others? Is there a formula to use when praying in order that our prayers may be answered? Should we gather in groups of three or more to have a prayer answered? Should we seek counsel first with the church elders? Should we stop sinning first? Should we fast first? What does it take to pray correctly?

My friends' twin children were struck with a terrible disease. One of them survived; the other did not. They asked why God didn't answer their prayers for healing. Another friend asked God in prayer to save her marriage but divorce ensued, nevertheless. We can all relate to so-called unanswered prayers. We consider ourselves to be Godly; yet God appears sometimes to lend a deaf ear to our supplications. Some lose faith in God when their prayers go unanswered.

Do you pray throughout the day – for things very important and for "the small stuff"? Or, are you more selective? You only "hit God up" for the big stuff – those items you consider to be life-altering? You figure that it is something of an imposition to bother God with petty items. You feel, too that God is more apt to respond if you only beseech Him when there is a matter of crisis proportions. You don't want to be the boy who cried wolf. Your logic is that, when God hears your voice, He'll know for certain that this one really counts. It's a sad case to think God is selective on who He chooses to answer their prayer.

God has made it clear that He wants us to pray to Him all of the time and whenever you are moved to do so, regardless of the relative importance of the item that brings you to prayer. Jesus wants to be one with you in Spirit as He is with His Father, and you will only achieve this through the constant use of prayer. Pray to Him for all occasions and for all reasons and for all times. That's what He wants from you and that's what will give you His Spirit. Don't screen your prayers to God according to weighty matters or certain conditions. Talk to God from your waking moment to your retirement at night. He wants to hear everything from you. You'll experience His peace and calm assurance. Live a prayerful life by following Jesus' example, for that is what God has asked of you.

What an encouraging command to follow. God has given you His formula for a prayerful life. **Won't you pray to Him right now? God cannot wait to hear from you.**

## HYPOCRITICAL PRAYER | JUNE 11

*"When you pray, don't be like the hypocrites who pretend piety by praying publicly on street corners and in the synagogues where everyone can see them. Truly, that is all the reward they will ever get."* Matthew 6: 5

After enjoying a rousing Sunday afternoon concert, a group of us went to our favorite Chinese restaurant to eat and enjoy our camaraderie. Three of us arrived first, and we asked for a table for eight. I expected the others to arrive shortly; so I decided to place our order so that we would not have to wait long for our meal. When the others arrived, we were informed that one of the guys in our group would not be coming due to an earlier commitment.

The restaurant began to fill up, and we noticed that those who arrived after us were beginning to be served while we were still waiting. The minister, who was a member of our group, commented about the slow service, and his wife was quick to echo similar sentiments. I decided to alert the hostess, and she sent our waiter over to our table. He informed us that he was waiting for our eighth party to arrive before he served us. Obviously, there had been a disconnect somewhere, and we were likely a bit too harsh on the waiter, who was only trying to please us. When the waiter was clued in on our situation, the appetizers came, post haste. It was apparent that we had made the waiter feel as if he were second-rate. Nevertheless the waiter continued to serve us with kindness and grace. Whether he was living a prayerful life or it was his duty to act that way, the truth is, it's always best to treat your neighbor with a Godly Spirit.

Before we partook of our meal, the minister led us in prayer. I had an uncomfortable feeling in my gut that, here we were, praying like righteous Christians, right after we had disparaged a well-intentioned waiter. I was immediately impressed by today's text. Wasn't it Jesus who said: "Don't be like the hypocrites, pretending to be one thing and, at the same time, doing another." Our hypocrisy was not that we prayed but that we had not lived up to the prayer we were about to recite.

How do you live your life? Is there a distinction from your public and private life or are they the same? We are confronted daily on how to treat our neighbor. You can choose a role of servant or master. Whichever you display may it be consistent with God's character.

There is more to being prayerful than the mere recitation of words. Words may come readily, **but the heartfelt prayer must be felt and lived in our actions and not merely recited.** What an invaluable lesson to learn.

## DON'T WORRY | JUNE 12

*"Who of you by worrying can add a single hour to his life?" Matthew 6: 27*

"Don't worry... be happy." Do you remember that Grammy-winning, feel-good song? Do you remember who sang it? If not, are you worried that you may be losing your memory? After age 50 or so, it's one of the most common worries reported.

The fact is that, when it comes to worrying, none of us has an exemption card. We all worry about something. It seems to be in our DNA. Moreover, despite the fact that many of us have everything anyone could ever want insofar as wealth, possessions, and even health are concerned, we are no less likely to worry than those whose problems are numerous and substantial. It's the American way. (Actually, it's the way of the entire world. Americans do not have a monopoly when it comes to worry).

Whatever it is that you are worrying about; Jesus tells us that we are worrying for nothing. We worry excessively, and, more importantly, our worrying is, more often than not, to no avail. He asks us whether worrying will add a single hour to our lives. The question, of course, is rhetorical. Just take a minute (you can time it, if you are worried that you may be off by a few seconds), and think about something that is of great concern to you. Now, start worrying about it for one minute. When time is up, reflect on the outcome of your worrying. Has the worrying relieved your concern? Probably not, in fact, very likely, it has set your mind to worrying even more. If you are worried that the minute's duration was insufficient time to prove anything, be my guest, and worry this time for half an hour. Did the incremental 29 minutes do the trick? Feel better now? I didn't think so. Lest you be worried that your end result was different than everyone else's, rest assured that it was a "trick question."

God sent His Son to dispel the worries about all things and to replace them with the knowledge of His love. I know when you're smack in the middle of a tumultuous situation it's difficult not to worry or be anxious. Doesn't it also seem like you are secure and comfortable when life is going smoothly but you revert back to your old cantankerous ways when things get rough? What does that tell you about yourself?

Acknowledge the issue, pray to God and then leave it at the altar. God is perfect. **His love is perfect, "Perfect love casts out all fears."** God is in total control, and He never worries; so, you don't have to worry. You'll be happier.

## ALL-YOU-CAN-EAT ETERNAL FOOD | JUNE 13

*"Jesus said, 'Have the people sit down.' There was plenty of grass in that place, and the men sat down, about five thousand of them. Jesus then took the loaves, gave thanks, and distributed to those who were seated as much as they wanted. He did the same with the fish." John 6: 10 & 11*

---

Ever hear the phrase: "I'm dying of thirst" or "I'm starving to death?" Sorry to disappoint you, but, if you've only gone a few hours without liquid refreshment, you are hardly dying of thirst. In fact, most of us would survive eight to fourteen days without water. As for starving to death, assuming that you were hydrated, you'd likely be able to last four weeks without food. Mind you, these might not be the most joyous weeks of your life. During an early '80's hunger strike in Northern Ireland, the ten prisoners who died lasted from 46 to 73 days. Bet you're glad you weren't a contestant in that one.

In today's text, Jesus doesn't test man's endurance without nourishment but rather test just how far a very small amount of food can go when that food's provider is the Most Holy of purveyors. Jesus' feat of feeding 5,000 with but five loaves and two fish is all the more remarkable when we consider that the loaves were really dinner-roll-sized and the fish were more the size of modern-day McDonald's McNuggets. Try sharing a couple of McNuggets with 4,999 of your closest friends, and see how many friends you still have after the feast is over.

The point of all of this...If we have faith in the Lord, He has the power to feed the many full portions, even when the initial ingredients would appear to satisfy just one or two. Jesus wanted to impress those gathered that they would never be filled (He meant both physically and spiritually), unless they knew the true source of their sustenance, and that, of course, is God, the Author of Love.

Jesus proclaimed in verse (35): "I am the bread of life. He who comes to me will never go hungry, and he who believes in me will never be thirsty." Are you experiencing hunger pangs even after you've eaten? Are you still starving after having a holiday feast? I remember going to a progressive dinner and eating various meals but after each meal I felt something was missing. I could not satiate my craving. After eating a banana split, I finally admitted it "hit the spot." Maybe it's time I savor another type of food. Maybe I should try eating eternal food.

**To know Him is your eternal food as well as your eternal life.** He is inviting you to sup with Him. And it's all you can eat.

## WALKING ON THE WATER | JUNE 14

*"When they had rowed three or three and a half miles, they saw Jesus approaching the boat, walking on the water; and they were terrified. But He said to them, 'it is I; don't be afraid.'" John 6: 19 & 20*

---

Another miracle that Jesus performed was walking on water. How would you have reacted if you saw someone taking an evening stroll on the water? No doubt, it would catch your attention.

Jesus performed this little feat for a rather limited audience, his disciples. Why not a larger audience – perhaps on whatever the Ed Sullivan show of the era was? Jesus had just performed the act of feeding 5,000. Those who partook of the food were not convinced that their host was indeed the Son of God. They grumbled, almost in unison: "How could this man, born of Joseph and Mary, claim to be the Son of God?" They had seen Jesus grow up in their midst, and, now, all of a sudden, He proclaims that He is the Son of God and the bread of life. Perhaps, had He performed the walk-on-water "stunt" for His dinner guests, He'd have won a few converts, but that was a limited-engagement performance, only for the benefit of the disciples. Jesus knew that He was beginning to lose the confidence of His closest followers, and He performed this act, not as a Houdini-type stunt, but rather to affirm their trust in Him and His divinity.

The disciples wanted to crown Him a political king. His unwillingness to assume such a role was a disappointment. As E.G. White explains ("Desire of Ages," pp. 379, 390): "Unbelief was taking possession of their minds and hearts. Love of honor had blinded them. They knew that Jesus was hated by the Pharisees, and they were eager to see Him exalted as they thought He should be. Another method humankind has been advocating since the Saul and David era, to crown Jesus as King, so He could save them from their oppressors, but look what it got them."

However, even with all of the miracles, they failed to recognize Jesus' true nature, which was not a magician or an earthly king, but rather one who is their Savior and redeemer that spreads His love unconditionally to everyone who receives Him. God is willing to work miracles in your life today but He has a deeper agenda. He wants you to have eternal life.

**You need to focus, not so much on the miracles God performs in your life, but rather on His Son, who is love eternal.** That, after all, is where the true miracle lies.

## A CELEBRATION FOR PRODIGALS | JUNE 15

*"So he got up and went to his father. But while he was still a long way off, his father saw him and was filled with compassion for him; He ran to His son, threw His arms around him and kissed him." Luke 15: 20*

---

Many people believe the story of the prodigal son is the summation of God's love for humankind. You've heard the story many times. A father had two sons and one of them asked for his inheritance early because he wanted to enjoy it immediately. The father divided the inheritance between the two sons. The eldest son kept his inheritance and stayed home and worked faithfully in his father's estate while the younger son took his share, went to another country and lived a lavish life, but soon he squandered all his money and lived in dire poverty. He took a job feeding pigs. He finally realized his mistake and decided to return home.

While he was still far away his father saw him and was filled with compassion. He ran to his son and threw his arms around him and kissed him. After being away from home, there is no greater longing than to feel welcomed back home by your father, mother or loved one.

We are all prodigal sons and daughters. We have all gone astray from our heavenly father. Some of us eventually return to our senses, as the prodigal son did, while others continue to resist God's invitation. They think they are living godly lives until one day they discover that there are yet greener pastures beckoning them. Each of us whether we realize it or not, is on a prodigal journey of sorts. Each of us is beseeched by the Author of Love to come home. He is fully cognizant of your prodigal ways. However, while we seek what we foolishly believe are greener pastures, Jesus also lived a prodigal life of a different kind. He conceded His throne of comfort and glory so that He might redeem us and lead us away from our prodigal ways. The prodigal son, of course, lived only for himself. Our redeemer lived so that He might bless others. Our Father is waiting for you to come back home to Him. You'll be amazed at what He has in store for you. It's a party like you've never known or experienced.

**There is no father on earth that will love you as your Heavenly Father. Be ready to have your Father put His arms around you and kiss you. That is how God loves.** Let's celebrate our coming home by wishing God a very Happy Father's Day!

# DO EVERYTHING IN LOVE | JUNE 16

*"Do everything in love." I Corinthians 16: 14*

Alfred, Lord Tennyson (1809-1892) said: "I hold it true, whatever befall; I feel it, when I sorrow most, tis better to have loved and lost than never to have loved at all." If that is the case, then we are a nation of losers because most who have loved (and married) have eventually lost (and divorced). That doesn't count, of course, those who are miserable in their marriages but who hang on for the sake of their kids or for a host of other reasons.

The divorce rate in America for first marriages is in excess of 50%. One might think that the numbers improved for subsequent marriages – this, on the theory that people learn from earlier mistakes. If you think that, you'd be terribly wrong. The divorce rate for second marriages is somewhere in the 70% range, and nearly three-quarters of third marriages end in divorce. This is an amazingly-high number, given the fact that, by the time people enter into their third marriages; they are apt to be old enough that death would be expected to end a decent percentage of those marriages. These numbers, as high as they are, do not take into account the number of couples living together, UN-hitched. As attitudes shift, and, as unwed couples continue to gain ground insofar as benefits and other "marriage lite" perks are concerned, the numbers in this unwed-couple category can be expected to grow.

Now the $64,000 question is whether the numbers improve when both parties to the marriage have truly taken God to their hearts. Are these people more serious about their vows? Does a Godly person have a better shot at marital success? If there are meaningful surveys on this subject, we've not come across them. One would conjecture, however, that those who have truly joined forces, so to speak, with the Author of Love will have a deeper understanding of what love is all about. We might expect people in a Godly alliance to be more other-centered than self-centered, more giving, more caring. Do such characteristics make for better marriages? You would certainly expect that those who sign on with God would be capable of sustaining love under all circumstances. The key to doing everything in love is to be receptive to the Spirit of God controlling your thoughts and emotions. God's ways are godly with a peace within that surpasses all understandings.

**You will know love (God) when you do everything in love.** That type of behavior happens when you allow His Spirit to control your heart. The love of God will constrain you to love not only in words but in deeds.

## CAN YOU HEAR ME NOW? | JUNE 17

*"When he has brought out all his own, he goes on ahead of them, and his sheep follow him because they know is voice." John 10: 4*

Answer quickly: "Can you hear me now?" Is it AT&T, Verizon, Sprint, or T-Mobile? We've seen that commercials dozens of times, but we're not certain. We are all familiar with the bunny that beats a drum for that battery company. It has a tremendous level of recall. However, about as many claim that the Energizer bunny is the Duracell bunny as Energizer. We hear voices all of the time, but, as often as not, we don't know who's calling.

When we were children, my father had conditioned us to drop whatever we were doing and run home when he whistled. His whistle was distinct to us only. I can recall when we were in the middle of a game when father sounded his whistle. Me and my brothers stopped playing ball and ran home. My friends looked at us in amazement and disbelief. Later they attempted to imitate my father's whistle but they didn't fool us. To anyone else, it was just a loud whistle, but to us, it was unmistakably his whistle.

God tells us that He wants us to hear His voice and to follow Him. Can you recognize God's voice when He calls? Beware…there is one caller who is known to be a consummate actor. He can assume virtually any voice he chooses, and, if you're not careful, you may be lured to a life of damnation rather than to a life of eternal bliss.

God warns us not to listen to the pretenders to His throne; for they are villainous thieves. Their purpose is to steal, destroy, maim and murder. Their promises are false promises, but they can be oh so tempting, so very convincing. God, on the other hand, sent His Son as a shepherd to lead us to green pastures and safety. He sacrificed His own life that we might thrive.

When God calls each of us to enter the gate to His kingdom, He is beckoning us to follow Him to a life eternal. Are you still unsure which voice to follow? ASK God to reveal Himself. Then BE STILL and LISTEN to His SPIRIT speak to you. His revelation will come in so many ways, be alert and observant. You can't miss Him. God has evidenced His love for us by being our divine shepherd. Where love is demonstrated in your life, the Spirit of God is there.

**Can you hear Him now? Then follow His voice and you will become a member of His eternal flock.**

## NEITHER DO I CONDEMN YOU | JUNE 18

*"Jesus straightened up and ask her, 'Woman, where are they? Has no one condemned you?' 'No one sir,' she said. 'Then neither do I condemn you,' Jesus answered, 'Go now and leave your life of sin.'" John 8: 10 & 11*

---

This is one of my favorite verses. Have you ever felt unfairly persecuted or condemned? We all have. Sometimes, we fail to express ourselves well. On other occasions, our thoughts, though well-articulated, are, nevertheless, misconstrued. And then there are those times when we have indeed erred, but our misstep has been blown way out of proportion.

This story involves a woman who was caught in the act of adultery. There was never a question as to her guilt. A pious group of lay people and Pharisees brought her in front of Jesus and the crowd that had gathered so that she could be stoned for her transgression. The group was feeling holy and righteous; for the Law of Moses specifically stipulated that those caught in such an act were to be stoned to death. The fact is that, in some countries, this punishment is still meted out. It is called Sharia law. As the group continued to ask Him what His opinion was regarding this woman's sin, Jesus bent down and began writing on the ground with His finger. His response was: "If any one of you is without sin, let him be the first to throw a stone at her." He then bent down again and started to write. Theologians have conjectured that Jesus was writing about every person in the crowd's sins. Others have theorized that Jesus was writing the Ten Commandments. Whatever He wrote, the crowd came closer to read it, and, soon, every one of them departed from the scene. From the elders to the youngsters, they all left in shame. Only Jesus remained.

Jesus is telling you right now that you are free to live a life of no more guilt because He has pardoned you. He has forgiven your sins in the past, present and future. That is why He is your Savior. There may be stone hurlers in your life that can't wait to throw the first stone. Jesus, given that He was without sin, could have cast the first stone. Instead, He said to the adulterer: **"I do not condemn you.** Go now and leave your life of sin." Remember this, and regardless of your sin, if you condemn you are ungodly. Anyone who condemns you is ungodly. Condemnation is not of God. No matter how vile and heinous your sin may be, God saved you.

**God is extending His NON-condemnatory message to you today.** He is telling you He came not to condemn but to save you. You can now leave your accusers and walk in His light, for He has saved you from the condemnation of the ungodly.

## I COULD SEE | JUNE 19

*"He replied, 'the man they call Jesus made some mud and put it on my eyes. He told me to go to Siloam and wash. So I went and washed, and then I could see.'" John 9: 11*

Jesus healed a blind man. It created such a controversy among the Pharisees that they did an investigation. The issue, at least nominally, was that Jesus had undertaken this healing on the Sabbath, and apparently this was not the first time that He had performed a healing on that holy day. Many at the time believed that disability such as blindness was God's retribution for sins of either the parents or the actual sufferer. It's a notion that we see in any number of verses of the Bible. God is portrayed as judge, jury and executioner.

Jesus acknowledges that there is sin throughout the world, and those sins are virtually countless. Jesus was attempting to shift the focus from the sins committed to the saving power, the healing power of God. He underscores the fact that, while physical blindness can be debilitating, the malady that many more suffer from is spiritual blindness.

We live in an age of "gotchas." Many cities now have so-called red-light cameras. Before long, cameras will be watching our every move, waiting to pounce on us for the slightest infraction. Many feel that the age of "Big Brother" is virtually upon us. All too often, we place so much emphasis on apprehension and punishment and far too little on healing.

The United States has the dubious distinction of imprisoning a higher percentage of its population than any other nation. The recidivism hovers at 80% of them end right back in prison. We are merely warehousing them. It is obvious our country is not seeing the truth about how to rehabilitate prisoners. Fortunately, there are some prison ministries administering salvation for those incarcerated. That's a start.

God wants to change our spiritual blindness into spiritual sight. He wants you to see Him and know Him. When it comes to rehabilitating the most scorned in our nation, we have a rather poor track record. Perhaps we should seek the help of the Author of Healing. Clearly, His track record is a good deal better than our own. Only God is able to change the most hardened criminal. That includes not only those imprisoned in our penal system.

We all need a change of heart. And that comes only through God's Spirit. I pray you can see God for who He truly is. **He wants to heal your blindness so you can not only see again but see Him.**

## SAVED THE BEST FOR LAST | JUNE 20

*"Everyone brings out the choice wine first and then the cheaper wines after the guests have had too much to drink; but you have saved the best till now." John 2: 10*

---

John writes that Jesus performed His first miracle at a wedding at Cana in Galilee. During the course of the wedding celebration, Jesus' mother tells him they have run out of wine. Jesus replied to her that His time has not yet come, a response his mother appeared to brush aside. She next directs the servants to do whatever Jesus asked of them. Jesus then instructed the servants to fill six stone jars, the jars used for ceremonial washing. Each of these jars held between 20 to 30 gallons. The servants filled each jar to the brim. Then He instructed them to draw some out and bring it to the master of the banquet.

In the lengthy wedding celebrations that were traditional in the First Century, it was customary to set before the guests the best foods and drink early and as the guests imbibed in the drinks; their taste buds became less sensitive to the drinks which were being served. Their sense of taste became dulled. Now, it seems that the master of the banquet, most likely the father who was paying the bill, noted the difference in taste. The wine apparently was better than the wine served earlier. This was indeed an extraordinary occurrence. Have you noticed in social gatherings or in concert productions, the best food or performer is saved for last?

We are provided with some rather interesting insights here. First, it was the third day of the wedding celebration. Christ was resurrected on the third day. Second, the wine, typically red in color, was deemed to be symbolic of the blood Christ would shed for the atonement of our sins. Third, you'll recall that Jesus has proclaimed: "My time has not yet come." Jesus had a mission to accomplish and a timetable to fulfill that mission. He looked somewhat askance at matters that might distract Him from His mission. The master of the banquet declared: "You saved the best for last."

Throughout His earthly stay, Jesus always did the very best for us. **God, in His time, also saved the very best for last. He gave us His only Son.** God still has another best He's saved for us. He promised to give it to us and that's His soon return to take us home to be with Him.

That will be a celebration and feast that will top all parties ever thrown. God certainly has a way of giving the very best. I can't wait to experience it.

## HE WELCOMES SINNERS | JUNE 21

*"But the Pharisees and the teachers of the law muttered, 'This man welcomes sinners and eats with them.'" Luke 15: 2*

---

Have you ever felt as if you were out of sync, not fitting in, an outcast, unwelcome, unacceptable, cut off from those whom society tend to favor? It gives one the feeling of being alone, and that is an absolutely terrible feeling. During Jesus time, there were leaders who acted as though they were the gate keepers to mankind's salvation. They took it upon themselves to decide who would be saved and who would be condemned. Even to this day, we tend to draw near to the popular, the renowned because this underscores the notion (in our minds) that we belong. Conversely, by shunning those whom society deems to be less desirable – the derelicts, the convicts, the embezzlers and the like – we protect ourselves (again, in our own minds) from being thought of in a similar light – guilt by association, if you will.

Is there a chance that you may fall under one of the less-favored categories? Of course not, you are quick to point out. You are a regular churchgoer, you tithe, you feed the hungry during Thanksgiving and Christmas, you provide clothing to the needy. You're one of the "good guys," one of the "guys" in a white hat. The fact is that the tithing and donating clothes and the like are indeed good things; they are to be encouraged. They are, however, somewhat passive in nature. Moreover, the people who benefit from such acts of kindness are typically those who are down on their luck more so than those whom society would prefer to disregard.

Jesus sought out these very people. He not only sought them out to hand them food, clothing or healing but He wanted to sup with them. God did not come for the saint and sinless people. He came for sinners. God was their Savior. He wanted to save the sinner from the Pharisees and teachers of the law. In other words, He wants a close relationship with them. He wants to restore those whom society might cast asunder. He sees them all as children of God and worthy of saving. Luke 19: 10 says: "For the Son of Man came to seek and to save what was lost." Are you feeling lost and unworthy? Is your past haunting your thinking and stifling your relationship with others, with God? Friend, stop fretting and wrestling with God; He said, He loves you and wants to welcome you into His fold. Won't you take Him at His word? He really means it.

**Whether you are a sinner or saint, Jesus came to welcome you back home with Him. Won't you come back home to where you belong?** Now let's sup with Him.

## YOU ARE WELL AGAIN | JUNE 22

*"Later Jesus found him at the temple and said to him, 'See, you are well again. Stop sinning or something worse may happen to you.'" John 5: 14*

---

How old are you? Have you reached the ripe old age of 38? Today's text is a story of a lame man, a man who could not walk. Can you imagine being chronically ill for 38 years? Many of you have suffered for even longer and see no hope for a cure.

As an observant Hebrew, Jesus was in Jerusalem for one of the three required feasts. There is near the "Sheep Gate" a pool, which in Aramaic is called Bethesda. Jesus witnessed a great number of disabled people lying there: the blind, lame, paralyzed -- all types of invalids. The belief then was an angel would come and stir the waters at unpredictable times. The first to touch the water during this stirring moment would be healed. Jesus noticed this invalid and asked him, "Do you want to be healed?" The man reasoned no one was there to take him to the water when it was stirred. Jesus told him, "Get up! Pick up your mat and walk." Immediately the man was cured. He picked up his mat and walked.

Bethesda may be interpreted as "House of Mercy." Jesus shows mercy where people seek mercy. Are you suffering from a malady that's haunted you for the past year or a lifetime? Do you want to be healed? The same Jesus is asking you the same question today. We wait patiently as the man in the pool of Bethesda did. What is unique about this man is Jesus' comment on his sinful ways. Jesus warned Him, if he didn't stop sinning, an even worse fate would befall him. Jesus knew this man's heart. He knew the history of his disability. We can surmise this man must have done something to contract his malady. Some of our illness is preventable through proper health, moral and commandment keeping practices. Granted there is some illness that happens through no fault of the person.

I am reminded of a friend who contracted a social disease through his promiscuity. After receiving treatment and he was healed, I cautioned him to be prudent and avoid such practice. Six months later, he contracted the same disease. He confessed he was an addict and could not control his behavior. God wants us to live a sanctified life through His commandments and laws. He wants to heal your physical and spiritual maladies as well. God is the Author of health. **Even when your illness is a result of your own doing God can heal you. Trust Him.** When you place your trust in God you will "See, you are well again." Now stop doing what caused your illness before something worst happens to you.

## THE DESIRES OF YOUR HEART | JUNE 23

*"Delight yourself in the Lord and He will give you the desires of your heart." Psalms 37: 4*

What gives you pleasure? What gives you joy? What is the desire of your heart? I have a weakness for ice cream. There's something about ice cream that soothes away any cares for one brief shining moment. One of my greatest delights when I was on a mission trip in the orient was to enjoy mangoes for breakfast, lunch and dinner. In between meals I also enjoyed indulging in mango ice cream. Someone once speculated of the 12 fruits found in the tree of life in heaven, one of them would be a mango. I suppose you can conclude one of the desires of my heart is food.

The Author of Love wants nothing but the best for us. He knows your needs even before you ask Him. He knows what you lack and what can fill the empty feeling inside your soul. God is also merciful and longsuffering. He will wait for you and let you do your thing before you realize your mistake. God says He is the Way, the Truth and the Life. The only way you can know Him is to know His Son. He sent His Son in our world to mingle with us and to sup with us. God knew what would satisfy our longing and void in our lives. God wants you to experience the life in Him; for it is abundant and eternal.

If you are seeking your future spouse, longing for a child, wanting healing, in search of relief from poverty and spiritual disease, emptiness, wanting recognition and acceptance, whatever, you need to know the source of all of these things, His Son, Jesus Christ. God is inviting you to learn of Him; for His way is the right way, He speaks only the truth, which will make all His promises come true. And if you are missing something in your life that you can't understand, then remember He is the life. In Him are your life's desires. He wants to give you not only the abundant life but life eternal. To live forever with Him is a desire worth pursuing. We desire much in what the world offers. We are tempted to pursue things this world entices us. Sometimes things we desire are very difficult to let go. All these allurements pale in comparison to knowing God. I know, sometimes the road to salvation seems so difficult and discouraging. We feel like giving up. It's seems easier to just say "I feel better without God's rules. Keep doing what you're complaining about but give God equal time. Then you will see the difference in the life with God and the life without God. Either ways, you cannot fail. God is the guarantee of success. Can you delight yourself in the Lord?

Only when you accept the life He is giving you will you finally know and understand what the desire of your heart is. **Knowing Him will give you the desires of your heart.**

## THE RESURRECTION AND THE LIFE | JUNE 24

*"When Mary reached the place where Jesus was and saw him, she fell at his feet and said, 'Lord, if you had been here, my brother would not have died.'" John 11: 32*

---

I have attended a number of funerals of friends and relatives. The grief from the loss of a loved one can be unbearable. However, it wasn't until death came to one of my parents that I was able to identify with Mary's and Martha's statement to Jesus.

I was away on a trip when my brother called to inform me that our father had passed away. My immediate thought was similar to Mary's. Why, I asked, had the Lord not responded to my prayers that my father be healed? Mary had said: "Lord, if you had been here, my brother would not have died." Take note how Jesus responded: "When Jesus saw her weeping and the Jews who had come along with her also weeping, he was deeply moved in spirit and, at the same time, troubled," "where have you laid him?" he asked. "Come and see, Lord," they replied (vss. 33-34).

It wasn't until mother passed away that I identified with Jesus in verse 35, "Jesus wept." I wept for my mother's passing. I too have hope to see mother again when Christ returns to wake her up from the grave. I'm sure you have the same longing for a loved one who passed away. For everyone who has ever died, Jesus was there weeping. Some have questioned why, if Jesus proved His ability to raise man from the dead with Lazarus, why has He not done the same for all of the departed. God will. It is only a matter of time. You must believe Him and His promise of a resurrection day.

There is one key fact Jesus wanted us to know on the day He performed the miracle of Lazarus. He said in verse 25 "I am the resurrection and the life. He who believes in me will live, even though he dies; and whoever lives and believes in me will never die." What a wonderful promise. Jesus summed it up in this verse. He IS Life. Someday Jesus will call Lazarus' name out again and this time he will live forever. He will also call our loved ones from the graves to live forever. What a blessed hope. Are you convinced?

The real good news in the story of Lazarus is not the miracle in raising him from the dead but Jesus' statement that anyone who believes in Him will have life eternal. **Focus not on the dead person but on the resurrection and giver of life...Jesus.**

## SAMSON'S PASSION | JUNE 25

*"'O Sovereign LORD, remember me. O God, please strengthen me just once more, and let me with one blow get revenge on the Philistines for my two eyes.' Samson said, 'Let me die with the Philistines.' Then he pushed with all his might, and down came the temple on the rulers and all the people in it. Thus he killed many more when he died than while he lived." Judges 16: 28 & 30*

---

The life of Samson was certainly tainted with deceit, violence and tragedy. Here was a man dedicated as a child to God and yet he went astray from that blessing. Samson fell madly in love with a woman named Delilah. Day in and day out she nagged him to tell her the secret of his strength. Three times Samson gave her reasons for his strength that were false. Finally, Samson succumbed to Delilah's entreaties, and, during a moment of weakness, he disclosed is secret, and, in so doing, violated a sacred trust. "No razor has ever been used on my head. Because I have been a Nazirite set apart to God since birth. If my head were shaved, my strength would leave me, and I would become as weak as any other man." While he was asleep on her lap, she called a man to shave off Samson's seven braids of hair. When he awoke from his sleep his strength was gone. He did not know the Spirit of the Lord had departed from him. (In truth, I believe the Spirit never leaves us. I believe when we stray away from God, we will be vulnerable to the ungodliness of this world). The Philistines subdued him. They seized him and gouged out his eyes. He spent his time as a slave in prison.

God has set us apart to be called His chosen children. We are to be an example to the entire human race. Patiently God deals with each of us. God wants us to learn of Him. God constantly admonishes us to be vigilant and watchful, for Satan is a roaring lion who wants to devour us. Samson was physically the strongest man on Earth; but in terms of temperance, self-control, veracity and faith, Samson was among the weakest.

"The real greatness of the man is measured by the power of the feeling that he controls, not by those that control him." (Patriarchs & Prophets, by E.G. White, P. 633). **Samson's true strength was not from his hair but from God. His hair was symbolic of God. Whatever it is that controls your passion, make sure it's from God.**

**All power and strength comes from God.** When you remove God in your life, you become vulnerable to self. **Samson's passion would have saved him had it been for the LORD.**

## **REMEMBER LOT'S WIFE** | JUNE 26

*"But Lot's wife looked back, and she became a pillar of salt."* Genesis 19: 26

---

There are numerous interpretations of why Lot's wife is even mentioned in the Bible. She has no name. She is only referred to as Lot's wife. However, just her single act of turning around to look back reveals a great deal about the character of this woman.

In order to obtain a clearer picture of what led to her destruction; let's look back a few chapters before this catastrophe. Lot and Abraham lived in the same valley. Abraham was Lot's uncle. With their family and herds of cattle and sheep expanding, the resources in the valley could not sustain the two families. They agreed to go their separate ways. Abraham asked Lot to choose first. Whichever direction Lot chose Abraham would go the opposite way. Lot sized up the "better "land and chose the whole plain of the Jordan. It resembled the "Garden of Eden," lush, fertile and abundant. With every imaginable goods to make one's life effortless, Lot and his wife lived in luxury.

There is nothing wrong with living the good life. Yet, Lot's wife had her priorities backward. She desired the luxuries of Sodom more than the deliverance of God. She was destroyed because she looked back at the city she was leaving in direct defiance of God's command. Thus she was turned into a pillar of salt. God did not turn her in to a pillar of salt. It was her rebellion that turned her into a pillar of salt. She went contrary to God's word. She rebelled. Anytime you remove yourself from God's presence and choose your own will, you are inviting the wiles of this world. The wiles of this world is not life but death. Please place our entire confidence right now in God.

God wants you to trust Him, listen to His call and follow His word. It may be tempting to choose riches or fame or power over God, but these things are fleeting. They are of the season. God's kingdom is eternal. To choose Satan's path is to choose short-term gains over long-term bliss.

The Author of Love beckons you to make the right choice. God knows the end from the beginning. He knows your heart. Do not trust in your ways but rely on the God who knows best and cares for your well-being. You will be tempted each day like Lot's wife. The decision you make may have eternal consequences. Choose wisely. Let God choose for you.

When temptation beckons, **remember Lot's wife. Even more, remember the Author of Love.**

## SHALL WE DANCE? | JUNE 27

*"Then Miriam the prophetess, Aaron's sister, took a tambourine in her hand, and all the women followed her, with tambourines and dancing." Exodus 15: 20*

---

Years ago, I worked for a very large insurance company. This company had so many employees that, just in the room which I was situated, there were literally hundreds of employees. One day, I chanced upon a fellow employee who was of my faith. This, of course, gave us a common bond.

In one of our meetings, while we were exchanging information regarding a case on which we were both working, she happened to mention to me how concerned she was over the turmoil that had erupted over the issue of the appropriateness of the music which the young adults wished to play in her church. In fact, she said, matters had become so testy that there was real potential for the church's splitting up. She acknowledged that she was at once troubled and confused. On the one hand, she enjoyed the fellowship of the youth and counted many of them as her friends. However, she had doubts about the music they were playing – particularly, the use of guitars in church.

In our text today, we see a large group of people who had just experienced God's miraculous salvation. In their celebration, Miriam could barely contain the jubilation in her soul. She and several other women took up tambourines and began dancing while extolling God. Psalms 50: 23: "Whoever offers praise," says God, "glorifies." Miriam, with all sincerity, was in fact glorifying God.

Have similar debates arisen in your church? Have you debated the appropriateness of certain music or dance or even attire? Is there a "litmus test" here? Actually, there is, and it is rather simple. As it was with Miriam, ask yourself whether or not the purpose of the act is to glorify God. God does not look at actions alone. God knows what is in each and every one of our hearts, and, for Him, motive and intent is far more important than deeds. We may observe external dancing and conclude what is acceptable and what is not acceptable dancing but always remember, it's only God who knows the heart of each person. **Whatever you do, whatever your motives or actions, whatever you say, make sure you do it all for the glory of God. God wants to give you all of His good pleasures. God never holds back any good thing from you. Just know where your heart lies.**

"Not unto us, O Lord, not unto us, but unto your name give glory, for your mercy, and for your truth's sake. Psalms 114: 1.

## ON GOLDEN CALF | JUNE 28

*"Then the LORD relented and did not bring on his people the disaster he had threatened." Exodus 32: 14*

---

We seldom fail to blame God whenever disaster strikes. After all, if God is all-knowing, all powerful and in control, He can certainly prevent disasters from befalling his subjects. The above-referenced verse lends proof to that notion. But is this what God is really saying? When you read the verses prior to verse 14, you will understand the context in which this text was written. The Israelites who instigated the request to create a calf were a mixed multitude from Egypt. They were accustomed to seeing and touching a representation of their deity. They influenced Aaron to make the golden calf. Aaron made a call throughout the camp for gold. Once in his hands, he melted them all and fashioned a golden calf. The people then in mayhem and revelry worshiped the idol. Just that morning the people were fed manna from God. Last night they ate their meat of quail. They could see the cloud of the LORD hovering over the mountain and they could hear the mighty roar of God. Yet, they still wanted an idol.

Back during the Reagan years, certain insiders were known to use the letters W.W.J.D. Familiar? Actually, not. It meant "What Would Joan Do?" Joan was Joan Quigley, who was alleged to be Nancy Reagan's astrologer. Supposedly, the First Lady called on Quigley after the 1981 attempt by John Hinckley to assassinate the President. Quigley was rumored to have told Nancy that she (Quigley) might have prevented the attack, had she been consulted. Nancy was later reported to have said: "I was doing everything I could think of to protect my husband and keep him alive." No doubt, her motives were indeed pure. However, that astrologer has as much power over our futures as the golden calf or eras past.

Horoscopes, Ouija Boards, Tarot cards, and the like are like idols, and, although we may think we dabble in such practices just for fun, they are in fact an affront to God. Be extremely careful and cognizant on what you dabble in, for what you focus and worship or who you worship is a reflection of your faith in God. Yes, we all at one time or another had our "golden calf" moment. Thank God for His grace and forgiveness.

**God gives us the freedom to choose. When you choose God, there will be no need for false gods or tangible golden calf;** He is the TRUE LIVING GOD.

## THE LOVE OF MONEY | JUNE 29

*"For the love of money is a root of all kinds of evil. Some people, eager for money, have wandered from the faith and pierced themselves with many griefs." I Timothy 6: 10*

---

"Money makes our world go around, the world go round, the world go round." This was a famous lyrics from the musical "Cabaret." But alas, life is NOT a cabaret. Were it indeed money that made the world go round, we'd have titled this book: "The Author of Money," hardly an apt title.

It has been said more than a few times that every person has a price. Can you be "bought?" Do you have a price? I once read about a couple who sold their child for $25. They were desperate for drug money. Our society extols the almighty dollar. Some people work two or three jobs in order to have the things money can buy. There's nothing wrong with having money. It is a means to an end. It's when it becomes a focal point in your life that makes it harmful for you.

Can you imagine planning a vacation in which one spouse stays home to tend to business? David did precisely that. He had his own thriving electronics business. He had everything his money could buy. One Easter weekend, David's wife and kids were away on one of their "family" excursions…without David. After dining out by himself, David rushed home to work on an especially large order. He promised himself that, once he landed this one, he'd begin to take things easy. Right before bedtime, he began to feel out of sorts. He figured that it was indigestion. He phoned his wife and vowed to phone the doctor in the morning if he didn't feel better. By 3 a.m., it was evident that this was not a case of indigestion, and he dialed 911. His indigestion was in fact a heart attack. Ultimately, David needed a heart transplant. He survived, but it was a costly miscalculation on his part. Are you in the same boat as David? Has the dollar become the center of your life? Money in and of itself can do wonders for your social life and social justice. But set your foundation on Him who is your true provider.

Remember, you cannot take one penny with you, and furthermore, in God's kingdom, your bank account will be to no avail, and they don't take plastic cards. Remember, too, that you have already been bought, so to speak, not with legal tender, however.

Jesus has already paid a price for your salvation. **Love God, use the money He blesses you for His service.**

## FIRST LOVE | JUNE 30

*"For where your treasure is, there will your heart be also." Matthew 6: 21*

Do you remember your first love? As teenagers, our first "crush" or "puppy love" was probably the most unusual emotional feeling you've ever experienced. You may not remember all of the particulars, but you likely remember how you felt. You had butterflies in your stomach whenever you were near the object of your affection. Your whole being was spent on knowing all about the person who desired. Unfortunately, the push to adulthood strained many first time relationships.

As you reached adulthood, the stakes became greater. You were playing for keeps… no mere puppy love. If you've succeeded, you'll end up growing old together. If the marriage ultimately fails, the law gives you a second chance, and, if necessary a third and so on. Some famous entertainers boast of the number of trips they have made to the altar. Ours is an era in which virtually everything is disposable, including relationships.

There was a time when people joined a company and stayed with that company until retirement or death, whichever came first. Today, you're a corporate veteran, if you have five years under your belt. And so are friendships. For too many of us, our relationship with God has become disposable. So-called inter-marriage should be encouraged, some would argue, because it evidences our willingness to treat people of all faiths, colors, nationalities, and, today, even genders with equanimity. However, when inter-marriage specifically involves faith, the compromise that is achieved is often that faith in God is lost. If no religion is observed, then the offspring of that marriage are apt to be raised devoid of Godliness.

That brings us full-circle to that first love who we remember so vividly. We forget sometimes, however, that our real first love was not that "sweet little girl" or that "strapping young lad" we left behind in junior high; our first true love was God. No true love should be disposable in nature. The one love, however, that will stand by us in good times and bad, in sickness and health, as the pledge goes, is the "one who 'brung' us to the party in the first place." God is your first love. God has made you His first love and priority. You are His first love as demonstrated by the cross. There is no one in your entire lifespan and for eternity that will love you more than God.

**Never forget your first love. It is He who teaches us how to love; for He is, after all, the Author of Love.**

## NAME HIM EL | JULY 1

*"O LORD, our Lord, How majestic is your name in all the earth! You have set your glory above the heavens" Psalms 8: 1*

---

What's in a name? How did you come up with a name for your child? Did you choose a popular name? Parents name each child according to what's popular but unique. According to the Social Security Administration statistics as of May 2010, the 100 most popular names for boys were: (I'll only list the top five) Jacob, Michael, Ethan, Joshua and Noah. The top six for girls were: Sophie, Emma, Isabella, Emily, Madison and Ava.

Your name is important. In some respects, it describes who you are. Certain names can have a negative effect on a child as he or she grows up. Children can be unmerciful when it comes to teasing a name. My parents named me James, which is an English name, related to the Hebrew name Jacob (Yaacov in Hebrew). Later, I added the nickname my father bestowed, Joc, in order to have my own identity.

There are 43 names in Hebrew pertaining to the name of God and over 400 descriptive names. The "El" before the name of God means power. Some of the names given to God are Elohim; the God who makes and keeps Covenants with His Creation. (Genesis 1: 1). El Shaddai means the Mighty One who nourishes (Genesis 17: 1). El-Elyon means the Most High God who reached down to save us (Genesis 14: 18-22). Adonai from Hababkkuk refers to Lord and Master or Husband. This word Adonai (God)is used over 6,800 times in the Bible. Then there is Yahweh which also means Jehovah. It is spelled YHWH because there are no vowels in Hebrew. God is called El-Gebor, the Mighty Warrior (Isaiah 42: 13).

Some Christians believe there is no other name under heaven that man can be saved except through the name of Jesus. Do you believe there will be people in heaven who were saved never knowing the true name of their God? I do. As Christians we know His name but there are many who per fate, grew up in societies that never had the opportunity to hear of Jesus but lived a Godly Spirit-filled life and then died. A just God does not save a person by their knowledge of a name but by their receptivity to God's Spirit that dwells in them. God's name is majestic and powerful when used in the context of His Holiness. Sometimes, we use His name in vain. When someone mentions your name, does your character precede you?

**Whatever name you call Him, what is most important is that you KNOW Him and understand the true character behind His name, which is Love.**

## FATHER FORGIVE THEM | JULY 2

*"Jesus said, 'Father, forgive them, for they do not know what they are doing.'" "And they divided up His clothes by casting lots." Luke 23: 34*

Recently, I had occasion to view Mel Gibson's movie "The Passion of the Christ." As you may be aware, the movie purports to depict the final 12 hours of Christ's life on earth. This movie has proven to be a magnet for critics, who have claimed that it exaggerates the Gospels, over-dramatizes the crucifixion and deliberately incites hatred against Jews. Abraham Foxman of the Anti-Defamation League was quoted as saying: "It's as if the Jews ruled, the Romans were only pawns in the Jewish hands." Gibson emphatically denied charges of anti-Semitism and insisted that the movie was a faithful Biblical account. His recent behavior proves contrary. No matter what one's behavior or thinking may be, one's motives can only be judged by God. God is a very forgiving God.

The four Gospels (Matthew, Mark, Luck and John) did not capture the visual effect Mel Gibson's movie portrayed. The controversy the film produced notwithstanding, it would seem to be a fact that Jesus tolerated a great deal of pain and humiliation, and one almost has to wonder why? Just hours before that scene (John 19: 9-11), Pilate met Jesus and inquired: "Do you realize that I have the power either to free you or to crucify you?" Jesus replied: "You would have no power over me if it were not given to you from above. Therefore the one who handed me over to you is guilty of a greater sin." Jesus was saying that, at any time, He had the power over Pilate to allow him to live or die. Pilate did not comprehend what Jesus was telling him. Jesus did not exercise that power. Why?

God's love for humankind compelled Him to bear the burden of the cross. When you love someone very deeply, you, too, might endure severe pain, even death, in order to save that person. Jesus best evidenced His amazing love for us when He said: "Father forgive them, for they know not what they do." There are times when it would appear that we, too, don't know what we are doing; for we, too, have, over the ages, forsaken our loving God. God's willingness to forgive us is quite amazing. That is how God loves us. Can you forgive like God? Are you still holding a grudge with a family member, relative, friend or stranger? Forgive them whether you feel like it or not. Start by forgiving yourself. If you're struggling to forgive then turn it over to God. To not forgive is because you are hardening your heart. Let His Spirit control that will.

**To capture the true essence of God's forgiveness, it can only be realized personally through the indwelling of His Spirit in you.**

## **AN EXAMPLE OF LOVE** | JULY 3

*"I have set you an example that you should do as I have done for you." John 12: 15*

Jesus' life was but an example. He poured water into a basin and began to wash His disciples' feet, drying them with a towel he'd wrapped around His waist. Jesus was the very antithesis of how we regard success today. The successful business person, for instance, demonstrates his leadership by way of being aggressive, dominant, crafty and cunning. To be subservient and placating are tantamount to failing. Have you heard of the phrase "He's a doormat"? That's a person that people walk all over. Do you ever feel used? Are you always the one giving in and never getting your way?

It would seem, therefore, that God's ways and the ways of modern business are polar opposites. Jesus declared that, in order to be first, you have to start out last. For those who recall the so-called Arab oil embargo of decades past, the image of lines of cars, literally stretched around the whole blocks, is a memory we've tried to erase. Can you imagine deliberately allowing all who chose to do so to cut in line ahead of you? Jesus would have done precisely that.

We've actually defined an entire generation based upon an egocentric, call it, outlook on life…the "Me Generation." Everything revolves around me. Self- esteem is where it's at. The sun rises and sets in my backyard. I worship at the altar of Donald Trump. You don't like it? You're fired. If things don't go right, don't blame me. I think every generation since the fall of man has been a "Me Generation."

This, clearly, is not God's way. Christ demonstrated that, for us to be fed, we must first feed others. For us to be clothed, we must first clothe others. If we are to be forgiven, we must first forgive others. How are we to love the unlovable – the outcasts, the incorrigibles, the aggressors, the back stabbers, the fakers and the misfits?

Jesus set the example. The same way He loved us, we are commanded to do likewise. God, through His Son Jesus, came to earth so that you might know His love for you and me. "Having loved His own who were in the world, He now showed them the full extent of His love." (John 13: 1) He is the very embodiment of Love. He is God. You can have that same love of God in you.

**God is love. Follow His example of love.**

## **FREEDOM** | JULY 4

*"Live as free men, but do not use your freedom as a cover up for evil, live as servants of God. Show proper respect to everyone: Love the brotherhood of believers, fear God, honor the king." 1 Peter 23: 16 & 17*

---

Today we celebrate our country's emancipation. The History of the United States of America is founded on freedom. Our constitution guarantees each citizen the right to life, liberty and the pursuit of happiness. The Bill of Rights is the first ten amendments to the United States Constitution. It was introduced by James Madison in 1789. The establishment of these rights plays a key role in government and American law. It is our nation's foundation.

God gave us the Ten Commandments, not to confine us, but rather to demonstrate His love for us. The Ten Commandments are in fact laws of love that govern God's universe. "Now all has been heard; here is the conclusion of the matter: Fear God and keep his commandments; for this is the whole duty of man. For God will bring every deed into judgment, including every hidden thing, whether it is good or evil." (Ecclesiastes 12: 13 & 14). God recognized that, absent certain rules, there would be chaos, and love cannot thrive against a background of chaos. To follow God's laws will bring peace, joy, harmony, and freedom. "Oh! How I love your laws, it is my meditation all the day." (Psalms 119: 91). David followed God's law daily and used it to govern his nation. This gave David his wisdom: "You, through your commandments make me wiser than my enemies." (vs. 98).

Jesus gave His life as atonement for our mistakes so we might enjoy the freedom and not be slaves to sin. God said to maintain that freedom we must follow His will and have faith in Him and His word. It seems God's freedom is in contra to man's freedom. To experience and be one in God's freedom you must trust Him and rely on Him in everything you do. You can feel free and in control of your life but without God's freedom governing your spirit, you are still imprisoned. You can also go through the motions of keeping His commandments but devoid of His Spirit. This true freedom is a daily process of faith in Him. Love is what motivated God to save us. That motivation should also be ours.

When God returns will He find Faith? Will He find a commandment-keeping people? "Here is the patience of the saints; here are those who keep the commandments of God and the faith of Jesus." (Revelations 14: 12). **It is a strong abiding faith in God that to live in freedom is to obey His commandments, respect everyone and live as servants of God's love.**

## HOW TO KNOW GOD | JULY 5

*"Now this is eternal life: that they may know you, the only true God, and Jesus Christ, whom you have sent." John 17. 3*

We are half way through these devotionals. Do you feel as if you have begun to know God or to know Him even better? Do you have a better picture of Him? Are you comfortable with Him? Has God drawn closer to you? It is not difficult to know God. He is constantly beckoning you with His Spirit. He is forever knocking at the door of your heart because He wants to sup with you. Do you hear His knock? Do you hear His voice? Do you feel his presence? God is the same God who walked with our forefathers. He is even closer to us today than when He was physically here on earth. He lives within your heart. If you feel as if you still don't know Him and you are still finding it difficult to comprehend who God is, then let's review what we've learned.

God is love. His whole essence speaks of His love for us. God has told you that He knew you while you were still in your mother's womb (actually even before the foundations of this world was created). He sacrificed His earthly existence so as to save you from sin. There are those who believe God performs wondrous magic every day, but God is not a magician. Do not expect Him to turn snowflakes into diamonds or deliver you a winning lottery ticket. Certainly, He could do any of those things, but this is not what your relationship with God is based upon. God has in fact revealed Himself throughout history and even in our day. However, it is not always by way of parting seas and burning bushes.

God sent His only Son to live among us and to serve as an example of how to live a life full of meaning and purpose. Jesus' words, as captured by His disciples, still ring true. The Gospels are a wonderful lesson plan for us to study, reflect on, and, most importantly, act upon. However, we must first be willing to receive God in our hearts if we are to accept both His word and His Spirit. TO KNOW GOD is first to have faith in Him. It is impossible to please God without faith. That faith does not stem from witnessing miracles or feeling it, but rather from the lesson plan that His Son lived and has given us. God initiates the first move by giving us the desire to know Him. His life served as an example for all of us. Follow the Author of Love. Go share His love to your neighbor.

As Pastor Aiden Wilson Tozer said **"You can see God from anywhere if your mind is set to love and obey Him."**

## HANNAH'S VOW | JULY 6

*"And she made a vow, saying "O Lord Almighty, if you will only look upon your servant's misery and remember me, and not forget your servant but give her a son, then I will give him to the LORD for all the days of his life, and no razor will ever be used on his head." Samuel 1: 11*

---

The story of Samuel takes up two books in the Bible. Hannah was the wife of Elkanah, who also had another wife, Peninnah. Peninnah had children but Hannah had none. Penninah mocked Hannah for being barren. Hannah in her pain and sorrow pleaded to God to give her a child. She made a vow that she would return her son to the Lord for a lifetime of service. God heard her prayer and she bore a son and named him Samuel.

Being a childless woman was considered a curse from God during those days. My "auntie" lived a few houses down the same street from us. She was about the same age as my mother but she never had children. One day, I came home and saw mother comforting my aunt. She was in tears; for she wanted to have a child but could not. She asked mother if she would give up one of us because mother had six kids and she had none. In ancient societies, children were bought and sold like an item in the market. As much as mother pitied and sympathized with my aunt, she could not part with any of her children. However, mother in her wisdom and compassion found a way to placate my aunt. She allowed her to babysit our youngest sibling as often as she wanted to.

Why do we blame God for barren wombs? Do you think it is God who creates such anomalies? This world is not perfect. We have inherited the "barren sin." My aunt was no exception. However, through the years many children went through her household and to this day many refer to her as "ma." She even adopted some of them. There are some who are even closer to her than their own biological mother. She learned the valuable lesson of God's way and kept her faith and trust in God.

Whether you be childless, loveless, penniless, God has filled your barren life through His Son. There is nothing more God can do or give you that He hasn't already done. Stop moping and feeling empty, He has already answered all your doubts. Focus on His goodness. Share your knowledge of God to a barren soul.

**Receive His Son and you will never be barren ever again.** Your life will be full and complete. You no longer need to pray "Hannah's vow."

## WHO IS MY MOTHER? | JULY 7

*"He remarked, 'Who is my mother? Who are my brothers? He pointed to his disciples. 'Look!' he said, 'these are my mother and brothers.' Then he added, 'anyone who obeys my father in heave is my brother, sister and mother.'" Matthew 12: 48-50*

---

If you have noticed our world is imperfect, upside down and out of sync. There are ideals that appear unrealistic. Certain advocates agree that the ideal home is a two parent home with children being raised by a stay at home mother while the father is the bread winner. However, that is not realistic in today's society. Families are broken, parents have become irresponsible and children are disobedient. Countless children have grown up in a one parent household, which often affects them throughout their lives. Sadly some never recover from this void.

I can recall having lunch with a friend of mine who expressed his sorrow that his parents never said "I love you" to him. His parents told him he was an inconvenience. His brother was favored over him. He felt discounted. This man is now middle aged. He is displaying the effects of his unloved childhood. There are homes where children grew up in an intact family. But even those ideals have flaws. Jesus knew the heartache of being rejected. He also knew there would be households without love. He knew there would be children orphaned or from dysfunctional parents and homes.

God sent His Son to gather in the scattered, to love the unloved, and to comfort the dejected. There may be mothers who abandon their new born or children and fathers who go astray. But God said He would never leave us nor forsake us. "Can a mother forget her suckling child, yea they may forget but not God." Love has no blood lines or boundaries or categories or caste systems. Christ was trying to teach His disciples and us that the whole world is one family. Can you treat your enemy, nemesis, stranger or competitor as though they were your mother? The love you crave for sometimes may not come from your biological parent but a stranger, a brother, a sister, a friend or an acquaintance. All who have shown you compassion, mercy, grace and love came from the true source of pure love, God. Wherever love is God is.

**Whenever love is shown or demonstrated, that is your "mother."** Can you accept this? Stop cherishing the ideal of a loving mother or father from your immediate bloodline. They will disappoint you. That is not how God thinks or work. He will send the love you need through a stranger, an acquaintance or a neighbor. Treat them all with love. God is there. So, rise above this earthly fantasy of love only through bloodline and reach out and be a "mother" or "father" to your neighbor. That is real Godly love.

## JOB'S PRAISE TO GOD | JULY 8

*"At this, Job got up and tore his robe and shaved his head. Then he fell to the ground in worship and said, 'naked came I from my mother's womb, and naked I will depart; the Lord gave and the Lord has taken away, may the name of the Lord be praised.' 'In all this, Job did not sin by charging God with wrong doing.'" Job 1: 10-22*

---

Job was a godly man. He shunned evil. He was blameless and upright; he respected God. He had seven sons and three daughters. He was a wealthy man who lived in the land of Uz. Job was so prominent and well known; he was considered a great man in the East.

The story of Job revolves around faith and trust in God. Job did not know God had a meeting. A host of angles were holding a meeting, and Satan happened to be one of the angels in attendance. God asked Satan: "Where did you come from?" Satan answered, "From roaming through the earth and going back and forth in it." Satan's territory is earth. He roams about trying to ascertain who he can destroy. God asked Satan, "Have you noticed my servant Job? There is no one on earth like him; he is blameless and upright, a man who fears God and shuns evil." Satan replied, "Yeah, but take away everything he has and he will surely curse you to your face." God said, "Very well then, everything he has is in your hands, but on the man himself do not lay a finger."

Satan left God's presence and immediately wreaked havoc on his household. Just as one servant reported to Job that all of his 500 oxen and 500 female donkeys were taken by the Sabenas, another servant came to tell him "fire" from God fell from the sky and burned up the 7,000 sheep and servants. A third servant came and reported the Chaldeans raided all his 3,000 camels. The third servant had not even finished reporting to Job all the calamities besetting his household when a fourth servant came and said a mighty windswept in from the desert and struck the four corners of his eldest son's house. All Job's sons and daughters were in the house having a party and they were all killed. At these reports, Job got up and tore his robe and shaved his head and fell to the ground and worshipped God.

Although Job mourned for his lost children, his attitude toward God did not falter or change. He knew His Maker. He concluded his fate was in God's hands. He resolved to trust His maker no matter what. What a man of undeniable faith. The whole history of man is summed up in Job's life experience. We are all Jobs of our day. **We are tested daily and the faith we exercise will reveal the God we serve. When you go through a Job experience, you too can have that undeniable faith.**

## JOB'S SECOND TEST | JULY 9

*"Then the Lord said to Satan, 'Have you considered my servant Job?' There is no one on earth like him; he is blameless and upright, a man who fears God and shuns evil. And he still maintains his integrity, though you incited me against him to ruin him without any reason.'" Job 2: 3*

---

Our story continues with Satan contending that, if he strikes Job's flesh and bones, Job would surely curse God. Yesterday, our story described how Job had lost all of his earthly possessions as well as his children. Job does not know why all this is happening to him. He continues to worship and praise God, nevertheless. Now Satan comes back with what he is certain an ingenious scheme – to wit, if God allows him to inflict physical harm upon Job, Job most certainly will throw in the proverbial towel and blame God.

Some would argue that this is one of the more controversial passages in the Bible. To the casual observer, it might appear that God and Satan are engaged in some kind of sport or contest. Each has apparently placed his bet, so to speak. The only problem is that they are not gambling for chips or money; they are gambling with a man's life – a righteous man at that. Obviously, such behavior is right up Satan's alley. But doesn't this seem out of character for God? Clearly, if He needed to test Job, the first test was test enough. Is this just an ego trip from God?

Most agree that God is NOT on an ego trip. After all, He is God. What is there to prove? Then why indulge Satan's appetite for things sinister? The argument here is that God needs to let Satan and the entire universe, as well as the hosts of angels, know, loud and clear, that when the final tally is taken, righteousness will prevail. God knows that Job is living proof. God also knows that every "Job" experience we are playing out, we will prevail because we have placed our trust and faith in God. There is nothing new under the sun. We are going through a "Job moment" each waking and sleeping day of our lives. History is continually repeating itself with our Job trials. God knows the end from the beginning. You know the outcome of Job's trials. His kingdom doubled. That is the outcome of ours too but a hundred fold.

Even with his wife prodding him to blame God. Job was steadfast in his faith in God. ( Job 2: 9-10) "'Are you still holding on to your integrity? Curse God and die!' Job replied, 'You are talking like a foolish woman. Shall we accept good from God and not trouble?'" **Job knew God. He defended God. A lesson we can all learn when trouble comes our way.** This is the answer to all your questions about the senseless troubles in this world.

## JOB'S TRUE FRIEND | JULY 10

*"When Job's three friends, Eliphaz the Temanite, Bildad the Shuhite and Zophar the Naamathite, heard about all the troubles that had come upon him, they set out from their homes and met together by agreement to go and sympathize with him and comfort him. When they saw him from a distance, they could hardly recognize him; they began to weep aloud, and they tore their robes and sprinkled dust on their heads. Then they sat on the ground with him for seven days and seven nights. No one said a word to him, because they saw how great his suffering was." Job 2: 11-13*

---

Job's friends were shocked at the sight of their friend's sickness. They could hardly recognize him. His body was covered with sores. Sometimes the pain was so unbearable that he would scrape the sores with a shard of pottery. His friends meant well. They stood by him for seven days and nights in total silence sympathizing and empathizing with their friend. Eventually, they could no longer keep silent. In this instance, silence was indeed golden. Hindsight shows that they should have maintained their silence.

Seeking answers to Job's condition, each friend offered his opinion as to why Job was going through this affliction. All three concluded (Job 4: 8 Eliphaz; Job 8: 20 Bildad; Job 11: 14 Zophar): "Those who plow evil and those who sow trouble reap it." Job had sinned and he was being punished for those sins, they exclaimed unanimously. Do you have friends like Job's friends – friends who rush to judgment without fully comprehending the truth? Are you that type of a friend to your friends when they have troubles in their home? When you entertain such thoughts, you do not have a strong faith in God. Right now, clear your mind of such thinking. God is not and never will be the bearer of bad things in your life.

Job, as we know, was righteous and, in these instances, clearly blameless. He was a godly man. He disagreed with his friends' contentions that his situation was recompense for his own sins. He did not, however, blame God. In fact, he defended God (Job 13: 15 KJV): "Though He slay me, Yet will I trust in Him; but I will maintain mine own ways before Him." Quite apparently, Job knew God better than his friends did.

God is your Friend and Savior. He does not want that any should suffer –or perish. **Whenever you are uncertain about God and you have a need to curse Him, remember Job's resoluteness.** (Job 19: 25-27): **"I know that my Redeemer lives and that in the end He will stand upon the earth. And after my skin has been destroyed, yet in my flesh I will see God; I myself will see Him with my own eyes – I, and not another. How my heart yearns within me!"** What manner of faith and trust! You too can be a true friend.

## SPEAKING ABOUT GOD | JULY 11

*"After the Lord had said these things to Job, he said to Eliphaz the Temanite, 'I am angry with you and your friends, because you have not spoken of me what is right, as my servant Job has.'" Job 42: 7*

---

Job's later years are worthy of note. After Job lost everything he had, save for his being, God restored that which Satan had taken. Job regained his health. God blessed Job with seven more sons as well as three more daughters. Moreover, God saw to it that Job's wealth was restored, more than two-fold. Job, of course, would have remained God's faithful servant, had God done nothing of the kind, and the Lord was well aware of this.

Job was troubled that Eliphaz and his friends blamed God for Job's suffering and, at the same time, blamed Job for alleged sins that they assumed were what led to Job's anguish. Clearly, his friends did not understand God. They had the wrong picture of God. They lacked the faith of Job. Oftentimes, when a neighbor or relative falls on hard times, we are quick to play the "blame game." I am guilty of such thinking too. I sometimes cannot help but wonder what this person did to encounter such a malady. We sometimes can't help ourselves, after all that's how we were raised to think. God punishes those who have done wrong. We need to throw out such conclusions from our minds. It's ungodly and comes from the father of lies.

I think back to when my mother was diagnosed with colon cancer. I promised God I would return to Him and do right by Him, if only He would cause my mother to overcome this ordeal. With God, there is no quid pro quo. We scratch His back, so to speak and expect Him to return the favor. God indeed healed my mother, but He never came knocking on my door with a reminder: "You owe Me big-time." I too practiced the "Eliphaz faith." I did not know my Maker as Job knew Him. I am glad God showed me the truth about Him. God is so good. He waited patiently and comforted me through my Eliphaz moment.

God knows our hearts, and God can readily distinguish His fair-weather friends from those who hold Him close to their hearts. **Fortunately for us, the Author of Love is a forgiving God.** God was saddened the vote of no-confidence He had received from Job's friends. He forgave them, nevertheless. Job knew that, one day, he would reunite in Heaven with both his original as well as his new family.

The Author of Love is preparing a place for you in Heaven. Someday you too will reunite with a loved one(s) you've lost. **Can you stay faithful as Job until then? Can you finally speak about God truthfully?**

## THE GOD OF ALL | JULY 12

*"For there is no difference between Jew and Gentile-the same Lord is Lord of ALL and richly blesses ALL who call on him, for EVERYONE who calls on the name of the Lord will be saved." Romans 11: 12 & 13*

---

I remember when I reached my teenage years and everyone started experiencing the new excitement: dating the opposite sex. Those were fun years for some of us and quite pressuring for others. As the years passed and the dating became a bit more serious in nature, I recall my mother's admonition that I should be careful to choose a mate of the same faith.

Her reasons were both social and spiritual. Her words, which I recall almost precisely, were: "Believe me…I know. I've seen enough of these failed marriages." Was my mother correct in her assertion? Does it really make a difference? What is Paul saying in this text? Paul's point is that God loves us ALL. He cares not about race, nationality, gender, social standing, religion, sexual orientation, and the like. He loves us all equally and unconditionally. If that is the case, then why can't we marry of different faith, of different race or different status? Paul is talking beyond earthly nuptials. He wants to elevate us to a higher level of love. You want to marry a person of a different faith, gender or race? Make sure you do it in the Spirit of God's love.

We are ALL welcome in His circle. We are ALL loved and can find grace and acceptance, no matter who we are. The theme of the verse above is that God does not exclude anyone in His kingdom. He is a loving God, and He condemns no man, woman, or child. He is an ALL inclusive God. There is no other God like Him.

God invites us ALL; ALL are offered salvation. What does this mean? You may be a thief or a giver, a person whose generosity is without bounds. You may be obese or skinny, tall or short; brown, yellow, black or white; it matters not. You may be divorced for the third time or married for half a century. You may be rich or poor, straight, or gay, bisexual or even asexual; it is of no matter to God. You may be a bigot, a racist, or a person who is totally devoid of prejudice. You may live in a mansion or live on the streets. You may be devout or agnostic or even atheist. Whatever you are whoever you are, the invitation to come and drink the water of life is extended to ALL. Even the holiest amongst us have sinned and will benefit, therefore, from God's mercy and grace. Do you still left out? Do you believe your "sins" will cost you eternal glory? Are you doubtful of God? God understands. He is an ALL God. In other words, He died for ALL. You are welcomed in His kingdom.

**God welcomes ALL in His kingdom. He is the God of ALL and EVERYONE. (Now, did I miss anyone?)**

## GIFTS OF THE SPIRIT | JULY 13

*"We have different gifts, according to the grace given us. If a man's gift is prophesying, let him use it in proportion to his faith. If it is serving, let him serve; if it is teaching, let him teach; if it is encouraging, let him encourage; if it is contributing to the needs of other, let him give generously; if it is leadership, let him govern diligently; if it is showing mercy, let him do it cheerfully." Romans 12: 6-8*

---

When someone is particularly adept at something, it is not uncommon to refer to that person as "gifted". Typically, we mean by this that the individual has a special talent. People are gifted, too, however, in an entirely different sense, which is to say that they are gifted spiritually. People who are blessed with that first category of talents are typically in it, so to speak, for themselves. Others may in fact enjoy or benefit from that talent, but, more often than not, if others are pleased by or benefit from the talent, it is an unintended consequence.

A spiritual gift, on the other hand, reflects the Spirit of God and has as its foundation a belief and an unconditional trust in God. If your talent happens also to be a spiritual gift, then you are indeed doubly blessed.

My mother was one of those rare people whose talent fit into both categories. She had a tremendous talent for cooking and won frequent praise for her culinary skills. She could make a simple dish taste like a blue ribbon winner in a cooking contest. Her secret, by the way, was in her seasoning. Mother also used her talent as a means of serving her church and her God. Her spiritual gift, you might say, was that of hospitality. When she cooked, she prepared her meals for all of the church members, not just for a select few, even strangers who came to our house. I remember coming home from school encountering total strangers that needed shelter and mother would take them in. She had no trepidation or fear. She trusted and cared because she knew her Maker. She lived the gift of her Spirit.

Do you have a spiritual gift? By definition, if you have such a gift, then you must be using it for God's glory. Some of us are destined to teach, others to heal, still others to prophesy. What is important is that these gifts must have their ultimate objective, the glorification of God. Jesus set the example of how to live in the Spirit. He lived to bless others. His life glorified His Father. The gift of the Spirit becomes evident when you welcome God's Spirit into your heart.

**In truth, if the Spirit dwells in you, you have all the fruits of the Spirit. God is all.**

## IT IS FINISHED | JULY 14

*"When he had received the drink, Jesus said, 'It is finished.' With that, he bowed his head and gave up his spirit.'" John 19: 30*

---

One of my favorite sports in high school was track and field. I ran both track and cross-country and trained morning and night in order to excel in my sport. I was highly competitive. The training wasn't always fun. Each step I took was agonizing both physically and mentally. There were thoughts and voices saying for me to quit. What kept me going, however, was a competitive spirit that urged me to complete what I had set out to accomplish. I looked toward the prize before me at the finish line.

In life, each of us has a race to finish. We are running for our life. At each step in our journey are obstacles and roadblocks as well as detours. Along the path, there are temptations. Take a shortcut. Nobody will notice. You'll arrive sooner or have more time to enjoy life's pleasures.

Jesus came to earth to accomplish what our first earthly parents failed to accomplish. You see, they took a shortcut when very clearly none had been sanctioned. They learned (the hard way) that obedience to God has no shortcuts. No detours are permitted. Jesus, on the other hand, was resolute in purpose. He gave not unto temptation; for His mission was to save us from eternal death and, very importantly, to reconcile us, who had sinned, with His Heavenly Father. No doubt, Jesus, too, heard voices that urged Him to forego this torture and come down from the cross. Jesus, however, kept His faith as well as His focus, singularly on His Father.

He was not motivated by the future accolades of mankind, but rather by His Father's love for us. When Jesus cried out: "It is finished," He knew this represented triumph over sin and death. He knew that His determination would mean ultimate salvation and eternal life for us. He did not know if He would rise again. He did not know if He would see His father again. He left His fate in His Father's care. He placed His whole trust in His Father even if it meant never seeing Him or us again. He literally sacrificed His life for us. What manner of love is this!

Jesus has made our race easier for us. We have already won. **When Jesus cried out "It is finish," He had forged our reconciliation with God. His task was completed. You may now cross the finish line to His waiting arms.**

## A FIRST BABY STEP | JULY 15

*"For the LORD your God dried up the Jordan before you until you had crossed over. The LORD your God did to the Jordan just what he had done to the Red Sea when he dried it up before us until we had crossed over. He did this so that all peoples of the earth might know that the hand of the LORD is powerful and so that you might always fear the LORD your God." Joshua 4: 23 & 24*

---

If you have seen the movie "The Ten Commandments," one of the most spectacular scenes is when Moses lifts his hands and parts the Red Sea. Most people forget that God performed the same miracle again when after 40 years the Israelites crossed the Jordan River. However, unlike Moses motioning with his hands the parting of the Red Sea, this time God instructs the people to take the first step into the Jordan River and then the river would part.

If you read Chapter 3:15 you will note the essence of this story. "Now the Jordan is at flood stage all during harvest. Yet as soon as the priests who carried the ark reached the Jordan and their feet touched the water's edge, the water from upstream stopped flowing. It piled up in a heap a great distance away, at a town called Adam in the vicinity of Zarethan, while the water flowing down to the Sea of the Arabah (the Salt Sea) was completely cut off. So the people crossed over opposite Jericho."

Yogi Berra is famous for the line: "When you come to the fork in the road, take it." Virtually every day of our lives, we face forks in the road of life. Sometimes the decisions are of little importance: Do I order the fettuccine Alfredo or the broiled salmon? Many of those road forks, however, are more serious: Do I take the job that keeps the family where it is currently situated or the one that pays a good deal more but requires a long-distance move? Do I go the chemo-radiation route or additionally go for the mastectomy? My marriage is essentially over. The spark is gone, and the differences are irreconcilable. Do we keep the marriage together for the kids' sake, or do we call it quits and begin anew? All difficult choices and we must choose one path or the other. The key is to take the first step in faith with God. He asks you to make the first move. God does not expect you to perform a large measure of faith. He does not want you to feel overwhelmed. Just as He came as a babe, totally unthreatening and harmless; He wants you to exercise a "baby's first step of faith."

If your first step is taken with faith in the Lord, then He who parts the seas and rivers will be with you. He cannot give you His blessing unless you initiate the first step. He is waiting for you to make the first step.

**Your step in faith will be your salvation.**

## RIGHT PLACE AT THE RIGHT TIME | JULY 16

*"For if you remain silent at this time, relief and deliverance for the Jews will arise from another place. But you and your father's family will perish. And who knows but that you have come to royal position for such a time as this?" Esther 4: 14*

---

Ever wonder whether you'll be at the right place at the right time? Timing is considered everything. No one has perfect timing but God. Perhaps you are having an "Esther moment".

Today's verse is about a young lady, Esther, who was chosen from many beautiful candidates to be the king's favorite and future wife. King Xerxes was considered a great ruler in his day. One day, however, he allowed his drinking to get the better of him and, in his inebriated condition, decided he wanted to show off his queen, Vashti. She declined the king's request, and the King's advisors convinced him to replace her so that a queen more respectful of his wishes might be installed.

A beauty contest was conducted throughout the kingdom, and the prettiest virgins of the lot were paraded in front of the king. The king was most attracted to Esther and selected her to be his next queen. Esther had been raised by her uncle, Mordecai, who, one day, overheard two of the king's officers conspiring to assassinate the king. Mordecai relayed this information to Esther, who in turn alerted the king. The conspirators were summarily executed.

The plot shifts to the king's appointing Haman to seat of honor higher than all of the other nobles. This position swelled Haman to the point that he expected everyone who came in contact with him to bow down to him. Mordecai refused to pay him homage. This infuriated Haman, and he plotted not only to do away with Mordecai but all Jews in the kingdom. Esther was told of the plot, and Mordecai counseled her to speak before the king.

Today's text explains the reason Esther was placed in the king's palace: to intervene on behalf of her people. The story ended with the Jewish people being spared and Haman hanged on the very gallows he built for Mordecai. To this day the Jewish people commemorate the defeat of Haman during the holiday of Purim. God has called each of us for one purpose, and that is reconciliation with Him.

If you're wondering what you should be doing or your purpose is in this whole scheme of things, wonder no more. Regardless what your calling is or the decision you must make, if you are willing, God will use you to save His people. **Now go in faith for your "Esther moment" is now.**

## GOD'S FAVORITES | JULY 17

*"Then Peter began to speak: 'I now realize how true it is that God does not show favoritism but accepts men from every nation who fear Him and do what is right.'" Acts 10: 34 & 35*

---

In 1949, India formally abolished the so-called caste system, although sociologists are quick to point out that remnants of the system exist to this day. Throughout the world, and, even in our own country, hierarchies, perhaps less formal, continue. It is said that, in the U.S., the gap between the wealthiest few and the large number of poor continues to grow. While none of these approaches the structure that Aldous Huxley describes in "Brave New World" (five groups labeled Alpha to Epsilon), there is a real question as to whether pure democracy exists anywhere on this planet.

In today's verse, Peter (Acts 10: 9-16) describes a vision he had. He envisions heaven opening and something like a large sheet being let down to earth by its four corners. The sheet contained all kinds of four-footed animals as well as reptiles and birds. A voice demands of Peter that he "…get up, kill and eat." Peter replies: "Surely not, Lord, I have never eaten anything impure or unclean." The voice replies: "Do not call anything impure that God has made clean." After three such occurrences, the sheet is taken back to heaven.

Peter was puzzled as to the vision's meaning. One interpretation: God had done away with the dietary laws. Another interpretation: God permits inter-marriage between races and cultures. Yet a third: The right of one class to dominate over or enslave another is rescinded. Peter's own interpretation was that God was simply declaring that He did not favor one group or person over another. Peter then seized this opportunity to testify about the ALL-inclusive God; the God who offered His Son's sacrifice so that ALL people might enjoy His salvation.

God has opened His arms to embrace ALL of us into His kingdom. Not one person is exempted. No not one. Your salvation is accepting His Son's offer. Yes, it's that simple. Remember the thief on the cross. All he asked Jesus was to remember him when Christ comes to His kingdom and Jesus said "today you will be with me in paradise." The thief did not have to prove his worthiness for God's kingdom by living a lifetime of goodness. There is absolutely nothing you can do to earn your salvation. God has paved the way for your salvation; all you need to do is accept Him.

**God has, in essence, declared that each of us is His favorite.**

## JUST SAY YES OR NO | JULY 18

*"Simply let your 'Yes' be 'Yes' and your 'No' be 'No;' anything beyond this comes from the evil one." Matthew 5: 37*

There seems to be a satisfying feeling inside us when we can curse freely when someone offends us. The thought of using four letter words to describe a bad behavior from someone towards us gives us a feeling of superiority. The trouble with this behavior is that it becomes a part of who you are. Cursing not only demeans its target, but its user as well. Soon it defines your essence, your personality and character.

Jesus knew a thing or two about the deleterious effect of swearing. He gave the commandment not to take the Lord's name in vain. A lot of our swear words are intermingle with the name of God. You know what I'm talking about. Using curse words like "God -----" and the last word is not God's last name. Jesus says to swear is to desecrate God and his throne (verse 34). It's an affront to God to use four letter words to express your disdain. Swearing does not comfort your restless nature but intensifies the moment to the point of detriment to your well-being.

Ever been cut off in traffic by a careless driver? Your first instinct is to evidence your disgust by means of the use of one of your fingers and then to curse the offender, either out loud or under your breath. When you curse, you reveal the true nature of who you are within. Do you feel better for these actions? Actually, you end up getting so caught up in the event that you ruin your entire day. What is worse, a good many of the swear words are used in combination with the name of God. Jesus warns (verse 34) that to swear is to desecrate God. He says, too, that when you employ such language you are siding with the source of all evil and that, ultimately, you become evil.

The next time you are driven to curse someone pray to God to give you the Spirit to just say yes or no. You can live a life of yes or no simply by having the Spirit of God with you constantly and at all times in your life. There will be relapse moments when you falter and curse instead of yes, but don't lose hope. God will change your heart to be like His. If someone provokes you to anger you will be able to say "You Yes" and "You No." The ability to speak these words from the heart does not happen over-night. **It takes a receptive heart and humility to have God's Spirit dwell in you.** You will be tested in mind and speech to curse, instead praise God.

Saying yes or saying no is a righteous response.

## LOVE YOUR ENEMY | JULY 19

*"You have heard that it was said, Love your neighbor and hate your enemy. But I tell you: Love your enemies and pray for those who persecute you." Matthew 5: 43 & 44*

---

Wow. This one sounds like a toughie. Do we really want to love the very person we despise – a person who returns the compliment many times over? I don't recall any mention in Ann Frank's diary of her praying for the soul of Adolph Hitler. Surely, there must be exceptions to this rule. Actually, NO!

Jesus wanted to teach His disciples a lesson. They were gathered in a village for the purpose of healing and preaching when a woman jostled her way up to Jesus and virtually demanded that He heal her demon-possessed daughter. Jesus pretended to ignore her, knowing full well that one of the very worst things you can do to another human being is to ignore that person. Psychologists refer to this type of behavior as "discounting", which is to act as if the person does not even exist. This, of course, is the ultimate insult. Have you ever been treated in such a manner? It's certainly feels awful. Have you treated someone in like manner?

The disciples, having observed the behavior of their spiritual leader, got into the act and suggest to Jesus that He send her away. After all, she was, they said, a low-life, utterly devoid of class. In fact, they argued, she was truly an annoyance. (You may read the entire story in Matthew 15: 21-28.)

Jesus' lesson here was actually two-fold. Obviously, He wanted to test the subject's faith. Perhaps more importantly, however, Jesus wanted to make it clear to His disciples that God is indiscriminate in His love. God in fact loves their enemies every bit as much as He loves them. When someone expresses hatred toward you, the only way you can truly love that person back is first to receive God's Spirit. This may seem like a hard thing to do, especially if you are innocent. You will learn to look at your enemy through the compassionate, merciful and forgiving eyes of God. I can hear you saying, "Sure, easier said than done!" I concur. But the more you cling to your Savior, every time you falter, the easier it gets to love your neighbor. God's Spirit will change your attitude, temperament and most of all your heart. You will be calm and at peace when God's Spirit is in you.

**When you have God's Spirit in your heart, you will love your enemy and pray for that person the same as if that person were a friend and ally.**

## NOT BY BREAD ALONE | JULY 20

*"And Jesus answered him, saying, "It is written, that man shall not live by bread alone, but by every word of God." John 4: 4 (KJV)*

Man cannot live by bread alone. Actually, American men and women appear to be doing rather well in the bread department, but, by the looks of things, they are doing especially well in the donut, ice cream pasta, Frappuccino and super-sized hamburger or "vege-burger" departments, too. How many of our 50 states have adult obesity levels of less than 20%? (Mind you, we're talking obesity, not just overweight). The answer...only one state, Colorado. In every other state, more than one-fifth of the adult population is obese. Clearly, man is NOT living by bread alone.

Now, John was not talking about diet in the above verse. His point was that the bread or Big Macs on the table will sustain us for but a day, but our true sustenance comes from God; for His WORD sustains us in this life and for life eternal. God has told us that our earthly life is but a day compared to the Heavenly life that awaits us. Our earthly bodies are essentially on loan from God. When we finally meet our maker our bodies will not be what you think they are today. We'll be neither skinny nor obese, neither tall nor short. We shall be as angels. And yet, while we spend our days on earth, we put more focus into what goes into our stomachs than what enters into our hearts.

How much time do you spend every day, shopping for meals, preparing meals, eating out, and eating at home? For the average person, it's likely a very significant portion of one's waking hours – perhaps four or five hours. Okay now, how many waking hours of the same typical day do you pray to or so much as think about God? Strange, isn't it? Your real sustenance doesn't come from the supermarket. It doesn't come from McDonald's. It certainly doesn't come from Starbuck's caramel Frappuccino. Your real sustenance comes from every word of God. God's word is His character. When you take Him at His word, you are taking Him in faith. This goes not only for food but everything in your life, relationships, careers, wisdom, health and even your faith. **All your existence is because of God's word. Never take His word for granted for they are life to your soul.**

Take God's WORD to heart. It will not only sustain you today but eternally.

## GREATER THAN JOHN | JULY 21

*"I tell you, among those born of women there is no one greater than John; yet the one who is least in the kingdom of God is greater than he." Luke 7: 28*

---

John the Baptist was mentioned by Isaiah the prophet in Isaiah chapter 40: 3-5 "A voice of one calling in the desert, prepare the way for the Lord, make straight paths for Him. Every valley shall be filled in, every mountain and hill made low. The crooked roads shall become straight, the rough ways smooth, and all mankind will see God's salvation." Also in Malachi 3: 1 "I will send my messenger ahead of you, who will prepare your way before."

Some people thought John was the messiah. However, John knew and recognized Jesus when He came to the Jordan River to be baptized. It was not until the Holy Spirit revealed to John that the One about whom he prophesized was Jesus that he declare, "Behold! the Lamb of God who takes away the sin of the world." John's message of repentance and good news about their salvation in Jesus was very compelling.

However, after John rebuked Herod for his adulterous affair with his brother's wife and the other evil acts he committed, Herod locked John up in prison. In Luke 7: 18-22, John became despondent and uncertain. Do you become discouraged and despondent when things look bleak? Do you sometimes wonder if Jesus will come again and save us finally from this earth's woes? Things only appear murky at this time but God's promise is as sure as His word.

John sent two of his disciples to ask Jesus "Are you the one who was to come, or should we expect someone else?" Jesus had been laboring all day, healing the sick from their disease, and casting out evil spirits. Jesus healed the blind, the lame, the deaf, and the lepers and reiterated the good news that John had been preaching. Jesus then urged John's disciples to share with John what they had witnessed. John's faith in Christ was not only renewed but strengthened. You are like John, too. You can pave the way of God's goodness. You can start by sharing the Good News of Christ's saving grace for all humankind. You can usher Christ's return and have a great part in the salvation of humankind.

Jesus said about John (verse 28) "I tell you among those born of women there is no one greater than John." **When John heard the disciple's message he was assured of his salvation and of Jesus who was the ONE greater than himself.** You too can believe you are saved even if things appears ominous, as in the case of John, but rest assured God will save you. John will see His Savior again. You too can have John's faith.

## THINGS WHERE THERE IS NO LAW | JULY 22

*"But the fruit of the Spirit is love, joy, peace, patience, kindness, goodness, faithfulness, gentleness and self-control. Against such things there is no law." Galatians 5: 22 & 23*

---

How important is the Spirit in your life? It should be so important that it's a matter of life or death, hell or heaven, Christ or Satan. There is something in the nature of man to want to go against the Spirit of God. Have you ever noticed that, when you are irritable, unpleasant, onerous, mischievous, vindictive, self-centered, temperamental, impatient, unsociable, brooding and destructive you do not have the Spirit of God dwelling in you? Who do you think is dwelling in you?

What does it mean to have the fruits of the Spirit? The fruits of the Spirit are contrary to the nature of man. The fruits of the Spirit are: love, joy, peace, patience, kindness, goodness, faithfulness, gentleness and self-control. As Paul insisted, I need to "die daily" to self. Not paying attention to the Spirit's leading means ungodly behavior. Do you notice ungodly behavior around you? How we deal with these unruly people will help us know whether or not the Spirit dwells in our lives.

How can we be certain to retain the fruits of the Spirit at all times? Well, for starters, you must place Christ #1 in your life. The Spirit will reveal to you what you are lacking in this regard. Every time you hear the Spirit of God talking to you, stay still, listen and pray. Ask the Spirit to guide your thoughts, your ways, and your desires. Ask the Spirit to show you how to be more gentle, kind, loving, patient, faithful, joyful, peaceful and controlled. Sometimes this can be trying because the nature of the beast in us wants to reign supreme. Don't resist the Spirit's guidance; even if it means eating "humble pie." Let the Spirit of God reign in your life.

When you are told to go last in line even when there is little or no food left, thank God that the others were fed first. If someone cuts you off in the freeway or highway, be glad that you are safe in God's care. If you encounter a rude individual in your church, school, work or home, don't treat them in kind. If someone cheats you, belittle you and slaps you in the face, turn the other cheek and pray for them. If you are going through a divorce and your spouse is acting unkindly treat them kindly. For by doing that you are behaving like Christ.

**It's of utmost importance to never neglect the fruits of the Spirit in your life; for against such things there is no law.** That's the law of love. Know this message for today and cherish it daily in your coming and going; for this is a matter of peace or turmoil, joy or sadness and life or death.

## ONLY ONE COMMANDMENT | JULY 23

*"The entire law is summed up in a single command: Love your neighbor as yourself." Galatians 5: 14*

---

According to C.S. Lewis' "Four Loves," there are four types of loves humankind displays towards one another.

The first love is: Eros." This refers to romance, to include but not be limited to physical attraction. Mind you, however, that Lewis is NOT talking about sexuality here. This type of love is about "being in love". It deals more with the emotional aspects of that love. There is actually a fifth category (separate from this discussion) referred to as "Venus", which treats the sexual connection.

The second love is from the Greek for "storge". This one speaks to affection – specifically, affection that is bred by familiarity. This affection is not necessarily of a romantic sort. It may, for example, be between family members.

The third love is "Phileo", which speaks to friendship. It treats people who have certain interests or activities in common. It refers to brotherly/sisterly love. We love people because it is the Christian thing to do. There is obviously a connection between Phileo and Philadelphia, which, not by chance, is referred to as the City of Brother Love.

The fourth category is "Agape", which refers to unconditional love. Lewis extols this type of love as the greatest type of love, and he believes it is the most Christian of the four categories. It is the love which Christ bestows upon us. It is love that is given without an expectation of like in return thus, unconditional. To be Christ like in character and action is what this love is all about. Do you know people like this? Do you agape your neighbor?

God loves us unconditionally. He expressed that love toward us through His Son. His Son, Jesus, sacrificed Himself so we may know and experience Him, who is the Author of Love. He did not ask us to love our neighbor, He commanded us to do so. He said, "If you keep on biting and devouring each other, watch out or you will be destroyed by each other." (verse 15). To stipulate that we should love our neighbors as we do ourselves is, therefore, only common sense. Can you try living for just one day loving your neighbor?

One commandment is all you need to follow to live a Godly life, love your neighbor as yourself. **It's all about love. Love fulfills all God's law.**

## WHAT MORE COULD HE DO? | JULY 24

*"What more was there to do for my vineyard that I have not done in it?" Isaiah 5: 4 (NRSV)*

You've no doubt heard the expression "Monday morning quarterbacking", even if you don't watch football. It refers to the second-guessing coaches, commentators and even fans do the day after a football game—the "what-ifs". What if we'd gone for the first down rather than punted? What if we'd gone for two points instead of only one? What if the quarterback had thrown to a different receiver? At one time or another – whether it be in sports, in politics, in business, in church, or in other activities, we have all second-guessed the behavior and performance of others and of ourselves.

In golf, players have been known to take a mulligan after they hit a poor first shot. This is essentially a do-over. Regrettably, there are relatively-few opportunities for do-overs in our real lives. At one time or another, we've probably all wished we could take a mulligan. I certainly have. Probably one of the most-oft-used phrases in the English language is: "Hindsight is 20/20." In other words, if I knew then what I know now, I would have behaved or acted very differently. Would you? How many times have you repeated your patterns of destructive behavior? Unfortunately, for most of us at least some of the time, hindsight is less than 20/20. This is to say that we don't learn from our mistakes. We keep making the same ones over and over again. I have noted that especially among divorcees who rebound so quickly that they choose a similar spouse patterned after their ex.

Today's verse tells us of a God who loves us to the point of waiting patiently as we decide which choice to make. The beginning of verse one of chapter five says: "I will sing for the one I love a song about his vineyard. My loved one had a vineyard on a fertile hillside. He dug it up and cleared it of stones and planted it with the choicest vines. He built a watchtower in it and cut out a winepress as well. Then he looked for a crop of good grapes. But it yielded only bad fruit." We produced bad fruit. Do you think there was something else or something different God could have done to harvest good fruit? If you know better than God, why not tell Him?

This parable tells us that God gave us all we asked for and more. He watched over us. He gave us love, His Son. Yet despite all of the things He did for us, we often proved unequal to the task. **What more could He have done for us?**

## UNDESERVING LOVE | JULY 25

*"The Lord said to me, 'Go, show your love to your wife again, though she is loved by another and is an adulteress. Love her as the Lord loves the Israelites, though they turn to other gods and love sacred raisin cakes.'" Hosea 3: 1*

What would you say is the vilest thing your spouse could do that might warrant your initiating divorce proceeding. Perhaps murder? How about lying and deceit? Disdain for his or her in-laws? Infidelity or child abuse? Today's text speaks to one act that would rank high on most of our lists, and that would be adultery.

The Seventh Commandment stipulates under NO uncertain terms: "Thou shall not commit adultery." (Exodus 20: 14). This one is a headline-grabber. It's also the one that hits you right in the gut because, if you are the one betrayed, it is insulting. It is embarrassing. It seems to challenge your manhood, if you are of that gender and your feminine qualities, if you are a woman. It is a violation of a trust you had. And, oh, by the way, it is a sin, and not one of us wants to be a party to an activity that is sinful, even if we are merely the victim of the sin.

The book of Hosea deals with a woman named Gomer. She is the wife of Hosea. She is not only caught in an adulterous act, but she flaunts her lack of fidelity to her spouse. In fact, Hosea considered her behavior so blatant and so egregious that he felt he had no alternative but to leave her.

God, however, had a different take on the matter. God urged Hosea to return his wife's loathsome behavior with Love. Is God for real? You have to be kidding? What is God telling Hosea? Have you gone through a similar situation which left you bitter and angry? Did you contemplate on leaving too? Did you return kind with love instead? That's not an easy task to do given the emotional investment you have.

God beseeched Hosea to love her as God loves His people. Hosea believed God's counsel. He trust God and did exactly what he was asked to do. He loved his wife unconditionally. He expressed his love for her by heeding God's advice and taking her back. This is really about our story. We were the adulterer that left God. How did God treat our unfaithfulness? He took us back. How often can you take back your unfaithful spouse? Can you do it once or twice? How about seventy times seventy? Let's go for infinite love. We have a long way to go to express God's love if we can't even forgive once or twice. God forgives us infinitely more. Stop being stubborn and obstinate in your heart and let go and let God love that animosity out of your heart. I guarantee you'll be glad you did. Your new found love will rise above earthly love.

**Hosea understood that God loves us even though we are often undeserving.**

## BLESSED IS THE MAN | JULY 26

*"Blessed is the man who does not walk in the counsel of the wicked or stand in the way of sinners or sit in the seat of mockers. But his delight is in the law of the Lord, and on his law he meditates day and night. He is like a tree planted by streams of water, which yields its fruit in season and whose leaf does not wither. Whatever he does prospers." Psalms 1: 1-3*

---

You've heard the story of King Midas of Greek mythology. Whatever he touched turned to gold. Would you like that ability? There are people who have the gift of making money. My mother, with her sixth-grade education and broken English, had the uncanny ability to succeed in whatever business venture she pursued. She was highly successful in real estate. Sometimes, without any capital, she would purchase a piece of property by convincing the owner to carry the mortgage. Her success she attributed to her daily walk with God.

I sometimes studied mother's Godly life. She was up at the crack of dawn, meditating on God's word and praying for His guidance. She counseled me God's way is always the way of life. To depart from that is death. God does not take pleasure in the death of anyone, wicked or righteous. In His compassion and love for us, He warns us of the danger of following the ways of the wicked and unrighteous.

God's law is neither confining; nor prohibitive; it is a law of love and freedom. Following God's law demonstrates your love for Him. You love His ways, and you love your neighbor as yourself. When you establish your ways according to His laws, you will be like a tree planted near the streams of water which "yields fruit in season and whose leaf does not wither." You will prosper and be blessed.

Your prosperity is in the attitude and peace you will derive from knowing Him. Your delight is an awareness of the presence of the Spirit of the Lord in your daily walk. The material things are secondary to the pleasure you will reap in knowing God and doing His will. Have you noticed there are people you encounter in your daily life that just seem to exudes warmth and compassion. You feel so at home and at peace. Then there are those you just can't stand to be around with. Everything that comes out of their mouth is complaint and accusations. Nothing good comes out of their mouth. It's so unpleasant to be in their company. You want to stay away from them. They're high maintenance. It's obvious they are suffering from the lack of God's Spirit in their life. Which one do you profess to be? Do you prosper?

**"Blessed is the person who delights in the law of the Lord. Whatever he or she does prospers."**

*"You will seek me and find me when you seek me with all your heart." Jeremiah 29: 13*

Last Sabbath, I witnessed the baptism of my nephew. It was quite a moving and spiritual moment for all of us, but especially for Mark. Mark, on his own volition, decided to make a public statement about his commitment and relationship with God. Mark was ready to give his all to the Lord.

Baptism is a very personal commitment, and the baptismal event itself is merely a symbol of that commitment. Your relationship or marriage, call it, with God only begins that day. The ceremony, the papers commemorating the event are meaningful only to the extent your life from that point on evidences your commitment to God. I was baptized when I was 16 years old. I made a personal commitment to God and vowed to Him I would be faithful, honest and live a godly life. There is an unspoken feeling when you walk with God, you feel invincible. All is well in your life and you wish the same for those struggling with their faith and walk with God.

Of course, not all of our life journeys are quite so blissful. I am the first to admit that my sanctimonious life faltered in less than a week after baptism. Many of us have or develop baggage and demons that become more and more difficult to hide as the calendar years advance. Certainly, it may appear easier to deny these issues, but there is no hiding from God; and He wants our lives to be full and fulfilled, NOT half-full and unfulfilled.

The good news is that when you committed to partner up with God, He signed up with you. He is as conscious of the roadblocks and detours you face as you are, and, if you commit to stay the course and keep Him in your heart, He will be there with you as you endeavor to overcome these obstacles and as you cross the proverbial finish line. I guarantee you that there will be times when your faith in God will wane, especially when you face death, whether by natural causes, accidental or illnesses. You gather family and friends and church leaders and ask for prayers be lifted to God on behalf of the dying but sometimes that person will succumb to death. **You will be tried. DO NOT LOSE FAITH. God is faithful. His word is true**. God will make all things new again. **You must reach that point in your life where you can believe God with ALL your heart.**

The Author of Love operates only in love. He is love. He cannot express any other emotion but through love. That is who He is. To understand love you must KNOW your Creator. He has given His ALL for you. All you need to do is respond to Him with ALL your heart.

## ALL KINDS OF FISH | JULY 28

*"Once again the kingdom of heaven is like a net that was let down into the lake and caught all kinds of fish."* Matthew 13: 47

---

How certain are you of your salvation? Well, once again, there is good news, for Jesus tells us that "ALL kinds of fish were caught from the bottom of the lake." This, of course, suggests that there is a place for everyone in God's kingdom – sinners and "saints", Democrats and Republicans, straights and gays…Catholics, Muslims, Buddhists, Protestants, etc…you get the point. It is said that an all-inclusive God invites ALL to come to Christ.

Ah, but that begs a question: Are the gates of Heaven open to those who practice other religions as well as those who come to Christ? There are many Christians who strongly believe that only those who have Christ in their heart are welcome into God's kingdom. A Christian sinner is welcome, but a Moslem or a Jew, even if they be righteous and god-fearing, would be unwelcome. Hmmm…yet another "toughie".

For years, certain groups (typically, Jews, African-Americans and Latinos) were unwelcome in certain country clubs and even in certain communities. So-called restrictive covenants in the club charters or the house deed underscored these policies. Are there restrictive covenants respecting the entry to Heaven?

The noted philosopher, George Santayana said: "What religion a man shall have is a historical accident, quite as much as what language he shall speak." Yes, some people do, over the course of their lives, change their religions, but, for the most of us, our faith was determined at birth. The odds are that, if you are born in India and spend your life in that country, you are not likely to come to Christ, however righteous your behavior. We would be presumptuous to do more than set the stage for this debate, except to remind the reader that our God is an inclusive God and that there are no restrictive covenants in His house. There will come a day when you will know the truth about God and His salvation of humankind. You will learn and understand that God is just, fair and true. Man excludes according to their bias beliefs but God includes all regardless of their beliefs and background. You will be surprised who will be in God's kingdom. Be glad you do not make that decision. Someday every mouth will confess God is just.

When multitudes from every tribe and nation shall enter into the New Jerusalem, it's been noted that some will say to Jesus, "So, that's your name." **Yes, my friend, you will see every kindred, tongue, people and religion in the new earth. They will all have one thing in common. Their salvation was because of God's gift to you and me, His Son.**

## GREAT IS GOD'S FAITHFULNESS | JULY 29

*"Because of the Lord's great love we are not consumed, for His compassions never fail. They are new every morning; great is your faithfulness." Lamentations 3: 22 & 23*

---

Do you have someone you can depend on to help you in time of trouble? Most of us have such friends. However, there are those who prefer not to ask for help. Sometimes, it's a matter of pride.

I have a close friend who refuses to depend on anyone. No matter what his circumstances, he will not ask for help. He will starve before he borrows money. He told me that, growing up, he was on his own by age 16. He lived in city parks and used public rest rooms to shower. He slept on park benches. Fortunately, he befriended a classmate who discovered his plight and told his parents. They invited him to live with them until he was able to be on his own.

My friend did not realize that God was the silent friend behind his care. We have earthly friends who are faithful and others who are merely fair-weather friends. There is one friend who is there for us, fair weather or stormy, a friend who will never fail us. You can trust Him and count on Him to be there when you're down and out. He will always come through for you.

God has promised to eradicate all of our sins, our miseries and our sorrows. Verse 21 says: "Yet this I call to mind and therefore I have hope." When you think back to those times when your best friends came through for you, be mindful of the fact that God was working in your life. All good things come from God.

The next time you are wondering if your prayer is being heard, remember to recall the good things that you have experienced in your life. Sometimes the good may outweigh the bad but sometimes they may not. Rather than focusing on the balance scale, focus on Him who has always been there for you. God has never failed you nor will He ever. You must place all your cares on Him. He is the faithful one for now and forever. He is a friend you can really depend on. The goodness you have experience in your life through, family, friends or strangers was because God had a great influence in it. Your salvation, in part, will be because of these people who allowed God to use them to share His love to you. He is an amazing, great and faithful God.

God's love and compassion have greeted you every morning. **There is no greater faithfulness towards us than God's.**

## ON TWO OF A KIND | JULY 30

*"Because of this, God gave them over to shameful lusts. Even their woman exchanged natural sexual relations for unnatural ones. In the same way the men also abandoned natural relations with women and were inflamed with lusts for one another. Men committed shameful acts with other men, and received in themselves the due penalty for error" Romans 1: 26 & 27*

---

This text has been quoted and cherished by zealot Christians as proof that homosexuality is an abomination to God. During that time, anyone caught lying (having sex) with a gender of the same sex was condemned to death. The punishment was to stone them to death. There were other practices that warranted the death sentence: doing any work on Saturday, wearing cotton and wool at the same time, eating pork or lobster, charging interest on loans, cursing father or mother; taking advantage of a widow or an orphan, adultery, sorcery, mediums or spirits, fornication with relatives or in-laws, destructive person, and prostitution. Why does zealot Christians only focus on the abomination and not these other acts?

Every year, at election time, one or more states places an amendment or proposition on their ballots, either allowing or prohibiting same sex marriage. The law of the land clearly stipulates that discrimination based on race, religion (or, for that matter, non-religion), disability, gender age, or national origin is prohibited. Homosexuals are not a protected class insofar as Federal law is concerned. Recently, the U.S. Supreme Court ruled DOMA as unconstitutional and the 9th Circuit U.S. Court of Appeals lifted a stay on the California Proposition 8.

This is to say that, in California and actually throughout the nation, there is a slightly stronger sentiment in favor of protecting gays, lesbians and transgender people as a class (and thereby allowing them to marry). Moreover, the sentiment on this issue seems to correlate with age. The younger people tend to favor affording gays class protection. Older people tend to hold a contrary position. This would suggest that the acceptance of gays will gain momentum in years to come. Given the re-election of President Barack Obama for a second term in office, and his inaugural message that his gay brothers and sisters journey is not complete until all are given equal rights under the law, there seems to be hope favoring gays in this issue. It would seem, too, that the abolition of the military's "don't ask, don't tell" policy has not met with dire consequences that some had feared.

The question that is begging to be answered once and for all, is homosexuality a sin? Before we delve into homosexuality let's define sin. "Whoever commits sin transgresses also the law: for sin is the transgression of the law." 1John 3:4. What is the law that Paul is referring to? the Ten Commandments. What did Jesus say about the Ten Commandments? "Jesus replied: 'Love the Lord your God with all your heart, and with all your soul and with all your mind. This is the first and greatest commandment. And the second is like it: Love your neighbor as yourself.'" Matthew 22: 37-39. **God calls His laws the law of love. [16] "And so we know and rely on the love God has for us. God is love. Whoever lives in love lives in God, and God in them. [17] This is how love is made complete among**

**us so that we will have confidence on the day of judgment: In this world we are like Jesus. [18]There is no fear in love. But perfect love drives out fear, because fear has to do with punishment. The one who fears is not made perfect in love. [19]We love because He first loved us. [20]Whoever claims to love God yet hates a brother or sister is a liar. For whoever does not love their brother and sister, whom they have seen, cannot love God, whom they have not seen. [21]And he has given us this command: Anyone who loves God must also love their brother and sister". 1 John 4: 16-21. A most unique part of this verse is "In this world we are like Jesus."** How did Jesus treat each of us? With love. "For God so love the world." Jesus treated Adam and Eve with love when they sinned, "The Lord God made garments of skin for Adam and his wife and clothed them." Genesis 3: 21. Jesus treated the prostitute ready to be stoned by a crowd with love, You can read the story in John 8:2-11. Jesus treated the thief on the cross with love, "truly I tell you, today you shall be with me in paradise." Luke 23: 39-43. The whole Bible is full of stories of God's love for us. Does He excuse are sins? No, He forgives us and loves us. How does all this tie in to Homosexuality. God wants us to treat one another as He treats us; with love, grace, compassion and mercy. Yes, but what about all those verse in the Bible that says homosexuality is an abomination to God? Remember, there are man's laws and there are God's laws. Whether in the Bible or not, there is a distinct difference. Man condemns, God NEVER condemn, John 3: 17. You decide which word you believe. Whichever you choose, if you hate the homosexual you'll be called a liar.

A case can be made, of course, that God's law and man's law don't always coincide. Some argue that homosexuality is a choice. Others maintain that gays are born with that disposition and can no more change that disposition than an African American person can change his or her skin color. What position should we as Christians take on this matter? We need to look at this from a couple of perspectives. First, we need to ask whether the quotation from scriptures cited above is to be taken literally. <u>If</u> (and you'll not that the word "if" is underscored) you conclude that the quotation accurately reflects God's law, then there still remains the question as to how we as Christians should deal with those who exhibit homosexual tendencies. Should they be allowed to worship alongside us without renouncing these tendencies? Should they be required not to act upon this disposition? And then there is the question we have come to ask over and over again: <u>If</u> we deem these dispositions and behaviors to be sinful, how would Jesus have dealt with those who are disposed? In order to clarify what God meant, He personally came down to earth, through His Son, to show us how to love one another. Jesus summed up all His commandments into two laws, the first is Love God and the second love your neighbor as yourself. Therefore if we follow these commandments are we not living a Godly life?

Love between two people, regardless of gender, is pure and holy when it is demonstrated in God's law of love. Sin is antithesis of Love. Sin is defined as not loving your neighbor as yourself. Love is genderless**. Love is God. God loves all peoples. He is the Author of Love. He demonstrated how we ought to love one another through His Son, Jesus**.

**If Jesus has shown you love, mercy and compassion, why can't you?**

## YOUR WISH IS MY COMMAND | JULY 31

*"At Gibeon the Lord appeared to Solomon during the night in a dream, and God said, 'ask whatever you want me to give you.'" I Kings 3: 5*

---

What if you had the same opportunity that Solomon had when God appeared to him and said, "Ask whatever you want me to give you?" What would you ask from God? Many, perhaps most, of us wish virtually every day that our proverbial ship might come in. My father had that dream. He became an avid gambler whenever the opportunity came his way. He always felt he was one step closer in hitting the "jackpot." My aunt considered herself a faithful Christian, but she played the lottery in the hope that wealth would bring her happiness. She rationalized she would use the money to help those in need. We even got caught up in the frenzy by sneaking to buy a lottery ticket, especially when the amount reached above $300 million dollars. We even started dreaming what we would do with the money if we won.

We claim we believe in God; yet we nevertheless rely on other sources to fulfill our dreams. Some people go an unfortunate step further and fulfill their dreams at the expense of others. Some depend on that "love of my life" person or "Soul-mate" to bring us wholeness or happiness. We want it now and not moment sooner. Are you unfulfilled in your life? Do you have something you wish God would grant?

Solomon asked for the wisdom to know how to rule his kingdom wisely. He knew that wealth and life's other so-called pleasures were at best fleeting. He knew, too, that his legacy would depend on how he ruled and what he accomplished in behalf of his subjects. To this day, Solomon is highly regarded for his wisdom – not for his lofty rank or his wealth.

God, it turns out, was moved by Solomon's choice and granted him not only wisdom but wealth as well. Solomon asked God to rule His kingdom through him. God was pleased with his request and helped him in all His ways. Solomon however, got too arrogance and haughty with his God given talent and abused it with so much indiscretions. Even a good thing from God can turn self-serving. He forgot his Maker.

God is giving you the same opportunity today. The only difference between your circumstances and Solomon's is that you already know that God has granted you salvation. You lack nothing. All of your other dreams pale in comparison. That's how caring God is toward us. Even before we ask He not only knows but has already provided. Yes! **Whatever your wish, remember He has already fulfilled it, through His Son.**

## DO NOT LET YOUR HEART BE TROUBLED | AUGUST 1

*"Do not let your heart be troubled, trust in God; trust also in me. In my Father's house are many rooms; if it were not so I would have told you. I am going there to prepare a place for you. And if I go and prepare a place for you, I will come back and take you to be with me that you also may be where I am." John 14: 1-3*

---

This is an oft-quoted verse. It has meaning for many of us at one time or another in our lives; for there are few of us who have not dealt with depression – either momentary or chronic. This passage offers comfort to any of us feeling uncertain, perhaps even hopeless, about the future.

Several years ago, I was on a mission to Jamaica with our pastor, who served as the group leader. We were expecting over 300 children over a three-week period, and we were busy readying the camp facility prior to the children's arrival. We had a number of opportunities to drive through the countryside, and we marveled at the lush jungle as well as the houses built along the mountain top. Each house was meticulously designed and painted in white or beige. One of our members was from Jamaica, and she informed us that Jamaicans were known to go all-out when it came to building their houses. This, as you know, is not a wealthy country, but its people take special pride in building and maintaining their homes.

The fact is that these homes, as nice as they are, do not compare with the homes that our God is preparing for us in His Kingdom. That time is likely soon. One of our members reminded us that a sure sign of the "last days" is when the people turn away from the truth, when they become discouraged and lose faith that Christ will return for us. Don't focus on His return, focus on Him. He is your salvation. He is your heaven. He is your everything. You lack nothing when you really know Him. Stay faithful and you will witness His return.

The truth IS that He will return. God is preparing, not little houses of white or beige, but mansions where you will live with Him. He urges us not to be discouraged as He hints at the things He has in store for us. He says: "He who overcomes will inherit all this, and I will be His God and he will be my son." (Revelation 21: 7). What will we inherit? His entire royal kingdom and universe as well as everything He has ever created. God has also said you will be His son and daughter. Do you understand what that means? We will be embraced in the circle of the Trinity. We will be one with them.

**This is secondary in comparison to the ultimate gift He has already given us, His Son.**

## **DEEP LOVE** | AUGUST 2

*"Now that you have purified yourself by obeying the truth so that you have sincere love for your brothers, love one another deeply, from the heart." I Peter 1: 22*

---

Do you know how to love deeply? Have you ever loved deeply? There is the love between two lovers, like Romeo and Juliet. Most would agree their love was very deep. What about the love between mother and child? No doubt I have heard parents say they would give up their life in order for their child to live. What about when someone hurts you? How can you love them deeply? God knows all about love. After all, He is the Author of Love.

Today I received an email forwarded to me from my pastor about a misunderstanding. Apparently one of our brothers in the mission field was accused of misappropriating funds. The money was to be used at his discretion on the mission's needs. He is being accused of using those funds for his personal gain. His defense: "They're jealous." This has caused much hurt and sadness within his family and the conference. When the problem is ultimately resolved, there will be no winners; both sides are fractured.

The seed of jealousy has its roots, not surprisingly, with Lucifer. What did Jesus do? 1Peter 2: 23 says, "When they hurled their insults at him, He did not retaliate; when He suffered, He made no threats. Instead, He entrusted himself to Him who judges justly." Jesus handled each insult in love. He did not seek vengeance or retaliation.

Does this describe your current circumstances? Do you consider yourself the victim of character defamation? As a rule, we are slow to forgive and slower yet to forget. It may seem counter-intuitive at the time, but, instead of allowing the rage to overtake your very being, treat your accuser with respect and brotherly love rather than with hatred and contention. When you take this course, you will find that your burden is shared with God. When you fill your life with enmity, the burden is yours alone. If you let God carry your burden, it will prove to be manageable and, if not light, certainly a good deal lighter. You can only treat your enemy as God did by allowing His Spirit to take control of your life. To love the unlovable is the deeper love. That is how God loves.

How deep is your love for your neighbor? Don't be discouraged if you cannot love like God. Only look to Him. Your deep love for your neighbor is in Him. God has shown us His deep love for us. His love runs deeper than any human relationship we have ever experienced. **When His Spirit dwells in you, you can love others as deeply.**

## PLANS TO PROSPER YOU | AUGUST 3

*"For I know the plans I have for you," declares the lord, "plans to prosper you and not to harm you, plans to give you hope and a future. Then you will call upon me and come and pray to Me, and I will listen to you." Jeremiah 29: 11 & 12*

---

Its' been nearly three years since my friend Susan found and kept a job. Her stint at telemarketing lasted five days. She was, by nature, an independent person until she hit the downward spiral. As hope faded, she developed ulcers and become despondent. She recently returned to Texas to be with her parents. She never considered herself to be suicidal, but the thought of ending it all has entered her mind a few times. Susan's dilemma is not unusual, especially when the economy goes into a tailspin. Many of us have, at some point, felt like Susan. What's your dilemma? Is it your inability to land a suitable job? Is it a marriage that's faltered? Is it home foreclosure? Is it your neighbor? How about your boss? A friend who betrayed you? Maybe you've been diagnosed with stage 4 cancer? How about uncertainty about your future? Are you feeling down and out without a hope in sight?

In the early years of television, there was a weekday afternoon show called "Queen for a Day". Five contestants would each tell host Jack Bailey a tale of woe, and the audience voted to determine which story was the most gut-wrenching. That person would be crowned "Queen for a Day". The winner would be awarded a prize that responded to her specific need as well as clothes, jewelry, a night on the town, etc. By today's standards, the show would appear rather ghastly, but it was like a precursor to today's so-called reality T.V.

Today's text tells us that, long before T.V. and to this very day, there is another emcee, a much grander one, who has plans to prosper you and to make every one of us queens and kings, not for a day, but into eternity. Moreover, He listens, not just for 2-3 minutes, but always and forever. His goal is to prosper you.

In these days, we have help lines for almost everything imaginable. We can take a pill for every mood swing. We have doctors for what ails you. There are even hotlines that will tell you your future. Whatever your needs are, someone out there has a cure or answer. Whether it's true is another matter.

There is one help line that has always been there for you. He wants to listen to your voice. His warranty is good for a lifetime and even beyond. He's available every second, 24/7, 365 days a year. **The Author of Love awaits your call. He has hope and a future to give you. What are you waiting for? Call Him.**

## THE FEAR OF THE LORD IS WISDOM | AUGUST 4

*"The fear of the Lord is the beginning of wisdom; all who follow His precepts have good understanding. To him belongs eternal praise." Psalms 111: 10*

---

What college or university has produced the most U.S. Presidents? Answer: Harvard College. What law school has produced the most Supreme Court Justices? Harvard Law School (by a wide margin). That may have been easy...now, what do Robert Frost, Howard Hughes, Matt Damon, R. Buckminster Fuller, Edwin Land (Polaroid), Eugene O'Neill, Pete Seeger, Bill Gates, Ogden Nash, and William Randolph Hearst have in common? Yes, they're all famous in one way or another, but not that. True, they are all men, but not what we're looking for. No, they didn't all play for the Chicago Cubs. Give up? They're all Harvard dropouts.

So, what's the point? The point is these ten men and a good many others realized at some point during their college years that they had a different calling. Not to knock Harvard education, but it's indeed a good thing when we recognize that calling and writing our own career tickets, or for that matter, life tickets. This is especially significant because studies show that some 70% of the working population are dissatisfied with their jobs.

Now, it is a fact, unfortunate or otherwise, that not all 10 of the people on this list were religious people. One thing that they indeed had in common was their discerning minds. Where do you think their intelligence came from? It is notable that, during Jesus' time, there were many who witnessed His wondrous miracles but failed or refused to recognize the Son of God – clearly not the sign of discerning minds. They were obviously blinded by their own self.

Today's text says to revere the Lord is the beginning of wisdom. In all matters of life, God must be first in our lives for us to have wisdom to make the right choices. You can experience wisdom to know where to go, what to do, which way to lean on all affairs of your life. When you stay focus on the Author of wisdom, you will never feel inadequate or uncertain.

If you feel you lack the wisdom to make the best life choices (career or other), you have been granted access to the best counselor of them all, God. When you respond to His Spirit beckoning you to seek Him out, then you will have good understanding and wisdom. The wisdom we all need to have is to know our Maker. **Fearing God means to respect, reverence and worship Him. God is the source of true wisdom. You want wisdom from above? Remember, all wisdom starts and ends with God. He is after all, the Author of all wisdom.**

## FOUR HUNDRED NINETY | AUGUST 5

*"Then Peter came to Jesus and asked, 'Lord, how many times shall I forgive my brother when he sins against me? Up to seven times?" Jesus answered, 'I tell you, not seven times, but seventy times seven.'" Matthew 18: 21 & 22*

---

I received a frantic call the recently from a family member asking if he could stay at my house. He'd just been served divorced papers from his wife. I replied: "sure." He came over, and we talked at length about his relationship with his wife. He confessed that he'd had an affair with another woman. He requested I contact his wife and ask her to forgive him. He was willing to return to her and make things right. I asked how serious was he, and he said very serious. He said he'd do anything!

I told him I would convey his sentiments to his wife. The following day I spoke with his wife. She was very angry. She proceeded to tell me her husband's philandering ways. She said they reconciled a year ago, and she'd forgiven him… until, that is, she received a phone call from an art dealer inquiring when to deliver a $5,000 art painting her husband had purchased for the "other woman". She confronted him regarding the matter, and he vehemently denied it. After further inquiries and a detailed investigation, she confirmed that he'd lied to her. He had continued to cheat behind her back.

She was angry, not only for being deceived, but also for being made a fool. She further added she had taken him back three times. How much more forgiveness should she be expected to extend, she asked. She knew that, in the Bible, Jesus said to forgive 70 times seven, but she'd had it with him. She even counseled with her therapist, friends and pastor. They all urged her to move on without him. I asked her: "Do you love him?" Her response: "The love is gone. He killed it." She said: "I want to punish him so that he realizes what he put me through." Her limit of forgiveness had reached maximum threshold. She had been hurt too deeply and she had nothing left in her well to try one more time. I must confess I understood where she was coming from. I too have been there. They say "time heals all wounds". There may be a modicum of truth to that. But with God's Spirit dwelling in you, you can forgive 70 times seven and more. That is how God forgives us.

How often can you forgive? Can you forgive 490 times – that's an awfully lot of forgiveness. Based on my past experience, boy do I have a long way to go! **However, just like our Father who forgives us not only seventy times seven but infinitely, we are to do likewise. You will only be able to forgive like God if you are one in His Spirit.**

# THE LOVE OF GOD | AUGUST 6

*""But the Lord called to the man, 'Where are you?'" Genesis 3: 9*

To write about God's love in a single page does God an injustice. Today's text is the first in the Bible to treat God's love for humankind. Ever since the fall of man, God has been on a mission to re-establish that which was lost on that fateful day in the Garden of Eden. Man has been running away from God, and God has not stopped pursuing man. The one who loves most is the one who pursues most.

This calls to mind a story of a young man named Pablo, who, in a fit of anger with his father, left home, vowing never to return. Pablo set out to live a glamorous life, but, before long, his became a life of squalor. He lived in the streets, scavenging for food and shelter. He longed to return home. Given how inauspicious his departure was, Pablo was not sure that his father would take him back. Meanwhile, his father waited every day for his son's return.

One day, the father devised what he thought was an ingenious plan. He took an ad out in the local paper with an note saying: "Pablo, if you read this notice, I want you to know that all is forgiven. I love and miss you. Please come home. I will meet you at midnight at the town square. Love, Father." Pablo was elated to read his father's message. When he arrived at the town square, he discovered 800 other Pablos, each seeking to return home to his respective father.

God has posted a similar message to tell us that He is coming to take us home to be with Him. He sent that message, not in the traditional way but rather through a baby born of a virgin on that clear night in Bethlehem. His journey on our behalf began as a babe wrapped in swaddling clothes. He waited 30 years to begin His quest for our salvation. He recalled our vulnerability to His sinless state and thus assumed a human form so that we cannot be overcome by His purity.

The love of God is seeking you right now. He has focused His whole attention on no one but YOU. You are the love of His entire being. God has not stopped loving you, nor will He stop waiting for you to come home to Him. He is reaching out to you right now with His tender mercy and compassionate grace.

**To realize the love of God, it is imperative that you reciprocate.** Don't wait for one moment or attempt to do right, come to Him exactly as you are. He will embrace and caress your filthy rags and fractured life. He loves you just the way you are. Won't you begin your journey back home to Him today and respond to the God who is asking: "Where are you?"

## COMMIT | AUGUST 7

*"Commit to the Lord whatever you do and your plans will succeed." Proverbs 16: 3*

---

Ever find yourself short of cash by month's end? Are you uncertain about your future? Do you simply feel down on your luck? Don't lose heart; you will succeed.

I recently attended a friend's birthday party. A long-time friend of the hostess, a woman with whom I was unacquainted, for some reason confided in me. She told me that she and her family had recently relocated to our area because of her husband's job. Before long, she was revealing information regarding her personal life. It seems that she had been married to her husband for approximately 20 years. Their only child, a son, had just started college. She had been a stay-at-home mom, all relatively-harmless data.

Then, virtually out of nowhere, she told me of an affair she was having with a man who was also married. She was quick to point out that she loved her husband but that he was not fulfilling her needs. She insisted that she didn't love the man with whom she'd been carrying on. Moreover, she had no plans to leave her husband for this man. She insisted that she was totally committed to her husband and to their family. Her rationalization for this behavior was that she was merely bored with life and needed a little excitement. As I indicated, I was rather surprised that this stranger would confide in me this way. Although this was not the first time this happened to me, I also knew this would not be the last. I couldn't help but wonder about her commitments to her family (most significantly, her husband) and to God. Nevertheless, I listened and discovered a woman looking for a deeper love than she has ever experienced. I told her what she was looking for was a deeper walk with God. I reminded her of today's text. She needed to first commit all her desires to God.

She listened and I did hear from her months later. She decided to leave her affair of twenty years and focus on her marriage. Noble gesture and sounds promising; however, I reminded to commit first to God, not her marriage and everything else will fall in place.

Do you ever make decisions, only to realize later that your choices were based on the emotions of the moment and not a longer-term outlook? One of the greatest gifs God gave us was freedom of choice. There was but one qualifier, and that was to choose Him. If we do that, that is, **if we walk in faith and commit our plans to Him, we cannot help but succeed.**

## WHAT'S THE DIFFERENCE | AUGUST 8

*"For there is no difference between Jew and Gentile-the same Lord is Lord of all and richly blesses all who call on him, for everyone who calls on the name of the Lord will be saved." Romans 10: 12 & 13*

---

There is no difference between you and me. How can that be? When our forefathers wrote the constitution they included a clause that stated, "All men are created equal." Did they honestly believe that? Clearly, some of us have tremendous intellect; others are, I believe the term is, mentally-challenged. Some of us are extraordinary athletes; others seldom exercise more than the fingers which push the buttons on their cell phones. We are so different in so many ways. What then is this "created equal" gibberish? The founding fathers were not suggesting that we are all clones of one another; they were merely arguing that we should have equal rights and equal protection under the laws of the land.

God's law, in this instance, is not terribly different than the so-called law of the land. God never intended for all of us to be the same. He not only acknowledges our differences, He made certain that there were differences. However, He treats all of His children without prejudice. He is not interested in comparisons. He loves us all – rich and poor, intelligent and less intelligent, Christian and Jew, Black or White...God only cares where our faith lies.

Recently, The Learning Channel (TLC) aired a show entitled "The Girl Born with No Face". A five-year-old girl was born with what many would consider a hideous-looking face – no nose, no mouth...I'll spare the gory details. She acted and played like any normal five-year-old. She accepted herself, and largely because her parents loved her unconditionally, she learned to love herself. Obviously, her parents were very much on the same page as God.

With God, regardless of how different you are with regard to intelligence, appearance or any one of a number of characteristics, we are treated equally. The truth is, there is no difference with God. Listen to Him. He knows everything about you and accepts you with open arms. You don't have to change a thing about you. **If you could see God's future for you, you would not hesitate to follow Him. Trust Him and you will see the difference. He has invited ALL of us into His Kingdom of love and acceptance. You may enter just as you are.**

## A CHEERFUL GIVER | AUGUST 9

*"Remember this: Whosoever sows sparingly will also reap sparingly, and whoever sows generously will also reap generously. Each man should give what he has decided in his heart to give, not reluctantly or under compulsion, for God loves a cheerful giver." II Corinthians 9: 6 & 7*

---

How might you be eulogized – as a giver or a taker? It was once said of John Wesley that, when he died, he left three things as his legacy: a well-worn pastoral coat, a saddle on which he'd traveled thousands of miles preaching the Good News and the Methodist church.

Wesley told the story of how he rode from village to village spreading the Good News of God's salvation. One day, as he rode out of a certain village, a highwayman held him up, demanding his bag of money. John Wesley wasted no time in giving up his recent collection. After giving his money, the highway robber rode off only to return a few minutes later and demanded he give up his fancy preaching coat.

Although John was reluctant to give it up, like Joseph's coat in the Old Testament, it was a coat he cherished; he immediately gave it up when the robber pointed a gun to his stomach. As the thief rode off, he threw his own tattered coat to the preacher and rode away. When John Wesley arrived at the next village he got up to preach and tell of his ordeal and began to explain why he was wearing an old tattered coat. He began to illustrate how he reached down into his own coat pocket to give the robber the moneybag and to his surprise and the joy of his congregation he pulled out the moneybag the thief had taken from him. John Wesley must have quoted today's text. God does love a cheerful giver, though John must have been reluctant to let go of his fancy coat, in the end, he was rewarded for his cheerful deed.

Whether you realize it or not giving is a rewarding experience. Some people prefer to receive rather than give. Try giving sometime. Give and see how it makes the receiver feel. They are overjoyed and overwhelmed. More so, feel the joy in your heart. That's how God feels for us. Giving is Godly love.

**The greatest gift you can give to God is yourself.** For God so love the world that He GAVE His only begotten Son. God gave His only Son to us without reservation. And He gave Him with a cheerful heart. God loved us without reservation or condition. You can experience the cheerful art of giving when you accept His gift (son) to you. For God Himself is a cheerful giver.

## YOURS BE DONE | AUGUST 10

*"Father, if you are willing, take this cup form me; yet not my will but yours be done." John 22: 42*

Jesus is on the Mount of Olives, beseeching God to remove the suffering that He was about to experience. When it comes to our own suffering, there are two events that top most people's lists. The first, of course, is the death of a loved one. The second is divorce.

With divorce, you ask yourself: "What went wrong?" That's soon followed by: "What did I do wrong?" The guilt trip lasts only a short while, followed in fairly rapid-order succession by the blame game. "Clearly, it's not my fault. I was the one always willing to compromise. She (or he) always had to have it her (his) way."

My friend Dave was a prominent, well-respected community leader, who was just starting his ministerial career when his wife asked for a divorce. Not only was the break-up of the marriage painful, but he was embarrassed that one who is called on to counsel others in times of marital difficulty could not hold his own marriage together.

Stories such as his are regrettably becoming the rule rather than the exception. Society today takes divorce for granted. In fact, the institution of marriage is very much on the rocks. The incidence of divorce keeps increasing. At the same time, more and more unwed couples are cohabitating. There are conflicting data respecting the impact of religion on divorce.

You must allow God to work His will in your life. It is all right to say "not my will but your will be done Lord." Jesus set the example for us. He showed us how to handle each desperate and foreboding situation in our life the same way He did. You ask your heavenly father to let the cup pass but if God sees best to have you go through your ordeal then let Him know that His will be done. Though Jesus' experience of separation is remarkably different from a divorce, the emotion is still very painful. But your pain will be eventually more rewarding when you place your will in God's hands. God will give you His peace.

Let Him know that you accept His plan for your life with full trust and confidence in Him. This may not be an easy process at first. You will never understand His plan for you unless you take the first step in faith. **You must be willing to walk in faith even if the road before you is uncertain. God's will is for your salvation. Now, can you say "yours be done."**

## THE THINGS ABOVE | AUGUST 11

*"Set your minds on things above, not on earthly things." Colossians 3: 2*

What you focus on is what you will live by. Our thoughts govern our actions, our disposition, our temperament, our motive and our way of life. Maybe you don't realize, but we can choose your thoughts. No one can make you think about something. You have the choice of what you will entertain in your mind. Granted there may be powerful influences in our lives. Even the media can snare your thoughts with provocative images in their advertisements.

I am reminded of a story I read about a positive farmer and a negative farmer. When the rain fell on the land, the positive farmer would say, "Thank you, Lord, for watering our crops." The negative famer said, "Yeah, but if this rain keeps up, it's going to rot the roots away, and we're never going to have a harvest." The sun came out and the positive farmer said, "Thank you, Lord, for the sunshine. Our crops are getting the vitamins and minerals they need. We're going to have a great harvest this year." The negative farmer said, "Yeah, but if it keeps this up, it's going to scorch those plants. We're never going to make a living." One day the two farmers went goose hunting together, and the positive farmer brought along his new bird dog. He was so proud of that dog; he couldn't wait to show him off. They went out in a small boat and waited. Before long, a big goose flew overhead. Boom! The positive farmer brought the bird down in the middle of the lake. He turned to his friend and said, "Now watch what this dog can do." The dog jumped out of the boat and ran on top of the water, picked up the goose, ran back all the way on top of the water, and put the bird down perfectly in the boat. The positive farmer was beaming from ear to ear. He turned to his friend, and said, "What did you think of that? The negative farmer shook his head in disgust. "Just what I thought," he said. "That dog can't even swim."

Do you know negative people like that? Maybe that's you too. I have friends who look at the glass half empty and friends who look at it half full. Those that see the negative in their life seems to possess internal ailments as well. Which one are you? Somehow it feels safer to look at the possible disasters in our life than the positives because then we're not surprised. I suppose it's the unexpected surprises that's scary for us. Whatever you want to focus here on earth that's what you'll live by.

**The Author of Love says to set your minds on things above, not on earthly things. Above means your God.**

## TO FORGIVE OR NOT TO FORGIVE | AUGUST 12

*"For if you forgive men when they sin against you, your heavenly Father will also forgive you. But if you do not forgive men their sins, your Father will not forgive your sins." Matthew 6: 14 & 15*

---

A prominent pastor talked about a former Baptist minister who was a member of his church. The man's hands were so crippled with arthritis that he could hardly use them. For as long as he'd known this man, his condition was always that way. He couldn't even see his hand to open a car door let alone shake someone's hand.

One day he paid a visit to his pastor. He showed him his hands, they were perfectly normal. He could move them as a normal person can. It almost seemed as though he had a new set of hands. The pastor was surprised and happy for him. The pastor inquired what happened. The man replied. Several months ago you were preaching about forgiveness. You stated how God's power is inhibited from operating in our lives, and how it keeps our prayers from being answered. I began to pray to God to show me if I had any areas of un-forgiveness and resentment in my life. And God began to deal with me. He brought to light several situations that had happened to me down through the years in which people had done me great wrong. I didn't even know it, but I still had anger and resentment in my heart toward those people.

The old man decided to forgive those wrongs and to let go of them. One by one, his fingers began to straighten out. One week went by and this finger would get healed, the next week this finger got healed and the next week this finger. As he continued the process of letting go of the bitterness that lay in his heart, God brought complete healing to his hands. Healing starts when you learn to forgive not only others but also yourself. As the saying goes, do not go to bed angry, go and forgive the one that hurt you or you hurt before the morning breaks.

Even the most righteous among us bear the burden of anger, bitterness, resentment. It's certainly not easy to let go. "I have heard of people saying I forgive but I don't forget." Some of these people harbor the spirit of un-forgiveness for many years, sometimes a lifetime. Don't let these harbored resentments eat you alive. Forgive. When you do, you will be following in the steps of He who is the most forgiving, God, the Author of Love. And **there is absolutely nothing you can do that God could never forgive.**

**Friend, stop harboring that resentment and forgive whoever hurt you; even if it means forgiving yourself.**

## EVERYONE IS LOOKING FOR YOU | AUGUST 13

*"Very early in the morning, while it was till dark, Jesus got up, left the house and went off to a solitary place, where He prayed. Simon and his companions went to look for him, and when they found Him, they exclaimed: 'Everyone is looking for you!' Jesus replied, 'Let's go somewhere else to the nearby villages-so I can preach there also. That is why I have come.'" Mark 1: 35-38*

---

When was the last time you went away in a solitary place to be with God? I don't mean going to church retreat or seminar. I mean totally alone with God, just you, God, and silence. Some of you have, but I venture to guess that most of you have not. There was a time when I counted myself among the "have not" group.

A few years back, I went on a mission trip with a group from our church. Given the spiritual environment, I woke up very early in the morning, well before sunrise; I would read my Bible, sit there and hear God speak to me from within the silence. It was during these private audiences with God that He was able to set my spiritual world afloat. If you find that you are going through some rough times and are struggling to rid yourself of depression, it is high time that you find some time for you and God to have a heart-to-heart. You needn't have to go on a mission trip to find time alone with God. You can do it in the privacy of your own home.

God is well aware of your difficulties as well as your sorrows, and He alone can grant you peace and comfort. He hears your prayer and will speak to you, but it is important that you listen, not only with your mind and body, but also with your heart and soul. If you are having a difficult time trying to commune with God, then you are not setting quiet times alone with Him. Quiet times alone means spending time with God in solitude, just like His Son Jesus did. Even when he was amidst crowds and attention seekers, Jesus could still spend quiet times with His Father. His mind, body and Spirit were attuned always with His Father. You too can have the same relationship with His Father. Receive His Spirit right now.

Jesus set an example for us. He, too, sought time away from His everyday affairs so he could be alone with His Father. Even before the sun rose, while it was still dark He would leave His house to spend solitary time with His Father. Afterwards, His disciples caught up with Him. Simon exclaimed: "Everyone is looking for you." Many continue to search for Him. Many look at all the wrong places. God dwells in you. Be aware that God is also looking for you. He wants to spend time just with you.

**You will find Him when you stop what you're doing and take time out for a one-on-one.**

# BE KIND AND COMPASSIONATE | AUGUST 14

*"Do not let any unwholesome talk come out of your mouths, but only what is helpful for building others up according to their needs, that it may benefit those who listen. And do not grieve the Holy Spirit of God, with whom you were sealed for the day of redemption. Get rid of all bitterness, rage and anger, brawling and slander, along with every form of malice. Be kind and compassionate to one another, forgiving each other, just as in Christ God forgave you." Ephesians 4: 29-32*

---

Pride can be a wonderful thing. The person who is proud of his or her accomplishments is apt to be more motivated than someone who is indifferent to or, worse yet, ashamed of his or her achievements. On the other hand, pride, can be a very negative force when the focus of our actions is to protect one's name, feelings or reputation.

Sometimes we ignore the promptings of the Holy Spirit and allow pride to take over. There is not one among us who hasn't wished he or she could take back words that proved to be hurtful, condescending, spiteful or even malicious. Even when reasonable people would agree that the words you have spoken are factual, you must consider how those words will ultimately affect a friendship, a family tie, even a marriage. The fact is that you do not score extra points for being right. Sometimes, it is wrong to be right. You may be able to declare victory with respect to a particular skirmish, but the damage you have inflicted may cause you to lose the war (a so-called Pyrrhic victory). Sometimes, the best revenge is no revenge at all. By acting "cool" in the face of being wronged, the unsaid words may hit home more than the words that might have been spoken. It would behoove each of us to contemplate on this text each morning before you come in contact with your neighbor. Always listen first before responding. Use this text to answer any misgivings or discussions. You will find you will accomplish and benefit much when you say and treat others with kind and compassionate conversations. Kindness is a Godly trait. Try it next time you encounter an unpleasant situation.

I am reminded of the text (John 4: 1-42) where Jesus meets the Samaritan woman at the well. She feigns innocence, but Jesus goes straight to the heart of the matter and tells her that she's had five husbands and the one she was with was not her husband. What was significant here was that **Jesus was not condescending or condemning in His manner and tone of voice; rather He spoke in tones that were supportive. He exuded love. In other words, He treated her kindly.** She was attracted to His kind and compassionate spirit. Another loving trait of God's character is His willingness to forgive. He forgave her. She finally found her true love.

## "WHAT'S LOVE GOT TO DO WITH IT?" | AUGUST 15

*"Wives, submit to your husbands as to the Lord. For the husband is the head of the wife as Christ is the head of the church, his body, of which He is the Savior. Now as the church submits to Christ, so also wives should submit to their husbands in everything. Husbands, LOVE YOUR WIVES, just as Christ loved the church and gave Himself up to her." Ephesians 5: 22-25*

---

Much earlier in this book, we spoke of the possible need for a so-called "newer testament". Suffice it to say that this is one of those passages that begs that question. The preceding passage, arguably suggests sexism. Some claim that organized religions are sexist. Moslem women must cover their faces. Catholic women are ineligible for the priesthood. Orthodox Judaism is, some have argued, a men-only club.

How can we subscribe to the notion of the Bible's being Divinely-inspired without accepting female subjugation, slavery, bigamy and the like? It all gets back to the perception we have of God as the Author of Love. Today's verse DOES speak of subjugation of women, but it all but orders the men to LOVE their wives. Moreover, love is defined rather explicitly: it is the kind of love that Christ had for the church and His people. A love that has God as its foundation is one in which each of the parties subjugates her or his own needs for the sake of the other. Certainly, Christ demonstrated this by sacrificing His very life for us. This text is not about submitting wives but about Godly love towards your spouse.

Nevertheless, there's no denying the first part of the verse. The fact is that there are Biblical passages that reflect the character of the day. What is, however, consistent through the centuries is the notion of Godly love. Man, not God, has demeaned women over the years. God urges us to love our spouses, just as He has loved us. It is a love in which both spouses play leading roles as well as supporting roles. It's O.K. for the woman to take lead in a family if the husband is incapacitated or does not have the drive to lead. It's OK for the wife to submit (relent) to the husband if the wife does it in love and vice-versa. It's all about the love that is shared between couples, family, friends and even total strangers. Love governs your actions. Love is self-less. That is how God loves us and set the example for us on how to love one another.

I have discovered in my observation of love relationships, that the submissive wife exudes the Spirit of love towards her husband in the same manner the husband demonstrates his love towards his wife by placing her first, even above his life, just as God gave His life for His church. God is love. His whole essence is about love.

**"What's love got to do with it?" EVERYTHING!**

## A COMPLETE HEART LIFT | AUGUST 16

*"Being confident of this, that he who began a good work in you will carry it on to completion until the day of Christ Jesus." Philippians 1: 6*

---

I saw a bumper sticker the other day which read, "Please be patient God is not finished with me." It's a message worth heeding.

I have an 88 year old friend who decided to undergo a face-lift. Her physician convinced her she would look considerably younger. After the surgery my friend was in so much pain she second-guessed her decision to undergo such a procedure.

My relative decided to undergo stomach stapling in order to lose weight. After the surgery, he was hospitalized for over one month due to complications. He confessed that, if he'd foreseen knew the consequences of the surgery, he'd have avoided his hardship. He lost much weight but the prize he paid both emotionally and physically was, to him, not worth it.

A recent documentary from China hyped the notion that tall men were most desirable to women. In order to stretch their height, men were allowing physicians to break their bones in several places and then separating the break with braces to all new bone to fill the gaps. Gaining a few inches brought about much self-esteem and confidence, but the pain and new gait was suspect.

Regrettably, most of us are not entirely thrilled with the reflection we see in the mirror. Thus the hair implants, tummy tucks, nose jobs, and the like. Some psychologists believe that a physical change can help increase self-confidence and bring about a higher self-esteem. There is, however, an alternative: love and accept yourself as you are. Paul stated: "He who began a good work in you will carry it on to the completion until the day of Christ Jesus."

God is not finished with you and me. He wants to do a total makeover, but His makeover will focus on the spiritual. God will create a new you if you are willing. God wants to give you a heart like His. His heart knows how to see and love beyond the realm of the exterior. His heart loves the unlovable. His heart sees the person and has total acceptance. His heart loves unconditionally. His heart loves you just as you are. He wants to instill in you a heart like His. His heart cares about your completion. Won't you trust Him with your heart?

**God wants to do a complete "heart-lift". You're looking good!**

## IN ALL THINGS BE CONTENT | AUGUST 17

*"I am not saying this because I am in need, for I have learned to be content whatever the circumstances. I know what it is to be in need, and I know what it is to have plenty. I have learned the secret of being contentment in any and every situation, whether well fed or hungry, whether living in plenty or in want. I can do everything through Him, who gives me strength." Philippians 4: 11-13*

---

Viktor Frankl's (1946) book entitled "Man's Search for Meaning: An Introduction to Logotherapy" (Therapy through Meaning) intensely searched for the purpose of his existence and the meaning of his life while a prisoner at Auschwitz concentration camp. The Suffering he witnessed and those that survived were tantamount to his conclusions. Frankl saw the meaning of life is found in every moment of living, life never ceases to have meaning, even in suffering or confronting death. He also noted that those who had no faith in the future were doomed. He discovered the answer to his search for meaning when he and a fellow prisoner began to reflect on the image of their wives. He stated he could see, hear and feel her presence as vivid as the stars twinkling at night or the sun rising in the day. Those images allowed him to survive and have faith because of his love for her. He found the truth-"that love is the ultimate and highest goal to which men can aspire. The salvation of man is through love and in love."

Only God can reveal the truth about the meaning of life and Frankl was well aware of this. He realized that God is love. Yet, Frankl may have been in the most morbid situation in his life, just as Joseph in prison, or John the Baptist who met his death in prison, but all these people had an inner peace and calm assurance that God was in charge of their life and they relied solely on Him for their salvation. They learned to trust God. They placed their whole heart and soul in Him. They did not give up their faith and hope on Him who is the author and finisher of their faith. They learned to be content in any situation, environment or predicament they were in.

In today's text, Paul learned the secret of being content through all circumstances. Whether he had food on the table or not, whether in had material wealth or not, whether he had love or not, Paul concluded without reservation or doubt that God fulfills Him completely and gives him strength to live content. **Your contentment, regardless of your circumstance or fate is in knowing, trusting and believing God, The Author of Love.**

You will never want or strive for anything this world has to offer you if you have the Spirit of God dwelling in you. God is your peace.

## FULL OF JOY | AUGUST 18

*"Out of the most severe trial, their overflowing joy and their extreme poverty welled up in rich generosity." II Corinthians 8: 2*

---

I have discovered that the secret to lifting oneself out of poverty is to give. Talk about a contradiction in terms...right? Actually, no.

Each quarter, our church takes a collection for the less fortunate. This is in addition to the traditional tithe and the free-will offering. We are amazed that, even in the bad times, people continue to give. Sometimes, people will give or give more when they have a little extra in their purses and wallets. True giving however, is to give when, by all reasonable standards, you have nothing to spare.

I recall when my mother retired and began collecting social security, she would not only tithe from her Social Security check, but she would double it. I, frankly, wondered why she was so generous, given the fact that that check barely covered her necessities. I must tell you that I was embarrassed because I was making ten times her income, and she was donating as much as I was. Mother was always giving, irrespective of her personal circumstances. Very importantly, she was not merely a giver; she was a joyful giver. She gave freely and joyously. You want to experience joy, then give.

Mother was forever of the mind that, whatever her plight, there was always another whose situation was more pressing – in some instances, more dire. Recently, there have been announcements of donors giving literally hundreds of millions of dollars to various schools. Typically a building or program is named in their honor. Some question their motives. They claim it's for tax purposes, or it's an ego trip. Others argue that we have no right to question motives. Suffice it to say that such acts are indeed acts of generosity. However, the joyful giver is the one who gives and then does without. That is certainly the kind of love God bestowed on us.

God knew about the joy of giving. Even though the road to giving was marred with jealousy and persecution, He saw beyond the portals of this earth's poverty and gave His life for us so we might be rich in His glory.

**You can experience the full joy that comes from God simply by giving not only of what you have saved but especially of yourself.**

## TIMING IS EVERYTHING | AUGUST 19

*"When the time had fully come, God sent forth his Son, born of a woman, born under the law, to redeem them those under the law, that we might receive the full rights of sons." Galatians 4: 4 & 5*

---

God had a plan for us long before there was "an us". Christ's coming was not something God conjured up last-minute after man sinned. God had intended to send His Son long before the earth was created. When Eve gave birth to her first child, they thought that he was the fulfilled promise of the Deliverer. Millennia passed and still no savior. Even the prophets became somewhat disillusioned. Ezekiel 12: 22 said: "The days are prolonged and every vision fail." Many generations handed down the story of a savior whose mission it would be to save us. Many of them went to the grave not knowing for certain that the promise would be fulfilled. "Just like the stars in the sky and the planets that follow their appointed pathways. God's purpose is not hastened or delayed."

Have you ever wondered why you were born in such a time as this? Or have you looked at the love of your life and wondered how you met at the very instant that you did and what might have happened had you altered your routine just a trifle? And how about those who suffer, is that, too, part of God's plan?

There is an important nuance here – to wit: God knows the beginning and end of our lives and all that is between. He is, after all, all-knowing. God has, however, given us free will. Did He know that Adam and Eve would disregard His warning respecting the fruit of the Tree of Life? Yes indeed. However, as we discussed earlier, God is not a puppeteer. The decision to eat of the tree was theirs.

There is a significant difference in time and perspective between God and ourselves. We want everything now. God thinks in terms of eternal. We see what is in front of us. God sees the big picture. God's timing is perfect. Even knowing the consequences of His creation of us; He still wanted us in His life. When the fullness of time to send His Son had come, God sent His Son to save us. What perfect love, what perfect time and what a perfect God.

Everything God does is governed by His love for us. **Since He is perfect, His love is perfect, His timing will be perfect when He comes again to finally take us home to be with Him.** Eternity would have come to its full time.

## THE CHILD JESUS | AUGUST 20

*"And the child grew and became strong; he was filled with wisdom, and the grace of God was upon him." Luke 2: 40*

Most of the first four books of the New Testament focus on the last years of Christ's earthly sojourn. The above verse is from a text that speaks to His formative years. There is another text that provides a vignette from Christ's early teens (verse 42), "When he was twelve years old, they went up to the Feast, according to the custom. While at the Feast of the Passover, the boy Jesus stayed behind in Jerusalem while his parents left for home. Thinking perhaps He was traveling with relatives or friends in the caravan, not until they were a day's journey away did they discover He was missing. They immediately returned to Jerusalem to search for Him. After three days of searching they found Him in the Temple courts, dialoging with teachers and listening to them and asking them questions. Everyone who heard Him was amazed at His keen perception and wisdom."

To understand His in-depth grasp of the Bible, one needed to look no further than His first teacher, Mary. It is the parent who educates (or fails to educate) the child about all matters Godly. Jesus grew up in Nazareth, a poor, rough town which, according to John: 46 had "...nothing good to come out of it." Because of who He was, He bore the added burden of being targeted by Satan and his legions, who threw one temptation after another at Him. God loved His Son and sent angels to protect and minister to Him. God was also instructing Jesus each step of the way.

Can you imagine Jesus' pondering every star, leaf, bird and animal as if they were like you and me? Are you aware that the Author of Love wants every child to experience the same knowledge which Jesus experienced as a child? Yes, your child has an opportunity to know God, much the way that Jesus did. It is incumbent upon you to instill the knowledge of God in your child. Thus, when your child is called upon, he or she will be ready to accept the task which God has called upon him or her to perform. **Just like the child Jesus, your child can experience the joy and fullness of His presence in his or her life.** You can represent God in their lives by introducing them to Jesus. You needn't worry about misrepresentation. Just like Jesus depended on His Father for all things, you can do likewise. Just like Mary, the mother of Jesus, their picture of Jesus will first come from you.

In giving of His Son, God gave us a perfect role model to emulate. Remember, His education and knowledge of God started way before His adult ministry.

## **FAITH EXPRESSED IN LOVE** | AUGUST 21

*"For in Christ Jesus neither circumcision nor uncircumcision has any value. The only thing that counts is faith expressing itself through love." Galatians 5: 6*

---

I read a parable from Darwin Forster about a handsome prince who was the envy of all who knew him. He was gentle and kind and real friends to those he met. One summer he threw a ball and there he met a beautiful princess who captured his heart. In time they were married and began a life together. Their first project was to beautify their village. They planted trees and flowers and landscaped the entire village. Everyone admired their handiwork.

One day, as the prince was returning home from a journey, he saw his princess on the side of the road weeping. He asked her why she was crying, and she pointed to the garden, where everything had withered and died. The prince was shocked that their effort to beautify the kingdom was apparently for naught.

It was just about that time a wise man came by and provided them with a plan for reviving their garden. They must, he instructed, spend time in the garden regularly. They needed to tend to the weeding the raking of the leaves, the trimming of the bushes and the watering. He added that it was essentially the same for human relationships. Plants and humans, both, require care and attention.

Having a relationship requires faith that is grounded in love. God came to save us. He lived among us and tended to our needs. He continues to express His love toward us, and He has promised to love us eternally. There is nothing more important to Him than you. Your own relationship with God is somewhat like gardening. You can plant a few seeds, water the soil every so often and marvel at the beautiful outcome. However, if you want your garden to flourish year after year, you must prune the plants, fertilize, and sow more seeds. Your relationship with God requires much the same kind of nurturing. **Expressions of love evolve through a daily nurturing/pruning of your relationship with God.**

Take the time to know God. Savor the moments you spend with Him. Learn from Him. There is much to learn from your Maker. Listen to His voice guide your daily living. Be still and know God. Shun the distractions of this world. You cannot serve God and mammon. "Choose ye this day whom you will serve. Let it be the Lord."

**Receive the faith He wants to bestow on you, and your faith will express itself through His love.**

## THE TRUTH WILL SET YOU FREE | AUGUST 22

*"Then you will know the truth, and the truth shall set you free." John 8: 32*

I had an uncle, who was pastor to the first Filipino Seventh Day Adventist church not only in the United Sates but in the Western Hemisphere. I recall a sermon of his, which told of a slave auction in which a strong and healthy but stubborn slave was placed on the auction block. The man unceremoniously let it be known that he was born a free man and that he had no intention of being a slave to anyone.

The bidding began, and the price kept increasing. Bidders figured this strong, young man could do the work of several men. A rather meek and humble-appearing man joined the bidding and made what turned out to be the final and winning bid. He took the shackled slave home. Once at his master's home, the slave was quick to reiterate that he would not work for him. The humble man unshackled the slave and told him that he was free to go. The slave proceeded to fall to his knees in joy and gratitude and said: "I will be your slave for life."

Today, virtually all of us consider ourselves to be free. However, many – some would say, most – of us are slaves of a different kind. We are slaves to sin, to habit, to superstition, to obsession. Sometimes, the slavery is readily apparent, as is the case of the drug addict, or it may be more subtle, like the child who is a slave to the approval of his or her peers.

There is, however, one way to be truly free, and that is to know the truth. Jesus said: "I am the WAY, the TRUTH and the LIFE." To know the truth is to know God. Do you know God? Does He reign supremely in your life? If He does, you can consider yourself free. Follow His way and you will have life eternal. There is no other way to freedom than through your Maker.

God's way is freedom – freedom from sin, from addiction, from obsession, from anything which makes you a slave. He has paid for your freedom from sin through the sacrifice of His life. Whatever enslavement you are experiencing today, you can be set free right now by asking God to be the master of your whole life. His mastery is total freedom. His whole purpose was to set you free. If you accept His freedom then you will be free from the slavery of sin. God's freedom is totally devoid of any shackles or encumberances.

**God is your passport to freedom. Accept His gift to you, His Son, Jesus Christ? He's your freedom.**

## FAITHFUL AS THE RAIN | AUGUST 23

*"Come let us return to the Lord. He has torn us to pieces but He will heal us; He has injured us but He will bind up our wounds. After two days He will revive us; on the third day he will restore us that we may live in his presence. Let us acknowledge the Lord; let us press on to acknowledge him. As surely as the sun rises, He will appear; He will come to us like the winter rains, like the spring rains that water the earth." Hosea 6: 1-3*

---

When Jesus was in Capernaum early in His ministry, the news of His miraculous healing power spread rapidly throughout that region. The people did not come to see Jesus until after sundown for fear that the rabbis would condemn them and Christ for healing on the Sabbath. Once the sun set, the people came to see Jesus at Peter's mother-in-law's home. Everyone that came to see Jesus was healed. Every minute, Jesus saw a person in need of healing, from the blind, the lame, the possessed, those with secret sin or the addicted personality. His mere touch rendered them whole again. Not one was left hopeless. The healing continued throughout the night until the last person left healed. It was a scene of pure joy. Even Jesus rejoiced in His power to restore them, not only to health but happiness.

Very early in the morning, after everyone was asleep and stillness hovered over the home and the city, Jesus journeyed to a solitary place and prayed. It had become a pattern for Him. Whenever He had the opportunity to be alone with His Father, He would spend hours praying and meditating with regard to His mission. He was concerned that there was developing an almost single-minded focus on the healings. Even though He delighted in healing the sick, He knew that such miracles were of the earth and, therefore, temporary.

God wanted them to focus on a greater healing, one that is eternal. Are you waiting for an answered prayer today? Are you having second thoughts about God's healing grace? Do you sometimes feel God is selective on whom He gives healing, wealth or justice? Are you experiencing doubts that cloud your mind and trust in God? Are you tired of asking but never receiving answers? Do you feel like throwing in the towel? Sometimes our faith wanes because we don't see evidences of His healing power. You must not lose hope in Him.

As today's text reminds us, like the rain that comes in the winter or spring, and as sure as the sun rising each morning, so is God's love and care for each of us. **God is ever steadfast and faithful to us. No one is exempted from His faithful love towards us. The question is, are we as faithful to Him?**

## A PRAYER ANSWERED | AUGUST 24

*"Then the angel continued, 'Do not be afraid, Daniel. Since the first day that you set your mind to gain understanding and to humble yourself before your God, your words were heard, and I have come in response to them. But the prince of the Persian kingdom resisted me twenty-one days. Then Michael, one of the chief princes, came to help me, because I was detained there with the king of Persia.'" Daniel 10: 12 & 13*

---

The Bible instructs us to "pray without ceasing." Have you prayed and never received an answer? I have. I have prayed for many things, and, many times, I was delighted when the prayer was answered immediately. What about the times you prayed and there were no answers? Whatever your response is to prayer, the Bible counsels us to pray without ceasing.

God wants us to pray to Him. He wants us to have a prayerful life. The text today reminds us that God hears our prayers and He responds. There was a minister years ago who said the art of praying is as simple as ABC (Accept, Believe and Claim it). Prayer is more than ABCs. It is an attitude of faith that is relational and a life commitment to your Creator. Sometimes we have answered prayers and sometimes it takes time. Regardless of the outcome, let us not waver in our faith in God. Our future is in God's care. He will deliver and redeem us into His promise kingdom. You must wait in faith.

The story of Daniel is one of a life of prayer. Daniel was thrown in the lion's den for refusing to stop his daily routine of praying to God. Today's text shares with us another answered prayer of Daniel. He was given a vision that he could not understand. Daniel prayed continuously for 21 days. He neither ate nor drank anything during that time. On the 24th day of the month, while he was standing on the banks of the Tigris River with some of his fellows, he saw a man of unusual appearance. Although the men with Daniel did not see what he saw, they sense a presence that so overwhelmed them with terror that they fled. Daniel was told by this man not to be afraid. He went on to explain to Daniel his prayer was answered the very moment he prayed. But this "angel" was detained for 21 days because the "prince" of the Persian kingdom resisted him.

It was no different in Daniel's time as it is today. God wants you to have a prayerful life. Our trust in God is what will see us through those times of what seemingly seems to us an unanswered prayer. God has answered your prayer even before you asked Him. Don't fret or be dismayed if you do not see what you want instantly.

Jesus was a great example of living a prayerful life. He waited on His Father in faith and trust regardless of His present circumstances. **To Jesus, a prayerful life was His link to His heavenly Father. You can have that same prayerful as Jesus.**

## LORD THE ONE YOU LOVE | AUGUST 25

*"So the sisters sent word to Jesus, "Lord the one you love is sick." John 11: 3*

The story of Lazarus was a story of love. Jesus loved Lazarus, Martha and Mary. He would go out of his way to spend some time with these people. He loved taking a break and just fellowshipping with them at their home. Today's text tells us about the love of God for not only Lazarus but for all of us.

When Jesus received word that the one He loved, Lazarus, was sick, Jesus did not immediately go to his friend's side to rescue him from his illness, instead He tarried awhile in Judea. In fact He stayed away for four days. Jesus regarded death as sleep. He discusses this in verse 11: "Our friend Lazarus has fallen asleep; but I am going there to wake him up."

Though we regard death as final, Jesus saw death as falling asleep. Even His disciples assumed that Jesus meant that Lazarus was in a natural state of sleep (verse 12) but He corrected them and said Lazarus was dead (verse 14). We have lost loved ones through sickness here on earth. We even prayed for God's healing. Some were healed, like in the case of Lazarus, others went to sleep with the LORD. God loved them all. He is the God of Life Eternal. Someday, God has promised us we will no longer experience earth's death. We will have His external life.

The story of Lazarus is more than raising the dead. It underscores God's word that the dead are indeed asleep and that they will arise when God speaks those words, "Come out!" E.G. White's book "Desire of Ages" p, 528 Says, "Christ remained away. He suffered the enemy to exercise his power, that he might drive him back, a conquered foe. He permitted Lazarus to pass under the dominion of death; and the suffering sisters saw their brother laid in the grave. Christ knew that as they looked on the dead face of their brother their faith in their Redeemer would be severely tried. But He knew that because of the struggle through which they were now passing their faith would shine forth with far greater power. He suffered every pang of sorrow they endured. To all who are reaching out to feel the guiding hand of God, the moment of greatest discouragement is the time when divine help is nearest. We will look back with thankfulness upon the darkest part of our way." "The Lord knows how to deliver the godly." (II Peter 2: 9). The Lord loves us more than His own life.

**The one the Lord loves will someday hear His voice "Come Out!" and all our loved ones will awake from their slumber and will be united with us forevermore.**

## A SILENT FRIEND | AUGUST 26

*"They asked each other 'Were not our hearts burning within us while He talked with us on the road and opened the Scriptures to us?" Luke 24: 32*

---

Two disciples of Jesus were walking to a village name Emmaus. This journey was about seven miles from Jerusalem. Along the way, a stranger came up and walked along with them. They did not recognize Jesus. He asked them: "What are you discussing so intently?" They replied: "Are you only a visitor to Jerusalem and do not know the things that have happened there in these days?" "What things?" He inquired? The two disciples, one named Cleopas and the other named Simon, recounted the events that occurred. They spoke of how Jesus had been handed over to the chief priests and rulers, sentenced to death, crucified. They related how a woman saw the empty tomb and was informed by an angel that Jesus was indeed alive. They spoke of how the people had hoped Jesus would establish his kingdom and be their ruler here on earth. They wanted Him to redeem them from their oppressors. Jesus had answered the people by declaring: "How foolish you are, and how slow of heart to believe all that the prophets have spoken. Did not the Christ have to suffer these things and then enter his glory? And beginning with Moses and all the prophets, He explained to them what was said in all the scriptures concerning Him." Luke 24: 19-27.

The two disciples were moved by the words Jesus spoke; yet they still did not recognize Him. As they neared their destination, the two men implored Jesus: "Stay with us, for it is nearly evening; the day is almost over." So Jesus stayed with them.

We are all on a journey in this world. Each day we work, go to school, to church, to social events, we watch TV, play sports, enjoy nature, and gather for special holidays and occasions. Each day we experience good times and bad times as we go about our daily living. Once in a while we get jarred by the news of a death in the family, maybe the birth of your first infant, a tumultuous divorce can be depressing or a debilitating illness. All these events can distract us from God.

Whatever road you are traveling today, are you aware that Jesus is with you? Yes, He is so close that He even dwells in your hearts. Do you notice Him nearby? **Ask God to tarry awhile with you today, and you'll probably want Him to stay a little longer. He is your silent friend. And remember, God can reveal Himself in so many ways, be sensitive to His Spirit. It may be that neighbor or stranger.**

## WHO TOUCHED ME? | AUGUST 27

*"At once Jesus realized that power had gone out from him. He turned around in the crowd and asked, "Who touched my clothes?" 'You see the people crowding against you,' his disciples answered, 'and yet you can ask who touched me?'" Mark 5: 30 & 31*

---

"Seeing is believing," so the saying goes. Jesus came to visit a ruler in the synagogue named Jairus. Jairus pleaded with Jesus to help his little daughter who was dying. So, Jesus set out to the ruler's house. On His way, He found himself surrounded by a crowd, anxious to hear His words and witness His miracles.

There was a woman in the crowd who had an illness which was a burden to her in her life. She had a "bleeding" illness that was in its 12th year. She had spent all those years in the hands of physicians that could not cure her disease. They had pronounced her incurable. Have you ever felt that way? Have you or a love one ever received news from your doctor that you've contracted an incurable disease. That is an ominous feeling.

This woman's faith was strengthened when she heard how Jesus cured others. She believed that if she could just touch Jesus' garment she could be healed. Amid the crowd and confusion, she could not be heard or get near Him, and she only caught a glimpse of Him as He passed by. An opportunity occurred when He passed by her and she reached in desperation and succeeded in touching a piece of His garment. Immediately her pain and disease left her, and she was in perfect health. She wanted to withdraw quietly and not seek attention but Jesus stopped His forward progress and asked, "Who touched me?"

There is a meaningless jostle touch and a touch of faith. The disciples and people around Him did not understand Jesus' words But Jesus felt power leave Him. The woman could not hide her act. She came forward and told her story of years of suffering and how she was finally healed. Jesus said to her, "Daughter your faith has healed you. Go in peace and be freed from your suffering." (Verse 34).

Do you long for healing today? Whether the healing is physical or spiritual, God is longing to heal you right this minute. Just be sure to tell Him, His will be done. God wants to heal you today. He is waiting for you to answer His question "who touched me?" If you exercise the kind of faith the woman in the story did, you will be healed not only physically but spiritually. **Jesus is passing by you. Have faith in Him. Touch His garment now.**

## A HOLY KISS | AUGUST 28

*"Greet Philologus, Julia, Nereus and his sister, and Olympas and all the saints with them. Greet one another with a holy kiss. All the churches of Christ send greetings." Romans 16: 15 & 16*

---

Have you ever been on a mission trip? Each year our church pastor goes on one. I have been to five of them. I have been to the Philippines three times, Thailand twice and Jamaica once. Every trip consists of building, repairing or painting churches, schools or camp grounds. Every trip is memorable. Lifetime friendships are forged.

There are many needs in these places. Some needs are so urgent that spontaneous offerings are taken from among the group. We have paid for wedding, bought motorcycles for some pastors, stoves for the kitchen and commitments to send a child to school. The list is long. Aside from renovating schools and churches we hold evangelistic meetings every night. The highlight of these meetings is the people who commit their lives to God. They seek to be baptized. This was very moving for me.

Today's text talks about Paul's experience during his missionary travels and the people he encountered. Paul devotes a whole chapter in Romans, sending greetings to all these people who one time or another helped him in his journey. In fact, in certain verses of that chapter, he attributes to them saving his life (verse4).

God lived among us and demonstrated to us how we ought to care for one another. There is nothing a friend would not do for his friend or love one. ***This holy kiss is an expression of God's selfless love that is to be a guide on how we are to relate to one another. In your daily journey, you will encounter all types of people. Treat them as though you were dealing with God.*** In following God's example of loving each other, you are truly saving not only the lives of others but your own life.

We are one family under God. We are a community of saints who share a common faith. This is what God was teaching us all along. We are all God's family, and we need to love one another as God loved the Church. Stop the bickering and in-fighting in our home, school, church or community. Instead, when you have the urge of dissension, stop yourself, go to the person that hurt you and give them a holy kiss.

**Always remember to send greetings and greet one another with a holy kiss. In doing so, you are spreading the gospel of God's grace to everyone you come in contact with.**

## GUARD YOUR HEART | AUGUST 29

*"Above all else, guard your heart, for it is the wellspring of your life." Proverbs 4: 23*

---

How well do you know your heart? "Out of the abundance of the heart the mouth speaks." Before you answer that question, notice that the heart, from a physical standpoint, is centered in your body. God knew a thing or two when He created us. The heart is the person. The heart is what makes you "tick." How you treat each other reveals volumes about us. Next to God, the heart is the second-most-popular subject matter in the Bible.

What does God means when He says, "Guard your heart?" Proverbs admonishes us to place this guardianship of the heart above all else. Who is first in your life? I suppose it would depend on your circumstances. During Christ's ministry, people were stricken with leprosy and He healed them, some were demon possessed and He freed them. Then there were the blind, the paralyzed, the mentally-challenged and those with a broad array of other afflictions. Whoever came to Him, He healed.

Word of His healing powers spread quickly, but God wanted for man a greater healing, not only the healing of their afflictions, but a healing of the heart. The heart is where it's at, so to speak. It's who you are. Above all else, it is your heart that God wishes to heal!

Just how much do you value your heart? We tend to be careless with our heats. We have been known to bury our hearts so deeply that we deal only in surface relationships. We deny ourselves the real us that we end up living "lives of quiet desperation." Are you guarding your heart? Are you slow to share your heart? Does it hurt too much to give a little bit of your heart to someone in need? I know, "it's easier said than done," especially if we've been hurt deeply. I don't blame you if you're cautious as to who you allow in your heart. Who sits at the center of your heart?

Your heart is you. God does not want a half-hearted heart. God wants all of your heart. He loved you enough to give all of His for you. You are the center of His heart. He proved that by sending His Son to show you His love for you and how to guard your heart. Don't be careless with your affection and especially your heart. Cherish your heart with much awareness and sensitivity. And never treat another person's heart with contempt or flippantly. God loves them just the same as you.

**Your heart is what makes you tick. Don't be careless with your heart. God did not take you lightly. Look, He died for you. He was dead serious. Then guard your heart as much as He does.**

## RECONCILE WITH THE HOLY SPIRIT | AUGUST 30

*"Therefore, if you are offering your gift at the altar and there remember that your brother has something against you; leave your gift there in front of the altar. First go and be reconciled to your brother, then come and offer your gift." Matthew 5: 23 & 24*

---

I have a friend who is taking care of his elderly mother, who is bedridden and requires 24/7 care. He has the power of attorney as well as the deed to his mother's house. He was able to convince his mother to sign the deed of the house over to him. His brothers and sisters discovered he has the deed to the property and it created a feud between them. Sides were taken and now half the family is not in speaking terms with him. Not only were they angry with what he did "behind their back" but they also brought up "skeletons in his closet" which added more fuel to the fire of their hatred.

At one time or another, we've all been angry at someone to the point that we find it impossible to forgive. We're certain that our anger is justified. Why then, we ask ourselves, should we be the first to extend the hand of reconciliation? Moreover, even if we do, will that stifle the feeling of resentment that resides in our hearts. Worse yet, what do we do if we make that first attempt and the other party does not so much as acknowledge us. Have we gone far enough?

Asking forgiveness or forgiving is not an easy task. We tend to be prideful beings. We must remember, however, that the father of pride is Lucifer. He had the same problem. Until this day, he has been unable to come to terms with his pride. He refuses to reconcile with God. Ask yourself whether you want to go to your grave carrying pride. Is this a weight you choose to carry throughout your earthly days? God tells us that anyone who hates his brother or sister has committed murder in his or her heart. Ouch! That's awfully deep.

God is patiently waiting for us to reconcile with Him. Before you can reconcile with your neighbor, you must receive God's Spirit of reconciliation. Is there someone you are feuding with right now? Or is there some resentment you are harboring on someone. Day in and day out you go to church but that thought of an estrangement with someone lurks at the back or you mind. Do you want reconciliation? Go to God first on your knees. Allow His Spirit to calm your spirit. Then go to that person and forgive him or her. Don't wait to feel it. **He is even knocking at the door asking you to open your heart to receive Him.**

**Just as He has opened His heart to us, it is imperative that we do the same to others. Let His Spirit in.**

## CITIZENSHIP PAPERS | AUGUST 31

*"Our citizenship is in heaven. And we eagerly await a Savior from there, the Lord Jesus Christ." Philippians 3: 20*

---

There has been a good deal of discussion of late regarding the approximately 20-million so-called illegal immigrants living within our nation's borders. Some see this as a potential threat to our security. Others see this as a severe economic problem, given the services that these people avail themselves of. The State of Arizona's decision to tighten the proverbial screws on illegal aliens is seen by many as a long-overdue step to protect what is rightfully ours. An equally-vociferous group believes that the Arizona law is tantamount to racial profiling. They do not want to see law enforcement officers stopping individuals based on their appearance and requesting proof of legal status. They argue that it is selfish and ungodly.

Our nation has, by virtue of its First Amendment, endeavored to separate matters of church from state. Some regard this as surrender to heathenism. By most measures, however, this is a good thing. When the state injects itself into matters of religion, it cannot do so without favoring certain religious thoughts over others. Moreover, while our own religious beliefs are indeed fervent, our Constitution does grant citizens the right not to practice any religion. We may find this morally repugnant, but the freedom to choose is fundamental to this nations' being.

For us Christians, it is imperative that we remember that our earthly stay is but a visit. When we are called to enter God's Kingdom, we shall be one people, devoid of borders, where every man and woman will have Godly love for one another. We live today – temporarily, of course – in an imperfect world. However, God has demonstrated how we might render this world more perfect. The Author of Love has demonstrated how we might extend our love to all, regardless of who they are and what their background. We can begin a heavenly attitude to others while still here on earth. Treat each neighbor, regardless of their origin or border with a Christ-like spirit of inclusiveness. How do you treat a person dressed differently than the accepted norm? How do you relate to people of different skin tones? How do you show respect to those with limited English or thick accents? Would you believe that someday they may be your neighbor in heaven? You can treat them godly and with fervent respect if you are connected to God's Spirit.

**Remember our citizenship is not in the greatest country in this world; our citizenship is in heaven where we eagerly wait to be with our Lord and Savior Jesus Christ.**

## HATE THE SIN LOVE THE SINNER | SEPTEMBER 1

*"Hate evil, love good; maintain justice in the courts. Perhaps the Lord God Almighty will have mercy on the remnant of Joseph." Amos 5: 15*

---

There is a proverb that says "hate the sin but love the sinner." It's easy to say...but not quite as easy to achieve. The truth of the matter there is no Biblical verse that says this. But many zealot Christians have used this adage to reflect God's way of dealing with us. Several years ago, I received a call from a very close friend whose family I considered part of my extended family. Martha was distraught. She sought my counsel. It seems that she and her husband had recently returned from her homeland of Vietnam. By the way of background; Martha had fled the Communists as a child. She went with her mother to France to live and study there. When she came of age, she traveled to America. It was while working in a nursing home that she met her husband, Don. They have five grown children. They worked hard and lived well.

The first visit together to Vietnam was for a month. Martha visited the village where she was born. She even found her elementary school teacher and a few classmates. It was a joyous reunion. They so loved the country that they decided to go back there three months later. It was in this second trip that she discovered that her husband was having an affair with another woman. She was devastated. She loved her husband but could not maintain a relationship with him as long as he was disloyal to her. She felt betrayed. She could not separate the sin from the sinner. She hated his behavior as well as him.

No matter what the outcome, it is evident that she must not rely on Don but rather upon God for her completeness. How does one continue to love the person that offended you? through the constant daily receptivity of the Spirit of God. The sooner you stop resisting God's Spirit to heal your wounded heart, the sooner you will learn to love. In due time the wounds will heal and you will be able to look at the sinner with compassion.

God would have been justified to had "divorced" and done away with us because we, too, committed adultery of sorts by turning away from Him and having an affair, call it, with the "father of lies". However, though we be sinners, God loves us, nonetheless. He could not bear to live eternity without us. He gave His life as payment for our errant ways so that we might eventually see the wisdom of His ways. His display of love for us is virtually incomprehensible.

**God showed us how to love the sinner. Through God's Spirit and guidance, you will learn to hate evil deeds, love the person and maintain justice in all of your affairs.**

## HEAR WHAT GOD SAYS | SEPTEMBER 2

*"He who belongs to God hears what God says. The reasons you do not hear is that you do not belong to God." John 8: 47*

---

I learned recently that a very dear friend for over 25 years is planning a divorce – this, after 27 years of marriage. Their parting is fairly amicable, although my friend (the wife) would prefer to salvage the marriage. The husband wants to have the freedom to play the field. In counseling her, we speculated as to what went wrong – everything from midlife crisis to a loss of sensibility. We'll never really know.

I inquired as to whether she has asked God for strength and guidance, and perhaps due to her feeling of upset, her reply was: "I'm in no mood to talk to God." It is unfortunate that, when we most need to listen to God – marital dissolution, death of a loved one, major medical difficulties – that's when we shut Him out of our lives. It is ironic that we might feel this way because sometimes our present situation is the result of our failure to listen for God's prompts.

As if to aggravate matters even more, we sometimes find ourselves listening to an entirely different voice, the one who speaks no truth. Jesus does not mince words when He expounds on this subject (verses 33 & 34): "Why is my language not clear to you? Because you are unable to hear what I say, you belong to your father, the devil, and you want to carry out your father's desire. He was a murderer from the beginning, not holding to the truth, for there is no truth in him. When he lies, he speaks his native language, for he is a liar and the father of lies." Talk about telling it like it is!

We're likely all familiar with the Verizon spokesman who asks: "Can you hear me now?" The only equipment you need to hear God's voice is the innermost reaches of your heart. His voice is not condemnatory, nor is it harsh or accusatory (Romans 8: 1). If you hear words of blame and fault finding, that is NOT God speaking. If you feel guilt, and regrets and disillusion, that is NOT God. **God speaks only words of encouragement and hope.** Do not listen to other voices that speak contrary to His love. I have a friend who has been struggling with God's love for him. Some of his family, friends and church goers have told him he is going to hell if he does not stop his sinful ways. Yet, a kindhearted man has counseled him that God loves him with faults and all. He's confused. I told him Hear the word of the Lord. God loves you, God is love. Anyone who does not love does not know God. If you hear contra about God's love, then it's not from God. 1 John 4: 7-21

**His Spirit is kind, gentle and comforting**. You will know Him because He will speak grace. Listen to Him right this moment. Hear what He says for He speaks only in truth and in love. Can you hear Him now? If you do, then you belong to Him.

## A CURE FOR AIDS | SEPTEMBER 4

*"A man with leprosy came to him and begged him on his knees, 'If you are willing,' he said 'you can make me clean.' Filled with compassion, Jesus reached out his hand and touched the man.' 'I am willing,' he said, 'Be clean!' Immediately the leprosy left him and he was cured.'" Mark 1: 40-42*

---

The term leprosy comes from the Greek "lepra. " During Christ's day, anyone with leprosy was an outcast. Lepers were forbidden from mingling with other people. In fact they were to shout warning to other people: "Unclean!" In the early days of the AIDS epidemic, ignorance ran rampant, and people were afraid to so much as shake the hand of a victim of the disease. While we have never compelled AIDS carriers to shout "unclean", some in society go out of their way to avoid any kind of contact with people who are HIV-positive.

Jesus evidenced compassion for the man who begged Him to be healed. He actually touched the man, which, in those times, was considered to mean that you, like the leper, were also unclean. Were Jesus physically among us today, would He shake hands with a person who has AIDS? Without question! More importantly, He would have compassion for such a man, woman or child. Certainly one of the worst things we can do to another people is to shun and reject them. Worse yet is to ignore them, as if to pretend they do not exist. It seems logical to be wary and cautious when we are exposed to someone with a contagious disease. We are fearful of being contaminated.

We are all carriers of AIDS today, but that is AIDS of a different sort -- Acquired Individual Disease of Sin. Unlike AIDS, (at least for now) the disease of sin is curable. Whether a person has AIDS of disease or AIDS of sin, God loves them without bias. Fortunately for us, God has redeemed us from sin. We shall never have to shout "unclean" because God has cleansed us through His own Blood. Jesus urged us to have compassion for the leper, and He would counsel us today to have compassion for not only the AIDS person but all of the outcasts of our society.

The Author of Love has demonstrated tremendous compassion for us, though we be sinners (AIDS). He has embraced us with His arms and His heart. **There is absolutely nothing in this world (disease or sin) and in His universe that will keep Him from wanting you. He will not only touch you but embrace you, care for you, kiss you and heal you**. You can do likewise. Let His example be a lesson for us.

## **DON'T YOU CARE** | SEPTEMBER 5

*"Jesus was in the stern, sleeping on a cushion. The disciples woke him and said to him, 'Teacher, don't you care if we drown?'" Mark 4: 38*

---

How strong is your faith today? Are you equal to life's tests? Do you get discouraged and wonder when Jesus will answer your prayer? What are you asking from God? All through Jesus' ministry, His disciples were always wondering about their teacher. They too wondered if He cared for them. They undoubtedly had their doubts.

As I write this text, I know people who have mortgaged their futures with no solution in sight. I know of relationships that are so torn apart that it would seem that only a miracle might reunite the parties. Lest I begin to sound like the nightly network news, are we all especially in these times, hearing the cry: "Lord, don't you care if we drown?"

During the 19th Century, Nietzsche declared, to the consternation of most, "God is dead!" Now that Nietzsche is dead, has God indeed had the last laugh? In October of 1966, some 66 years after Nietzsche's demise, "Time Magazine" ran a cover story entitled: "Is God Dead?" Some accused the magazine of rendering the question rhetorical. The article bemoaned God's apparent absence from the history books that have chronicled the past millennium or more.

I suppose that there were times when similar thoughts entered into my mind. As a child, I had a problem that was so all-consuming (to me, that is) that I prayed and even fasted, not unlike Paul, when he had a "thorn in his flesh" which he asked God to take away. Well, I had my "Paul thorn of the flesh moment" too. I asked God to take it away but it was not to be. I'm glad I came across this verse that gave me much hope and grace. You'll recall how God responded "my grace is sufficient for you." When you accept God's grace you too will say God's grace is sufficient for me.

Some conclude that, if God turned His back on Paul, what chance do we stand? God did not turn His back on Paul or anyone of us. The fact is that God has already answered our prayers. In verse 40, He proclaims: "Why are you so afraid? Do you still have no faith?" God has already calmed the wind in your life. He asks you "why are you still afraid and worried. Do you still have no faith too?"

**He tells us to trust in Him, and so the question is: "Do we care?" Rest assured God does care.**

## MY BURDEN IS LIGHT | SEPTEMBER 6

*"Come to me, all you who are weary and burdened, and I will give you rest. Take my yoke upon you and learn from me, for I am gentle and humble in heart, and you will find rest for your souls. For my yoke is easy and my burden is light." Matthew 11: 28-30*

---

I came across a story during a mission trip to the Philippines that I want to share with you. Jose and Aaron, best of friends in a small village, were playing hide and seek. Jose hid so cleverly that Aaron couldn't find him. Hoping to drive Jose out of his hiding place, Aaron set fire to the grass. Jose climbed a tree to escape the flames, but the leaves burst into flames, and Jose plunged into the fire below. Terrified, Aaron carried his badly burned friend home to his parents, who rushed him to a hospital. Jose survived but lost both legs. He spent nearly a year in the hospital. A deep hatred took root in his broken heart. His father, too, plotted revenge on Aaron and his family. His boy's dreams of becoming an engineer had been burned in the fire as surely as were his legs. Perhaps murdering the whole family would satisfy a terrible lust for revenge. Aaron and his family heard of the plot and fled far away.

Years later, Jose's family attended an evangelical meeting in their village. Jose was carried on his father's back. Jose chose to be baptized. A similar even took place in Aaron's village, and he, too, sought salvation. It happened that baptismal candidates from both meetings came together for the ceremony, and the boys met for the first time since the tragedy. Under the influence of the Holy Spirit, a miracle of reconciliation occurred. Aaron carried Jose into the water on his back. Cheers of praise filled the air. Jose testified: "The heavy burden that pained my heart for so long has been lifted. Peace runs into my heart."

Do you have a burden that pains you? How long have you been carrying that burden? Once you realize that it was all in vain, you will look back and say "what a waste." Let God lift it from you. Jesus used the oxen image to address, at that time, the use of oxen as "burden of beasts". A yoke was used between two oxen to carry a person's worldly goods. The load appeared quite heavy for a person to carry and even the oxen labored. Jesus said take His yoke. It's easier and His burden lighter. That means following Jesus in faith and not running ahead of Him or lagging behind. **Faith in God is what will make all your cares easy because God's way is effortless. Try Him.**

**When you come to Him, you will learn the Spirit of forgiveness and reconciliation, and you too will say "My burden is light."**

## ARE YOU OUT OF YOUR MIND? | SEPTEMBER 7

*"When his family heard about this, they went to take charge of him, for they said, "He is out of his mind." Mark 3: 21*

---

What a fascinating text to meditate on today! Ever had someone exclaimed, "Are you out of your mind?" In other words "Are you crazy?" I know that I've been asked that at least a few times. Well, Jesus was asked that by His own family.

The problem was that Jesus' family as well as a good many people who witnessed His miracles truly believed He'd lost it. Whatever made them think such thoughts? Some would say that it was because, after Jesus healed the sick and cast out demons, He would go to a mountainside and summon His twelve disciples. He anointed them to preach the good news of God's salvation and to drive out demons, too. Perhaps on the theory that it takes one to know one, the learned scribes and Pharisees accused Jesus – He who rid others of demons –of being a demon Himself. In fact, His own family sided with His critics and proclaimed that He was indeed crazy. Some say that they were trying to protect Jesus by making excuses for Him.

It's been often said that there is but a fine line between genius and insanity. (Oscar Levant., whose witticisms do not often grace texts on religion, was quoted as saying: "There is a fine line between genius and insanity. I have erased this line.")

We do not need to defend Jesus. It is sad that the world often equates being different with being mad or insane. Have you ever thought about how Jesus might be received today if He showed up, say, in the middle of Times Square? If some questioned His sanity back in His own day, can you imagine how a world that has become as cynical as ours would regard a being so pure, so righteous, so full of love. It's a very sad commentary on our society, but there would likely be a movement to commit Him. How sad to consider that we might react to the ultimate manifestation of love in such a hateful way. God's love goes beyond this world insanity.

I think we are the ones who would be out of our minds to think or act that way. **Unless your mind is one with Jesus you too will be caught up in the insanity of this world. There is God's way and the world's way. Do you know the difference?** Can you see God in all your dealings? If not, then you are blinded by the world.

**God's ways are definitely not of this world.**

## TRADITION, TRADITION | SEPTEMBER 8

*"No one sews a patch of unshrunk cloth on an old garment. If he does, the new piece will pull away from the old, making the tear worse. And no one pours new wine into old wineskins. If he does, the wine will burst the skins, and both the wine and the wineskins will be ruined. No, he pours new wine into new wineskins." Mark 2: 21 & 22*

---

Today's text reminds me of a story, you'll not be surprised to hear. A lady was preparing a ham dinner. After she cut off the end of the ham, she placed it in a pan for baking. Her friend asked her: "Why did you cut off the end of the ham?" She replied: "I really don't know, but my mother always did; so I thought you were supposed to." Later, when talking with her mother, she asked her why she cut off the end of the ham before baking it, and her mother replied: "I really don't know, but that's the way my mom always did it." A few weeks later, while visiting her grandmother, she inquired: "Grandma, why is it that you cut off the end of the ham before you bake it?" Her grandmother replied: "Well dear, it would never fit into my baking pan."

During Christ's time, there were specific traditions handed down which most people would not even contemplate breaking. One such rule concerned mixing with Gentiles, tax collectors, prostitute and "sinners." Jesus addressed this point in verse 17: "It is not the healthy who need a doctor, but the sick. I have not come to call the righteous, but sinners."

The Pharisees, who were virtually married to their traditions, regarded these as their security blankets, and they scorned most others. They could not function without their handed down traditions. But their traditions made no sense. It became a burden and a drag to follow. What's sad is some of these traditions are still being followed today. There are many faiths and religions that follow tradition to the core. Much of what we observe as holidays of goodwill did not originate that way. Have you ever wondered why? Are you guilty of following such traditions? Isn't it time you changed the process?

We are all sinners in need of a Savior. **God came for all of us to show us how much He loves us. He came not for the righteous, but for the sinner. He also came to show us a better tradition – a tradition not handed down by man but by God.** He showed us how to accept and embrace everyone, regardless what their makeup, religion, sexual orientation or gender is. God reached out to us, and He wants us to reach out to those who are burdened with traditions that make no sense or hurtful. **The only true tradition is the one that comes from above.** Now, that's a tradition worth handing down.

## **I WANT TO SEE** | SEPTEMBER 9

*"What do you want me to do for you?" Jesus asked him. The blind man said, 'Rabbi, I want to see.'" Mark 10: 51*

---

It is amazing the technology we have today as it pertains to correcting one's vision. I recently went in for an examination because my right eye is farsighted and my left eye is nearsighted. However, my right eye is weaker and I am unable to read at arm's length unless I wear my reading glasses. The doctor explained to me the Lasik procedure. He added I would see clearly in both eyes but they would both be farsighted. If I wish to read at arm's length I would need to wear glasses. Inasmuch as I was considering the surgery so that I would not require glasses, I decided to pass on the procedure.

How well do you see? Can you see the poverty, bigotry, prejudice, greed, lust, and envy that are so prevalent in our world? You won't require glasses or Lasik surgery to see these issues. Nevertheless, sometimes the things that we see right before eyes we tend to look the other way because we do not want to be involved.

What is it that you want to see? Psychologists say that we don't really see what's beneath the surface. This is known as Freud's "tip of the iceberg" theory. Can you distinguish between the truth and a lie, between good and evil, between what's real and what's faked? What about seeing but not wanting to see? Do you turn a blind eye to injustice? Do you look the other way when you try to avoid a neighbor whom you cannot tolerate? Have you ever said to your child, "Tell them I'm not home" to avoid someone with whom you'd rather not see?

The blind man referenced in the verse merely wanted to see, and Jesus accommodated him. Can you imagine seeing for the first time, and the first image you behold is your healer and Savior? His eyes became fixated upon Him. He followed Jesus wherever He went.

Jesus wants us to see more than what our eyes behold. He wants us to see beyond the surface and know the depth of His love for us. He wants us to look beyond our tears and see the future He has planned for each one of His children. Close your eyes and pray to God right now. Let Him reveal His plan for you. You will be amazed. You will see everything clearly from now on. God will never hold anything back from you that is for your good.

Ask Jesus to help you see Him better. Be prepared to receive His answer for you. **When you truly see God for who He is, you will also want to follow Him.**

## TIMELY DEATH FOR AN UNTIMELY DEATH | SEPTEMBER 10

*"No man has power over the wind to contain it; so no one has power over the day of his death. As no one is discharged in time of war, so wickedness will not release those who practice it."* Ecclesiastes 8: 8

---

What a compelling verse for those of us who think we can control our present life and destiny. Today I just found out that one of my best friends died in a car accident. He was only 38 years old. He always lived life to the fullest and looked ahead for tomorrow until his life was taken. Conversely, I have another dear friend who will be 103 in a few months. She still has her faculties and loves life. She keeps wondering why God allowed her to live this long. Who has control of their life?

Death is no respecter of persons. We really can't predict when out time is up. When tragedy of this type strikes, we often ask why God would allow such an untimely death. Is God in control of each of our lives? Should we fear dying? Is death the final curtain?

When Eve partook of the forbidden fruit in the Garden of Eden, the serpent (Lucifer) declared that, when you eat of the fruit you will NOT surely die. As we know, she did not immediately die after ingesting the fruit; nor did Adam. What they likely didn't realize at the time was that, from that time forward, it was a downhill road for them physically. While the Bible tells us that it took over 900 years for their deaths to occur, their bodies began slowly deteriorating after they succumbed to temptation. Even though their death was untimely, Jesus' death came at a timely time. The pair believed in God's promise of a Savior.

What is important here is not precisely when they died but rather who said what to whom. Clearly, the serpent lied when he declared that the partaking of the fruit would not cause their deaths. God in His mercy did not allow them to die immediately. God's word eventually came to fruition. On the other hand, everything that God has said from the time of the fall of man until this day has been true.

God does not want anyone to die. God sent His Son to die in our behalf so that we might ultimately live. God's plan for each of us is to live forever.

**This whole death syndrome is only a detour in His bigger picture. You must trust His word, but even more, you must trust Him if you want to have life eternal.**

## **GOD IS OUR REFUGE** | SEPTEMBER 11

*"God is our refuge and strength, an ever present help in trouble. Therefore we will not fear, though the earth gives way and the mountains fall into the heart of the sea, though its waters roar and foam and the mountains quake with their surging." Psalms 46: 1-3*

---

None of us will forget the chilling pictures we witnessed on September 11, 2001, when both towers of the World Trade Center came crashing down. Those pictures are indelible. Our focus on nine-eleven was on the terrible loss of life – innocents, with little concern for international politics, out earning a living or just passing by the buildings and then …pow! Days and even weeks later, our grief was none the less, but many of us began to focus on a different issue: where was God? Some suggested, rather derisively, of course, that He had the day off or that He was out to lunch. Of course, such remarks were nothing less than blasphemous. However, in those days at a time when the perpetrators, the sponsors of this mayhem were claiming victory in God's name, it seemed that all were fair game for the press, even God.

Several weeks after the tragedy, Larry King assembled a panel of religious leaders to discuss, among other topics, where God was as events unraveled. Each religious leader was given the same question. One man in particular stood out, Rabbi Harold Kushner. He asked Rabbi Harold Kushner: "Rabbi, if God is omnipotent, He could have prevented this, could He not?"

Kushner response is instructive: "No, because I think at the very outset, God gave human beings the freedom to choose between being good people and being bad people. And at tremendous risk to God's creation, He will not take that power away from us, that freedom, because we stop being human beings if He does. I don't find God in that terrible accident…I find God in the courage of firemen and police. I will continue to find God in the willingness of the survivors to rebuild their lives. Remember, Larry, God's promise was not that life would be fair; God's promise was that even if life is unfair, we would not have to face it alone; for He will be with us in "the valley of the shadow." Remember the story of Job? God was not only with him but He restored him. All these calamities we are witnessing is temporary.

Since the fall of man from grace, God has dealt with every heinous act that man has perpetrated the same way He did on September 11, 2011. "God will be our refuge and strength, an ever present help in trouble." That is love in action. **Freedom of choice and love go hand in hand. Don't feel defeated. God's way will eventually win out. When we are finally established in the new earth, we will forget our past.**

## RIGHTEOUS RUMOR | SEPTEMBER 12

*"A perverse man stirs up dissension and a gossip separates close friends." Proverbs 16: 28*

We as a society just can't seem to get enough gossip; unless, of course, we are the subject of the gossip. A gossip is defined by Merriam Webster's dictionary as, "a person who habitually reveals personal or sensational facts; rumor or reports of an intimate nature." Are you guilty of spreading rumors? Do you have friends who update you on the latest gossip about such and such a person? Are you the bearer of gossip in a "Christian manner?" Welcome to the club!

A friend of mine failed to inform his wife that he was leaving her for another woman. It seems that the rest of the immediate world knew about it. One day, the wife ran into a friend of theirs, who matter-of-factly referenced the split-up. The wife was caught off-guard, but she played along as if she'd known about it. Gossip would be wonderful fun, were it not for the fact that there are always victims.

The fact is that nothing good ever comes from gossip. Believe it or not, God was the target of some rather evil gossip – this, at the hands of Lucifer, not surprisingly. Lucifer, of course, is widely regarded as the father of lies. Lucifer was bucking for a promotion, so to speak. He thought he deserved a shot at the number-one spot; thus he spread rumors to the effect that God was unfair, unjust, and exacting to a fault. Lucifer is a master of deception, and he managed to net one-third of the angels by means of his little scheme.

When Lucifer entered our world, he continued to spread these fabrications about God. Lucifer's style of gossip was not only convincing but appeared factual. He used the serpent to clothe his guile. The serpent before the fall was a very attractive creature. Obviously, his first targets, Adam and Eve, proved to be receptive to his guiles. God, of course, was well aware of Lucifer's tactics and had decided, long before the fall, to send His Son to earth so as to put these lies to rest. God lived among us and showed us His Father. Even His own disciples wondered about Jesus. They asked Him to show us the Father. Jesus replied, "I and my Father are one." The disciples must have been recipient of rumors and gossips too because even with Jesus at their midst they did not discern God.

The Author of Love dealt with false rumors by presenting us truth, His Son. The next time you are inclined to spread rumors, instead **spread the Good News of God and His saving grace. Now, that's a righteous rumor.**

## THE KEY TO SUCCESS | SEPTEMBER 13

*"Do not conform any longer to the pattern of this world, but be transformed by the renewing of your mind. Then you will be able to test and approve what God's will is-his good, pleasing and perfect will." Romans 12: 2*

---

Most of us have, at one time or another dreamed of accumulating fantastic wealth so that we might retire early and do all of the things we enjoy. I wanted to accomplish this fete by my 30th birthday. Note that the operative word here is "wanted". You see, it didn't quite happen, certainly not by 30 and, I'm sorry to say, not by 2 times 30.

First, I decided to become an airline pilot. I went so far as to take flying lesson. During one instruction flight, the instructor set me up for a stall maneuver. The vertigo I experienced was a sign to me that there were likely greener pastures elsewhere. My next pursuit was professional tennis. That dream was shattered when I lost a key match by the score of 6-0, 6-0. Next I decided to return to school and obtain a medical degree. Once I was exposed to the infirmed and had to perform tasks which exposed me to blood borne pathogens I developed a phobia at the sight of the hypodermic needle. Then the lure of celebrity fame got the better of me. I was told by a talent agent to record two songs and "come back and see me in six months." I left his office haughty, thinking to myself "well if he can't see my talent now, it's his lost." How delusional was that? The patterns of this world left me wanting. Somehow I needed to learn God's will.

It seemed that my life was a little more than a series of trial balloons, and, each balloon encountered a sharp needle. It was as if someone was going out of his way to render my career as difficult as possible. It wasn't only my career that needed revamping but my own personal life as well. Nothing seemed to be working. I began to lose faith in myself. It was then that I discovered that I was focusing on my own ego-centric will and strength to succeed in my pursuits. I needed a total transformation.

It wasn't long before I realized that I would never really achieve faith in myself until I was willing to place all of my faith in the Lord. Jesus showed us the way. Every step of His journey – from birth to resurrection – He depended on His father for guidance. In the same way that God cared for His Son, He wants to show you the way. God has called us to be His sons and daughters. He wants us to commit our ways to Him in whatever we do. **Place ALL your plans on the Lord and He will guide you to succeed. With God as your counselor, you can never fail. I realized God's will and it was perfect.**

With Him by my side, I cannot help but succeed. **The key to my success was to trust Him.**

# WHAT'S IN A NAME | SEPTEMBER 14

*"A good name is more desirable than great riches; to be esteemed is better than silver or gold." Proverbs 22: 1*

---

What's in a name? A name can conjure up awe, respect, reverence, mockery, fear, sentimental feelings or disgrace. What about your name? When people say your name what do you feel?

There's a popular talk radio call-in show, which routinely dishes out advice. A young man phoned in and asked if he should marry his fiancée without her parents' blessing. The host asked why the parents were against the marriage. He replied that he was a security guard. His fiancée, on the other hand, was a dentist. Her parents were judgmental and essentially felt that he wasn't in her league. Furthermore, the daughter had inherited two-million dollars, and the parents automatically figured that he was a gold-digger. Quite apparently, her parents had him labeled, notwithstanding the fact that their daughter was not about to marry a label.

The talk show host's response was that they were adults and were free to do as they pleased. She recommended that, over time, he demonstrate to her parents that he was marrying their daughter for love as opposed to money that in his mind character trumps riches. When people speak of your name, do they trust you? Does your name evoke a sterling reputation? Do people want to do business with you? Are you more apt to marry into a "good name?" It's not so much the name but the person behind the name that is esteemed.

God has a special name for each of us. Just as we give our loved ones "nick -names" or a special "love" name God does so for us. John 10: 3 "The watchman opens the gate for him, and the sheep listen to his voice. He calls his own sheep by name and leads them out." The Creator of our universe, who named each star and planet (Psalms 147: 4) and everything He has created also has a name for each of us. You will know your name because you will recognize His voice and the name He has especially given you. The name God calls you by reflects your character and will be with you for all eternity.

There is, however, only one name we will call upon that blessed day, and that is Jesus. "Therefore God exalted Him to the highest place and gave Him the name that is above every name, that **at the name of Jesus every knee should bow, in heaven and on earth and under the earth**," (Philippians 2: 9 & 10).

## TURNING YOUR BACK | SEPTEMBER 15

*"From this time many of His disciples turned back and no longer followed Him." John 6: 66*

---

Many of you have, at least occasionally, watched the television series "Survivor". It is a primer on influence peddling. Contestants jockey for position by colluding with one another. It is, to a considerable extent, a game of bluff. The last one standing, so to speak, wins the grand prize of one-million dollars. There is virtually no genuine concern for anyone else, except to the extent that one's trust may work to one's own advantage. The object of the game is to win at any cost. There is no consideration for the feelings or the emotional well-being of another. By game's end, it becomes apparent to the contestants that they can trust nobody but themselves.

During the recent explosion of so-called reality television, critics have argued that these shows do not replicate the real world. They are caricatures of the world in which we live. Most people, they argue, are trusting and loyal. They are not, the critics contend, nearly as self-centered as the reality T.V. characters.

The fact is that even Jesus had to test the loyalty of His disciples, the very same ones who had sworn an oath of fealty to Him. Some of them had seen Jesus grow up in their neighborhood, and, as a consequence, they regarded Him as one of them. This was an example of familiarity breeding, not contempt, but rather a sense of equality. At one point, Jesus turned to Peter and asked: "You do not want to leave, too, do you?" Peter responded: "Lord to whom shall we go?" Peter realized that Jesus was their only hope and answer. He urged the others not to turn their backs on the One who is their salvation.

We too have turned our back on Christ, especially in moments of despair. Doubt creeps in and we give up. Even when we play the "platonic attitude" towards God we are in essence turning our back on Him. Sometimes we cater to our self-sufficient, self-absorbing inherent behaviors and mind-set that God is relegated to the back burner. No one have been exempted from the turn your back syndrome. When times get rough and survival is the only option, we will turn our back on the weak. **It is time we made an about face and face the One who is our Lord and Savior.** To turn your back on the One who is your Savior would certainly be detrimental to your well-being. He is someone you can depend on. **You need never fear because He has your back covered. He will never turn His back on you.**

# EAT | SEPTEMBER 16

*"But they laughed at him. After He put them all out, He took the child's father and mother and the disciples who were with Him, and went in where the child was. He took her by the hand and said to her, 'Talitha koum!' which means, 'little girl, I say to you, get up!' Immediately the girl stood up and walked around (she was twelve years old). At this they were completely astonished. He gave strict orders not to let anyone know about this, and told them to give her something to eat."* Mark 5: 40-43

---

Today's text illustrates the same powerful message Jesus said to those present at Jairus' house. The men came to greet Jairus even before Jesus entered his home and told Jairus not to bother "the teacher." His daughter was dead. But Jesus begged to differ, He told them, "The child is not dead but asleep." Did you notice the reaction of the people outside? They laughed. Most likely the real reason they laughed was they didn't believe Jesus' words. They never saw a person raised from the dead. Jesus even countered the people's attitude of "why bother, she's dead" with, "shhh!, don't listen to what they're saying and don't be afraid; keep hoping and believing. Let's go to your daughter." Jesus took the parents and three of his disciples, Peter, James and John, then took the daughter by the hand and told her to get up. The child stood up immediately and walked around. **The words of Jesus brought healing to the child IMMEDIATELY**.

Three things stand out for me in this story. One is the laughter of the unbelievers. Because the unbelieving people lacked faith and the knowledge of God's power they were not blessed to witness Jarius' daughter raised from the dead. Never stop believing in God.

Second, Jesus honored Jairus for believing. Jairus had great faith in Jesus and His word. He knew something more about Jesus than his neighbors. He trusts God. Never lose your trust in God.

And lastly, Jesus told them to feed the child. Why would Mark emphasize such a minor act of this last phrase of Jesus? "Give her something to eat." Christ knew she needed nourishment to sustain her earthly physical being. God thinks of everything, even eating. That's how He cares for His Children. It's the little things that we seem to neglect in our daily living that we take for granted. But God sees and knows what we need to survive in this world and He never takes anything for granted. What does that tell you about our God? **He is so consumed with His love for us that there's nothing He missed.**

**A greater lesson God wanted to impress was that eternal life was only in Christ.**

## DO YOU UNDERSTAND? | SEPTEMBER 17

*"He said to them, 'Do you still not understand?'" Mark 8: 21*

We have, as you are well aware, five senses. (Some claim that there is a sixth sense – common sense. Others argue that it's not as common as we might think.) It is a tribute to God's incredible ingenuity how well the senses interact with one another. From the earliest moment of infancy, we learn to listen with our ears. It is only as we age that we forget why God blessed us with ears, and, instead, we listen with our mouths. We're so busy thinking of what we want to say next that we fail to listen to the other party's words. Then we wonder why there is misunderstanding in our world.

Even Jesus was misunderstood in His day. His wondrous deed went un-or under-appreciated. One such occasion was when He fed a crowd in excess of 4,000 with a mere seven loaves of bread and a few fish. It had to be abundantly clear, both to the larger group and to Christ's disciples that feeding a group that large with so meager an amount of food was an absolutely incredible feat. Despite the fact that they had just observed what could only be described as a miracle, neither the disciples nor the group was impressed. If Jesus was to convince them of His Divinity, He would, it appeared, have to do better than that. They said that nothing less than a very clear sign from heaven would make them believers.

Talk about a tough audience! They had witnessed this miracle of feeding; they had observed any number of healings; they had witnessed the casting out of demons; and, now, they wanted a sign. Tell me, is that what you're waiting for; a sign from God? Just like the 4,000 people He fed, are you still not convinced? I must admit I'm guilty of the sign from above syndrome. I have tested God and asked for a sign too. Once again, we do not see as God sees. Or we forget to notice how God really cares for us. Look at your present life, where do you think your food, shelter, resources, the rain, sunshine, life came from?

God had already given them a sign, and that sign, call it; was Jesus Himself. God gave us eyes to see, but we are blinded by our lack of faith. To demand more miracles is to miss the point. God is not a magician and certainly not an illusionist. He speaks only the truth, and His medium is not a magic wand but rather His love.

**Open your eyes and ears, and most importantly, your heart to God's Spirit. Then you will understand Him.**

## ALL OR NOTHING | SEPTEMBER 18

*"Love the Lord your God with all your heart and with all your soul and with all your mind and with all your strength. The second is this: Love your neighbor as yourself. There is no commandment greater than these." Mark 12: 30 & 31*

---

I have a friend who is going through a break up in his marriage of five years. His wife has not only left him, but has left the state. Six months after the split, he continues to mourn. He realizes that he's the principal culprit here. He was caught fooling around, and his wife would not forgive him. He desperately wants her back, and he phones her, but his words fall on deaf ears.

I suggested that he start over and attempt to court her as if it were the beginning of a relationship. He told me that he'd end up being rejected. Quite apparently, he was more concerned about how he might be perceived than he was in reigniting the relationship. It would be reasonable to conclude that his love for her was incomplete. He was not it seemed, willing to go all out.

To what extent are you willing to invest to capturing your love back? Are you willing to do it with all your heart, soul, mind and strength? Will you give it your all? Yes, there are certainly times when we in fact go all out and still don't achieve our goals. However, that's not a reason for not trying. To go all out means to do it with all of your heart, soul, mind and strength. To go all out means doing whatever you can to win at all cause, some people even do so to their death. How far are you willing to go? Are you an all or nothing person? That's certain a tall order to pursue isn't it? There is no halfway.

Jesus was faced with a similar dilemma. He had to choose between temporal things and eternal consequences. He knew that man's salvation was contingent upon His own willingness to give His own life. Jesus trusted His Father and placed His life in His hands. There could be no halfway. Obviously, we know how the story ends. The Author of Love chose to die for us so that we might ultimately have eternal life. He quite literally gave His all. Even in the face of not knowing if He would ever rise again, God decided your life was of more value to Him than His life. That is how God loves us. He is an "ALL" God.

**You too can love the Lord your God with ALL your heart and with ALL your soul and with ALL mind and with ALL your strength. Yes, you can do all things with God who strengthens you. Are you an ALL or nothing lover?**

## THE VALUE OF LIFE | SEPTEMBER 19

*"When Judas, who had betrayed Him, saw that Jesus was condemned, he was seized with remorse and returned the thirty silver coins to the chief priests and the leaders. 'I have sinned,' he said, 'for I have betrayed innocent blood.' 'What is that to us?' they replied, 'That's your responsibility.' So Judas threw the money into the temple and left. Then he went away and hanged himself." Matthew 27: 3-5*

---

I met Larry through a friend of mine years ago. He was a doctor of psychiatry. He was handsome, wealthy and divorced. Once in a while he would throw a catered party in his beautiful Malibu oceanfront home and I would be invited. His parties were lavish and exquisite. There were many attractive aspiring celebrities there. Other times I would see him at other social functions and humanitarian causes. Larry, it seemed, had it all. He made most of his money not in his medical profession but in business savvy. It was in the summer of 2004 that Larry threw a barbecue party at his home and invited not only friends but also family members. I met his sister and his children. They appeared to dote on their brother and father. I also saw beautiful aspiring actors who seem to relish Larry's lifestyle. I didn't see or hear from Larry after the party until I received a call from a mutual friend. He informed me Larry committed suicide by shooting himself in the head. What a tragedy. Who knew what the source of his anguish? (Some said it was financial.)

Judas committed suicide too. The story indicates he was filled with remorse for betraying Jesus for 30 silver coins. In the book of Luke chapter 22: 3 it says, "Then Satan entered Judas, called Iscariot, one of the twelve." Could it be that Satan made Judas commit suicide? Could Satan have entered Larry prior to his suicide? Did Satan enter all those who have committed suicide in the past or are now contemplating it? Be careful not to judge people who commit suicide readily because God is the only one who knows the heart of man. I wouldn't be surprise if I see Larry in heaven someday, or even Judas. Who makes it to heaven is not my decision. I know that God will be just and fair. I know all are welcome in His kingdom. I know the choice will be mine. My choice is to trust in God no matter what I witness here.

**The Author of Love does not want even one person to perish (Ezekiel 18: 23).** He values each life and is willing to do all He can to save you. He has chosen life eternal for each of us. Have you chosen the One who is life eternal?

## SHADES OF GRAY | SEPTEMBER 20

*"Listen to me, O house of Jacob, all you who remain of the house of Israel, you whom I have upheld since you were conceived, and have carried since your birth. Even to your old age and gray hairs I am He, I am He who will sustain you. I have made you and I will carry you; I will sustain you and I will rescue you." Isaiah 46: 3 & 4*

---

When you're young, every additional year seems an eternity. Eventually, you will learn patience. You must have patience when choosing a life mate. You've heard the phrase: "Marry in haste; repent at leisure." You must have patience, too, in the upbringing of your children. Treasure those years; they go by ever so quickly. Treasure your parents. As they lose a step or two and perhaps a memory or two, you may regard this as a preview of coming attractions, and, to an extent, it is.

Use advancing years as an opportunity to take inventory. Has your life been worthwhile, not only to yourself in terms of accomplishments, and assets collected, and kids raised but also in terms of how you have impacted others? There are no awards given to the one who can declare that he (or she) is the richest person in the cemetery. In God's eternal kingdom, you won't need your stocks, bonds or CD's. You can leave your checkbook behind, and, no, it's one place where they do not take your Visa card.

That, however, is tomorrow's concern…how about the period from now until your last day on earth. Do you know who will take care of you? Perhaps you have a care facility in mind or a willing daughter or son. Perhaps it's a bit of a predicament for you. As the shades of gray in my hair become more difficult to dye (as in my case) I know God will be there for me in my old age. God is in the nursing homes, private homes or strangers' homes caring for the invalids who are advancing in years. Those care takers who care from them is God clothed in human garb. They are really God in care mode. Wherever tender loving care (TLC) abounds, that's God.

One thing is for sure, and that is that God has assured us that He will sustain us. He was there from your beginning (actually, even before conception); He's watched you grow; and He'll be holding your hand as your earthly curtain is drawn. Would you believe He will not only rescue you but will carry you in your shades of grey years? Yes, the Creator of you will do all that for you. What an amazing God we have. **When God opens His eternal kingdom to all of us, that no-longer-very limber body of yours will be about as useful to you as the aforementioned Visa card.** You will leave them both behind. He will welcome the new you home.

## PRISON BREAK | SEPTEMBER 21

*"Then he touched their eyes and said, 'According to your faith will it be done to you.'" Matthew 9: 29*

---

When we think of imprisonment, most of us conjure up notions of steel bars, striped garments and exercise yards with guards looking down from watch towers. There is, however, an even more insidious type of imprisonment. It is of the mind, but it is every bit as real as the steel bars. In some instances, the imprisonment is merely being stuck in a rut…doing the same thing every day or every week.

In other cases, however, the behavior is far more troubling. It's the guy who puts on plastic what he can't afford to pay with cash and what he won't be able to afford when the bills start appearing in his mail box. It's the gal who just barely squeaks by every pay period; so she buys a lottery ticket. Soon, it becomes five-at-a-time. Next, it's the weekly trip to the casino, and you know the rest of the tune.

Then there are the more secret imprisonments such as porn, lust, greed, envy, shoplifting, and the like. In just about every instance, it begins with a casual, seemingly innocent indiscretion, and, before long, the person is living a self-imposed imprisonment. Do you fit one of those categories? Many, perhaps most, of us do.

What is your "sentence" in life? Are you mired in the things of this world? Do you feel there is no chance for your freedom? Are you ready for a "prison break"? For the healing process to begin, you need to place your faith in God. He is very much aware of your imprisonment, and He is ready to set you free. You must first evidence your faith in Him. You must place Him first in your life. He wants you to follow His lead. What will He do in return? He will give you all the reasons your life is worth living without the temptations that imprison you. Those are of Satan. Satan wants yours ultimately to be a life sentence. Don't get mired in a routine pattern of the same old stuff. Your admittance of your helpless nature, your acceptance of God's Spirit in your life will begin the prison break you've searched for all your life.

I've notice people ( me included) who continue to repeat patterns in their life that leaves them wondering why they continue to wallow in the same old mud. They need a break from their locked and unproductive choices. God can break your destructive pattern. God is there for you with reprieve in hand. Let Him touch your eyes so you can see your Redeemer.

**Allow Him to touch you and heal you right now. It's the prison break for which you've been longing.**

## PATIENCE IS GODLY | SEPTEMBER 22

*"And so after waiting patiently, Abraham received what was promised." Hebrews 6: 14*

---

Patience is a virtue. When someone asks you when you want something delivered or completed, how many times have you responded" "yesterday!"?

The other day, I received a call from my cousin, informing me that her father had passed away early that morning. He was ill with cancer for the past two years. He was 72 years old when he died. It was expected; yet it was a sad day for all of us. They had waited all of these years for their father to return to the Lord. They were left not knowing what, if any, was the state of his salvation. He never really attended church or showed signs that he gave his heart to God. For a while, he abstained from his smoking and drinking habits. However, he took a period of remission from his cancer as a license to revert to drinking. His family continued to love him. They waited, it seemed forever, for his return to God, but they never saw the fruits of their prayers. Their father truly tried their patience.

I am reminded of a story of the man who sold his prize mule. He had guaranteed the mule would be docile and obedient. He had certified that, anything you wanted this mule to do, he would do so without hesitation. The man who purchased the mule returned it to its previous owner, saying: "You said this was an obedient mule, but I can't get it to do anything." The seller said: "That can't be." He proceeded to pick up a two-by-four and walloped the mule over the head. "First," he declared, "You have to get its attention."

God, too, wants our attention. He urges us to be patient and wait on Him rather than asserting our independence. Patience is Godly. Abraham learned that. Ultimately, God's promise to him was realized. God did not use a two-by-four to get his attention. God operated in love. God wants you to wait patiently on Him. Our life here on earth is but for a season.

I still can't believe I am now a senior citizen. I thought the age of 60 was the "ancient of days". That was real old. My memory still reminds me when I was a kid playing in the streets of San Francisco. I feel like it was only yesterday. Where did the years go? Now what are we waiting for? A better tomorrow! **We wait patiently on God's soon return, just like our forefathers before us did. We too will receive what was promised.**

**God's promise will be realized when we accept His faith that He has gifted us through His Son.**

## YOU CAN COME BACK HOME AGAIN | SEPTEMBER 23

*"He will not turn his face from you if you return to him." II Chronicles 30: 9*

---

Much earlier, we talked of the prodigal son. My own life paralleled that parable. I was born into the Adventist faith, a third generation Adventist. My uncle, Pastor A. A. Alcaraz, baptized me at the age of 16. I recall coming out of that baptismal pool feeling blessed and, for at least a moment, holy. I vowed to myself that I would be careful of what I thought and said and circumspect in my behavior. I prayed to God that He would find favor in me and keep me safe, pure and acceptable. I considered this a life-long commitment, not merely a commitment for the moment.

When I became an adult, I grew envious of the lifestyle of many of my friends. They seemed to have everything they, or for that matter, anyone might want. However, at the same time, I yearned to remain faithful to God. I had recalled the pledge I made to myself and to God on that baptismal day. For a while, I was able to rationalize my actions. Hadn't Jesus lived among sinners? I still longed for the day of salvation, but, for the moment, salvation needed, or so I thought, to be back-burned.

I tried show business and various get-rich-quick schemes. I was in and out of love, a millionaire by age 40, and then it caught up with me. I'll spare you the details, but suffice it to say that I was penniless and homesick. And then I remembered what Peter had said: "Lord who can we turn to?" There is no one who will welcome us more than the One who loved us most. God has said to all prodigal sons and daughters: "You can come home again." My return to God was gradual but defining. I look back and see in details how God led me back to Him. It started with mother asking me to take her to church and pick her up after. She never asked me to join her. Then there was my brother's children needing a home. Soon I was taking mother and the kids to church. Then I was staying with them inside the church. Church did not make my life, but the warm fellowship did. Then the pastor extended his friendship. Suddenly, I felt at ease in my new surroundings. I felt welcomed back home.

Are you still wandering aimlessly without a goal or purpose in life? Does everything seem bleak and unforgiving? Do you feel like you're life is going in circles? Are there patterns in your life that's too difficult to break? Stop wandering, you can come home again. There is no better place on earth to be than home.

I was privileged the other day to witness my brother re-baptized. After more than 30 years out of the fold, He too has decided to come home again. Nothing is more rewarding than to come back home to God. **You too can come home right now. The Author of Love will not turn His face from you. He is waiting with open arms to embrace you.**

# FORGIVEN MUCH | SEPTEMBER 24

*"'Leave her alone,' said Jesus. 'Why are you bothering her? She has done a beautiful thing to Me. The poor you will always have with you, and you can help them any time you want. But you will not always have Me. She did what she could. She poured perfume on my body beforehand to prepare for my burial. I tell you the truth, wherever the gospel is preached throughout the world, what she has done will also be told, in memory of her.'" Mark 14: 6-9*

---

The story of Mary is deeper than this text reveals. Simon, the Pharisee wanted to express his gratitude to Jesus for healing him of leprosy. He threw a party for Jesus and his disciples. Mary, Martha and Lazarus were also there to celebrate Lazarus being raised from the dead. Mary poured an expensive perfume on Jesus' feet. (Remember in Jesus time, with dirt streets and sandals it was virtually impossible to keep your feet clean, and it was customary when receiving an honored guest to have the lowliest slave wash the guest's feet). It wasn't clear whether she did it out of gratitude for Jesus' bringing her brother back to life or whether she sensed that Jesus would not be with them much longer.

Mary's behavior exasperated Simon, but Jesus knew what was in each of their hearts. Jesus tells the story of two debts being forgiven, one large and one small. He asks Simon which debtor would love the forgiver more. Simon, of course, responds: "the one who had the bigger debt canceled." Jesus then compares Mary's and Simon's behavior. He tells how, when he entered Simon's house, Simon did not so much as offer water for His feet, but Mary wet his feet with her tears. Simon had given him no kiss, but Mary did not stop kissing His feet, a sign that she was completely in His power and debt. And so forth.

Jesus proclaimed: "I tell you, her many sins have been forgiven," much to the astonishment of the guests. Jesus said to Mary: "Your faith has saved you. Go in peace."

It doesn't matter how much debt you owe. It doesn't matter the degree of your sin or what your past has been. Whatever sin you have committed in your past, you can be forgiven. There is nothing you can do to make God not forgive you. All you need to do is accept His gift of forgiveness right now.

You will be forgiven. Just come to Him as you are. He is calling your name. God is offering His pardon and grace to you. **When you see His mercy and forgiveness for you, you, too, at least figuratively speaking, won't stop wiping His feet with your tears.**

## **WALK WITH GOD** | SEPTEMBER 25

*"I pray that you may be active in sharing your faith so that you will have a full understanding of every good thing we have in Christ. Your love has given me great joy and encouragement, because you, brother, have refreshed the hearts of the saints." Philemon 6 & 7*

---

My sister asked me how Enoch could be translated to heaven and never experience death. I suspect she was envious. She asked, too, why God chose Enoch specifically to avoid the death experience. The verse in question is found in Genesis 5: 21-24. "When Enoch had lived 65 years, he became the father of Methuselah. And after he became the father of Methuselah, Enoch walked with God 300 years and had other sons and daughters. Altogether, Enoch lived 365 years. Enoch walked with God; then he was no more, because God took him away."

By walked, we don't mean strolled, but rather to follow a course of action humbly in the sight of God. Enoch was allowed to live 365 years while here on earth. During that time frame Enoch nurtured his relationship with God. Each of us, whether we know it or not, has a story to tell regarding our personal walk with God; for some, the walk is one of denial, but it is a walk, nevertheless. For others it is a walk of faith.

Which one are you walking on? Do keep the faith and walk with God regardless of the circumstances you face daily. No one is exempted from the travails of this world. Yet, we can still have a walk like Enoch had with God. I believe there are many "Enochs" in our midst that have a wonderful walk with God. A great deal of that walk is sharing your faith in Christ with others.

Some of us, no doubt, are disappointed with God. We focus on the negative rather than life's joys, and God becomes our scapegoat. We crave free choice but when our choices don't work out for the better, God gets the blame. Does all this sound familiar? I know "I've been there and done it" too. There is an invitation that is used at the end of every Alcoholics Anonymous (A.A.) meeting; (they know people will relapse but they always tell them) "Keep coming back." **I invite you to keep walking back to God, no matter what.**

Philip Yancey wrote a book entitled "Disappointment with God". Among other topics, he deals with the notion that God is unfair. Life may indeed be unfair, but Yancey later points out that we ought not to confuse God and life. In the earlier-referenced Book of Job, we see that God "weeps" for Job more than Job weeps for Job. God's perspective with respect to time is, of course, not the same as ours. His day is but a moment, and He knows that any pain we suffer today will be but a distant memory when we reunite with Him in His Kingdom. **How's your walk with God?**

## WAIT ON THE LORD | SEPTEMBER 26

*"Wait on the Lord; Be of good courage, And He shall strengthen your heart; wait, I say, on the Lord" Psalms 27:14*

---

Waiting it not one of my strengths, yet I have to do it every day. I wait in car from one to two hours when driving to work in traffic. I wait in line at the bank, supermarket, or airport. I wait to see the doctor or dentist agonizing in anticipation of what they may discover. Then there's the anticipatory wait for the next paycheck, next vacation, next birthday, next holiday or social party. When Monday comes we can't wait for Friday. There are gut wrenching waits like; did you pass your national board examination; waiting for the birth of your first child; waiting for your bride to come down the aisle. There's something about waiting that seems to go against our human nature.

There is another period of waiting that may not cross our minds every day, but it is a good deal more important than the others, and that is the wait for our Lord's return. Ever wonder how God feels about waiting? He waits for the sinner to turn to Him. He waits for the entire human race to repent and be saved. Other than taking care of His universe, does it seem odd for God to wait?

The Bible takes note of some very long waits. Abraham's waiting 100 years for his heir. Jacob waiting seven years for the one he loved to be his wife and yet another seven because of his father-in-laws deception. God has been waiting an awfully long time for us to reunite with Him. But have you noticed God's time is not the same as our time.

We live within the context of clocks and calendars, but God is outside of these. He did, however, send His Son to join us in our time frame. He had to wait nine months before exiting His mother's womb. We see Him preparing at the age of 12 years when His parents found Him in the temple learning from and questioning the elders. But He was 30 years old when He started His ministry. He waited three days in the tomb before He rose from the dead.

Why did God do all this? God's wait of love is like Jacob's wait for Rachel, each day was cherished. **God is governed not by time but by love.** If you've ever been in love, time is blissful. It flies by fast and you feel you're just beginning. **We wait in love because God too is waiting in love to be with us eternally.**

## SOMETHING TO CHEER ABOUT | SEPTEMBER 27

*"Son be of good cheer thy sins be forgiven thee." Matthew 9: 2 (KJV)*

Although this is a story of physical healing, true healing begins with the healing of our hearts. We are all sinners in need of a Savior.

The paralyzed man was suffering from an illness which made him bedridden for life. He probably felt helpless and unworthy. He likely sought help from doctors and Pharisees who declared him a hopeless case. He could not walk to see Jesus for healing. He may have heard of Jesus healing lepers and all kinds of diseases. He longed for the same healing. However, as much as he yearned for physical healing, his greater yearning was to be relieved of the guilt he had harbored all of these years. His greatest need was to be healed of sin.

We read of the same even in Luke 5, where we learn: "the power of the Lord was present to heal the sick." Yet the house where Jesus visited was too crowded to approach; so this man's friends literally tore a hole in the roof to lower him down. When Jesus saw the man coming down through the roof, He was moved with compassion. The Holy Spirit had already heard his prayer. When Jesus told him: "Son, be of good cheer; thy sins be forgiven thee," he felt forgiven. His whole being was released from the burden of the guilt he had carried. He lay there in blissful silence, speechless and totally at peace. He received not only spiritual healing but physical healing as well. Would you like to be guilt-free and have peace?

There are many today just like the paralyzed man, anxiously waiting for healing. You may be physically fit and enjoying good health, but are you carrying a guilt that's burdensome. Is it affecting your inner most soul. Do you crave relief? I recently went through an ordeal that left my neck and shoulders in muscular pain. Every time I thought of a dear friend threatening to betray me if I didn't acquiesce to her whim, I felt this pain radiate from my head to my back. I asked God to help me learn to deal with the issue according to His way. God wants to heal more than just the physical. He also wants to heal our guilt-laden souls. He wants to give us spiritual healing. All I could do was rest in God's promise.

Finally, God wants us to be happy. He is a very cheerful giver. He gives freely without hesitation or reservation. God's great love for us motivates Him to give everything good for us freely. God cheers us with His hope, love and care. **God has heard your plea and has already forgiven you. Now that's truly something to cheer about.**

## IMITATE GOOD | SEPTEMBER 28

*"Dear friend, do not imitate what is evil but what is good. Anyone who does what is good is from God. Anyone who does what is evil has not seen God." III John 11*

---

Have you ever been slighted by someone and wanted to get even? Who hasn't? I remember when I owned a small company with my partner. We had an especially-good rapport with one client and received a good many case referrals from them. At one point, one of their claims adjusters left them, and a new claims adjuster took over a case on which she had been working. This new claims adjuster from the get –go flexed her authority. She was vicious and demeaning to one of my staff. I confronted her and she wrote a scathing letter contrary to our discussion. I responded in kind. I literally imitated her letter but with, in my ever so humble opinion with facts. Nevertheless my motive was not kind. I imitated evil because I did not see God.

It's common to give back to the offender some of their own medicine—typically, with the dose doubled. In essence, we are imitating their behavior, but, ultimately, it is ourselves we are demeaning. It is often said that imitation is the sincerest form of flattery. Yes and no.

Today's text places these matters in a better focus. We must be careful regarding what it is we are imitating. When a kid sees his parent take delight in receiving too much change during a purchase transaction, he or she regards that as acceptable behavior and will do the same when the situation arises…keep the ill-begotten gains…what they don't know won't hurt them. When that same kid observes his/her parent returns the extra change, a lesson is learned.

God has shown us how to treat one another. He treated us kindly when we deserved punishment. God knows our character. He sees our wayward ways. He blesses us with His goodness, nonetheless. God never met anger with anger but always retaliated in love. His character is altogether lovely.

God would have been justified to have returned evil for evil when Lucifer falsely accused Him of being unfair, unjust and untrue. God did not imitate Lucifer. He treated Lucifer with love. God's character is love. He governs and deals with everyone and everything He created only in love. God cannot operate any other way.

**Next time you're caught in a dilemma, respond not with evil, but with good. When you do good, you are from God.** Focus on God because He is good. **Learn from Him and imitate His goodness.** Anyone who does what is evil has not seen God.

## A FRIEND LOVES ALL THE TIME | SEPTEMBER 29

*"A friend loves at all times." Proverbs 17: 17*

---

Do you have a best friend you can go to whenever you have a need? Who would you contact if your car got stuck in the middle of the night? Who would you ask to take you to the airport at 4:00 a.m.? If you have such a friend, even one friend, you are fortunate. A friend that loves at all times is today's verse. Are you that type of friend?

I have a good number of close friends. One friend in particular who stands out from the rest is Dana. We were childhood friends. When we became adults we continued our strong friendship until a disagreement about housing tore us apart. We haven't spoken to each other in over 20 years. It was about that time when Jesse came into my life. He became a true friend until this day. He took over where Dana left off. I will admit I have failed to live up to the standard of true friend. As the adage says "It takes two to tango." I'm the first to confess I have not always carried my end of the friendship bargain. Now, whenever I note a discord in my friendship, I attempt to vow to my close friends to try and nip the problem in the bud before it blossoms.

I've learned a valuable lesson with regards to friendship. All too often, they are of a season. Most of us have difficulty in keeping good friends. Sometimes, there are spats that cause a friendship to end. Other times, it may just be a matter of circumstances. Two friends go off to college in different states and eventually find themselves thousands of miles apart. They try to maintain the bond, but, gradually, the bond loosens. It is rare when you have a friend who sticks with you over the decades. But no matter how long we remain friends, sooner or later some incident occurs, and we're left friendless. I've had friends from both sides of the fence. I noticed that friends come and go. Some stay for a while others disappear when things are uncomfortable. Is there a true friend that can love me at all times? Can I be a true friend all the time?

Today's verse just doesn't seem to apply most of the time. Friends simply come and go. Is there a true friend who can love me at all times? I believe there is, and that friend is Jesus. He has never failed me as a friend. His friendship exceeds that of any earthly friendship. Here is a friend who gave His life for us so that we might live. "Greater love has no one than this that he lay down his life for his friends." John 15: 13. Jesus is your true best friend who loves at all times.

**Every earthly friend you have encountered who has treated you kindly and showed you love came from your best friend, Jesus. He is a friend that loves at all times. He is the Author of Friends.**

## **POSSESSED** | SEPTEMBER 30

*"Just then a man in their synagogue who was possessed by an evil spirit cried out?" Mark 1: 23*

---

I have seen a documentary of a possessed man shrieking and playing "mind games" with his audience. I was fascinated by a program on the cable T.V. which portrayed a person possessed in real life. The show was about to reveal how they exorcised a possessed man. It took two days of intense exorcism rituals to rid of the man of his possession. The whole process left me exhausted. Have you ever witnessed a person possessed by an evil spirit? I have. It happens and it is very real. In Jesus' time, it was prevalent. He healed many of them. Jesus did not take two days of rituals to heal the possessed man in this story. Jesus told the evil spirit to "be quiet" and "come out of him." There were displays of shrieking and shaking before the evil spirit left the man.

Whether we wish to believe these things happened, or it's just a myth is your choice. The fact is evil surround us. It may not jump out at us like a possessed person. We may not recognize it if we become too caught up with the distractions of daily living. "God is love. Whoever lives in love lives in God, and God in him." (I John 4: 16).

We are constantly exposed to good and evil. While we don't see people walking around shrieking or foaming at the mouth, we are witness to a more subtle form of evil. Envy, lust, greed and vanity run rampant. Deeds of kindness and compassion come from God, but deeds of jealousy and lying comes from the evil one. Sometimes motives of altruism can be clothed in sheep's clothing all the while the wolf inside the clothing is waiting to paunch on you. Sometimes, the evil is disguised as an angel of light, but if God is in your heart, you will be able to discern the evil one.

Remember: anyone who loves is from God. Are you experiencing love from another person that's too good to be true? Do you feel your love is God-sent? How do you know if this is the real thing? God is your answer. He will show you the truth, the way and a God-possessed life. You must allow Him to illuminate your mind to distinguish the truth.

**Let your heart and soul be possessed by the Spirit of God. His Spirit is meek, lowly, humble, benevolent, peace, joy and love.**

He is waiting for you to receive His spirit into your life. He is your protector and shield. Let Him drive the demons from your life. He will tell them to be quiet and to leave you. No other can save you but Jesus.

## GOD LIVES IN YOU | OCTOBER 1

*"No one has ever seen God; but if we love one another, God lives in us and His love is made complete in us." I John 4: 12*

---

There are a number of stories in the Bible of God's love displayed through healing. One of my favorites is the story of the centurion, found in Luke 7: 1-17. The Centurion was well-respected in Capernaum. His servant, whom he much valued, was near death. This centurion was powerful and generous. Even though he was not Jewish, he helped build the Jewish synagogue in town. The Jews were eager to return the favor. They pleaded with Jesus to heal the centurion's servant. The centurion himself sent friends to Jesus to proclaim in his behalf that he considered himself unworthy of Jesus. Jesus was stunned by the centurion's faith and healed the servant.

What would make a centurion of another faith show love and mercy to a servant, a slave? Today's text addresses that very question. If we love one another, it demonstrates our love for our fellow man. Since God Himself is love, it serves as evidence that we know God. When God dwells in each of us, we have God's love. When we are receptive to His spirit dwelling in our hearts, we exude God's love. The centurion had God dwelling in his heart. Why? Because he was receptive to the Spirit's guidance, counsel and love. It is not a person's religion that gives a person knowledge of God's love. It is the indwelling of the Spirit of God that gives a person the ability and desire to love another human being regardless of their race, creed, color or status.

The centurion knew God. Even though he was not a Jew, he knew God. The fact is that there are many people in this world who know God because they demonstrate the spirit of love in their everyday dealings with other people. They may not practice your particular "brand", call it, of faith. God recognizes that our brand of faith relates both to where we were born and our parents religious affiliation. He doesn't care if you're of Christian or Jewish or Islamic heritage; He cares about what is in your heart. He cares how your treat your neighbor, your spouse, your child or the stranger in your midst. **Wherever love is shown there is God. Wherever, evil, destruction or death is shown that is not of God.**

When God lives in you, you mirror His treatment of us in the way you treat others. **Do you know God? If you respond in the affirmative, then you have love in your heart. His love is complete in you when you allow Him to reside in you.**

## HOW DEEP IS YOUR LOVE? | OCTOBER 2

*"Above all, love each other deeply, because love covers over a multitude of sins. Offer hospitality to one another without grumbling. Each one should use whatever gift he has received to serve others, faithfully administering God's grace in its various forms." I Peter 4: 8-11*

---

There was a singing group back in the 70's that had a hit song entitled "How Deep is Your Love?" How do you love? There are various forms of love. Your "love" for that person may range from mild affection to fiery passion, from passing fancy to lifelong commitment. Someone once said that the love between mother and child is the strongest love between two human beings. Others contend it is the love between husband and wife. The story of Romeo and Juliet exemplified the deepest love. These were two people who gave their lives for one another. "Greater love has no one than this that he lay down his life for his friends." John 15: 13. How deep have you loved? Deep love does not necessarily equate to giving your life for the one you love.

Would you lay down your life for a loved one? God loved us to the point of forgoing His Godly nature in favor of human skin. With all the vulnerabilities, limitations and shortcoming of a human being, God eventually gave His life for us so that we might have life eternally. His love for us demonstrated the deepest love anyone can ever experience.

A story circulated on the Internet about the Pope's being ill and needing a heart transplant. Many of his followers gathered at St. Peter's Square to pay homage and offer their life for him. "Choose me," they yelled. The Pope was so overwhelmed with joy and compassion that he decided to drop a feather from his balcony window, and whomever the feather landed on, that would be the person chosen to give up his or her life for the Pope. As the wind gently carried the feather through the air, the closer it got to the heads of the people below, you could hear the sound of puckered lips blowing the feather to avoid its landing on them.

We may be caught up in the emotions of the moment to offer our life for another, but when faced with the true test; we cower amidst second thoughts. Jesus did not cower when He gave up His life for our salvation. He did not know whether or not He would rise again. He only knew that He wanted to save the one He loved deeply more than His life. He trusted His Father more than anything. If you don't see God in your life, then you have not opened your eyes and heart to His Spirit.

**What matters most is not your love for God but your acceptance of His deep love for you.**

# SUBMISSIVE WIVES | OCTOBER 3

*"Wives, in the same way be submissive to your husbands so that, if any of them do not believe the word, they may be won over without words by the behavior of their wives," 1 Peter 3: 1*

---

"Wives…be submissive to your husbands…" Not exactly what the 19th Amendment had in mind when it granted women the right to vote. But, there it is, in the Bible in black and white: wives should be submissive to their husbands.

Many scholars have rationalized that this is not forced submission but rather voluntary and an act of selflessness on the part of the wife. Others argue that Christ Himself submitted without any reservation to His Father's will. Submission itself is not necessarily demeaning. There is no arguing that men and women are not equal in a good many ways. God saw to it that a mother's role would be different than a father's. Clearly, He equipped them differently. And if all of the preceding is insufficient reason to allow for the subservience of women, we should remember that, in God's order of things, man came first. Some maintain that woman was an afterthought, a response to Adam's loneliness. So what's wrong with the notion of wives submitting to husbands? Doesn't someone need to take the lead? EVERYTHING is wrong with that notion.

It's unlikely that very many women would regard the preceding as anything more than rationalizations. Some would argue: "That was then, and this is now." If that be the case, then we are back to the question of the Bible's relevancy in our time. Yes, the Bible is indeed relevant today. Its lessons are as meaningful today than they were two millennia ago. However, the context has changed. If slavery was evil then, the same applies to the issue of submissive wives. We can rationalize all we want but the verse says: "Wives, be submissive." That verse seems to be the prevailing practice of many religious sects. They stop looking for the true meaning beyond those words and stick to its command. **The trouble with man is that he does not know how to love as God loves. And until he can demonstrate God's love to his wife, he needs to submit to God first. There is an overriding message throughout the Bible, and that is to love each other as God loves us.**

**Submissive means to love as how God loves us.** You will understand how to submit and love only when you truly KNOW God. **Husbands must love their wives as God loves us. God's love for us is boundless, selfless and unconditional. God loves the wife and husband equally. That theme is consistent throughout the Bible. We ought to follow God.**

## SEEING IS NOT BELIEVING | OCTOBER 4

*"And without faith it is impossible to please God, because anyone who comes to him must believe that He exists and that he rewards those who earnestly seek Him." Hebrews 11: 6*

---

Thomas sought visual proof that Jesus had risen from His tomb. He was of the "seeing is believing" school. Thomas had that opportunity a week after the resurrection when he was with the disciples as Jesus appeared. Jesus said to him: "Put your finger here; see my hands. Reach out your hand and put it into my side. Stop doubting and believe." Thomas then exclaimed: "My Lord and my God!"

We have not had the privilege of seeing Jesus as the disciples and hundreds of others before He ascended to heaven. Today's text is extremely important. Your salvation hinges on your believing, NOT on your seeing. Jesus proclaimed that it is impossible to please God without faith. Unless you have faith, you will not see God.

**What is faith? "Faith is being sure of what we hope for and certain of what we do not see." (Hebrews 11: 1). "We live by faith, not by sight." (II Corinthians 5:7). Seeing is NOT believing.** Hebrews 11 begins with a description of faith as well as a history of faith from Abel to Enoch, to Norah, Abraham, Sarah, Isaac, Jacob, Joseph, Moses, Rahab, Gideon, Barak, Samson, Jephthah, David, Samuel, Daniel, and the list goes on. Can we add your name?

They were all commended of their faith, notwithstanding the fact that NONE OF THEM RECEIVED WHAT HAD BEEN PROMISED. Why is all this important? because this is what will separate you from God. **"But the man who has doubts is condemned if he eats, because his eating is not from faith; and everything that does not come from faith is sin." (Romans 14: 23). "Consequently, Faith comes from hearing the message, and the message is heard through the word of Christ." (Romans 10: 17) Jesus declared: "Whosoever BELIEVETH in Him will not perish but have eternal life." (John 3: 16). What a compelling verse.** Everything we do that is not of faith is sin. Ah! But we hope; our hope is our belief in Him. We must trust Him whether we see or not.

Though we have not seen Jesus we must believe He exists. We must believe on what He has promised in His word. It is not about seeing Him that matters most. Whether we see Him or not we must believe. Our belief in God is manifested on how we love one another. God is a Spirit. Who resides in you will determine the Spirit within you. The physical realm is temporary but the Spiritual realm is eternal. **Believe in God. You cannot please God without faith in Him. You cannot see God unless you believe in Him.**

## WHERE ARE THE OTHER NINE? | OCTOBER 5

*""As he was going into a village, ten men who had leprosy met him. They stood at a distance and called out in a loud voice, 'Jesus, Master, have pity on us!' When he saw them, he said, 'Go, show yourselves to the priests.' As they went, they were cleansed. One of them, when he saw he was healed, came back, praising God in a loud voice. He threw himself at Jesus' feet and thanked him-and he was a Samaritan. Jesus asked, 'Were not ten cleansed? Where are the other nine?' 'Was no one found to return and give praise to God except this foreigner?'" Luke 17: 12-19*

---

My friend is a grandfather and uncle. Every holiday and birthdays as well as anniversaries he sends each of his grandchildren and nephews and nieces a card with money to wish them well and warm greetings on their special occasion. He complained to me he never receives a thank you note or a letter of acknowledgement.

A dear friend was diagnosed with breast cancer. During her ordeal she went through a metamorphosis that looked bleak but in the end she was declared in remission. My friend threw a huge thank you party to honor God and all her family and friends who prayed for her. She had a thankful heart to God. What about the one who dies? Can you still trust God? Can you still praise Him when things don't go your way? "In ordinary life we hardly realize that we receive a great deal more than we give, and that it is only with gratitude that life becomes rich." Dietrich Bonheoffer

Today's story represents the number of people who give thanks to God. Out of ten only one returned to thank Him for healing him. That is a poor representation of our gratitude to God. Have you ever prayed to God to strictly say thank you to Him? How often do you think on the Lord and ponder on His goodness to you? Just as you anticipate a thoughtful word of thanks, God also appreciates a thankful heart. His love for you does not alter just because you forget to thank Him. God's love for you is steadfast and sure. That's something to really be thankful for.

The Greek word for thank you is "eucharistia." Earlier I mentioned to you charis in Greek means grace, therefore the center of eucharist is grace, and the center of grace is chariro, which means "to rejoice." Thank you then means to rejoice in God's presence. Jesus asked Him, "did I not heal ten, but where are the other nine?"

God wants you to remember the Giver more than the gift. Will you be one of the ten who returns and give thanks to God? God will still love the other nine who did not return. Rejoicing in His glory is the ultimate love.

**"Thanks be to God for His indescribable gift!" ( 2 Cor. 9:15) That gift is Jesus Christ. Now thank Him.**

## GOD THE WOMAN | OCTOBER 6

*"Or suppose a woman has ten silver coins and loses one. Does she not light a lamp, sweep the house and search carefully until she finds it? And when she finds it, she calls her friends and neighbors together and says, 'Rejoice with me; I have found my lost coin.'" Luke 15: 8 & 9*

---

Each of us remembers special occasions. We even remember the exact date of our birthday, our anniversary, our graduation or the date of the birth of our first child. Do you remember the date you were baptized? How about the date of your divorce? Do you remember the exact date you left the church? I do. It was a traumatic event. I felt lost. I felt abandoned, alone and unwanted. I decided church, God and church people did not fulfill me. I thought the world offered a better deal. So, I ventured out there and indulged in the pleasures the other side had to offer. In the process I got really lost and even more confused.

Today's Bible text talks about the parable of the lost coin. God in His care and love for us will forgo everything He has and will earnestly seek the lost coin until it is found. We, of course, are the lost coin. The book of Luke, Chapter 15, also talks about the lost sheep and the lost son. God is like the woman who went and sought the lost coin. She had several coins and valued each one equally. When she lost that one coin, she placed all her might and soul in finding the one lost coin.

Can you picture God as a woman? not a very palatable allegory of a deity as a woman given the male dominant culture we live in. Yes, we male and female were created in the image of God. We, as human beings have character traits that originated from God. God as a woman is really the greatest comparison and depiction of God we can understand in human language, character and life. Jesus came to earth to reveal to us the Father. Jesus was male. Jesus wanted to dispel the male dominant mentally pervading our world. God met us in our own sphere and thinking. We neglected to love one another as He loved us. Therefore, the role of man as the head and God as male reigned throughout earth's history. He was birthed not by a man but by a woman. A woman is most responsible in rearing the infant from birth to adolescent.

In Matthew 24: 37, God says "how often I have longed to gather your children together, as a hen gathers her chicks under her wings, but you were not willing." Jesus again is depicted as a mother hen protecting and caring for her young chicks. It's hard to picture God as a woman isn't it? All our indoctrination when we were children was that God was male gender therefore the man in his household is not only the head but the bread winner. Rest assured that the rearing of children and the first picture of God is usually the woman or mother of the household of faith. **God is not only depicted as a woman in these parables but She is your search party, protector, security and salvation. God's nurture is Her nature.**

## FEAR, POWER, LOVE AND SOUND MIND | OCTOBER 7

*"For God hath not given us a spirit of fear; but a spirit of power and of love and of a sound mind." II Timothy 1: 7*

---

What a very encouraging and uplifting text we have to meditate on today. God wants to empower us with His Spirit. It is a Spirit of no fear, of power, of love and of sound mind.

My brother has been training for his first marathon. He joined a track club which runs every week. He fought through shortness of breaths, aches in is muscles and mental frustration. Early on, he felt like quitting the running, but he did not give up because he was determined to overcome these obstacles. Since then he has run in numerous marathons. I applaud him and anyone else who can endure such a difficult race.

God wants us to have the same Spirit. Only His Spirit can accomplish those tasks that you set your mind to accomplish. We are running a race that is longer than a marathon yet shorter than a heartbeat. We are running for our lives. We do not know when out time here on earth will be up. It can happen in an instant. One of my friends got into a car accident recently and perished at age 28. He crossed his finish line prematurely. Are you aware of your time here on earth? Do you feel you are running out of time?

Virtually every day, we encounter an array of temptations, even in the privacy of our own homes. It may be tempting to quit the race. Nobody will know you rationalize. Then there is the race to love your neighbor. God commanded us to love them. It's easy to love the lovable, but what about the unlovable? We ask God "Do we have to?" Boy! That's a real hard task to do, isn't it? I mean there are just some people we don't want to "hang around with," at least not very long.

God operates only in love. God did not let us down. He is a seeker of the lost, the unlovable, and the prodigal sinner. God chose to imbue us with the Spirit of no fear, love and wisdom. He is with us as our shield, armor and strength. He gave us love of our neighbor, self-discipline in our daily struggles and wisdom to make the right decision in facing our challenges.

**You can live as He lived when you allow His Spirit to dwell in you. Are you willing to receive His Spirit? If so, you will have no fear, much power, unconditional love and a very keen and sound mind.**

# MERCY AND GRACE | OCTOBER 8

*"At one time we too were foolish, disobedient, deceived and enslaved by all kinds of passions and pleasures. We lived in malice and envy, being hated and hating one another. But when the kindness and love of God our Savior appeared, He saved us, not because of righteous thing we had done, but because of his mercy. He saved us through the washing of rebirth and renewal by the Holy Spirit, whom he poured out on us generously through Jesus Christ our Savior, so that having been justified by his grace, we might become heirs having the hope of eternal life." Titus 3: 3-7*

---

It was a wonderful Mother's day. The weather was perfect, and restaurants were teeming with people treating their moms on this special occasion. My friend Donna refused to join us because she was waiting for her children to call her. At seven o'clock, I checked on her to inquire how her Mother's day had gone. She asked me to come over and dine with them. Her children were at her house and she made dinner for all of them.

I asked the kids why Donna was cooking on her day. They informed me that she was in a grouchy mood. It's been three years since her divorce. She ran across boxes of pictures that needed organization and filing. Memories of her life welled up inside her. She asked herself those daunting questions. "Why me? What did I do wrong? Have I failed as a mother, wife and Christian?" I asked her; "How could you blame yourself for something over which you had no control? He was the one who had the affair and left the family." I told her she took out her misery on her children. I further added "How could you blame your innocent children too?" She said one of her children reminded her of her ex-husband. "What!?" I said "and that justifies your treating her that way? You need to apologize to your children." She recognized her jaundiced thinking and committed to show her love to them.

Can you identify? We have played the blame game. Yes, we were once foolish and enslaved to all kinds of "baggage." We lived a life of malice, envy, hatred and finger pointing. We made poor choices and lived a life of regrets and guilt. We ended up blaming God too. That was before we were renewed by His Holy Spirit. Yes, we were undeserving of God's grace yet He gladly showed us mercy and grace. We have a role model in Jesus Christ. His heart is devoid of blame. He has saved us, not for what we did but because of His mercy.

**Undeserving though we be, when we are open to Him, He will bestow upon us His mercy, His Spirit and most of all His grace. What a blessing!**

## I DON'T KNOW YOU | OCTOBER 9

*"Someone asked him, 'Lord, are only a few people going to be saved?' He said to them, 'Make every effort to enter through the door, because many, I tell you, will try to enter and will not be able to. Once the owner of the house goes up and closes the door, you will stand outside knocking and pleading,' 'Sire open the door for us.' But he will answer, 'I don't know you or where you come from.'" Luke 13: 23-25*

---

In 1974, William E. (Bill) Miller did one of the more memorable spots in the American Express advertising campaign which always began with: "Do you know me?...I ran for Vice-President of the United States in 1964; so I shouldn't have trouble charging a meal, should I? Well, I do. That's why I carry the American Express card." We don't know many people. Sometimes we need a card to identify who we are.

Some time back, I was in line at a fast food store, and I'd noticed that the cashier's routine always included: "here or to go?" The rather corpulent lady in front of me ordered a bucket of chicken. The lady was offended by the "Here or to go?" question. She replied: "Do you think I could eat a bucket of chicken here?" The cashier's respond was: "Girl, I don't know you."

The "suits" in your company may not know you. By gone friends may forget you. Family members may even disown you. To engage in any kind of transaction, you must present two forms of identification, at least one of which must have a photo. It's so rare these days to be able to walk up to a teller window at a bank and be greeted by name. Don't you wish you could be recognized without having to produce an ID card? It's such a hassle and an inconvenience isn't it?

My friend asked me to go with him to a wedding. I did not know anyone at that wedding. When the parents of the groom came around to greet their guests, She said to me, "I don't know you? Have I met you before?" I replied, I am with my friend, "Jesse" and she said, "Oh! nice to meet you." What an awkward moment!

There is One who knows you very well, and He knew you even before your parents knew you. God wants to take you to His home where you won't need an ID to enter in. He has promised that one day soon, He will open the doors to His kingdom. He will greet you personally. He tells us to make every effort to be there. Your effort is to place your faith in Him.

**Yes, God knows you. Why not return the compliment and get to know Him?**

## PAYBACK TIME | OCTOBER 10

*"And we urge you, brothers, warn those who are idle, encourage the timid, help the weak, be patient with everyone. Make sure that nobody pays back wrong for wrong, but always try to be kind to each other and to everyone else. Be joyful always; pray continually; give thanks in all circumstances, for this is God's will for you in Christ Jesus." I Thessalonians 5: 14-18*

---

This is the Christian life in Christ Jesus. Can you be patient with everyone? Today's society gives in to the notion that it is good to live with someone before you get married. It is known as a trial period before committing to marriage. It is during this period that the "true colors" of a person are exhibited. There is a saying: "You don't know a person until you live with them." Live-in trials often raise a plethora of issues because we don't know the other person well. The key factor in any relationship is commitment and to what extent are you willing to commit?

What about the neighbor you detest or avoid? It doesn't have to be your next-door neighbor; it can be your classmate, your co-worker, a friend, an acquaintance or relative, or even the stranger you cross paths with. How do you treat these people? Are you kind to them? Do you help them in their time of need? Do you give encouragement to the timid? Are you patient with everyone you meet? Do you love your enemies or do you seek revenge? Do you "collect stamps" and plan to pay them back for what they've done to you? After all we're only human. None of us are perfect. If you carry that attitude, have you ever wondered what heaven would be like when we all live together? Will we carry the same attitude there? I think not.

Today's text gives us guidance and hope. We are to treat our neighbor as God instructed us -- with love and care. His Spirit longs to bless you and give you His Spirit of love, patient, kindness and understanding. **When you discover the true God of love there will be no pay-back time ever. You will give thanks in all your circumstances because you know God. You will see and treat others as though you were dealing with God.**

Whenever you are wronged, instead of vengeance you will pray for them. His Spirit will bring you the joy of His salvation. There will be relapses along the way; but don't lose heart, always return to the One who is the fruits of the Spirit and you too will express His love to everyone. Above all, be patient with everyone and treat them kindly. If you can't see them or be with them, pray for them. Rejoice always and never forget to give thanks.

**May God's Spirit reign always in your life because this is His will for you in Christ Jesus.**

## WHO'S YOUR BOSS? | OCTOBER 11

*"Whatever you do, work at it with all your heart, as working for the Lord, not for men, since you know that you will receive an inheritance from the Lord as a reward. It is the Lord Christ you are serving. Anyone who does wrong will be repaid for his wrong, and there is no favoritism." Colossians 3: 23*

---

The late Elizabeth Taylor had a reputation for being fashionably late; so it was no surprise when her remains arrived at her funeral service at 2: 15 p.m. for a scheduled 2 p.m. service. It turns out that Elizabeth planned it that way. She knew that she wasn't going to there in the flesh, but she wanted to be accountable for the service, nevertheless. Today's verse speaks of accountability.

There was builder who worked very hard and rather diligently for his boss. He was meticulous in everything he did and was uncompromising with respect to the quality of his work. When the final house project was complete, his boss was proud of him and told him "great job." The builder was expecting some kind of tangible reward or bonus for his extraordinary effort, but, instead, his boss asked him to take on one more project. He begrudgingly obliged, but his heart was never in the project. He approached the job half-heartedly, and he even hid flaws with inferior work and materials. He was attempting, quite apparently, to get even with his boss. When he completed the project, his boss thanked him and proceeded to give him the keys to his new home. It was a tangible expression of the boss's gratitude for a job well-done.

What is your attitude when it comes to work? What is your attitude in life period? Do you have the Spirit of God or the spirit of halfhearted? Whatever task you are assigned to do, do it with all your might knowing full well you are working for the Lord and not man. Don't try and cut corners or produce inferior work, for whatever you are doing, there will be a reward. And that reward may be your inheritance. Your reward from God is more than a house; it's a character consistent with His kingdom. The Lord is really your boss.

The next time you attempt to impress your boss or anyone for that matter, remember the One who is your ultimate boss. It is not your immediate supervisor at work, your wife, your friend or the president of the U.S.A. **Treat each individual as though you were dealing with God. For God is your boss. You must always serve God first. You are accountable to Him above all others.**

**When you place Him first, you are acknowledging your real Boss.**

## BE CONTENT WHATEVER THE CIRCUMSTANCES | OCTOBER 12

*"I am not saying this because I am in need, for I have learned to be content whatever the circumstances. I know what it is to be in need, and I know what it is to have plenty. I have learned the secret of being content in any and every situation, whether well fed or hungry, whether living in plenty or in want. I can do everything through him who gives me strength." Philippians 4: 11-13*

---

It is not easy to praise God and give him thanks when one's belly is hungry. Whenever we go on mission trips, we encounter poverty. Chronic hunger is near epidemic in our world. The World Bank estimates that 1.4 billion people live at or below the poverty line. Mind you, their poverty line is $1.25 per day. At, say, $1.25 per day, nobody is likely to be out painting the town red.

With perhaps 20% of the world living in abject poverty, there's a lot of misery to spread. It is amazing just how many of these people have managed to achieve contentment, no matter their financial plight. It is interesting, too, that so many American hit rock-bottom insofar as contentment is concerned, just as their earnings peak. Call it midlife crisis or whatever; it sometimes seems that contentment and wealth have an inverse relationship.

Paul tells us he was content, regardless of his circumstances, and that is because his strength came from Christ. If your faith in God is dependent upon the outcome of your prayers, then contentment is apt to be elusive. God works in ways that we are incapable of understanding and in a time frame that is unlike ours. We must rely on His word, therefore, whether or not we see evidence.

Knowing God is an important first step, but contentment in all circumstances lies not only in knowing God, but also in having a trusting and working relationship with Him. Our definition of contentment tends to rely on a feel good mentality. God's contentment focuses beyond earthly satisfaction. Paul learned the truth about being content through his relationship with God. He did not always have this kind of attitude. It took an awakening from God's Spirit to show Paul his priorities. When He discovered the true God, he was satisfied, content. All His wants and desires took a back seat to His Maker. He found the answer to all his longings. Everything else was secondary when it came to his relationship with his Maker.

**God's contentment is an abiding, internal calm assurance. God wants you to learn of Him and you too will be content, whatever your circumstances may be.**

## FIRST COMMANDMENT WITH A PROMISE | OCTOBER 13

*"Children obey your parents in the Lord, for this is right. Honor your father and mother-which is the first commandment with a promise, that it may go well with you and that you may enjoy long life on the earth." Ephesians 6: 1-3*

---

While we get to choose many things in life, parents are not among them. Not all parents, of course, are model citizens. I remember accompanying my friend to visit her father. He was an elderly man. Every time she spoke to him, she had a condescending, abrasive and curt manner. She was disrespectful toward him. It was a shock to me the first time I witnessed this. I was raised to respect the elderly. The resentment and hostility with which she treated him disturbed me until she shared with me her deep dark secret. The question is: Does even the most flagrant offense by a parent warrant disrespect? When a parent seems unworthy of respect, do we have a right to react in kind?

Our text gives us a promise of a long life and things going well if we respect our parents. Parents sometimes can be overbearing to their children. Verse four tells parents to treat their children in kind. "Fathers, do not exasperate your children; instead bring them up in the training and instruction of the Lord." This goes not only for parents but also for you and me.

Clearly, not all people deserve respect, but the fact remains that we all need it. This was abundantly clear from the way that Jesus treated the least-accepted people of His time. He looked for the good in each of them. Sometimes, it is not readily apparent, but, usually, there is an ounce or two of decency in each of us.

As a people, we are sometimes so intent on playing the blame game that we forget to focus on the good. Sometimes we may be justified to treat others with disdain because they wronged us. After all, "we're only human," right? There is some good in every parent/person. It may just take a leap of faith to find it. Faith, after all, is what it is all about. It will take a God-like faith to treat an undeserving person. God is able to change even the most harden heart. The change begins with you. **There is hope when you allow God's Spirit to dwell in you. The greatest miracle you will witness is your change of heart and attitude toward God. Focus on Him and not your change of heart and everything else will fall in place.**

God has shown us favor, kindness and goodness in spite of our sins. He is always ready to forgive us. Let that same Spirit guide us in how we treat our parents and, for that matter any person.

## DO EVERYTHING WITHOUT COMPLAINT | OCTOBER 14

*"Do everything without complaining or arguing." Philippians 2: 14*

---

When was the last time you complained? When was the last time you argued with someone? Did it result in a bitter dispute that left a wound that still hasn't healed? Can you go just one day without complaining or arguing with someone? Have you noticed it's the petty, little mundane things that seem to affect our equilibrium the most? Forgive me for saying this but I hate complainers or complaining! Don't you? It's so divisive.

The biggest complainer of them all, of course, was the father of lies (Lucifer), who complained that he was not consulted regarding the trinity in the plan of salvation. His complaint, as you know, led to his downfall. God warns against complaining. It is destructive. When you complain or argue, it leads to no good. Even when you resolve the issue, it always seems to leave a bitter after taste and things are never quite the same. Instead, He advises, you should reason together rather than complain. Unless you have the Spirit of God dwelling in you, you will be caught off guard and the spirit of dissension will prevail.

Argument is often the easy way out; for it typically seems easier to denigrate another than to lift up ourselves. So often he (or she) who has the weakest argument endeavors to out-shout his opponent. We are a society that deals in half-truths. How many times have you watched a car commercial in which they flash on the screen three paragraphs of disclaimers which, even if you had perfect vision, you could not possibly read in the half second allowed? It is the way we deal with one another. We adhere, ever so tenuously, to the letter of the law without any regard for the law's spirit.

Well, there is a Spirit who focuses much more on intent than on legalese. He knows what is in our hearts and is not fooled it we attempt to mince words. He's heard our complaints. He's read all of the disclaimers. He knows too that His only Son gave His own life without so much as a complaint. "He was oppressed and afflicted, yet He did not open his mouth; He was led like a lamb to the slaughter, and as a sheep before her shearers is silent, so He did not open his mouth" Isaiah 53: 7. Are you a complainer? Do you always seem to have something to complain about? It's time to bag it and store it. **Put away the spirit of negativism in your life. Stop arguing. Stop complaining. Listen to the Spirit of God. He brings forth the fruits of the Spirit.**

God never complained or mumbled a word and we ought to do the same.

## A LOVE THAT NEVER SEPARATES | OCTOBER 15

*"For I am convinced that neither death nor life, neither angels nor demons, neither present nor the future, nor any powers, neither height nor depth, nor anything else in all creation, will be able to separate us from the love of God that is in Christ Jesus our Lord." Romans 8: 38 & 39*

---

"They say that breaking up is hard to do. Now I know, I know that it's true." Most of you won't remember the song that went to #1 on the charts in 1962. Typically, when we think of breaking up, we think of romances gone astray, but there is the breaking up that occurs when a father goes off to war, a child heads off to college, a parent or grandparent loses his or her faculties and becomes a very distant object. Death, too, of course, brings with it a feeling of separation.

The feeling of separation is always a difficult one with which to cope. Typically there is shock and then anger, perhaps vengeance, and, in some instances reconciliation. If reconciliation falters, there is resignation or acceptance of the fact, and hopefully one restarts his or her life again.

As a people, we have not only tolerated separation, we have, over the years, compelled people to remain separate from one another. In many states, African Americans had their own places in restaurants, parks, buses, and the like. In fact, in 1896, in the U.S Supreme Court Plessy v Ferguson decision, the court upheld the notion that separate but equal public school facilities were constitutional. It wasn't until some 58 years later (1954), in Brown v. Board of Education of Topeka that the court ruled that separate facilities were inherently unequal. As a people, we have endeavored to separate ourselves from different ideologies, different nationalities and even different religions. Where there is no love separation abounds. Separation does not come from God. Separation is one of the most heart-wrenching emotional known to humankind. There is nothing more painful. God is love, anything not of God separates. Remember who the father of separation is, Lucifer.

**God knows about separation. He understands what it means to be separated from a loved one. God says; not even death or life, angels nor demons, neither present or future, powers, infinite distances, nor any thing He has ever created will be able to separate His faithful love for us.** Doesn't that love just brags you deeply. Who on earth can love you like that? What manner of love is this that the Father has told us? Even all eternity could never fathom or exhaust this love of our Father.

That tremendous and inexhaustible love is in His Son, Jesus Christ our Lord.

## ROBBING YOURSELF | OCTOBER 16

*"Will a man rob God? Yes you rob me. But you ask, How do we rob you? In tithes and offerings. You are under a curse-the whole nations-because you are robbing me. Bring the whole tithe into the storehouse, that there may be food in my house. Test me in this, says the Lord Almighty, and see if I will not throw open the flood gates of heaven and pour out so much blessing that you will not have room enough for it." Malachi 3: 8-10*

---

Yesterday a friend of mine lost his job. He had been working for his company for many years. They had a massive lay-off. Another friend asked me if my friend pays tithe. I said "no." She replied that's why he lost his job. Does God punish the person who does not give tithe? This seems to be the belief among stalwart tithe givers. Just last week, a close friend received a huge check and confessed to me "now I can pay tithe."

Today's text doesn't say a word about God punishing the sinner for not paying his/her tithe. Instead, God promises that He will open the floodgates of heaven such that you will not have room enough to receive it if you do. Does God need our tithes and offerings? Does He need our money? I don't think so. What is God saying? God has no boundaries when it comes to giving. He wants to give us the best and the most. God wants our tithes and offerings so we can experience the joy of giving. This reminds me of a story:

Three men were boasting of their charitable giving. The first said: "I tithe, not 10%, but 15%, of my salary every week." The second man proclaimed: "That's nothing. I give 25% of my earnings annually." The third man did them one better: "I take all of the money I have and throw it up in the air. God takes what He wants, and I keep the rest."

Yes, "God loves a cheerful giver." In fact, God is a cheerful giver. God wants us to share not only our money but also ourselves. If you hold back in giving, you will have nothing. You will only be robbing yourself, not God. God wants you to give yourself as He gave Himself. There is no greater joy than to give. God is a giver. His nature and character is all about giving. When you practice giving, you will soon discover the secret to life's happiness. That happiness originated from the true source of joy, God. Don't rob yourself by not giving.

**Giving is a very deep expression of love. The deepest of all expression of love came from "God so loved the world that He GAVE." He gave us His Son unreservedly.**

## IF MY PEOPLE | OCTOBER 17

*"If my people, who are called by my name, will humble themselves and pray and seek my face and turn from their wicked ways, then will I hear from heaven and will forgive their sin and will heal their land." II Chronicles 7: 14*

How does God answer prayer? Does He arbitrarily choose whom He will answer? Today's text is explicit on the condition of answered prayer. He says we must humble ourselves, pray, seek His face and turn away from our wicked ways and God will then answer our prayers. That shouldn't be too difficult a task to accomplish.

Does He favor one sick person over another? I remember when some church elders came to anoint my mother when she was first diagnosed with colon cancer. Her physician told her that she had only two to three months to live. Others claimed she first needed to repent of her sins to be healed.

God said in Isaiah 65: 24," "Before they call I will answer; while they are still speaking I will hear." God has already answered all our prayers, even before we asked. Yet we conjure up excuses and rationalize why our prayers are not answered. We begin to look inward on ourselves and think "what must I do to obtain God's favor." The problem is that you are looking inward instead of above. You have a totally wrong picture about God. Our understanding of God plays a major factor in how we perceive our prayers to Him.

God sent his Son to live among us so we could see God and know Him. During His earthly ministry Jesus healed many that were sick. He did not turn away anyone who called on Him for healing. Yet He tells of the time when many in Israel had leprosy in the time of Elisha the prophet (Luke 4: 27), but only Naaman the Syrian was cleansed. Why was that? Faith played a key factor. Does it mean when you are not healed and you die or someone you prayed for dies that you lacked faith? No. In Luke 18: 1 "Jesus told his disciples a parable to show them that they should always pray and not give up." Likewise God is telling us the same thing. We need to pray and be humble and contrite and follow God's ways before healing can be granted. **The greater lesson here is not the healing but the relationship of faith one has with God. Faith is trusting God no matter what we see, hear or experience. We trust God because we know He has already delivered**.

The Author of Love is telling us that He has already answered our prayers through His Son. Get to know His Son and be healed.

## NO BREATH IN IT | OCTOBER 18

*"Of what value is an idol, since a man has carved it? Or an image that teaches lies? For he who makes it trusts in his own creation; he makes idols that cannot speak. Woe to him who says to wood, 'Come to life!' Or to lifeless stone; 'Wake up!' Can it give guidance? It is covered with gold and silver; there is no breath in it." Habakkuk 2: 18*

---

I have a very dear friend of a different faith. She has a heart of gold and is always concerned about other people's well-being. Recently, right after experiencing a devastating blow to her marriage, she sought guidance from a fortune teller, who counseled her that her husband was going through a mid-life crisis. My friend knows my stance on fortune-tellers. I shared with her the story of King Saul in the Bible and how he, too sought the advice of a medium, and it ended tragically for him. My friend rationalized that this fortune teller had the uncanny ability to know what she was going through without her telling him anything. He was "right on the money," she insisted. In the end, she and her husband divorced.

What does the Bible say about seeking counseling with soothsayers, mediums, witchcraft or fortune-tellers? In Deuteronomy 18: 10-12, "Let no one be found among you who sacrifices his son or daughter in the fire, who practices divination or sorcery, interprets omens, engages in witchcraft, or casts spells, or who is a medium or spirits or who counsels the dead. Anyone who does these things is detestable to the Lord." These practices have been going on since the dawn of man, but certainly NOT with God's approval.

The issue here is trust. Whom do you trust when it comes to life counseling? Remember that He who breathed life into the lifeless form of clay when He created us is the same God who wants you to depend upon Him. He is your Maker, your Creator, your Counselor. No one knows you or your future better than God. He has all the answers to your questions. You needn't depend on fortunetellers, idols or good luck charms to guide your life. They are unreliable, lifeless and godless. Listen and 'Wake up!' before it's too late.

**Don't depend on things that are lifeless and tenuous because there is no breath in it.** I must confess I too, became enamored to watches and fine jewelry. They were attractive, addicting to pursue and own, but after awhile they became a lifeless disappointment. When I was hungry I could not eat them. When my monthly financial obligation came due, I could not use them to pay my bills. If I needed to buy gasoline for my car, I could use them. If I needed medical attention, they had no redeeming value. It was useless.

**The Author of Love is your true guidance and also the Creator of the breath in you. He alone is the way to all your needs and life eternal. He is the Author of your breath.z**

## A REFUGE IN TIME OF TROUBLE | OCTOBER 19

*"The Lord is slow to anger and great in power; the Lord will not leave the guilty unpunished. The Lord is good, a refuge in times of trouble. He cares for those who trust in Him. Whatever they plot against the Lord He will bring to an end; trouble will not come a second time." Nahum 1: 3 & 9*

---

Another tsunami hit Japan on March 11, 2011. The devastation and havoc it wreaked was mind boggling. Video footage shown during the news showed communities hit with uncontrollable force. Homes, cars, boats and ships and buildings collapsed in the wake of the tidal wave. People who were fortunate were clinging to debris to stay afloat while those less fortunate were buried in the rubble. Days after the clean-up, carnage was found everywhere and the count of lives lost continues to climb in the thousands. To add insult to injury, the earthquake that preceded the tsunami, which registered 8.9 in the Richter scale, also did considerable damage to three of the four nuclear plants. Radiation was leaking and affecting the environment. Even after eight days of cleaning, a ray of hope, a grandmother and child were found underneath the rubble alive. One year later, after floating thousands of miles from Japan, the debris from the tsunami hit the shores of California.

We live in a fractured world. Earthquakes, tsunamis, global wars and unrest abound, hurricanes and natural disasters happens unexpectedly. God, however, wants to assure us that He is a good God and will be our refuge in times of trouble. God knows there are evil forces plotting against Him and those who trust Him. Remember April 16, 2013 when someone planted two bombs during the Boston marathon? President Obama called it an act of terrorism. It was definitely an ungodly and evil act. God has promised to put an end to all our troubles, deaths, devastation and woes.

You can count on the Lord to be your refuge. We must place our trust in Him to benefit from that care. God has promised not one hair or blemish will afflict you. But the question remains, how could those innocent lives have been lost? "Where was God?" God is in total control. He operates only in love. Trust Him, no matter what.

Rest assured that He will return soon and all those innocent lives lost since Earth's history will be restored anew. He will make all things new again. He even promised that sin will not rise a second time. **Can you wait patiently for our Lord's return? All His promises will come true. In the meantime, stay faithful and remember He will be your refuge even in your times of trouble.**

## WHO IS A GOD LIKE YOU | OCTOBER 20

*"Who is a God like you, who pardons sin and forgives the transgression of the remnant of his inheritance? You do not stay angry forever but delight to show mercy. You will again have compassion on us; you will tread our sins underfoot and hurl all our iniquities into the depths of the sea." Micah 7: 18 & 19*

---

There must be one type of sin that is so heinous that even God cannot forgive it. Would it be adultery – clearly a violation of the Ten Commandments? How about idolatry? if you're looking to lay a great big insult in God's lap, that one wins the prize. Certainly, the perpetrator of a holocaust must be at or near the top of God's list of unforgivable heinous acts.

Well, both David and Moses committed murder and were forgiven. Peter lied on three different occasions and was forgiven. The Israelites turned to false gods and idols, but God took them back. Jacob stole Esau's birthright and was forgiven. However, I can recall when I was a child my adult family and friends handed down to me a sin that was unforgivable. They even quoted a specific Bible text. "Grieving the Holy Spirit" was the "unpardonable sin."

Since knowing God, I personally believe there is no sin so heinous that God will not forgive it. Our God is a God who pardons all of our inequities and forgives all of our sins, and as the above passage states (figuratively, we assume), He hurls them into the depths of the sea. Very likely, you have friends and family who will never let you forget your indiscretions, but God operates on a different plain, and He is prepared to forgive each and every sin. Not only is He merciful but He does not stay angry very long. Do you stay angry very long? Do you like to wallow in self-pity and anger? Human nature has a long memory and don't easily forget. But God not only easily forgets your transgression but He also remembers them no more. God develops "dementia" when it comes to forgetting your sin. God's forgiveness, of course, is what truly counts.

God has declared that He will bring an end to all suffering and heartaches. Moreover, He has declared that, when we enter into His Kingdom, sin will not rise again. What an unbelievable and amazing God to know. His mercy and compassion are incomprehensible. The way that He loves us is indescribable. **We will never fully comprehend His matchless love. The incredible truth about God is that we will have eternity to savor His goodness.**

**There is no other God like Him; now that is so comforting and alluring.**

## WHY BLAME GOD? | OCTOBER 21

*"But the Lord replied, 'Have you any right to be angry?'" Jonah 4: 4*

Sometimes, we believe that we have every right to be angry, especially at God. How many times have we blamed God for our lot in life? How many times have we attributed our misfortune to God? God is supposed to be mighty, strong and on our side. Why are we losing? Why do we still see suffering, pain, wars, diseases and death? Why can't God just get rid of all the wickedness in this world and restore a new order where there is no more pain, no more suffering and no more death?

Jonah felt the same way. There is more to the story of Jonah than the belly of the whale. God called Jonah to preach a warning message to Nineveh that "wicked" city of Nineveh. Jonah was instructed to tell the Ninevites that if the people did not repent and seek the Lord, they would be destroyed in 40 days. Keep in mind that God is not a destroyer, the truth is the people were on a course of self-destruction if they did not desist their evil practices. Well, the Ninevites listened to Jonah's warning. From the greatest to the least they fasted and put on sackcloth. Even the king listened and followed instructions and took off his royal robe and fasted. Everyone from the royal family to the lowly fasted and repented from their evil ways. Even the herds, flocks and beasts were not allowed to eat or drink.

God was moved with compassion and did not bring destruction on the city. But Jonah got angry with God. He wanted to see his prophecy fulfilled. Jonah was so embarrassed that his prophecy did not materialize that he ran away sulking. Jonah wanted to save face. "See, I knew you would do this!" He fumed. Jonah forgot about the selfless nature of God but instead wallowed in his own self-pity. He craved the attention of the people He warned. He wanted to tell the people, "See I told you so!" The greater story here is not about Jonah but about a loving God who does not want anyone to perish. God is patient and longsuffering showing mercy to everyone who would heed. God is very slow to anger. How slow is His anger? so slow that He is still waiting for us to return to Him. He will wait your lifetime to save you. Stop blaming God for your mistakes, own up to it.

**It is our nature to blame God when things don't go our way. Being a compassionate God, He always readily forgives us for we really don't know what we're doing.** Let's not blame a most loving God for the bad choices we make. We really don't have any right to blame God. Yet, because of His love for us He relents.

## MAN'S BEST FRIEND | OCTOBER 22

*"You are to bring into the ark two of all living creatures, male and female, to keep them alive with you. Two of every kind of bird or very kind of animal and of every kind of creature that moves long the ground will come to you to be kept alive." Genesis 6: 19 & 20*

---

I am reminded of a story I read about a couple who were told she could not conceive. She had a dog which she had bought when he was seven weeks old. The dog was lovable and brought them comfort. Pam was 41 years old by the time their pet dog reached the age of 15. One day, the dog was diagnosed with a small tumor near his liver. Pam could not let the dog suffer, although the bill was going to be a large one, she allowed the veterinarian to surgically remove the tumor. The dog soon recovered.

It was a few months after the dog's recovery that Pam and her husband discovered she was two months pregnant. Pam and Doug decided to assimilate their dog to the scent of the newborn baby even before they brought the baby home. They felt this would allay any jealousy. She let the dog smell the blanket that the child was wrapped in from the hospital. The dog dragged the blanket to his bedding and slept with it. When the child came home, their dog immediately bonded with the child.

At 5:00 a.m. one morning Pam was awakened by the baby's cry. He was likely hungry, she assumed. She went to the kitchen to prepare the baby's bottle. Suddenly, the dog came running into the kitchen very agitated. Pam had never seen him so upset. The dog led her into the baby's room. Pam saw her baby boy turning blue and gasping for air. She frantically attempted to revive the child while her husband dialed 911. The child eventually recovered. However, had just a few more seconds lapsed, the child would have died.

There is something comforting in having a dog for a pet. Some studies reveal having an animal for a pet increases one's longevity. Others believe the unconditional love they receive from their pet brings joy in their lives. I have witnessed pet owners cater to their animals in such a doting way that their own children would display jealousy. Some people have even admitted their love for their animals surpassed that of their children. A Sad but true case isn't it? That's what happens when we forget our Maker.

God knew man would benefit from His creatures. He saved them also from the flood, even the dog. It's little wonder people refer to a dog as man's best friend; actually, second-best friend. There are many stories of animals saving human lives, especially man's best friend. **The Lord gave us animals to show us how to love us unconditionally, but He also gave us our true best friend in His Son.**

## **FIXATED** | OCTOBER 23

*"Therefore, Holy brothers, who share in the heavenly calling, fix your thoughts on Jesus, the apostle and high priest whom we confess."* Hebrews 3: 1

---

When I was in Viet Nam during the Christmas holidays I met a wonderful family, who were kind, hospitable and endearing. They had two young children, a boy and a girl. They lived the good life and did not lack anything. My friend informed me that the woman wanted to speak to me privately. I was surprised by the unusual request, but I obliged.

In her broken English she asked me what America was like? I described my country as best as I could. I told her we had tall buildings and skyscrapers that seem to reach the sky. We had freeways and millions of cars that travel throughout the vast country on those freeways. There was plenty of food to eat from every known country. It was a melting pot of people from all corners of the world. I told her the country is beautiful with its mountains, rivers, lakes and sandy beaches. Our government allowed us freedom of religion, to worship the God of our choosing. Women supposedly had equal rights as men. She was surprised by that statement.

I inquired as to why she was asking all these questions. She replied: "I want to go to America." It seems that, no matter where you are, you see people looking for a better life. Even in the U.S., poverty, while not the rule, is definitely a very serious problem. Very often, the poverty is masked by the excess that surround it. Whatever you think about this great land of ours there is an even a better land that you can't even imagine. Eye has not seen nor ear heard of what heaven will be like.

My new Vietnamese friend knew nothing about the heaven that has been promised us. She did not yet understand that our stay here on Earth is but a season and that our true homeland is with God in heaven. As much as the U.S. is looked upon as an earthly heaven, it pales in comparison to the heavenly home. I further explained that no matter where one resided, it's the person you're with that makes a home. I shared with her a Savior whose name we call Jesus who will bring us home to a heavenly place that we can't imagine.

**It is, for that reason that we eagerly await the return of our Savior, who is preparing a permanent home where we can live with the Lord. That is our focus, what we are fixated on and our true hope,** I explained.

## AWAKENING LOVE AT THE RIGHT TIME | OCTOBER 24

*"Daughter of Jerusalem, I charge you: Do not arouse or wake love until it so desires." Song of Solomon 8: 4*

---

The book of Song of Solomon is attributed to the wisest man that ever lived on this earth, King Solomon. Yet, what did Solomon know about love? Actually a good deal, Solomon had over a thousand wives. Ultimately, they were his downfall, for they brought with them the gods of the surrounding nations. Their gods influenced Solomon and he began to worship them.

God has commanded us to stay faithful to Him only, but Solomon thought he was wiser than God. There was someone before Solomon who also thought he knew better than God. He was jealous of God; so he decided to take matters into his own hands. He even convinced a third of the angels to join his "team". His followers became partners in crime (literally and figuratively). They were there when Adam and Eve fell to temptation, and they have been his accomplices ever since.

It is often asked: "Why didn't God intervene?" Life would have been a lot easier and a good deal happier, had He done so. The Author of Love loves us so much that He granted us free will. Without free will there would be no love. It would be an automaton relationship. God could have made perfect robots that look exactly like us but without free will. God only operates in love. Human love, thanks to Lucifer, can be deceptive and complicated. God's love, on the other hand, is perfect because He is perfect.

When it comes to earthly love, timing can be of paramount importance. Have you ever wanted someone so badly that you blew your chances, so to speak, because your timing was not propitious. I have a dear friend who was pursued by the love of her life, but six months into the relationship she felt he was overbearing. She told him to leave. A year later, she realized her mistake but it was too late. He had already moved on and found someone else. She was devastated. She tried to lure him back to her but he was already committed to his new found love. She asked me "why couldn't we love each other at the same time?" She later confessed that her timing was off.

God's timing bears virtually no resemblance to our earthly calendars and clocks. His timing is perfect and always right-on. The sad part to all this is our timing can sometimes be imperfect. **We would do well to wait on the Lord. Awakening love at the right time can best be accomplished when it's on God's time.**

## **TWO WAGERS** | OCTOBER 25

*"Rid yourselves of all the offense you have committed, and get a new heart and a new spirit. Why will you die, O house of Israel? For I take no pleasure in the death of anyone, declares the Sovereign Lord. Repent and live." Ezekiel 18: 31 & 32*

---

Is God a killer? Why do we suffer? Never have these questions been more meaningful and provocative than now. Even the staunchest in faith have been known to question God during especially trying times such as the passing of a loved one.

Philip Yancey in his best-selling book entitled, "Disappointment with God," wrote of his own struggles with these questions. In the last chapter, he talks about two wagers. The first wager is found in the book of Job. There, God took a risk and wagered, so to speak, that Job would not lose his faith in God despite the calamities that befell him. Yancey remarks that probably none of us fully understands that wager. Jesus, however, summed it up in his comment that, at the end of human history, it will all come down to one specific issue: "When the Son of Man comes, will He find faith on earth?"

The second wager involved not God's but man's point of view. When Job's faith was challenged, he could not see, hear, feel nor touch God. He had no clue whatsoever what was going on in his life. He was at a total lost for answers. Even his friends tried to help him on the reason for his misfortunes. Job, nevertheless, placed his entire faith in God.

Are you still a bit skeptical? You, too, must make a wager. You can conclude that there is no God and live your life according to that belief. Alternatively, you can wager that there is a God who is true to His promises. At stake, of course, could be your eternal destiny. What causes many to wager against God is that they see insufficient evidence of His presence. They come up more than a little short in the faith department. God doesn't need to pop up in Times Square for us to see evidence of His divinity. That evidence is there to behold in the wondrous planet He made for us and in the Son He sent to redeem us of our burdens.

No matter what your wager is, God knows the end from the beginning. He said every mouth will confess that He is just and true. Just as Job trusted God, you can too. There will be times in your life when God will seem not to answer your prayer for healing. Your love one may pass away. Don't be dishearten or lose faith. **Learn from Job because in Job's story, it has a happy ending. God has promised the same for you and me.**

**Wager on God. It's a sure bet.**

## **OPEN THE DOOR** | OCTOBER 26

*"Here I am! I stand at the door and knock. If anyone hears my voice and opens the door, I will come in and eat with him, and he with me." Revelations 3: 20*

---

The Author of Love has been pursuing us since before our birth. God is a pursuer. He makes the first move to extend His love toward us. We do not come to God naturally. God comes to us. God's love for us is evident in the fact that, while we have been out in the world pursuing our desires, He has patiently waited outside the door of your heart to come in. God operates in love only.

There is a custom in the Middle East that, when relatives or strangers visit your home, you prepare a meal. Hospitality is one of Eastern societies' most serious obligations. Even with your enemies, the hospitable thing to do is to feed them. When Jesus was here on earth He fed thousands. He regularly broke bread with His disciples. When He raised the little girl of Jarius from the dead, one of the first things He instructed her parents to do was to feed her. God has even planned a banquet feast for us when He welcomes us home in the new earth. Now that's something to really look forward to.

Most of our social lives center around food. We as a nation enjoy socializing with our family and friends. Food is always involved when we gather together. There is something about dinning with family or friends that seem to "break ice" and disarm any hostility. One's guard is down and people tend to be more receptive and open when dinning. God knows that supping with us will give us joy and pleasure.

What is it about food that is so important? God knew something about eating. It was one of His best ideas. That's because eating is the natural process of taking the substance of what you eat and making it into the substance of your life, your body. "You are what you eat." We often forget that we must "eat" spiritually as well. In fact, Christ taught that we must eat His flesh and drink His blood if we are to enter the kingdom. Was He teaching cannibalism? No. He was describing the process by which His nature, both human and divine, would gradually become our nature as we continue to abide in Him, drinking of His life and eating of His nature.

Dine with the Lord. He is knocking at your door right now. He knows you need food for sustenance, but He also knows the conversation and time you spend with Him will be an amazing delight, and the food you eat will taste even better. **The source of all our substance and life is not in the earthly food we eat daily but in Him.**

**Do you hear Him knocking at your door? Open your heart and invite Him in. He wants to sup with you.**

## SEEK GOOD, NOT EVIL, MAINTAIN JUSTICE | OCTOBER 27

*"Seek good, not evil, that you may live. Then the Lord God Almighty will be with you, just as you say He is. Hate evil, love good; maintain justice in the courts. Perhaps the Lord God Almighty will have mercy on the remnant of Joseph."* *Amos 5: 14 & 15*

---

Evil surrounds us. We've all fallen prey to evil at one time or another. These days, evil's threat is multiplied because of modern-day technology. The Internet can be a virtual mine field.

A friend of mine is a frequent user of Facebook, which, as most of you are aware, enables you to stay in touch with friends anywhere in the world. One day, he received a live chat message from an old high school friend named Amanda. After the exchange of a few niceties, the conversation turned urgent. Amanda said that she and a companion were touring Germany and were mugged at gun point. She said that she had lost all of her cash and credit cards as well as her cell phone. She was apparently in dire need of help, and my friend, who is as kind-hearted a guy as there is, asked if he could help her.

She asked if he would send her a specified amount of money so that she could pay for her hotel room and her return trip home. My friend offered to phone the hotel and cover the bill with a credit card. Amanda kept insisting on a wire transfer to her. My friend grew suspicious and asked her questions about classmates and about mutual high school friends and as well as who was their geometry teacher. Amanda was stumped. She grew silent. She flunked the test and hung up. A pastor of mine sent me an email saying they were in the Philippines doing missionary work in a remote part of the country when they were robbed. He requested I wire him money because their credit cards and passports were stolen. I immediately contacted his brother here in America and he said don't send the money, someone hacked his brother's computer. His brother was actually here in the states safe and sound.

Yes, evil surrounds us. God has warned us to be vigilant at all times because the devil awaits the perfect moment to pounce on us. Evil sometimes appear alluring, it can even come in the guise of a "heavenly angel," but God urges us to seek good. Surround yourself with goodness and good people, and pray to God for strength and the wisdom to distinguish good from evil.

**When you seek God and follow His counsel, you will always see good not evil, you will hate evil and love good. You will maintain justice not only in the courts but in all your dealings.**

## DON'T BE FOOLISH | OCTOBER 28

*"But avoid foolish controversies and genealogies and arguments and quarrels about the law, because these are unprofitable and useless. Warn a divisive person once, and then warn him a second time. After that, have nothing to do with him. You may be sure that such a man is warped and sinful; he is self-condemned." Titus 3: 9-12*

---

I threw a party a few years back and invited a number of my close friends. My friends know that I go all-out for them so they can have a wonderful time. However, there are a few friends who always ask: "who's going to be there?" I tell them some names and some have literally said they won't come if so and so is there.

On this particular occasion, a birthday party, I invited a dozen of my very close friends, and one of the invited guest asked that very question. I began to recite the list of invitees, and, when I got to a certain name, she said: "I'm not coming. I can't stand Him." I responded: "Can't we all get along?" She laughed but still refused to attend.

I then said to her: "It's your choice. I invited you, and your decision will not make a difference in our relationship. I will still love you and miss you." The next day, she phoned to say she was coming. She realized that she was attending the party, not for the other person, but for me. There are some things not worth arguing about, and this certainly was one of them. Do you know which battles or arguments to pick? Don't you think all arguments are foolish? When you look back and think about it they are.

I then started thinking about the number of times I'd started an argument, just for the sake of coming out on top or scoring. I have argued over garbage, whether to throw it in the recycle or the garbage bin. Yes, it sounds silly but it is. All that argument ended up being just that, a bunch of garbage. Today's text urges us to admonish friends who are contrary and divisive at least twice, and if that fails on deaf ears, avoid that person. I ask you: is this how God is telling us to treat such people? Does God leave us two warnings? of course not. Whenever an argument ensues, you can rest assured that someone will be a fool because of their warped mentality. In the final analysis, a person who argues is self-condemned. I believe that this text is saying that we should distinguish between the fool and the person who may be suffering and that we should be Godlike in our approach.

God is never argumentative or divisive. **He never once succumbed to any argument because He knew it would be foolish and useless. We ought to follow His example. God is harmony and peace.**

## LEFT OR RIGHT HEART | OCTOBER 29

*"The Heart of the wise inclines to the right, but the heart of the fool to the left." Ecclesiastes 10: 2*

We tend to live by the creed: "What you see is what you get." We rely too much on our eyes and not nearly enough on our hearts.

When God sent Samuel to the house of Jesse to anoint a king to replace Saul, He looked from the left of his heart and, therefore, failed to discern that his choice was not a man of God. It took him seven tries, and, with God's guidance, he finally got it right and anointed David as King.

How many relationships were you engaged in before you found your future spouse? Were you choosing from the right heart or the left, and from which side was that ultimate choice? Regrettably, sometimes we don't get it right the first time and end up making second or third choices, which leave a trail of regrets and sorrows. With each choice that you make, ask yourself: "Is this choice from God or not?" Ask God to guide your thoughts and, most importantly, your heart.

What does it mean to choose wisely from the right or foolishly from the left? Our eyes fail to capture a person's spirit. It is better to pause and let the Spirit of God lead our hearts to make the right choices. I have a close friend who dated a man for two years. Each time she broke up with him she would always end with the statement," I love you in my heart but my mind tells me it won't work." Eventually she severed the relationship with her head and not her heart.

A commonly-used phrase these days is "the total package". A person who has the total package is perceived to be top-notch from head to toe, a real looker. However, a package is nowhere near total if it doesn't include a good heart. When you've found someone who has a true total package, you need to ask whether your affection is momentary or does it have staying power. Staying power means is this person solid in their faith in God. Do they live a consistent and unwavering godly life? I have had friends share with me their dating experiences in meeting a gorgeous-looking guy or gal, but once this gorgeous person opens their mouth to speak, they have no substance.

**You will know that you've made the right decision when you allow God's Spirit to guide you.** God's heart always inclines to the right. **Choose God first in all your decisions and you will choose right.**

## WHICH IS BETTER TO SACRIFICE OR TO OBEY? | OCTOBER 30

*"Does the Lord delight in burnt offerings and sacrifices as much as in obeying the voice of the Lord? To obey is better than sacrifice, and to heed is better than the fat of rams." I Samuel 15: 22*

---

We all make sacrifices to obtain our objectives. Some sacrifices are extreme, like sacrificing a child to the "gods." The Israelites perfected the art of sacrifices. They sacrificed animals, grain, oil, etc. However, their sacrifices held no true spiritual value. They were merely going through the motions. In no way were their sacrifices grounded in faith.

God told the Israelites that the act of obedience is far more important than sacrifices. What does God mean "To obey?" It means simply to follow instruction. Our parents trained us as children to obey. That was likely our first lesson in trust. If we did not obey, we faced the consequences. Our parents wanted us to honor and respect them. They knew right from wrong, and they instilled obedience in us for our own sake. Sometimes we did not know their motive but we had to obey if we were to be safe.

God, too, wants nothing but the best for His children. The Israelites went through many animals for their daily ritual sacrifices. In the meantime, they behaved rather despicably during their long journey through the desert. They behaved like bratty children who want their own way, and, when they don't get their way, they throw tantrums. They griped about everything – their food, water and shelter. On those occasions when they lost faith in God, they would create idols, not so much for the sake of worship, but more to annoy their true God. God, however, behaved like a doting parent and forgave them more times than they deserved.

God cares more that we obey than we offer Him sacrifices. We must learn to trust God and obey His counsel. Everything God does for us is for our own good and protection. Like a parent who cares for their children, God wants us to know He can be trusted at all times. Sometimes a child will want to know why he or she must obey a parent's order, and usually a parent's response is "because I said so". Trust and obedience of the child toward their parent is vital for that child's well-being. Our obedience to God is vital for our well-being.

**We must never lose sight of the fact that all our sacrifices are moot if we do not obey His commands. God has shown us the way. Trust and Obey Him.**

## COMBATING DEPRESSION | OCTOBER 31

*"Whenever the Spirit from God came upon Saul, David would take his harp and play. Then relief would come to Saul. He would feel better, and the evil spirit would leave him." 1 Samuel 16: 23*

---

Depression is a mood disorder with emotional displays of sadness, feeling low and a bleak outlook in one's life. We have all faced moments of depression, but for most, these moments are passing. For some, however, the condition is chronic. Have you ever been depressed? Did you feel tormented? Maybe even hear accusing voices robbing your peace?

I have a friend who confessed to me recently that his mind sometimes goes "a hundred miles a minute." He jumps rapidly from one thought to another. He is bombarded with thoughts that range from bizarre or unmentionable to coherent and creative. I asked him if he had peace of mind amidst these thoughts and he replied, "Yes." He has a mood disorder but the opposite of depression, his condition is called "mania." All these dominating emotions fall under mood disorders. Anger is also a form of depression.

The Bible is full of people who have had depressive states in their lives, such as; Moses, Nebuchadnezzar and Saul. Abraham Lincoln confessed that he suffered from episodes of depression. In 1842 he wrote to a friend "I am now the most miserable man living. If what I feel were equally distributed to the whole human family, there would be not one cheerful face on earth."

In today's verse, Saul hears voices in his head, and he is tormented. I Samuel 16: 14 "Now the Spirit of the Lord departed from Saul and an evil spirit from the Lord tormented him." Psychologists today would likely diagnose Saul as paranoid. But the Bible said an evil spirit tormented him. One person I know was so depress he committed to suicide. There appears to be evilness in our world that haunts every soul to give up.

How do you combat depression or other emotional disorders? Have you gone through therapy? Do you practice meditation, yoga or easy listening music? What about exercising? Maybe medication is your solution. All these have their merit. Saul however, found relief when he heard David play his harp.

How about considering the Lord? Today's text informs us that, when the Spirit from God came upon Saul, he found relief and felt better. Anxiety, turmoil and fear are not from God. We live in a world where the evil one wants to stir up turmoil in our lives. **Go down on your knees and pray to God to send you His Spirit. Don't get up until God's Spirit has soothe your tormented soul.**

## **RIGHTEOUS ENVY** | NOVEMBER 1

*"As they danced, they sang; Saul has slain his thousands, and David his tens of thousands." I Samuel 18: 7*

---

Throughout Saul' life, he was tormented. What a way to live your life being tormented daily. That would have driven me insane. Saul became even more vexed by believing that David was his rival and enemy. He plotted ways to kill him. He even attempted it himself. Saul's efforts proved fruitless. Saul knew that David was with God, and God protected David. Saul, in his arrogance, would not permit the Spirit of God to rule his life, and it all stemmed from his jealousy of David. He got jealous when the people mocked him with the victory song of David.

Saul and David were loved by God. Saul, however, let the spirit of jealousy -- in his case, his jealousy of David – into his life. Jealousy is a strong emotion which has ruined many lives. Jealousy may begin as a passing thought and turn into obsession.

Evil arose as Lucifer entertained the thought of what it would be like to be God. He was jealous of Christ, even before God created us. Jealousy stalked Cain and Abel, Jacob and Esau, Leah and Rachel, Joseph and his brothers, David and Saul and it reigns undiminished to this day.

Don't be like the father of lies, who cherished jealousy to the point that it ruined him eternally. Satan's spirit is not godly. Don't let his spirit in your life. In verse 9, "And from that time on Saul kept a jealous eye on David." Saul was prophesying in his house while David played the harp. Saul allowed an evil thought to enter his mind and hurled a spear toward David in hopes of pinning him to the wall. But David eluded Saul's assignation attempts twice. God protected David. In verse 14, "In everything he did he had great success because the Lord was with him." Do not allow the sun to set tonight without you giving your jealousy to God. God can heal you.

**The Author of Love is also a jealous God. But His jealousy is a righteous one.** God's love is more than to protect you. He wants a deeper walk with you. God wants to bestow His love that passes all understanding. He wants to be one with you. He wants a very intimate relationship with you. A relationship that is secure and faithful. God wants you to have the best things He can offer. He proved that by sending His only Son to rid us of evil emotions. **Righteous envy is of God.**

# GOD IS LIFE | NOVEMBER 2

*"Like water spilled on the ground which cannot be recovered, so we must die. But God does not take away life; instead, he devises ways that a banished person may not remain estranged from him." II Samuel 14: 14*

In rich countries, the average lifespan is around 70-80, though many die prematurely. I am sure some of you have had a loved one die before reaching their senior status. Some people blame God for premature deaths. Others console one another by saying, "He (or she) went to be with the Lord." Or some say, "It's God's will." Others, however, erroneously believe that comfort will come from abandoning God altogether.

Let's set the record straight. God does not take away life. God IS life and His life IS eternal. Today's text affirms that. God is the very antithesis of death; He is the Author and Giver of Life. Okay, then, why, many have wondered, is there death? Death is the result of sin. Our first parents chose to disobey God's counsel. "The wages of sin is death."

As today's text says, God devises ways to help us avoid death. God does take away life. He is life. He devised a plan that would save us from death. The wages of sin may be death but the gift of God through Jesus Christ is eternal life. God took Adam's place and in doing so saved us from eternal death.

The reality of this world is that there are death, pain, suffering and sorrow. Ah, but there is once again good news: God devises a "million ways " to lure us back to Him. He has planned ways for us to enjoy eternal life. You must first choose to believe His word and follow His lead. God has promised to make all things right again, including the eradication of death completely. In God's heaven, there will be no more dying. We can live pain-free and never grow old.

Trust in God's promise that He will return and wake up those who have died in His name. Those loved ones of ours that died (even prematurely) will rise again. Their bodies will be incorruptible and perfect as you've never seen before. We will have a great reunion with all our loved ones who have passed away. He has promised to take us home to live with Him forevermore. What an amazing God! He reveals His love for us in a million ways.

**Remember, God does not take away life; instead He creates ways for us to live. He devised a way to save us from eternal separation. The connection was His Son. God does not want to be separated from us. God knows all about separation. His Son became separated from Him on the cross. God is truly the God of life.**

## **ONE WISH GRANTED** | NOVEMBER 3

*"At Gibeon the Lord appeared to Solomon during the night in a dream, and God said, 'ask for whatever you want me to give you.' Solomon replied, 'Give your servant a discerning heart to govern your people and to distinguish right and wrong. For who is able to govern this great people of yours?'" I Kings 3: 5 & 9*

---

There is a fable that tells of a sailor named Sinbad who gets stranded in a deserted island due to a ship wreck but finds and picks up a bottle washed ashore. He opens the bottle and out comes a genie. The genie tells Sinbad that since he has released him from the confines of the bottle he would grant him three wishes.

If you discovered God and He granted you three wishes, what would you ask for? Think carefully, you don't want to waste your wishes on frivolous matters. Let's say like Solomon, God grants you just one wish, and what would you ask God? This time you must be real careful because one wish is all you have. Before you answer this question, picture yourself in the middle of a desert without food or water and you are in your last leg. What if you were driving home in a blizzard and your car skidded off the road and you were stuck in your car for days without any help in sight? Picture yourself in the ICU ward struggling to survive after being diagnosed with cancer. What if? The scenarios are endless. We want that special wish granted. Sometimes we look at God as our Genie or Santa Claus to grant us our wish.

There is a worthy organization in America known as the "Make a Wish Foundation" which grants terminally ill children one wish. Most kids request a trip to Disneyland or contact with their favorite celebrity. Whatever your wish maybe, when we are placed in a life and death situation our priority is not to go to Disneyland or dine at the finest restaurant or receive the most exquisite diamond or to find the love of our life, You choose to live. When you're dying of thirst you'll wish for water; when you're starving to death you'll wish for food; when you're diagnosed with an incurable illness you'll wish for healing; when you're tired and needing sleep you'll wish for rest. When you are in excruciating pain, you will wish for relief. Whatever discomfort you may be experiencing, you will make it a priority to resolve.

Whatever you wish for God knows your needs even before you ask Him. You too will have a discerning heart and wisdom to know right from wrong when you have allowed God to be the center of your life.

**If you could be granted one wish in your life, what would it be? Well, take heart, your wish has been granted. All the things you wish for have already been granted through His Son, Jesus.**

## SIGNS AND WONDERS | NOVEMBER 4

*"The Pharisees came and began to question Jesus. To test him, they asked him for a sign from heaven. He sighed deeply and said, 'Why does this generation ask for a miraculous sign? I tell you the truth; no sign will be given to it.'" Mark 8: 11 & 12*

Have you ever prayed to God and asked for a sign? How do you know what you're praying for is God's will? Everyone wants a sign to solidify their faith. Even Satan wanted a sign. Satan tempted Jesus to produce a sign. He said: "If you are the Son of God, throw yourself down," Jesus replied: "You shall not put the Lord your God to the test." Matthew 4: 6 & 7. Satan continued to tempt Jesus and Jesus answered each temptation with the word of God.

The trouble with asking for signs is there may also be false signs. In lieu of signs, establish a relationship with God. You can trust Him to keep His promise just by His word. Jesus said, "I am the way the truth and the life." John 14: 6. All your needs for signs and wonders are rolled up into one person, Jesus. "Trust in the Lord with all your heart and do not lean on your own understanding. In all your ways acknowledge Him, and He will make your paths straight. Do not be wise in your own eyes; fear the Lord and turn away from evil." Proverbs 3: 5-7.

Neil T. Anderson in his book, "Finding God's will in Spiritually Deceptive Times" gives 10 keys to wise decision-making. 1. Have you prayed about it? 2. Is it consistent with God's word? 3. Can I do it and be a positive Christian witness? 4. Will the Lord be glorified? 5. Am I acting responsibly? 6. Is it reasonable? 7. Does a realistic opportunity exist? 8. Are unbiased, spiritually sensitive associates in agreement? 9. Do I have a sanctified desire? 10. Do I have a peace about it? He says if you can answer yes to ALL 10 questions, then go for it. This is a great tool to consider. Man wants concrete and tangible evidence to follow in order to feel comfortable that they are on the "right track". There is something innate in human nature to feel secure when they follow something tangible. Sometimes you can follow all of the above and still feel uncertain. What do you do? May I add number 11.

The better way is to place your trust in God through a relational faith. Be still. God will speak to you and you will know what to do. **You will be able to walk with peace and calm assurance because you know God. Wait on the Lord because greater than the sign and wonders is the One who gives the sign and wonders.**

## GAMES PEOPLE PLAY | NOVEMBER 5

*"'Do I bring to the moment of birth and not give delivery?' Says the Lord." Isaiah 66: 9*

---

Does games people play exasperate you? In 1964, Eric Berne's book "Games People Play: The Psychology of Human Relations" introduced "Transactional Analysis" as a method of interpreting our social interactions. He categorized three ego states that we possess: the child, the parent and the Adult. He postulates that many undesirable behaviors stems from the interaction and switching of these roles. An example, your boss talking to his staff about implementing new company policy and procedures takes on a parent role while the staff listens and produces behaviors of self-abased obedience, tantrums, or other childlike responses. Underneath all these superficial behaviors are predictable series of "transactions" that conceal motivations that are counterproductive.

People play games and the games are predicated on the role that a person plays. Berne may have discovered what God has known all along, people are not what they actually show themselves to be. We have both public and private persona and these dictate behavior. Some people have been married to each other for many years and never know their spouse because of fear of being discovered. I had a friend who was married for over 25 years and when the divorce was final he said I didn't know she was that kind of a woman.

Do you blame God for your lot in your life? Do you think God is playing games? True, we live in a fractured world. We want what we cannot have and don't want what we have. Our God is NOT a game player. Games were invented by man. Games people play generally result in a winner and a loser. It's hurtful. The only way you can truly believe that God is not a gamer is to know Him. He says He will not have a woman pregnant and then not (the baby) deliver. He will not have us go through life in this world and not deliver us. He will not have death be the final word. He will not have the blind and deaf not see and hear. He will not have the sinner be lost. God has given us enough proof of His love and good intention that we have nothing ever to worry about again. He says you can count on Him to keep His promises.

**God is not playing around. He is dead serious. Everything He said will come to fruition. You can count on Him to deliver on His word. He will complete what He has begun in you. Stop playing games. The Author of Love will deliver, believe Him and be ready.**

## DIVORCING THE LOVE OF YOUR LIFE | NOVEMBER 6

*"Anyone who divorces his wife and marries another woman commits adultery against her. And if she divorces her husband and marries another, she commits adultery." Mark 10: 11 & 12*

---

Divorce is fast becoming the rule in our society. The fact that it is almost fashionable renders it none the easier. The issue was debated even in Moses' time. It had become an informal process, and he decided to provide guidelines: "When a man has taken a wife and married her and it comes to pass that she finds no favor in his eye because he hath found some uncleanness in her, then let him write her a bill of divorcement and give it in her hand and send her out of his house. And when she is departed out of his house, she may go and be another man's wife." Deuteronomy 24: 1 & 2. (Note that it is assumed to be his house. Times have changed).

One of the most painful issues to confront us in our society or church is the subject of divorce. Since it's more prevalent today, new standards and by-laws are being adopted by the church to address this matter. Where at one time a pastor who divorces is usually grounds for dismissal, there are exceptions to the rule if certain criteria are met.

Divorce is devastating. It is a heart-wrenching experience that you wish on no one. God never intended for anyone to go through a divorce. Divorce is man-made. During Moses' time, "uncleanness" was interpreted in many ways. If a wife burned a meal, that was grounds for sending her away. The meaning of uncleanness continued even in Jesus' time. But Jesus made it clear the only ground for divorce was adultery. He clarified it even further by stating either party, man or woman as noted in today's text can file for divorce. The text in Deuteronomy appears to indicate that a man can put away a woman but a woman cannot put away a man. Few countries today grant true equality to men and woman. Man once again created divorce and its ground rules. Jesus cared not about gender superiority. Because of our stubbornness God relented and permitted us to practice divorce. You can blame God for all the divorces that ever happened in this world. You could tell him it wasn't your fault, but if you were smart, you'd know where the truth about divorce lies, with each of us.

God never intended divorce to enter this world, but He will never override our free will. Love is a choice. God is patient with humankind's choices. You may divorce your earthly spouse for unfaithfulness or irreconcilable differences or loss of affection but don't ever divorce the love of your life, Jesus.

**No matter what, Jesus would never divorce or leave you. He is committed to you forever.**

## ONE HUNDRED TIMES | NOVEMBER 7

*"Jesus said, 'Mark my words, no one who sacrifices house, brothers, sisters, mother, father, children, land-whatever-because of me and the Message will lose out. They'll get it all back, 100 times in homes, brothers, sisters, mothers, children, and land-but also in troubles. And then the bonus of eternal life! This is once again the Great Reversal: Man who is first will end up last and the last first.' "Mark 10: 29 (Message & NIV)*

---

What an amazing and unbelievable promise Jesus said. In today's verse for meditation, Jesus makes a promise: Those who love God and share that love to others above all else will be rewarded a "100 times." This includes sharing in the persecutions that a faithful follower of God may encounter here on earth. And finally God promises eternal life. What a promise! Does a hundred-fold return motivate you to share the "Good news" of God's love for us? Be careful you don't get caught up on the rewards rather than the "Rewarder."

The prior text explains what Jesus meant. There was a very rich young man who ran up to Jesus and asked Him what he had to do to be saved. Jesus counseled him to keep the commandments. Jesus even specifically pointed out which commandment, "Don't kill, don't commit adultery, don't steal, don't lie, don't cheat, respect your father and mother." The young man stated he never once broke any of those laws. Jesus looked him straight in the eye and loved him. Jesus then told him: 'There's just one thing left to do, go and sell whatever you own and give it to the poor." The man was discouraged. That was the last thing he wanted to hear. He walked away with a "heavy heart." This young man was holding on tight to a number of things, and he was not about to let it go to follow Jesus.

What are you holding on to? Can you let go? Are you able to trust Him now for the greater reward later on? Unless you know and believe Him, when He asks you to sell all that you have and follow Him, will you be able to? Don't let your earthly possessions ruin your salvation. If you're holding on to a lover, a house, a career or gold, that's O.K. But be ready to let it go when Jesus tells you to sell all that you have and follow Him. He has for you "100" times more than what you're hoarding or can ever imagine. Oh, if you only knew the truth about Jesus's love for you, you wouldn't ponder or hang on to your possessions, like the rich young man did. You'd let go of everything you have and follow Jesus' command.

**God's promise of what you'll get back is only a figure of speech. It will be even greater than 100 times.**

## ABOVE ALL ELSE GUARD YOUR HEART | NOVEMBER 8

*"Above all else, guard your heart, for it is the wellspring of life." Proverbs 4: 23*

---

There was an elderly patient awaiting a heart transplant. His physician came to him and said: "I have good news. Not only is there one heart that matches your needs, but there are three. The first belongs to a mid-40's businessman, who never smoked or drank. He died in a plane crash. The second belongs to a healthy, young athlete, who lost his life in a car crash. The third is an attorney, who died of gunshot wounds after practicing law for 40 years." After successful transplant surgery, the doctor asked the patient why he'd chosen the attorney. "It was a no-brainer," he replied. "I wanted a heart that hadn't been used."

God knew the best area of your entire body to place the heart, right in the center. The heart is what makes the person. Next to God, the heart is the second most popular subject matter in the Bible. What does God mean when He says guard your heart? Proverbs emphasizes this point by admonishing us to place the guardianship of the heart above anything else in your life. Your heart is what makes you. It is your entire being. Out of the heart springs everything of who you are. This is where the real you resides.

During Christ's ministry, people would come to Him to be healed. Everyone that came to Him was never turned away. Some were stricken with leprosy and He healed them, some were demon possessed and He made them whole again. He also healed the blind man, the paralytic, the prostitute, the hypocrite, the legalist, the temperamental or passive-aggressive. Whoever came to Him, He healed. Though God healed everyone's immediate malady, He wanted to give them more than healing. God wanted to heal more than their immediate need. God wanted to heal their broken heart as well.

God wants you to know that He values your heart. He will treat it with tender loving care (TLC). God identifies with you. He knows, firsthand what it is like to have one's heart broken, because His heart indeed ached when we gave our hearts to someone else. Despite our careless handling of our hearts, the Author of Love remains steadfast in His care and concern for our hearts. You mean so much to Him that He gave His life for you to save your broken heart.

**Whatever you do, think or say, above all else, guard your heart for that is the center of your whole life. God cherishes you "above all else."**

## WHO IS MY NEIGHBOR | NOVEMBER 9

*"But he wanted to justify himself, so he asked Jesus, 'And who is my neighbor?'"* Luke 10: 29

My family and I live in a rural area outside Riverside, California on about three acres of land. The whole environment almost suggests we are living in a quasi-farm. The land behind our property was seldom used and it abutted against a neighbor whose house we never see because it was down the hill. One day mother was cooking in the kitchen and happened to glance out the kitchen window when she noticed a herd of goats grazing on our back property. She came to me and said "There are goats grazing in our backyard." I looked, and, sure enough, there were several young goats chomping away on our grass, and their parents were tied to a tree. Our rear fence had been torn to allow these goats to wander and graze on our property. Needless to say, I wondered how anyone could have the gall to let their goats loose on our property without asking, much less tear our fence to let them in. How un-neighborly.

I decided to confront our neighbor. As I walked to the back of our property I started to think about our verse for today. I said a prayer to God to allow his Spirit to handle this unpleasant situation and pray our neighbor would be civil about the whole matter. "Betty" and her family have lived behind us for the past four years. However, I'd not met them until that day. Betty informed me that my neighbor to our left, the one who refuses to speak to us, had told her the land was his and gave her permission to have her goats graze there. Now I don't know who to believe, but I asked her to remove her goats because we would be mending the fence and they could be corralled without an exit. She agreed to remove her goats.

Unfortunately this is not heaven. Someday these same people may be our neighbor in heaven, and our love here on earth will be the attitude we bring there. It's too bad we have to have fences, boundaries and markings to identify and safe keep our property. Love for our neighbor begins here on earth, right this moment. Jesus is our neighbor and how we treat our earthly neighbor is how we treat Jesus. This concept can only be perceived if you are attuned to your Marker. You have a lifetime to get to know God. Don't wait in your last year of your life to discover how really good God is. You will miss out on the joy of His salvation. Learn of Him starting right now. When you do you'll start welcoming goats in your yard today.

**Who is my neighbor? The one for whom Christ died.**

## THE LOOK OF LOVE | NOVEMBER 10

*"The Lord is compassionate and gracious, slow to anger, abounding in love. He will not always accuse, nor will He harbor His anger forever; He does not treat us as our sins deserve or repay us according to our iniquities. For as high as the heavens are above the earth, so great is His love for those who fear him." Psalms 103: 8-11*

---

Do you know the look of love? If love came your way would you recognize it? Love comes in so many forms, sizes and shapes that one would be fooled if he or she did not have an inkling of what love is.

In today's love column of a local newspaper a reader writes: "I have never been moved to write in to a letter until I read "Concerned about my girl in Kentucky." It was from a mom who was worried that while her daughter had no problem attracting men, she has a problem keeping them. My intelligent, caring, creative adventurous and beautiful daughter had successful, handsome and wonderful men throwing themselves at her. A couple of dates and they were never heard from again. When I asked, "What's the problem?" she would shrug her shoulders. One day, my daughter came to me and said she had met someone. I said, "Tell me about him." She replied, "Who said it has to be a 'him'?"

Love can be an enigma, especially if you are not secured in your own self-understanding of what love is. I know for one thing, love is no respecter of persons. Love can be blind or it can be crystal clear to the person longing for it. I am reminded of a dear friend who wanted to get married and was having difficulty finding the "right" person. He placed an ad in the dating section of a local newspaper. His main criteria was "no obese women, must be Caucasian and very feminine." This guy thought he knew what he wanted and was sure of the "love-image" he wanted to spend the rest of his life with. A few months later I saw him dating exactly what he did not want. She was obese, ethnic in color and quite masculine in appearance. I asked him "what gives?" He later confessed to me that when he got to know the "real" her he fell madly in love with her. They eventually married.

Sadly, we all have certain criteria or types we desire to make our love complete. Some couples look puzzling together but then again, love can be selective. Sometimes, people settle for what they can get while some prefer the company of themselves. God's love knows no color, size shape or gender. It is not selective or favored.

**What is the look of love? God knows; it's the widowed, imprisoned, derelicts, homeless, undesirables, minority, the rejected, the sinner. Everyone He has ever created.**

## **REMAIN IN MY LOVE** | NOVEMBER 11

*"As the Father has loved me, so have I loved you. Now remain in my love." John 15: 9*

---

When I was a child my parents reprimanded me for doing something mischievous. The punishment meted was meant to teach me a lesson and instill future good behavior. I can still hear my parent's remorseful saying: "Wait until you have your own children."

We can trace this dysfunctional upbringing to our first parents. After Adam and Eve sinned, rather than God reprimanding them, He went looking for them. If you ever had a squabble with your lover or mate, have you ever noticed how each one refuses to talk to each other afterwards? You get the silent treatment. No one wants to admit fault. One partner soon is lying alone, whether on the couch or room, hoping the other would sneak in and cuddle and say "I'm sorry." Sometimes, just a touch or assurance would suffice. Usually the one who loves most will be the first to approach the other person. Which one are you? the pursuer or the silent one?

God is the lover who doesn't give the silent treatment. It seems at times God is silent and doesn't answer our prayer. Read Genesis 3: 8 & 9, "the man and his wife heard the sound of the Lord God as He was walking in the garden in the cool of the day, and they hid from the Lord God among the trees of the garden. But the Lord God called to the man, 'Where are you?'" If you happen to stray, He will pursue you and woo you back to Him. He is compassionate, patient and benevolent. He is ever pursuing, ever the first one to extend His love. Even though He is not at fault, He will never rub it in. You say, "I'm not God, I can't be like Him."

Only God knows the true art of loving. However, you can know it too. You can experience the same love relationship He and His Father have, just by taking Him at His word. He is inviting you to dwell with them in their love for you. The way to love like God is to be receptive to His invitation of love. You don't have to act or be like God. All you need to do is accept His love and REMAIN in His love. Remain means to trust God and stay connected to His Spirit.

Won't you complete the love circle by remaining in their love? **God wants to include you and me with Him in His circle of love.** His circle of love is His Father, the Holy Spirit as well as a host of angels and other beings He has created. What a big universal family we will have. **Their love will not be complete unless you are in their family circle.**

## ACCEPTABLE | NOVEMBER 12

*"I beseech you therefore, brethren, by the mercies of God, that ye present your bodies a living sacrifice, holy, acceptable unto God, which is your reasonable service. And be not conformed to his world: but be ye transformed by the renewing of your mind, that ye may prove what is that good, and acceptable, and perfect, will of God." Romans 12: 1 & 2 (KJV)*

---

I wanted to be accepted when I was a child. I learned that, if I did well in school, behave and did right, I would be rewarded and accepted. That's how society treats those with acceptable behavior. As adults, the need for acceptance is undiminished. We want to be recognized for our good deeds and accepted for our physical attractiveness. We will go to great lengths to sculpt the ideal body. Millions of dollars are invested for hair plugs to cover that balding spot. Permanent ink is used to create a perfect eyebrow and eyeliner. Gastric by-pass surgery is performed to help us loose the weight our will power could not accomplish. One of the greatest needs in our fragile human psyche is the need to be accepted. More than half for our problems would be solved if we learned to accept each other. Acceptance begins with you. Unfortunately we don't accept or like what we see in the mirror. We see imperfections more than we see goodness. Isn't that sad? Why can't you accept yourself?

Acceptance must begin, not with pleasing others, but with self-acceptance. It is a fact, proven by hundreds of studies that, if you have low self-esteem, all of the tummy tucks and face lifts and the like will be for naught. We are all familiar with the phrase: "Beauty is in the eyes of the beholder." Beauty (outer or inner) must first be beheld by the one who wishes others to behold. Famous beautiful celebrities have confessed that they did not think they were beautiful while the rest of the world envied them for their good looks. How we perceive ourselves is detriment on how we accept ourselves.

There is a fine line, of course, between positive self-image and conceit. One can love him or herself without being overbearing. There's nothing wrong with wanting to be accepted. However, bear in mind that there is One who accepts you, no matter the circumstances – no cosmetic surgery or weight loss programs required.

God loves us just the way we are. God loves the whole you, faults and all, with God size, color, shape or gender does not matter. **God knows a thing or two about you and He sees beyond the external features. In fact, He said our "outer garments" will fade but who we are internally is what we'll bring to the new Earth.** His desire for now is for you to accept yourself as He accepts you.

## FREE FROM PAIN | NOVEMBER 13

*"Jabez was more honorable than his brothers. His mother named him Jabez, saying "I gave birth to him in pain. Jabez cried out to the God of Israel, 'Oh, that you would bless me and enlarge my territory! Let your hand be with me, and keep me from harm so that I will be free from pain,' and God granted his request.' "I Chronicles 4: 9-10.*

---

What is the worst pain you have ever experienced? Jabez's mother experienced such pain bearing him that she named him after the experience. Jabez too, cried out for freedom from pain. Yet, whatever pain Jabez experienced was probably of no comparison to the pain his mother experienced giving birth to him. She speaks of that pain in today's text. "I gave birth to him in pain."

I can remember my mother's words when she expressed her experience of giving birth to each of her six children. It left an indelible impression that forever bound her with each of her children. Mother can vividly explain the pain she went through when she gave birth to each of her children. Some were less painful than others. Do you remember the birth of your child? Was it similar to Jabez's mother?

Jabez's mother knew her pain in giving birth to her son. Jabez did not know the pain of childbirth, but he knew the God who gave him life. The pain Jabez is talking about is most likely not the pain of childbirth but the pain of a hostile environment, perhaps at home. There may have been sibling rivalry because the first sentence in verse nine states, "Jabez was more honorable than his brothers." Jabez's mother must have had a great influence on his spirituality and knowledge of God.

The interpretation of this verse has gone the gamut, from asking God to enhance one's financial well-being to keeping one safe from harm and danger. The key verse today is about a loving God who granted Jabez's request. This same God grants your requests, too. Even though our prayers may be self-serving, the Author of Love wants to say: "yes," as only a loving parent wishes for his or her child. Whatever pains a mother endures giving birth to their child, the love she showers on that child is many times more.

God loves us even more. Even with the pain we cost Him, He gave His life for us to free us from the pain we deserved. He has blessed us and enlarged our territory more than you can ever imagine. Can you measure the width and depth of His entire universe? God's territory is so vast that you can say it's infinite. It's an immeasurable territory as His love for us.

**When you know God, you will understand Jabez's answered prayer.**

## BRIDGE OVER TROUBLED WATERS | NOVEMBER 14

*"Therefore, if you are offering your gift at the altar and there remember that your brother has something against you; leave your gift there in front of the altar. First go and be reconciled to your brother, then come and offer your gift." Matthew 5: 23 & 24*

---

There is a story I heard of two brothers who worked in adjoining farms in harmony for many years. One day, a small misunderstanding blew up, and it became a major rift. They exchanged hurtful words, and insulted each other's families. It almost came to blows.

One day the younger brother decided to create a physical barrier between the two farms where heretofore there had been a psychological barrier. He diverted a stream into a meadow between the two farms, creating a permanent barrier between them.

Sometime later, a carpenter came to the older brother and asked for work. The older brother said: "I'd like to do my brother one better and erect a fence between our properties." "I think I understand the situation," said the carpenter as he began work. When the older brother returned that evening, he found a bridge over the stream. As he stared in wonder, he saw his estranged brother coming across, holding out his hand. "Thank you," he said, "for having this bridge built to bring us together." As they shook hands, the older brother saw the carpenter leaving. "Please stay," he said. "I'd love to," replied the carpenter, "but I have many other bridges to build."

Are you estranged with someone you once loved? Don't you think is time to cross that bridge and extend your hand of reconciliation? There was a time here on earth when we had a beautiful relationship with our Maker. The friendship and bond was strong. But one day we decided to do things on our own and in doing, tore a rift between us and our Maker.

God sent a lowly carpenter to make a bridge for us. His bridge became a cross. And our Savior hung on that cross to reconcile us with the Father. No matter what troubled waters you are crossing in your life, rest assured that you are safe in God's care. To experience that care, you must first follow His command and seek your brother or sister and reconcile with him or her. You cannot reach out to your brother or sister unless you allow the Spirit to dwell in your heart and move you to reach out.

**No greater love can God show us than to give up His Son as a bridge to win us back to Him.** Now, do likewise.

## **GOD'S TORMENTOR** | NOVEMBER 15

*"And the devil, who deceived them, was thrown into the lake of burning sulfur, where the beast and the false prophet had been thrown. They will be tormented day and night forever and ever." Revelation 20: 10*

---

One of my favorite spots to travel through is the scenic route along Pacific Coast highway in Big Sur and Carmel areas of Northern California. The views during the summer days are particularly stunning. The high cliffs and the ocean below are breathtaking.

In several places along the winding road, there are signs that warn of blind spots and sharp curves. If you drive too fast, you can easily miss a turn, sending you plummeting hundreds of feet below. There are numerous danger signs along life's highway with which God has provided us – signs that we sometimes ignore because we want a moment's pleasure, risking lifetime of woe. If you get away with your carelessness once, it becomes easier to ignore the next sign.

A friend has an affair because he is bored with his life. A neighbor is changing her career because she is unhappy with her present job. A church member is transferring membership because they did not elect him for the office he wanted. Several teenagers in school are caught experimenting with drugs. They were expelled from school. Not all of the danger signs in life are obvious; yet the law of averages is always at work. Lucifer will likely see to that. Are you experiencing a tormenting issue in your life today? Is it nagging at you daily that it affects your ability to function normally? Yes, the devil is relishing tormenting you. That's his M.O. (Modus Operandi).

John the Revelator says the deceiver will be thrown in the lake of fire with his false prophets and will burn forever! Is that edict coming from a loving God? What gives? Our faith in God's justice will be fair and just. Given the character of God, I believe God will operate only in love. The Author of Love sends us warning signs to prepare us for the onslaught of the devil's deceptions. He has been warning us from day one. A life apart from God is a life with God's tormentor. It is a life of torment and chaos. Left to themselves, God's tormentor and His accomplices would self-destruct. God is even merciful to them.

**Stay connected with God and you will be able to face your tormenters with an assurance that God will save you.**

## JUST THE BEGINNING | NOVEMBER 16

*"When he had received the drink, Jesus said 'It is finished.' With that he bowed his head and gave up his spirit." John 19: 30*

What were the defining moments in your life? Was it when you finally received word from your doctor that he detected no cancer cells in your body? Was it the day your divorce was finalized? Perhaps it was the day you moved out of your parents' house to be on your own? Freedom! Whichever you define as your defining moment it was the beginning of a new chapter in your life. The cross, however, signaled the beginning of a new chapter for the entire universe, when Jesus said "It is finished." Surely this was the greatest act of love we have ever seen.

By giving up His Son as a ransom for our sin, God died in our stead. He took on the punishment of eternal death so we may live eternally. This culminating act purchased once and for all our redemption, our hope of salvation. When Jesus declared: "It is finished," God fulfilled His promise in the garden where our first parents sinned. "I will put enmity between you and the woman between your offspring and hers' he will crush your head and you will strike his heel." Justice required the price for our mistake to be paid. God took it upon Himself to be your surrogate.

Are you still wondering about the efficacy of this act? Are you uncertain and in doubt because of the issues you are still facing in your life? You ask, "Lord, when will my dilemma end?" I understand your doubts and struggles. We are all engaged in something of a "rat race," and sometimes there doesn't appear to be an end in sight. You likely feel discouraged and hopeless, perhaps tempted to call it quits? What would it take to convince you to hold on?

God's redemption for us was accomplished on the cross but the complete and final product has yet to be realized. God has not finished His whole plan for us. There is one more task He promised to accomplish before we live with Him eternally. God promised He will return to take us home to be with Him. God has even planned a vacation that will be a phenomenon you've never dream of it. We will go on a space cruise that will last not 7 days or two weeks or even a month. He has planned a thousand years for us to enjoy that excursion. Wait until you see what He has in store of us. You will want to praise Him for eternity.

**Do not lose hope of His crowning glory. Remember this promise is for you and me. When it does occur, this is just the beginning.**

## NEVERTHELESS | NOVEMBER 17

*"They were from nations about which the Lord had told the Israelites, 'You must not intermarry with them, because they will surely turn your hearts after their gods.' Nevertheless, Solomon held fast to them in love." I Kings 11: 2*

---

Solomon was the wisest man that ever lived. He asked God for wisdom when God appeared to him in a dream and said "Ask what I shall give you." In answer to God's offer, the young and inexperienced ruler said, "I am but a little child: I know not how to go out or come in; give therefore your servant an understanding heart to judge your people, that I may discern between good and bad: for who is able to judge this so great a people?" God was touched by Solomon's response. "Lo, I have given you a wise and an understanding heart; so that there was none like you before you neither after you shall any arise like unto you. And I have also given you that which you have not asked, both riches, and honor, such as one of the kings has had that have been before you neither shall there any after you have the like."

Solomon was the son of David and Bathsheba. God made a promise to be with Solomon as He was with his father David during his reign. However, God also admonished Solomon to be sure to walk in God's way and keep his statues and commandments. God added He would lengthen his days on earth, if he obeyed. Solomon did his best to follow God's statues and commandments. However, he had a weakness for falling "in-love" too readily with women. When Solomon saw a woman to his liking he married her. He used his position to indulge his carnal appetite and it eventually influenced his heart. He turned away from the true God and began devoting his heart to the gods of Ashtoreth and Molech. These were "other gods' which his wives worshipped. He even built temples for these gods.

Are you having a "Solomon moment" in your life too? Are there things you want to have or accomplish before you turn to God? Those things you want are not adverse to God's plans. However, like Solomon, don't make them a priority that you forget God. God is the source of all your wants and needs.

Even with God's admonition, Solomon decided nevertheless to indulge in his passion. God allowed him to reign in his kingdom during his lifetime. God is loving and compassionate with us. He is also forgiving, patient and longsuffering with us. God always relents. He definitely is a doting Father. But even God cannot control your choices and wavering desires. The choices you make without God's leading will result in mayhem and destruction.

**One thing you can be certain of, nevertheless, God will never stop loving you or let you go.**

## IS ANYTHING TOO HARD FOR GOD? | NOVEMBER 18

*"I am the Lord, the God of all mankind. Is there anything too hard for me?" Jeremiah 3: 27*

---

This is a text worth meditating upon today. Is there anything too hard for God? I believe that, with God, nothing is impossible. I believe He can bestow on me all I desire. So, what does God mean when He challenges us with the question "Is there anything too hard for me?" Read the entire Bible and you will find throughout earth's history God performed miraculous deeds. His deeds transcend natural law or human nature. God is the Creator of nature. He embodies the law, and His works testify to His character. He is, as presumably is evident by now, the Author of Love. His love is so extreme that it goes beyond human comprehension.

Perry Como, a singer foreign to most under age 40, recorded the song "It's Impossible," a hit four decades ago. The song asks these questions; if you were to ask the sun to leave the sky, ask a baby not to cry or keep the sea from rushing to the shore, they're all impossible. The song may be correct, but, with God, nothing is impossible. He stilled the sun for one whole day. He calmed the sea with His words "Peace be still." He even raised the dead. There is absolutely nothing too difficult for God to accomplish.

Don't, however, try to test God. God knows your prayers even before you ask Him. There is nothing more God can do or give you that He hasn't already done through His Son. God will finish the work He has begun in each of us soon. We must trust His promise and stand firm in His word.

When you have a need to ask God for something you desire, ask Him and be prepared to receive His answer. There is nothing He will hold back to you and me. You can ask Him why your prayers weren't answered, why you didn't get that specific job, why you didn't have healing, why the accidents, earthquakes, catastrophes, wars, murders, unsolved mysteries and deaths. God has answers to all your questions. He will reveal all of them without reservations. I'll wager when you see the whole picture, you will be too embarrassed to ask God for any more proof. He is more than willing to give all the riches of His universe. But He will direct you to His Son, who is the author and finisher of all your wants, needs and desires.

God knows the best answer to all your desires, His Son. **Is there anything too hard for God? Yes, He cannot make you love Him. But you cannot stop Him from loving you.**

## I AM NOT A THIEF | NOVEMBER 19

*"The thief comes only to steal and kill and destroy; I have come that they may have life, and have it to the full." John 10: 10*

---

I sometimes reflect on the good old days when I was a child with no worries in the world. I was raised to watch television programs that were acceptable and influential to the glory of God. Every Saturday evening, after sundown worship and dinner we would gather around our black and white television to watch "The Lawrence Welk Show." I was particularly impressed by the tap dancer who moved with such agility, I dreamed of being a dancer. One day, I accompanied mother to a Salvation Army second-hand store, and I chanced upon a pair of tap dancing shoes. They were twice my shoe size, but I didn't know better. Mother tried her best not to be discouraging, but she reminded me that our denomination frowned upon dancing.

I saw my dream fade away. I was devastated. I often wondered where my life would be, had I pursued that dream. Has anyone stolen your thunder? Have your dreams been unfulfilled? Was it your spouse, your education, a neighbor, your job, your health that stole the opportunity right out from under you? Have you focused your anger on God? I did. I asked God why he wouldn't allow me be a dancer.

There are thieves in this world who steal; not only your physical possessions, but rather you're heart, your allegiance, your very being. Their mission is to distract you from God, and they will do anything – destroy your hopes, your dreams, even your life – to steal you away from God. God is the very antithesis of thievery. He is a giver. He gave His Son.

God wants for us a life fulfilled, and He wants you to have it NOW. The fact is that we have all been robbed. The good news is that we are being renewed every day. Our momentary troubles are achieving for us an eternal glory that far outweighs them all. Fix your eyes "not on what is seen, but what is unseen, for what is seen is only temporary, and what is unseen is eternal" (2 Corinthians 4:16-18.)

**Don't focus your eyes on your stolen dreams. Don't blame God for your poverty, sickness or misery. Don't dwell on the past or dream about the future. Your hope is only in the one who loves you. He is your Maker and Savior. Nothing bad comes from God. God is not a thief. He is the bearer of only good things. Focus instead on Him who is the fulfiller of life abundant.**

## **IF YOU LACK WISDOM** | NOVEMBER 20

*"If any of you lack wisdom, he should ask God, who gives generously to all without finding fault, and it will be given to him." James 1: 5*

Choosing a profession can be rather challenging and uncertain. For as long as I can remember, I gravitated toward helping people solve their personal and social problems. I earned my degrees in this field. I have other passions such as tennis, sports, entertaining and singing, but these became avocation. I dabbled a bit in these, but they would not have been productive careers for me. I believe my calling was the right one for me, but we all have at least some slight doubts.

I have read autobiographies of famous people – singers, actors, statesmen, people of the cloth – and virtually all seemed to know their calling at a young age. All were content in their professions. Many people, however, do not listen to what their hearts tell them to do, and this accounts for the fact that 70% of workers are somewhat or very dissatisfied with their jobs.

Of course, if I were blessed with the wisdom of Solomon, I would not have any second thoughts. God gives wisdom freely. While there are no limits respecting the wisdom He imparts, His "specialty", call it, treats those matters which steer us to His Kingdom.

During Jesus' time, there were many who marveled at the wondrous miracles that He performed. However, even with the evidence of His authority and power right in front of them, many, perhaps most, failed to recognize the Son of God.

The wisdom which God imparts is not intended to render you a more skilled doctor, lawyer or scientist. Some people enter a profession for reasons other than their calling. Some enter a career for monetary gain. Regardless of your motives seek the wisdom from above. God offers each of us the knowledge to help us know and understand our Maker. His wisdom is intended to point us toward our Savior and Redeemer, Jesus Christ. The wisdom that God wants you to have is the wisdom that leads you heaven-bound. Even more, He wants you to learn of the knowledge of His saving grace.

Grace is what He gives so generously. If you lack wisdom, ask God, but be prepared to receive it. God's wisdom, which He wants to give to us so liberally is the wisdom to know His Son. **Be prepared to receive the wisdom to know the Author of Love.**

## AVENGE REVENGE | NOVEMBER 21

*"For we know Him who said, 'It is mine to avenge; I will repay,' and again, 'The Lord will judge His people. It is a dreadful thing to fall into the hands of the living God.'" Hebrews 10: 30 & 31*

---

We are a vengeful society. Centuries (actually, millennia) of wars underscore this fact. In each of those wars, each side genuinely believed it had right on its side, and each was determined to stay the ground, no matter the cost in lives. World War I was dubbed "the war to end all wars". The war that might end all wars is the one which will reduce our planet to nuclear dust. Let's hope that God prevents that day.

One of my personal pet peeves is injustice. If I feel slighted or unjustly treated, I want vengeance in the worst way. The emotional upheaval and rage within my inner soul can't wait to wreak havoc. The desire to win is at any cost. Isn't that just awful and ungodly? Yes. Perhaps Lucifer felt the same way when he was not included in the council of the Father, Son and Holy Spirit during the creation of this world. Satan has been conjuring up ways to get even with God ever since.

In C.S. Lewis' "The Screwtape Letters", Screwtape is an experienced devil while his nephew Wormwood is an apprentice. Screwtape writes Wormwood letters to counsel him on the subtle art of deception. Wormwood, plots with Screwtape to ensnare a newly converted Christian man. One of the chosen weapons is to shake the man's faith in God. The young must deal with issues of good versus evil, temptation, repentance and finally grace. Satan is the prince of vengeance. He will use any means to befuddle man's faith in God. It is his principal weapon in his struggle to get even with God. Do you sometimes find yourself in a state of vengeance? Do you feel slighted and want to get even? If so, you are entertaining "Wormwood's" plot. How long will you harbor such resentment? Be careful you don't wallow in it too long or it will eat you alive.

When Jesus was born, Satan had King Herod slaughter every baby born during that time to try to kill the Savior and thus thwart God's plan for our salvation. God however declared: "Vengeance is mine." If you are contemplating getting even with someone, forget it. Let go and allow God to carry your burden.

God's revenge is perfect because He will handle it as only the Author of Love can. Be not an avenger. **Let God do what He does so very well. You see, God's revenge is always clothed in love.**

## GOD'S WAY | NOVEMBER 22

*"Now this is what the LORD Almighty says; 'Give careful thought to your ways. "You have planted much, but have harvest little. You eat, but never have enough. You drink, but never have your fill. You put on clothes, but are not warm. You earn wages, only to put them in a purse with holes in it." Haggai 1: 5 & 6*

---

In today's text, God warns us to give careful thought to our ways. Clearly, as He sees matters, we come up short in just about every category. He gives a handful of examples, but the first says it rather well: "You have planted much but harvested little." The unsaid but implied statement is that our ways differ significantly from God's way. Using modern-day jargon, we are spinning our wheels, but we're hardly getting anywhere.

There is a famous phrase that goes: "Those who forget history are doomed to repeat it." Actually, the original quotation is from George Santayana, who said: "Those who cannot remember the past are condemned to repeat it." Recently, we pointed out that the history of the world is essentially a history of wars. As a people, we seem not to have learned the lessons from earlier wars and have thus relegated our nations to positions in which they are either fighting wars or building up defenses in anticipation of wars. No one feels secure. Everyone is playing it safe and watching their backs. The "better safe than sorry" is the trust we rely on.

Our personal lives are not terribly different. It often seems that we are moving from misunderstanding to skirmish to divorce, separation and estrangement much of our lives. We have a tendency to want to control others according to our way. There is an unexplainable desire inherent deep within the recess of our soul to want power and be like god. The fear of losing that control leads only to uncontrolled behavior and eventually failure. This is not God's way. God's way always leads to the truth. His way is THE way. In John 14: 6 Jesus says "I am the way, the truth and the life." This is to say that, if we know God, we will indeed know right from wrong. We know our life is but for a season and then we wither and perish. But we know God is life eternal. That is what we hope and wait for. The "way" is what leads us to God. So, if you are following the same pattern all your life, going in circles and never feeling totally at peace and content, then "give careful thought to your ways." Remember God's admonition, the wages of sin is death. Anything apart from God is not God's way but the earthly highway. Anyway but God's way will perish. Stay on the highway that leads to heaven.

In his book entitled "The Jesus Way," (P. 37) Eugene H. Peterson says **"The way we come to God is the same way that God comes to us, and that is in Jesus. Jesus is the way we come to God. Jesus is God's way."**

## **DO YOU LOVE ME?** | NOVEMBER 23

*"The third time He said to him, 'Simon son of John do you love me?' Peter was hurt because Jesus asked him the third time. 'Do you love me?' He said, 'Lord, you know all things; you know that I love you.' Jesus said, 'Feed my sheep.'" John 21: 17*

---

Jesus asked Peter three times, "Do you love me?" Have you ever been in a relationship where you told each other, "I love you" everyday? I remember a friend of my coming to me and weeping because her future husband forgot to send her a valentine's card and express his love for her. She was devastated. She thought he didn't love her. She started to wonder if she should invest more time in their relationship. I have notice lovers and family members use the words "I love you" as they hang up on the phone or say good bye. The word was so overused that it became second nature to them.

Then you have the complete opposite. There are those who rarely use the word and when they do, it becomes a big production. Saying I love you can be both fulfilling or exasperating. For the recipient, it can be either comforting or uncomfortable to hear. Some psychologists recommend you look at your loved one's behavior rather than the words. You can have a person say the words but never actually demonstrate it through deeds. There are those who show love in deeds but can't express it in words. Love can be a very invigorating feeling to hear even when it makes you feel squeamish and awkward. I had a friend recommend to another friend to record "I love you" in a tape recorder and whenever she felt unloved to play the recording. That's so patronizing and impersonal, isn't it?

Jesus is now asking you the same question He asked Peter, "Do you love me? It is time to really look deep within your heart and ask yourself: "Do I love God?" Many say they know God, but do they really love God? Many do God's work but do they really feed His sheep? We can also get caught up in God's work but neglect the source of all love. The trouble with the answer to this question is do we really know what love is? What some feel love is may be insult to another person's point of view. There is one thing we can agree on, God's love is selfless, our love is selfish. Regardless of how you respond to God's question, He knows your heart and, whatever is in your heart, God will love you just the same. He wants you to have a part in the salvation of His sheep. We are all His sheep and need a Savior.

**Even though you may not feel it, won't you say: "Yes Lord, I do love you?" Now go spread God's love and feed His sheep.**

## BEAUTY IS NOT IN THE EYE OF THE BEHOLDER | NOVEMBER 24

*"Your heart became proud on account of your beauty, and you corrupted your wisdom because of your splendor. So I threw you to earth; I made a spectacle of you before kings." Ezekiel 28: 17*

---

The saying "Beauty is in the eye of the beholder" has never rang more true than when Eve encountered the serpent in the Garden of Eden. Have you wondered why Lucifer used the serpent to attract Eve? Let's go back in time when the world was perfect. Every creature which God created was a thing of beauty. Some writers have speculated that the serpent had wings with dazzling brilliancy and of burnished gold. Today some regard the snake as hideous in appearance, while others revere the snake and find them spiritually mesmerizing. It's all in the beholder's perception. Let's set the record straight here today.

First of all, Eve was pure and innocent, though that is not an excuse for her indiscretion. She had never seen an animal, let alone a serpent, speak. Before the fall this was one of God's masterpiece creations. As a matter of fact, all of God's creation before the fall of man was truly a masterpiece.

Lucifer used his sophistry to beguile Eve. He apparently studied Eve's ways and knew what would most likely get her attention. Fascinated by the serpent's ability to speak, Eve succumbed to Lucifer's deceptions. He was, after all, a master of deception.

It is believed, too, that Lucifer used his own good looks to his advantage. In fact, it is generally perceived that Lucifer's good looks were, to an extent, counter-productive for him because his good looks rendered him vain.

You must be careful in your life never to be deceived by beauty. Certainly, you do not want to repeat history. When you place your trust in a human, however beautiful in appearance, you take your chances. As the saying goes, "beauty is only skin deep." We place too much emphasis on looks and stature of a person from a physical stand point rather than character and heart. We are more prone to be attracted to the physical beauty than the substance of a person. That can be detrimental to your well-being in the long run. That person may not have enough "staying power" to keep you interested. Have you ever experienced that type of a person? We end up saying behind their back "he or she is not the one." God declared everything He created as very good.

**True beauty, however, is NOT in the eye of the beholder but in God. He is the source of beauty.**

## FOLLOW ME | NOVEMBER 25

*"As Jesus went on from there, he saw a man named Matthew sitting at the tax collector's booth. 'Follow me.' He told him, and Matthew got up and followed him." Matthew 9: 9*

---

In our text for today, Jesus went to a dinner party of a different kind. There were many tax collectors and sinners that ate with Him and his disciples. This puzzled the Pharisees; they asked his disciples, "Why does your teacher eat with tax collectors and sinners?" Have you ever sent out invitations to a party and some of your friends asked you whom you invite? Their excuses for not attending vary from, he's a leach, she's a gold digger, to, oh! I can't stand be around so and so. These reasons may sound idiotic and childish but we all have friends we don't particularly care to be around with.

Jesus went through a similar ordeal. He was criticized for hanging around with the "IRS" and those "sinners" we don't like to be around either. Jesus had an answer for His critics. He said: "It is not the healthy who need a doctor, but the sick, but go and learn what this means: I desire mercy, not sacrifice. For I have not come to call the righteous, but sinners." (Matthew 9: 12 & 13). Jesus came for the sinner and the sick. Are you a sinner? If not, are you sick? If so, then you need to follow Him. Jesus is calling you to follow Him. Following Jesus will not only heal you but you will be made whole. In Him is your completeness.

Everywhere Jesus went and every person He ministered to needed a Savior. The sad aspect of this whole scenario was the self-centered people who wanted the recognition of men rather than the humbleness of God. They did not see or understand what Jesus was doing because they were blinded by their arrogance, their haughtiness and their overbearing pride.

This was the reason why God sent His Son, to show us the ways of the Father. Our heavenly Father is a God of love and mercy. His Son came to redeem us from the mentality of "I'm better than you attitude." When He told Matthew to "follow me," He meant for Matthew and all of us to follow Him and His ways; for they are righteous, merciful and full of grace. His ways are worth emulating because it leads to eternal life.

Greater than His ways is who He is. He is your salvation. You must make Him priority in your life. God is your source for all your needs. **Don't wait for Him to tell you to "follow me." Follow Him right now.**

## THEY WERE BORN THAT WAY | NOVEMBER 26

*"Jesus replied, 'Not everyone can accept this word, but only those to whom it has been given. For some are eunuchs because they were born that way; others were made that way by men; and others have renounced marriage because of the kingdom of heaven. The one who can accept this should accept it.' " Matthew 19: 11 & 12*

---

Today's text addresses natural versus environmental. The Pharisees came to Jesus to test Him. They loved to put Jesus on the spot. They asked Him, "Is it lawful for a man to divorce his wife for any reason. "Haven't you read," He replied, "that at the beginning the Creator 'made them male and female,' and said, "for this reason a man will leave his father and mother and be united to his wife, and the two will become one flesh? So they are no longer two, but one. Therefore what God has joined together, let man not separate." "Why then," they asked, "did Moses command that a man give his wife a certificate of divorce and send her away?" Jesus replied, "Moses permitted you to divorce your wives because your hearts were hard." But it was not this way from the beginning. I tell you that anyone who divorces his wife, except for marital unfaithfulness, and marries another woman commits adultery." The disciples said to him, "If this is the situation between a husband and wife, it is better not to marry" (Matthew 1-7).

The original plan for man before the fall was perfect in every way. There were no divorces no anomalies of nature. Man created divorce, and God relented. Jesus even reminded them that Moses permitted divorce because "man's hearts were hard." In other words man insisted in doing it his way thus, disobeying God.

When you see eunuchs, this was either an anomaly, man-made or natural. God said they were born that way. There are many things made by man that God has relented for your sake. But there are also those born with abnormalities. Whether man made or by birth, God said accept them as He has accepted them. Many today are born hermaphrodites, eunuchs, some with no arms, no legs, extra fingers, physically challenged, mentally ill, single, celibate, adulterer, sinner, divorcee', addict, regardless of their malady, they were born that way. Do you see God's point of view? Not all of you can but for those who can, then you are godly. God wants you to love and accept them as He does. Is this a hard task for you to follow? You'll be much better off if you do. **No one is perfect. We ALL have anomalies. We were all born that way.**

**God's kingdom is ALL- inclusive. There is no one rejected or exempted to enter His kingdom. We are all welcome just as we are.** God knew man's frailties and showed us how to deal with them. Others were made by man, and God loved them all and said, "The one who can accept this should accept it."

## THANKSGIVING DAY | NOVEMBER 27

*"For everything God created is good, and nothing is to be rejected if it is received with thanksgiving, because it is consecrated by the word of God and prayer? I Timothy 4: 4*

---

I look forward to Thanksgiving. It is a time to reflect on the good things in one's life and to celebrate all God's blessings. What do you have to be thankful for? This time for family gatherings is both a delightful time to be with ones we most care about and a pensive time for those who've lost a loved one. Every year, people take the time to share their bounty to those less fortunate. There's a sense of gratitude in the air during this time of the year. We count our blessings and pray good will to our country and fellowman.

This is a solemn occasion that makes each of us pause to remember our Maker who supplies all our needs. Well, it used to be a solemn occasion. In 2010, if our information is accurate, K-Mart, Wal-Mart, Sears, Toys R Us, Gap banana Republic, Old Nay, and Walgreens, to name a few, opened all or some of their stores anywhere from the morning only to 24 hours. In recent years, Thanksgiving was perceived more and more as a prelude to Black Friday. If the current trend continues, it will be Black Thursday. God is being relegated to a position of also-ran to $499 42-inch flat screens and $49 DVD players.

I know how empty I feel when just one of my family members either cannot or chooses not to join us during this holiday of thanks. If you are estranged with a loved or family member, pray for them and then invite another person to take their place. It is sadder yet when the One we are forgetting is the One who is ultimately responsible for the bounty of which we partake. We can rant and rave all we like, but we're unlikely to stop what is the runaway freight train of retail greed. Whatever you do on this Thanksgiving Day, don't get caught up in the anticipation of those harrowing retail sales or bickering mood swings with strangers or loved ones.

We can, however, make certain that we act in a Godly way by focusing on those who are unable to care for themselves and those from whom we are estranged. **Take the time to extend the hand of fellowship to those in need. Caring embraces more than our family circle. Everyone God created is His family. Who we embrace in our family circle is a sign of the God you know and love. We must also give thanks not only today but every day of our lives. God has shown us how to care for one another.**

That is how we can best serve the One to whom our thanks are due on this wonderful holiday. The flat screens will be available tomorrow.

## **LOVE WITH KINDNESS** | NOVEMBER 28

*"Therefore, as God's chosen people, holy and dearly loved, clothe yourselves with compassion, kindness, humility, gentleness and patience." Colossians 3: 12*

I have an auntie who's a pillar in her church. She is in charge of the social committee. Her significant duties include preparing meals for church functions nearly every Sabbath.

One Sabbath morning, during the pastor's Sabbath school class, there was a distinguished guest from the local conference. He was there to observe the dynamics of church member relationships. The pastor went around the room, asking each person how they showed kindness to their fellow believer. When it came for my aunt's turn she said she showed kindness by assigning certain church members what to bring for potluck.

The guest from the conference was taken aback on the style of kindness. It gave him food for thought for his next sermon. Months later, when he returned for an update on his findings, he informed my aunt that she had taught him a valuable lesson: "It's not so much how you express your kindness verbally or what you ask for, but rather how you select the person to whom your kindness is directed."

I am reminded of the kindness our God showed the Israelites as they journeyed through the wilderness. No matter what God brought them, from the manna, quail, to the water, they complained like children. God was patient with them and dealt with them in a tender and compassion manner. In like manner God is telling us how to treat one another. Can you try a little kindness in your daily dealings? If so, you are being God's chosen people.

Kindness is an active demonstration of love. When you express kindness you are being clothed in God's Spirit of compassion, humility, gentleness and patience. They are all fruits of God's Spirit. Patience sometimes requires doing nothing and waiting, but kindness requires action not only in deed but in words. If you have difficulty expressing kindness when someone just humiliated you, stay silent. Silent speaks volumes of godliness. Our Savior was abused, humiliated and beaten but He never said or mumbled a retaliatory word. God showed compassion and sorrow towards His abusers but He always acted in kindness.

**Just as God has shown us kindness, even when undeserving, we are to do likewise because kindness is God's love.**

# THINK ABOUT SUCH THINGS | NOVEMBER 29

*"Finally, brothers, whatever is true, whatever is noble, whatever is right, whatever is pure, whatever is lovely, whatever is admirable-if anything is excellent or praiseworthy-think about such things." Philippians 4: 8*

---

Paul's counsel to find excellence in everything we do is praiseworthy but certainly easier said than done. It's not easy to be courteous and considerate when someone hurts you or a stranger cuts you off on the highway. How do you hold back your emotions and bite your tongue when you learn your spouse has been cheating on you? Do you think you could treat with equanimity a colleague who has taken credit for a cost-saving idea that he knows was yours? How do you deal with a boss who is intimidated by your business acumen and meteoric track record?

True, but God is telling you that there is a better way of handling a situation that is otherwise apt to push you over the proverbial edge. To react with rage or vengeance is only human. God tells us to act as He would, which, of course, is a big step beyond how humans typically act. If we exchange wrong for wrong, we are doing Lucifer's bidding. He'll be right by your side applauding. It's the person imbued with the Godly Spirit who can forgive the person who just cut in line at the bank or store. It's the person with the Godly Spirit who can approach the swindler with a caring heart rather than with a bludgeon. It's the person with the Godly Spirit who can warmly congratulate a person who edged her out in an election by virtue of chicanery.

You can do all of these things through Christ, who gives you the strength to do what is true and fair. Mind you, you don't take a couple of Godly pills before bedtime and wake up the next morning with a new spirit. It takes time for anyone to alter his or her behavior. There will be heartaches and shame along the sanctified life. You will feel the humiliation and guilt. God speaks to us daily. If we listen and obey His promptings we will possess His Spirit of grace. We must die daily in Christ. You will relapse from time to time, but each time you return to God, you will be humbled. The Spirit of God will imbue you with His Spirit. Never stop coming back to the Lord each time you stumble. He will welcome you back as long as you return back to Him. One of the mottos at the end of an Alcohol Anonymous (A.A.) meeting, before they leave, everyone in unison says "keep coming back."

In other words, God must be the center of your whole being. He doesn't ever give up on you, you are to do likewise. Your success in this effort will depend upon how willing you are to submit your will to Him. To do less would, of course, be un-Godly. **Think on these things that are praiseworthy then go and practice them.**

## **FORGIVE** | NOVEMBER 30

*"For if you forgive men when they sin against you, your heavenly Father will also forgive you. But if you do not forgive men their sins, your Father will not forgive your sins." Matthew 6: 14 & 15*

"The Hiding Place," by Corrie ten Boom is an autobiographical account of a life that included imprisonment at Ravensbruck concentration camp with her sister Betsie. Just days before her own release from camp, her sister Betsie perished. They were sent there by the Nazis for harboring Jews in their home during the Holocaust.

In memory of her sister's selfless love and forgiveness, Corrie founded a post-war home for other camp survivors who were recovering from the horrors of life in these camps. Corrie traveled throughout Europe as a missionary, preaching God's love and forgiveness and the need to extend the hand of reconciliation to one's tormenters. It's never easy to recount the horrors of your past life and to relive them each day, especially when you've lost loved ones and you're still alive.

One chapter in her book is entitled: "I'm Still Learning to Forgive." One day, she was in Munich, spreading God's love and the need to forgive, when she experienced a true example of practicing what one preaches. She noticed a balding, heavy-set man, who was clearly approaching her. As he neared, she had a sudden flashback of this man, a guard in the camp, confronting her frail sister Betsie.

Suddenly, the man began speaking to her: "You mentioned Ravensbruck in your talk. I was a guard in there." He claimed not to remember her. "Since that time," he went on, " I have become a Christian. I know that God has forgiven me for the cruel things I did there, but I would like to hear it from your lips as well, Fraulein,..." he extended his hand and said: "will you forgive me?" Corrie stood there numbed and immobile. She could not. Her thoughts began to wander about her sister Betsie. She wondered: could he erase her slow terrible death simply by asking. Although he was there for only seconds Corrie was still deliberating for what seemed hours. She knew she had to do it. She was reminded of the text "if you do not forgive men their trespasses," Jesus said: "neither will your Father in heaven forgive your trespasses."

Forgiveness is really from God. You may forgive your neighbor through lip service but still hold a grudge inside your heart. You may even forgive but not forget. This text really means you will understand God's love of forgiveness in your life when you allow His Spirit in your heart. He can melt your pain, anger and hatred toward the person who sinned against you. He will forgive any sin no matter how heinous and atrocious it may be. God will always forgive you even if you do not forgive your neighbor. But you will never experience His love of forgiveness unless you receive His Spirit in your heart. And that's what Corrie did. She trusted God to give her the Spirit of forgiveness.

She knew her heart felt cold, but forgiveness was not an emotion. She knew it was an act of the will, and the will can function, regardless of the temperature of the heart. She prayed "Jesus, help me!" "I can lift my hand. I can do that much. You supply the feeling."

"And so woodenly, mechanically, I thrust my hand into the one stretched out to me and as I did, an incredible thing took place. The current started in my shoulder, raced down my arm, sprang into our joined hands. And then this healing warmth seemed to flood my whole being, bringing tears to my eyes." "I forgive you, brother!" I cried, "With all my heart!" For a long moment they grasped each other's hands, the former guard and the former prisoner. She had never known God's love as intensely as she did then.

Alexander Pope once wrote, "To err is human, to forgive is divine." Are you struggling with a deep seated hurt that cannot be forgiven? Is your tormentor someone you know or a total stranger? How long have you been holding such anger and resentment? too long? Not forgiving will eat you alive inside. Don't take it with you to your grave. It's time to forgive. Friend, God is extending His hand of reconciliation to you today. **Stop punishing yourself. Grasp His hand of reconciliation and you too will be forgiven.**

## GREATER LOVE HAS NO ONE | DECEMBER 1

*"Greater love has no one than this that he lay down his life for his friends." John 15: 13*

---

I have a number of best friends. Do you? One best friend in particular that stands out is my friend I have known since I was 13. We grew up together in the same home church. This best friend of mine knows more about me than any friend I've ever known. We used to stay up until dawn talking about everything under the sun. We concluded we had all the answers. We also professed our undying loyalty and love until death do us part.

As adults we continued our friendship by going into business together. However, a disagreement regarding how to run the business changed things. We each became entrenched in our respective positions, and the line in the sand was drawn. We went our separate ways. She left the church, as did I. Eventually, I allowed the Holy Spirit to re-enter my heart, and I extended the hand of reconciliation. The healing, regrettably, came with a price. Our relationship has never been the same.

The undying feelings we once had for one another were, in the end, not undying. It was then that I realized that human love and friendship were ultimately unreliable. If your happiness is dependent upon earthly friends, or lovers, then beware. Earthly relationships are at high risk for failure because we are flawed-all of us. To place your whole life on a person for your happiness is foolish. They will disappoint you. They will fail. They are not perfect. There is no perfect relationship here on earth. What's really sad is to harbor such hurt for such a long period of time is un-godly. God said "I am slow to anger and I am also quick to let go of my anger." Try practicing such behavior and you will find your cares become easy and light.

Does this mean that we should give up on relationships? Absolutely not! Every relationship comes with faults. As the wedding vow oft quoted during the ceremony says "for better or for worse." There is One who is our true best friend. He will stick by us, no matter what. He teaches us how to love one another. He teaches us how to reconcile with estranged friends. He set the example on how to forgive. He is altogether lovely. He is a friend who loves you and me and is willing to stick by you to the very end. He is steadfast, unfailing and loyal. That friend's name is Jesus. You can learn all about Him through His Spirit.

**You can have His Spirit in your life. You must be willing and receptive before you learn of Him. And you won't be disappointed. There is no greater love than God's love. Give Him a chance.**

## **YES, I AM COMING SOON** | DECEMBER 2

*"He who testifies to these things says 'Yes, I am coming soon.'" Revelation 22: 30*

---

I remember feeling a sense of great relief when I finally passed my oral and written exam for my doctorate degree. It seemed as if a virtual lifetime of hard work had been rewarded. What was the moment of greatest relief in your life? Was it when your physician told you that you were cancer-free? Was it when you finally landed that dream job? Maybe it was finally coming home from war? Was it when you met your soul mate? What about when you reconciled with a family or friend after all these years? How about when you finally felt really forgiven?

It is wonderful to set and achieve goals. It is important, however, that our lives be more than a series of goals. There are many people in our world who live from one goal to the next, but they are seldom there for the moment. No sooner do they reach the corporate vice presidential level then they are focused on senior vice president and then president. Life is to be cherished and enjoyed and not squandered. So-called success is not necessary to a life well-lived. Oftentimes, we learn more and grow more through our failures. When your earthly days are over, it won't matter what run on the corporate ladder you reached. What will matter is whether you have let the light of the Lord be your example and taken Him into your heart.

The second phase of God's promise will be fulfilled. It is coming soon, and it may well be within your lifetime. Jesus said to the world: "It is finished," as He gave His life so that we might eventually enter His Father's Kingdom. We may enter tomorrow, or it may be years after our earthly existence has ended. Be ever mindful of the fact that God's love for us did not end on the cross. He has been patient with us. He has tolerated our evil ways and loved us nonetheless. We must never believe that He will not return. That is one goal you can be sure of. To give up now would be detriment to your well-being. One of God's greatest attribute in love is waiting. He is a patience God that waits for you to believe in Him. That's what He is waiting for before His return.

What would it take to convince you to hold on to His promise? Many have gone to their graves not seeing the second phase of God's promise fulfilled. Sometimes doubt will creep in our minds and we end up saying "not in this generation." Don't think for one minute that's true. God says He will come when you least expect Him. And He will eventually. **God said His word is as sure as His love.** When you have finally reached the level of complete trust in God, then you will testify of His soon coming.

**What are you waiting for? Trust Him and His promise now. Waiting for His soon return will require a trust like no other. Yes, He is coming very soon.**

## FIERY TRIALS | DECEMBER 3

*"When you pass through the water, I will be with you; and through the rivers, they shall not overflow you: When thou walk through the fire, you shall not be burned; neither shall the flame kindle upon you." Isaiah 43: 2*

Apropos of the preceding verse, we find that, sometimes, the choices we make in life become the fiery trials that consume our peace. Daniel and his companions faced just such a test when they elected to stand with God and refuse to surrender to a false god.

The King of Babylon, at the prompting of his advisors, allowed a golden statue of his likeness to be created and then situated in the courtyard so that all of the king's subjects might pay homage to their ruler. Whenever the horn was sounded, everyone thought the kingdom was required to bow down to the golden image.

Only Daniel and his comrades disobeyed the mandate. One person spied on them and reported their disobedience to the authorities. The king decreed that Daniel and his cohorts be thrown into a fiery furnace. That furnace was to be heated seven times hotter than usual. The soldiers who threw Daniel's group into the furnace were themselves burned to death. However, Daniel and his companions were not so much as singed. The king did not smell any smoke on either their clothing or hairs. Stunned, he released them.

Are you passing through flooded rivers and fiery flames in your life? Are you struggling to find a way out? Sometimes the choices we make in life become the fiery trials that land us in the furnace. When we least expect it, we are thrown in the fiery furnace by either our choice or through no fault of our own. God warns us of last day events where you will go through fiery trials. Take heart. God is with you, just as He was with Daniel's group. You needn't be fearful or feel abandoned or helpless. As long as you live in this world, there will be trials of rivers overflowing or fires that burn you. God has promised to protect you.

God said He would be with you and protect you. When you pass through your own fiery trials, there will be no hint of "smoke" on your person. The waters you cross will not overflow either. Whether you trials are now or in the end times God will be with you. You have nothing to worry or fear. Rest assured. You will be saved.

**Whatever problems you are facing, no matter how rough your life has been, and whatever your health condition is, God will see you through. If you end up sleeping in the Lord, that's OK. When you awake, the first one you'll see is your Savior, Jesus Christ. Whatever fiery trials you experience always keep your faith and focus on God.**

## **THE HOLY CITY** | DECEMBER 4

*"Then I saw a new heaven and a new earth, for the first heaven and the first earth had passed away, and there was no longer any sea. I saw the Holy City, the new Jerusalem, coming down out of heaven from God, prepared as a bride beautifully dressed for her husband." Revelation 21: 1 & 2*

---

John describes the City, which God has prepared for us as the Holy City, or New Jerusalem coming down from heaven like a bride beautifully dressed for her husband. Nothing can capture the beauty of a bride than on her wedding day as she marches down the aisle to meet her husband to be. She is regaled in all the splendor and glory that would seem fit for a king. God is the groom and we are His bride. Like a loving husband He has prepared a home for us. God does not hold back anything but has prepared a mansion like no other ever witnessed in His entire universe.

This is our dwelling place, a home to live with God for eternity. John further describes the city as like a square cube with equal sides measuring 1, 400 miles length and width with walls 200 feet high and the entire exterior of the city made out of gold. The great wall, made of jasper, has twelve gates, with twelve angels at the gates. On the gates were written the names of the twelve tribes of Israel. There were three gates on the east, three on the north, three on the south and three on the west.

Its foundation was decorated with every precious stone. The first foundation was jasper, the second sapphire, the third chalcedony, the fourth emerald, the fifth sardonyx, the sixth carnelian, the seventh chrysolite, the eight beryl, the ninth topaz, the tenth chrysoprase, the eleventh jacinth, and the twelfth amethyst. The twelve gates were twelve pearls. Each of the gates was made from a single pearl. The streets were made of pure gold, like transparent glass. The river of life was as clear as crystal flowing from the throne of God to the middle of the great street of the city. From each side of the river stood the tree of life, bearing twelve crops of fruit, yielding its fruit every month.

There are no street lamps nor the sun or moon to light the city. The Lord God will give them light from His presence. If you can't wait to see the Holy City, you will be in for a surprise when you walk through the streets of gold. Eye has not seen or ears heard of what God has in store for us. Even John could not express in words the holy city. John is asleep awaiting his resurrection, as well as those who have gone before us. We wait. We too will be astonished. All that He has prepared for us will pale in comparison to seeing our Savior, Jesus.

**As glorious as the holy city will be, a dwelling place is only complete and habitable when you are with the ones you love. We will finally call this place home because the One who loves us will reside with us. Even so, Lord Jesus come.**

# A WONDERFUL FRIENDSHIP | DECEMBER 5

*"I grieve for you, Jonathan my brother; you were very dear to me. Your love for me was wonderful, more wonderful than that of women." 2 Samuel 1: 26*

---

How would you characterize true friendship? Today's text speaks to the extraordinarily-strong bond that existed between David and Jonathan. What they had for each other was love, but not in the modern-day, carnal sense. Their commonality was of course their knowledge and relationship with God.

Who would you say is your best friend? Someone you've known for many years? Someone you can trust and rely with your life? Someone who attends all those special occasions with you? What are the qualities of a "best friend?" Who is on your "A-list" first when putting together an invitation list? Who would you call first in the middle of the night if you were stuck on the freeway or needed bailing out from jail? It's been said never loan money to a friend, if you want to keep that person as a friend. However, if you had your back up against the wall, who would you call for a loan?

According to psychologists, friendship grow out of situations in which two people discover that they have one, likely several, important (to them) attributes in common – race, education, religion, hobbies, food, sports or a host of others. The friendship thrives over time as the two learn of more things they have in common and assume the other person's passions. I have noticed when you speak a common language it immediately breaks the ice and doors open readily.

How many friends would you say you have? Do you look to have a long list of friends, or are you the sort of person who likes to have one or two good friends, and more than that is a crowd for you? Are you perhaps too slow to extend your hand in friendship? Being timid tends to limit one's circle of friends, and some argue that it is better to be somewhat aggressive in acquiring friends so as to avoid rejection. Sometimes friendship happens unexpectedly when you least suspect it. Sometimes friendship grows old with time. Time certainly plays a key factor in whether or not a friendship has staying power. One key factor in maintaining friendship is to nurture it. Staying in touch is one way to keep the fire of friendship burning. With today's social media Facebook, friends from years gone by have surfaced. We can re-connect. The key to keeping friends is to nurture them.

Jonathan loved David more than he loved his own family because he knew David's heart. David loved Jonathan because he was willing to risk his life for him. Their loved was based on the Lord. Whatever friendship you have experienced here on earth, you will understand the person behind all true friendships is our Savior. **Someday we will meet the Author of Love, who calls each of us His friend. That's a wonderful friendship we will enjoy for eternity.**

## WHO IS YOUR FAVORITE? | DECEMBER 6

*"Isaac, who had a taste for wild game, loved Esau, but Rebekah loved Jacob." Genesis 25: 28*

Family dysfunction existed in Isaac's household as revealed in Genesis chapter 25. Isaac favored Esau, the first-born and Rebekah loved Jacob. It is customary to look favorably on the first-born child. The first child typically receives the most attention. Cultural traditions place the first born as heir to the family throne when the father dies. Thereafter, the succeeding siblings are counted in the order of their birth.

Rebekah favored Jacob probably because he was closer to his mother. He was more domesticated in his behavior, while Esau was more the outdoors type of man. Here were two men with distinct differences in personalities coming from the same parents. Yet, their parents cleaved to them according to their proclivity and need.

Sad as it is, favoritism exists in many families. It's part of the fallen human condition. As much as parents try to remain impartial and unbiased, there is a predilection towards favoring one child over another. After all, we tend to gravitate toward the easy going, calm and pliable child as opposed to the hyperactive, independent and strong-willed child. And children seem to know who parents favor. I have witnessed it in my own as well as other families. Some children deal with it well, while others do not and the wounds and resentment can shape a child's character until his or her last days. Parents are fallible and as much as they try to love their children equally, children will display their insecurity whenever they feel un-loved. Then there are parents who give-in to every whim of their children. The children run their household. They allow them to make decision even at a very young age. Those types of households appear to be the least desirable way of raising kids.

If you are feeling slighted because of a parent's misjudgments, don't feel disheartened. The best-adjusted among us have learned that human beings will, sooner or later, disappoint us. We are, by nature, imperfect beings, and, try though we might to please others; we very often come up short. As hurt as you may feel for feeling un-favored, God has many ways of showing you love that you may not see because you are looking for love in the wrong places. Sometimes that love will not come in the form of your parents or blood relationships.

You must not feel disfavored or dejected because God has favored you among all of His creation. Yes, God created the universe and everything in it. Yet, His whole focus and goal is all about bringing you home with Him. He has always loved you even before you came into existence and will, quite dependably, continue to show you favor throughout your earthly stay. **When He returns to take us home we will finally understand the One who loved us most.**

**His love for you is without favoritism and is unconditional.**

## **WAITING IN GOD'S LOVE** | DECEMBER 7

*"Keep yourselves in God's love as you wait for the mercy of our Lord Jesus Christ to bring you to eternal Life." Jude 21*

The book of Jude gives us a background of how godless men defiled themselves and their environment to the point of doom and damnation. As men's hearts grow weary and impatient, it is easy to succumb to the temptations of the evil one. Even Christians who await their just reward may find it difficult to persevere.

Jude reminds us of this condition as prophesied by Enoch. He feels compelled to warn his fellow saints that: "…certain men whose condemnation was written about long ago have secretly slipped among you. They are godless men, who change the grace of our God into a license for immortality and deny Jesus Christ, our only Sovereign and Lord." (vs. 3 & 4). Jude warns that, if the people of his time are not circumspect, they will fall prey to the evil doer in their midst. He further admonishes that they will "…eat with you without the slightest qualm – even shepherds who will only feed themselves and forget others. They are similar to clouds that produce no rain or like autumn trees without fruit. They are wild waves of the sea, foaming up their shame, wandering stars, for whom blackest darkness has been reserved forever." Clearly, these are people without the Spirit of God in their souls. Outwardly, they are attractive because they feed on your emptiness.

Jude, of course, is prophesying the end times of the earth. He likens these men to the citizens of Sodom and Gomorrah. These are men who seek to divide us, who follow their base instincts and certainly do not have the "Spirit." As the Spirit of God is withdrawn from this world, un-godly behavior will pervade this world and those waiting for Jesus's return may become discouraged and forlorn. We are witnessing tumultuous chaos all over the world today. War, bombings, political unrest, uncontrolled religious fervor, murders, heinous acts unimaginable is posted in the news daily. Do you sometimes feel you have been waiting too long for Jesus' return? Have you been waiting in God's love?

Jude offers hope and encouragement by reminding the saints of the Lord to persevere by keeping themselves in God's love. To wait on the Lord's return means waiting in His love. We need to practice His love in our lives daily by allowing His Spirit to control us. That is the meaning of waiting in God's love. As for the evil doers, He says to be merciful to them for God is merciful. I know it's difficult to love someone who has offended you, murdered a loved one, stole your spouse or betrayed you. Instead focus on God. He will soothe your heart and soul with His Spirit. You will inherit His compassionate and forgiving nature.

**When you keep yourselves in God's love while waiting for His return; suddenly our Lord and Savior Jesus Christ will return to bring us to our eternal life. That's a love worth waiting.**

# HEAVEN'S GLORY | DECEMBER 8

*"In the past God spoke to our forefathers through the prophets at many times and in various ways, but in these last days He has spoken to us by His Son, whom He appointed heir of all things, and through whom He made the universe. The Son is the radiance of God's glory and the exact representation of His being, sustaining all things by His powerful word." Hebrews 1: 1-3*

---

On July 22, 2010, scientists discovered the largest star ever known yet. This star is 265 times the mass of our sun. They gave it a number to identify it instead of a name. They called it "R136a1." It is 165 million light years from our planet. Astronomers never contemplated a star so large. They thought this would be an impossibility given their knowledge of stars and their role, which includes burning up eventually. This star has shed some interesting light regarding our solar system and its relationship with other galaxies.

I have always been fascinated with space. I particularly enjoy watching and reading documentaries regarding new planets discovered or stars similar to ours that may be able to shed some light in the compatibility of our world with other life forms in other galaxies. Each night when I take the dog out for a walk I gaze at the heavens and look at the stars and planets in our solar system and ponder on our Creator's majesty. I long to be with Him.

I would venture to say that because of the infinite vastness of space, we have just discovered the very tip of the proverbial iceberg. The sun is registered at 93 million mile away from earth. The next nearest star to our earth is "Alpha Centauri." This star has been measured to be 4.37 light –years away (one light –year, with light traveling at 188,000 miles a second, in one year would equate to 5.9 trillion miles). If we built a spaceship that could travel at 200,000 miles an hour, it would take 14,500 years to get there. As vast and infinite is space, conversely if we probed into an electron microscope to study each individual gene cell, we would be baffled at the infinitesimal microscopic world that also exists under a Petri dish. Behind all these phenomenon is Heaven's Glory, our God. He made the suns, the universe and His glory is sustaining all these things simply by His spoken word. However, God has realized, even before all His creation that His universe is not complete until we are with Him to live with Him forever.

What is truly amazing, when you think about it, is that, as vast as God's universe is, He still has the capability and the interest to dwell in us, though we be the tiniest of specs in the universal scheme of things. In His vast universe He has made us the apple of His eye. Why? He saved us because that's how much He loves us.

**I can't wait to meet Heaven's Glory, His Son.**

## WHITE ROBES | DECEMBER 9

*"The one of the elders asked me, 'These in white robes-who are they, and where did they come from?' " Revelations 7: 13*

---

Last week I attended my best friend parents' 50th wedding anniversary. It was a quite an elaborate affair. She was dressed in formal gown while her children were dressed in suit and tie. The food was catered and a professional photographer was hired to capture the moment. Most of the guests were dressed in suits and gowns. I was remiss in calling him regarding the dress code and I came dressed in "preppy" semi-formal attire. I would surmise 90 per cent of the guests were dressed formally with a few stragglers dressed in jeans and sweats like tops. I wasn't the odd ball in the group but there were others who definitely needed a make-over. I learned a valuable lesson. One should always prepare beforehand so one is not left off guard and embarrassed.

Today's verse talks about a garment of white robes. I remember my professor in college, Madelyn Haldeman, conveying a story of a church lady she met in her church. When my professor entered her home, she noted the walls in the living room were covered in sheets of white paper with names of people written on them. My professor inquired what these names meant and she mentioned they were the names of the 144,000 mentioned in the book of Revelations 7: 4, "Then I heard the number of those who were sealed: 144,000 from all the tribes of Israel. This church lady had been writing names of people she thought would be "saved." My professor did not dare ask if her name was written there. Unfortunately this women did not read verse 9, "After this I looked and there before me was a great multitude that no one could count, from every nation, tribe, people and language. They were wearing white robes."

I thank God we do not have to wear formal or semi-formal attire to enter His kingdom, white robes will suffice. Yes, white robes are more than a garment, it symbolizes "These are they who have come out of the great tribulation; they have washed their robes and made them white in the blood of the Lamb." "For the Lamb at the center of the throne will be their shepherd, He will lead them to springs of living water, and God will wipe away every tear from their eyes." Rev. 7: 14 & 17. What a glorious day that will be. Our Shepard will lead us home and our tears will also be wiped away by our Shepard. God is really a good God. He comforts us.

**It is not our character or white robes on our part that saves us but our faith and acceptance of the Lamb's invitation.**

## HOLD ON | DECEMBER 10

*"I am coming soon. Hold on to what you have, so that no one will take your crown." Revelation 3: 11*

---

And here are the headlines. Three children, ages three, four and seven were killed in the crossfire between drug lords and Mexican authorities today. In Afghanistan, a Taliban-led band of grenade-toting soldiers decimated a mosque as over 200 were engaged in noon-time prayers. 127 perished. In Jerusalem, a busload of holiday shoppers was blown to pieces when a suicide bomber cast her shadow on an otherwise peaceful afternoon. In a Cincinnati suburb, two 16-year-olds rampaged through the halls of Pete Rose High School. Ten students, three faculties and a janitor perished. And, now for the good news…it's not raining, and there are 15 shopping days until Christmas. Well, so much for the holiday spirit. Wow!

I long for the good-old days…when family gathered and so many of those we loved most were still with us. Call it holiday blues; call it what you want. Sound familiar? Jesus was no stranger to the blues. He made it a point to live among those considered least worthy in our society, and any of us would have been terribly discouraged by these experiences. Throughout, His spirit was an uplifting one, and it was a contagious spirit indeed.

Jesus urged, back during His time on earth and urges to this day that we hold on to what we have. He warned that: "You will hear of wars and rumors of wars, but see to it that you are not alarmed. Such things must happen, but the end is still to come. Nation will rise against nation, and kingdom against kingdom. There will be famines and earthquakes in various places. All these are the beginning of birth pains. The love of most will grow cold. But he who stand firm to the end will be saved." Matthew 24: 6-11.

Can you hold on up to the last minute? Sometimes just giving up and walking away is so much easier and quick to do. God knows the outcome of our journey here on earth. Yes, it will be unbearable to watch. There will be tribulations never before witnessed in earth's history. But guess what? The all-knowing God has promised salvation. He is really coming back to finally take us home. I know you've heard this promise all your life but all your life will be like a blink of the eye in the whole scheme of things when it's finally over.

**God is asking you to "hold on." Don't wane and lose sight of His coming. Are you ready for His coming? Then don't let anyone steal your crown, stay faithful and "Hold on." He is just around the corner.**

## IT'S ALL ABOUT JESUS | DECEMBER 11

*"You diligently study the Scriptures because you think that by them you possess eternal Life. These are the Scriptures that testify about me, yet you refuse to come to me to have life." John 5: 39 & 40*

---

It's been a while, but I can vividly recall a conversation I had one morning with my track coach. We were discussing the Sabbath, and he insisted that the day for celebrating the Sabbath was nailed to the cross because Christ's resurrection occurred on the first day of the week. I refuted this argument by reminding the coach that Exodus 20: 8-11 says in no uncertain terms: "Six days shalt thou labor and do all thy work, but the seventh day is the Sabbath of the Lord thy God. In it, thou shalt not do any work…" It goes on to say: "…and (the Lord) rested the seventh day." "Gotcha," I was thinking.

It was not, however, a "gotcha" moment. We battled to a draw. I decided, therefore, to escalate the matter and present the "truth" to his pastor. He argued that the Sabbath was made for men and that it doesn't really matter which day of the week one worshipped, as long as Christ is the center. He made a very strong point. After all, isn't it all about Jesus and not the Sabbath? I continued my one-upmanship on Facebook. I've learned never to discuss religion, politics or pro-life/free choice on Facebook unless you can respect them.

It wasn't until I carefully studied the word and Spirit of God that I gained a better understanding of the relevant issues here. Jesus was directing His remarks (today's verse) to people just like me. It seems that many of us can recite the Bible virtually verbatim, but we do not know the Author of Love. Regrettably, as we discussed earlier in this devotional, I am not alone in this regard. Many (some would say most) of this nation's most prominent televangelists have done Satan's bidding. They have been guilty of embezzlement, self-aggrandizement, prostitution, lying, and too many sins to catalogue; yet, every week, they can be seen on nationally syndicated television, quoting scriptures. They too missed the mark. And yes, God has already forgiven their sins. God has also forgiven me for my Pharisaical ways. Sometimes lesson are learned the hard way because we do not listen to the Spirit of God's counseling. We need to focus on Jesus and not on the issues at hand.

We know our Bible backwards and forwards, we memorize the scriptures and can quote them verbatim but we do not know our Lord and Savior, Jesus Christ. We pay tithe, worship on the Sabbath, don't smoke or drink liquor but how well do we treat our enemies? **We know the message, but NOT the messenger. You must have your own personal walk with God. Yet, it's not about you. It's all about Jesus.**

## GLORIOUS CHILD BIRTH PAIN | DECEMBER 12

*"We know that the whole creation has been groaning as in the pains of childbirth right up to the present time." Romans 8: 22*

---

I recall Mother's disciplining us as children and declaring, "Wait until you have your own kids someday! Then you'll realize what I went through raising you." Of course we didn't believe her, but by the time our own kids were teenagers, we knew all too well the struggles of Christian parents. Parents raising teenage children are one of the most trying times of their lives. Their children are 13 years old going on 30.

We are prone to say that times have changed. Gone are the days of "Ozzie and Harriet" and "Father Knows Best", when a stay-at-home mom cooked the better part of the afternoon, waiting for dad to come home from work and join the family for dinner. In modern-day homes, the dinner table is an option often disregarded. I remember morning worship before school and evening worship before bedtime – all, as a family. Family worship has given way to texting and web-surfing and Tweeting. In an age of Wi-Fi and Bluetooth and iPads and iPhones and "I" everything else, many of our "I" children have lost their way. In a world that is supposedly ever-more connected, many feel ever-more isolated. Our answer to most of these problems – we've got a pill for that – prescribed, over-the-counter, or illicit.

It is ironic that we have more and more devices that render our lives easier and more pleasant, and yet the world seems to have a good deal more pain. Our text compares this ever-prevalent pain to a mother's going through childbirth. A mother exclaims the pain of birthing: "But you don't have to go through all of that horrendous pain." And then the mother is reminded of the joy that accompanied that pain and concludes it was worth it.

Similarly, God recognizes that there is much pain and suffering in our world today. He knows the troubles you've been through. God is not the Author of pain and suffering. He cares for you and me. He urges us to take heed of the fact that even the worst of this suffering does not compare with the "...glory that will be revealed to us." (verse 18).

**I can hardly wait. When I finally see Jesus, I will know it has been worth the pain and suffering. It will certainly be well worth the wait.**

## BELIEVE THE GOOD NEWS | DECEMBER 13

*"After John was put in prison, Jesus went into Galilee, proclaiming the good news of God. 'The time has come,' he said. 'The kingdom of God is near, Repent and believe the good news!' "Mark 1: 14 & 15*

---

Jesus went about preaching the Good News of God. What is the Good News of God? Does it apply to our present day? God had a purpose and mission when He came here on earth. He first came as a babe lying in a manger. The angel proclaimed the "Good News". "But the angel said to them, 'Do not be afraid, I bring you good news of great joy that will be for all the people. Today in the town of David a Savior has been born to you; he is Christ, the Lord." (Luke 2: 10 & 11).

The Good News was our Savior, named Jesus, who came to save us from our sin. He was the promised Messiah foretold in Genesis 3: 15, after man and woman fell from grace, as well as in Isaiah 53: 1-12. The message of salvation for all was carried to all of mankind from generations to generations as prophesized throughout the Old Testament Bible.

The recording of Jesus birth in the New Testament Bible brought great joy and peace to all who witness His presence here on earth. During His earthly ministry, Jesus preached the Good News. What was He preaching? Was it about Himself? Jesus never uplifted himself. It was all about His Father. Jesus came to earth to show us His Father.

God came in the form of man and dwelt among us. Jesus knew the sickness He witnessed while living here amongst us. Everywhere people needing every conceivable type of healing. Jesus was healing the crippled, the blind, the lame, the deaf, the leper, the demon–possessed and the spiritually sick; Jesus saw what sin manifested in this fallen world. He showed us the way to eternal life. God gave us His only Son to restore us back to the relationship we once had with His Father. You have only one life to spend in getting to know your Maker. Give Him a chance. You will never regret it.

The message of man's salvation and forgiveness continues to resonate today. God has one final Good News. He wants to fulfill His promise to take us home to be with Him eternally. The promise is about to be realized. He promised us the kingdom of God is very near. So near, it's just a heartbeat away. We must repent and believe His word. Now go and share the Good News of His salvation to all.

**He says the time has come for Him to return soon and that too is Good News.**

## SHOW ME A MIRACLE | DECEMBER 14

*"How long will these people treat me with contempt? How long will they refuse to believe in me, in spite of all the miraculous signs I have performed among them?" Numbers 14: 11*

---

When was the last time you saw a miracle? Was it someone cured of cancer? Was it a close call with death? Was it someone emerging victorious despite all odds? Some would say that the current use of the term "miracle" has cheapened the concept because so many events have been described as miraculous. In 1969, when the New York Mets won the World Series after a ninth-place showing in the National League the prior year, they were dubbed the "Amazing Mets" and the "Miracle Mets". No doubt, this was a spectacular accomplishment, but was it a miracle? While some religious bodies have established tribunals that rule on the specific appropriateness of the term's use, by and large, a miracle is in the eye of the beholder.

It is not important whether or not the miracle be sanctioned; what matters is that you believe the event was divinely inspired. Presumably, if the act or event is, at least in your mind, a miracle, then it should serve to strengthen your faith in God.

We as a society demand proof of every claim. If you say your product will make my teeth whiter, you better be able to demonstrate your claim's validity. We expect the same of God. It's the doubting Thomas syndrome: "Unless I see it with my own eyes, I won't believe it." Jesus proclaimed: "Blessed are those who have not seen and yet believe." It's called faith, and faith is the foundation upon which our belief set is based. It is taking God at His word without being a witness to tangible evidence.

You want evidence. Open your eyes and behold the wonders of the mountains and the seas and the deserts. Look up to the sky and witness the stars in His universe. Behold the miracle of the birth of a child. Behold the miracle that our universe is infinite in dimensions and that we have a Creator whose origin is literally forever ago. The miracles are there. God is asking you how long will you treat Him with contempt by asking Him to show you a miracle? What is it that you want? Is it healing, wealth, fame, security or salvation? What about asking Him a change of heart? That is a miracle. You can say people don't change but witness the change of heart when a person gives his or her heart to God. That is a miracle to behold. Unless your heart is renewed in Him, you will not see God. There is nothing more He could do to convince you. You must believe Him.

**He gave His greatest miracle by giving us His Son. Do you want to see a miracle, open your eyes to God.**

*"When Jesus spoke again to the people he said, 'I am the light of the world. Whoever follows me will never walk in darkness, but will have the light of life.'" John 8: 12*

---

In the beginning before earth's creation, the world was dark and void. Then God said: "Let there be light" and there was light. God divided the light from darkness and called the day morning and the darkness night. That was the first day. We have a 24 hour cycle each day with a division of night and day relatively equal hours. Some people love the darkness while other prefers more day light savings time. Jesus has also given us metaphors of darkness and light. We look at darkness to represent the ungodly, uninformed or wrong thinking. While light gives us truth, knowledge and wisdom.

Jesus said He is the light of the world. Whoever follows Him will never walk in darkness but will have the light of life. Light, therefore, represents Jesus. If you know Jesus then you have light. How well do you know Jesus? Jesus was in the temple discussing who He was and His mission with the Pharisees. The Pharisees were having trouble accepting what Jesus was saying to them. Jesus was testifying He was the Son of God. Knowing His upbringing from the lowly town of Nazareth they were shock at His bold assertions. Jesus further told them they used human standards to judge people but He depends on His Father if He were to judge. This claim further irritated the Pharisees but they continued to press Him.

Jesus told them "You are from below; I am from above. You are of this world; I am not of this world. I told you that you would die in your sins; if you do not believe that I am the one I claim to be, you will indeed die in your sins." (Verse 8: 23). This really puzzled them. They were not in the same "page" as Jesus. They operated in darkness and could not comprehend the truth speaking to them. They asked Jesus "who are you?'

This same question has been asked by all of us one time or another who is Jesus? Do you know Jesus? People will know if you know Jesus by your behavior and your actions. How you relate to one another, especially in terms of mercy, truth, love and justice will indicate if you are walking in the light of God or if you are in darkness. When you're in tune with God you can tell if a person is walking in darkness?

**Jesus is the Light of our world, follow the Light and you will never be in darkness.** To be without Jesus is to walk in darkness. You need to have the Light in your life always. In heaven there will be no darkness, there will be no sun or moon, because the presence of God will be our light.

## THE GREATEST OF THESE IS? | DECEMBER 16

*"And now abide faith, hope, love, these three; but the greatest of these is love." I Corinthians 13: 13*

---

In 1955 a year most of you will likely not recall, a popular, pre-rock-and-roll singer Don Cornell had a hit single that reached number seven on the mainstream charts. What was unusual was that the song was a religious one. Its' title was: "The Bible tells me so." Not a bad message – in those days and even today. However, there was one very important ingredient missing from the mix, and that was love. No doubt, there were more lyrics that rhymed with charity than with love. Today's verse underscores how important all three – faith, hope, and love are to being on God's "team." This is in no way to denigrate charity, but charity is derivative of love.

Let's talk first about faith. God made it clear that, absent faith, we're not apt to please Him. God voiced real concern as to whether He will find a faithful people when He returns to save us, and faith is a must for there to be salvation. Without faith, there can be neither trust nor belief in God.

Hope is a key for life. Without it, there is little to sustain us until our God returns. Amidst all discouragement, if you have Hope you can survive any gloom. Hope is what will keep you clinging on to God's promise.

Love is truly the trump card. It is the greatest of the three because it encompasses the other two. With love, there are always faith and hope. For a greater understanding of what love is (and is not), I commend to your attention I Corinthians chapter 13.

Jesus declared: "You shall love the Lord your God with all your heart, with all your soul, and with all your mind." (Matthew 22: 37-39). This is the first and great commandment. And the second is like it: You shall love your neighbor as yourself." (Matthew 22: 37-39 NKJV) Mark has a similar verse but added "strength" when pointing out all four variables from the human standpoint (Mark 12: 30). Above all else, I wish for you to experience love in its purist form. That type of love can only come from above. God is the love of our life. Get to know that type of love and you will want no other love.

**To know God is to know love. Love is God in action in our lives. Love is the greatest virtue. It is the foundation of our lives. When you love, you have accepted and embraced God. Faith, hope and love; the greatest of these is... God, who is the Author of Love.**

## **FAITH** | DECEMBER 17

*"And without faith it is impossible to please God, because anyone who comes to Him must believe that He exists and that He rewards those who earnestly seek Him." Hebrews 11: 6*

---

"Got faith?" The Bible is replete with stories of people who lacked faith and consequently failed at what they were trying to accomplish. God makes it clear: without faith, we cannot please Him.

What precisely do we mean by "faith?" Romans 10: 17 tell us that: "Faith comes from hearing the message, and the message is heard through the word of Christ." God gave His message of faith through His Son, Jesus Christ. God was faithful to us, even before there was an "us." Faith comes from listening to what God has said about His Son. God has provided us with ample evidence of His love for us.

God made a commitment to us early on, and His word is bankable. He specifically fulfilled His promise by sending us His Son. He did this as an expression of His love for us. "For God so loved the world that He gave us His only begotten Son, that whosoever believes in Him shall not perish but have everlasting life." (John 3: 16). You must believe in God in order to be saved. Belief is trust in God. Trust is a vital and integral part of having a relationship with God. Just as children have complete trust in their parents and lovers' key ingredient to a healthy relationship is trust, so should you have complete faith in God.

Faith is necessary for any relationship to evolve here on earth. Sometimes faith requires trust in evidence not seen. I remember as a child, my father would take us swimming at the beach. I was afraid of the ocean. But my father was not. He would call me to go to the deeper part of the ocean because he was there. He said he would take care of me; all I had to do was keep my arms around his neck. I believe my dad.

Bottom line: there is only One in whom you can place your complete trust and that, of course, is Jesus. With God, nothing is impossible when you place your faith in Him. He is the author and finisher of your faith. Whether or not you see evidence, you can believe in His promises and His word. He truly exists and will reward those who earnestly seek him. He will never disappoint you.

**Trust in Him and you will please Him. How much faith do you have? Enough I hope to take you to heaven and meet the Author of your Faith, Hope and Love.**

## FIRST LOVE | DECEMBER 18

*"For where your treasure is, there will your heart be also." Matthew 6; 21*

---

Do you remember your first love? Who has your heart today? As teenagers, our first "crush" or "puppy love" was probably an emotional tormenting time in your life. Do you remember how you felt? You would get butterflies in your stomach. You could not eat, sleep or function without thinking about the object of your affection. Your whole being was focused on your heart's desire. Today, your first love is but a memory.

When you became a mature adult those feelings continued but now you are supposedly more in control. You didn't act like a teenager, or did you? Your courtship and then wedding plans are more methodical and deliberate rather than spontaneous and impulsive. Soon you start a family and when the first child arrive your whole focus and family dynamics shift. The focus is on the child. You want to raise them to be godly and fearful. If all things work out you both end up growing old together as planned. Sometimes the best laid plans go awry and suddenly the script you have been following is not the script you planned with her earlier in the marriage. Soon you become another statistic in the marriage or separation of life. As we age, our values and interests changes with time.

Charles Darwin was a Christian and a zealot believer in God. When his daughter got sick, he prayed for healing. She died. He denounced his faith in God. You know the rest of his story. He left his first love.

Do you remember the tragic story of Lot's wife? She was a proud woman who persuaded Lot to remove himself from his Uncle Abraham and move to the fertile and prosperous city called Sodom. E.G. White's, Patriarch and Prophets, P. 154 the author teaches; "had Lot immediately followed the Lord's first pleading, she would have been spared. But Lot's hesitancy influenced her heart to tarry. While her body was upon the plain, her heart clung to Sodom, and she perished with it."

Guard the affections of your heart. Your heart is the center of your being. Without your heart you are lifeless and heartless. Your heart is what God wants. No matter what your circumstance is never leave God. "Yet I hold this against you: You have forsaken your first love. Remember the height from which you have fallen! Repent and do the things you did as first." Revelations 2: 4 & 5.

**Do you remember your first love? God was and always will be because He is the Author of love.**

*"So here's what I want you to do, God helping you: Take your everyday ordinary life-your sleeping, eating, going-to-work, and walking –around life-and place it before God as an offering. Embracing what God does for you is the best thing you can do for him!" Romans 12: 1 & 2*

---

The other day was like most days at work. A lot of routine "stuff" as well as a conversation here, a hallway encounter there, a coffee klatch at break time. Janice told me about troubles she's been having with her daughter, who, as if things weren't bad enough, had just been diagnosed with diabetes. Veronica is struggling with a bulimic daughter, who refuses to accept that she has a problem and hasn't been attending counseling sessions. Thomas informed me, on the QT, of course, that he was planning to retire because he can't take the pressure any more,

My brother interrupted one of these conversations with a phone call, telling me that he'd just lost a job with a company he'd been with a bit more than 20 years – during the Christmas holidays, no less. As soon as I hung up the phone, a friend called with a tone of desperation. He's been out of work for a few days shy of two years, and his prospects have gone from poor to awful. He is obviously growing despondent, and I pray that he doesn't do anything foolish. And, oh, by the way, my company is, I have on good authority, contemplating cutbacks, and I have butterflies in my stomach. Otherwise, it was a normal day at the office. How was your day?

Ah, but, you guessed it….there's good news. God wants us to take all of these mundane, everyday issues and share them with Him. Paul advised us that, when you accept God's willingness to care for you, that is the best thing you can do for God. In any relationship, there is a giver and a receiver. God is always ready to play the latter role. He loves us and wishes to establish a close relationship with us. Your problems may seem mundane to you, particularly in view of the cosmic scope of God's reach, but nothing is mundane in God's eyes. He is eager to hear from you. He lives to watch over you and to care for your every need. He loves your trivial stuff.

If you're too engrossed in your everyday living and don't want to bother God with these everyday ordinary things, think again. God wants you to share your everyday ordinary life with Him. He wants to hear all the little chatter like you have with your best friend. No matter whether the subject is inconsequential or devastating God is all ears. Why? That's what a person who is so in love with you wants to experience. "Embracing what God does for you is the best thing you can do for him!" Romans 12: 2. If you've ever loved, you know what God is talking about. Haven't you kept a meaningless photo, a souvenir or a ticket stub from a memorable occasion of your love one? To others it may seem trivial but to you it's a part of your love one.

**You want to do something for God that will please Him, bring ALL your cares to Him.**

## A LOVE WORTH CLOTHING | DECEMBER 20

*"The Lord made garments of skin for Adam and his wife and clothed them." Genesis 3: 21*

---

What a loving act from our gracious God. After Adam and Eve sinned, they were afraid God would punish them. They knew they had done wrong. They became aware of their nakedness and sewed fig leaves together as an act of modesty. While they may have deemed this sufficient at the time, God knew better and made coverings for themselves. Little did they know God had a reason for clothing them.

Despite their seemingly unforgivable misstep, God never stopped loving them. Like a loving parent, instead of spanking them or punishing them with severely. God in His compassion took several animals and sacrificed them. He then took the skins of these animals and fashioned them into clothing. God knew the season would produce distinct changes in the weather, which would affect their comfort. Through His Son, God's demonstration of His care for them foreshadowed the ultimate sacrifice He would someday make on their behalf. God in His mercy and grace clothed the two lost, trembling souls. For soon they would begin to experience hot and cold climates. God thought of everything and provided everything they would need to face the consequences of their disobedience. As God was saddened by the outcome of their error, God also knew of the promise He would fulfill in due time.

My friend Jeremy was a despondent man, whose weakness for the bottle was legend. No matter how belligerent and stubborn his behavior, he always acknowledged he was married to a saint. His wife loved him unconditionally and tolerated his drinking habits with nothing but love and understanding. Every morning when he awoke, thoroughly hung over, he would notice that he was wrapped in a blanket.

Have you ever had a parent or loved one place a blanket on you when you fell asleep on the couch or armchair? I have been both a recipient and giver of blankets. I remember a touching incident in my youth, after a long day of strenuous physical activity helping a friend move, I fell asleep on the couch. In the middle of the night I felt cold but I did not want to get up to find a blanket because I was so sleepy and groggy. Surprisingly the next morning I had a blanket over me. Not knowing mother had placed a blanket on me in the middle of the night. These small acts are a reflection of God's care. He covers us with His "blanket of love" to protect us from the elements of this world. Jesus also promised to send His Spirit when He left this world.

**Just like the care He proffered to Adam and Eve on that fateful night when they fell from grace, God is ready to show His love for you. God wants to give you His Spirit of love. His Spirit is life eternal. Won't you let Him into your heart? God knows you are His love worth clothing.**

## NO NIGHT THERE | DECEMBER 21

*"Then I saw a new heaven and a new earth, for the first heaven and the first earth had passed away, and there was no longer any sea. I saw the Holy City, the New Jerusalem, coming down out of heaven from God, prepared as a bride beautifully dressed for her husband. And I heard a loud voice from the throne saying, 'Now the dwelling of God is with men, and he will live with them. They will be his people, and God himself will be with them and be their Go. He will wipe every tear from their eyes. There will be no more death or mourning or crying or pain, for the old order of things has passed away." Revelations 21: 1-3; "There will be no more night. They will not need the light of a lamp or the light of the sun, for the Lord God will give them light." Revelations 22: 5*

---

One night, a few years ago, my mother came to my room to tell me that her father visited her a few minutes ago. Her father had died 60-plus years earlier. I asked her what she had said to him. Apparently, she was so frightened that she failed to respond to him. (Surprisingly, certain Asian cultures believe whenever a ghost appears to an elderly person, it is a sign that she will pass away within a year.)

A few hours later, my mother came into my room again and said much the same thing. I then asked her, "What did the man say? Where was he in the room? What did he look like? And what did you say to him?" Mother said he was tall, and sat at the foot of her bed. She suggested later that it indeed was not her father but rather a man, likely a Caucasian man, dressed in shirt and tie. I asked her if she felt this was from God. She said, "No!" that's why she did not respond to him. She did not believe in apparitions. The Bible taught her about spirits. However, each time I would check on her at bedtime, I would notice that she slept with her nightstand lamp on all night.

God has warned us that "our struggles are not against flesh and blood, but against the rulers, against the authorities, against the powers of this dark world and against the spiritual forces of evil in the heavenly realms." Ephesians 6: 12. They know our journey here on earth is temporary. We are pilgrims on this earth wandering towards a final destination where there will be no more pain, suffering, war, death, tears or night. Can you imagine a place where there will never be night? You will be up all day for eternity enjoying God's gifts. You will be able to visit planets in His vast universe and see His creations. You will never be tired of traveling and you can travel to your destination in a blink of an eye.

Since this incident mother has passed away. Her story on that fateful night has allowed me to ponder on what heaven will be like. I look forward to seeing her where she will no longer need a lamp to light her night. I think sleeping is a waste of time. There is so much more things to do when awake. It would seem like we will party all day and all day. Imagine an eternal party. I guess there will be no sleeping there too. For some of us this is unfathomable. But for others it's heavenly.

**Since we will no longer need a lamp to light our way, I understand the Lord's presence will be our light.** I'm already homesick, aren't you? Umm… no night there.

## PURE AND UNDEFILED RELIGION | DECEMBER 22

*"Pure and undefiled religion before God and the Father is this, to visit orphans and widows in their trouble, and to keep oneself unspotted from the world." James 1: 27 (KJV)*

---

Sometimes, it seems that there are more religions in the world than there are people. In some instances, so-called religions are established, not for the purpose of worship, but rather as a tax dodge. There are religions today that are dedicated, not to a supreme being, but rather to a concept such as man's goodness or righteousness. There are even religions – again, so-called – that are specifically predicated on the notion that there is no supreme being. Some would argue that they are not religions but rather anti-religions.

Religion is generally looked upon as an organized system of beliefs and rituals centering on a supernatural being or beings. Who's to say which religion is right and which false? Are there criteria one can use to identify the true religion that is pure and undefiled? Frankly, I am not a subscriber to the term religion because it describes a systematic reaching out to man by God. The term I prefer is "faith", which speaks of our response to God's reaching out to us.

**In today's verse, James suggests how we might best focus our religious zeal: to minister to those in the most desperate need; yet even as we serve in the midst of the worst situations imaginable, we are to remain pure.** Remember that, back in ancient times, widows and orphans were completely without support of any kind except the charity of strangers. To fall into this class meant that you had absolutely no one to care for you.

James has declared that pure and undefiled religion is best evidenced by taking care of widows and orphans, by visiting those in prison, and by keeping ourselves unspotted from the world. This is how Jesus ministered to everyone while He was here on earth. He cared for those in need.

Christ, you will recall, said that, if you did it to even the least of these, you have done it to Him. What type of religion do you practice? Do you have the true religion? Are you sure? **Do you want to know the true religion of God? minister to the neglected, undesirable and to the least of these. Show them kindness and mercy. Treat them as Jesus did. The truth of the matter we are all in the same boat. That's the religion Jesus practiced while He was here on earth. You ought to do likewise.** It was pure and undefiled religion. That is what His kingdom is all about.

## **THE HAND OF GOD** | DECEMBER 23

*"This Ezra came up from Babylon. He was a teacher well versed in the Law of Moses, which the LORD, the God of Israel, had given. The King had granted him everything he asked, for the hand of the LORD his GOD was on him." Ezra 7: 6*

---

Ezra does not come into the picture in his book until chapter seven. This was a tumultuous time for the children of God. They were being ruled by other nations. King Artaxerxes provided Ezra with a decree that all the people were to obey his orders. Ezra returned to Jerusalem to rebuild the Temple. He had insight and was well respected by the people as well as the king himself. As he registered all the men for the journey ahead, he proclaimed a fast, so that they might humble themselves before God and ask God for a safe journey for all the families and their children. Ezra didn't seek military protection, preferring instead to trust God for a safe journey, and God answered their prayer.

Ezra had a significant impact upon Jerusalem's culture. He recognized that his people were influenced by the lifestyles of other nations through intermarriage. This had been specifically forbidden by the LORD; for He knew they would pick up habits and practices that were contrary to God's way. Are you grounded like Ezra in the knowledge of God? But if you are in a marriage where your faiths are different or missing altogether, hold fast to God and He will guide your journey.

I have a dear friend who was married to a non-believer. As much as she prayed to God and hope that he would convert he continued to distant himself from her church and her God. There were days when she was discouraged and her faith in God waned. But she would not let go of her trust in God. She never pushed him or lectured to him. She continued to show her love and care for him. Last year, on Christmas weekend, he surprised her and announced he wanted to join her faith and be baptized. She was so elated. She confessed to me she had been praying for him for the past 43 years. Just as with Ezra, **the hand of the Lord her God was on him and her all these years.** The Spirit of God was wooing her husband patiently all these years. Are you waiting for God's return?

Trust in the Lord, for His promises are sure. It doesn't matter how long it takes before you realize your answered prayer, the key is the hand of the Lord is on you. God will "enlighten our eyes and give us a measure of revival in our bondage." Ezra 9: 8, NKJV. **When your eyes have been enlightened by God then your salvation would have been realized. Do you see that God has had a hand in your life all these years?**

## I WILL BE WITH YOU | DECEMBER 24

*"The Lord turned to him and said, 'Go in the strength you have and save Israel out of Midian's hand. Am I not sending you?' 'But Lord, Gideon asked, 'How can I save Israel? My clan is the weakest in Manasseh, and I am the least in my family.' The Lord answered, 'I will be with you, and you will strike down all the Midianites together.' "Judges 6: 14-16*

---

Have you ever been called by God to do His service? Can you distinguish between God's voice and the other voice? Gideon was called by God to lead his people out of bondage again. During this time, Israel did evil in the eyes of the Lord, and for seven years they were oppressed by the Midianites. But Gideon protested. He said his family was at the bottom of the totem pole of the ones most likely to succeed. Gideon counted himself as the least likely leader of his family. But that was exactly who God wanted, and He assured him He would be with him.

Whether we realize it or not, all of us are called by God for service. How we respond may be of much more consequence than we imagine. God called upon Gideon to fight an oppressive enemy. Gideon was scared, hesitant and insecure. He felt he was too weak for the task. He feared for his very life. God, however, assured him that he needn't worry. He said: "I will be with you." Before Gideon could obey, he wanted to know if it was truly God. Gideon set out to test God by laying out a piece of wool overnight and asking the Lord to make it wet while keeping the dirt dry. God accommodated Gideon – thus the term "lay out a fleece".

Are you hearing God's voice calling you for service? Are you uncomfortable with the call? Are you uncertain whether the voice you hear is truly from God? Do you need a sign as Gideon did? Are you feeling inadequate and afraid you will not succeed? Do you see yourself as the weakest and least in our circle of friends or family? Like Gideon, you're human. It's normal to feel insecure. We talk of "putting fleeces" before God, but it's better to have a simple faith that He who created our ears is fully able to speak to us. God has promised to be with us as we journey in this land. **You need not fear your adversaries. No matter how weak you are God said He will be with us, and He will strike down all our enemies**. Can you trust Him?

The angel of the Lord said on that night in Bethlehem. " Immanuel, God with us." You read this verse and heard it from the pulpit but do you really believe it? Are you for certain that God is with you? If you are uncertain then you really need to experience the presence of God in your life today. God is with us every moment of our lives. We especially look forward to the day when we can finally say Immanuel, God is with us forever. Believe it!

## CHRIST'S DAY | DECEMBER 25

*"But the angel said to them, 'Do not be afraid. I bring you good news of great joy that will be for all the people. Today in the town of David a Savior has been born to you; He is Christ the Lord.'" Luke 2: 10 & 11*

---

Christmas Day has finally arrived. By now you may have opened your presents and are relaxing with family and friends savoring the holiday. But can you picture yourself being a shepherd in the field and suddenly an angel appears. There is this bright light and a voice speaking from heaven. I think I would have been terrified. No wonder the angel said, "Don't be afraid." I have never seen an angel. The Bible says be kind to strangers because you never know if the person talking to you may be an angel.

Christmas is a season which, hopefully brings out the best in each of us. Many charities count on the spirit of giving during the season. Merchants depend on this time of the year to ring the cash registers. Diets are forsaken. Credit card limits are tested. We express gratitude for gifts that may not necessarily be to our taste or liking. People tend to be a bit more gracious and patient. It is a joyous time for all – well, almost all.

You see, not everyone participates in the holiday spirit of good will towards all. The spirit of Christmas is not a spirit at all if it lasts for just a day or a season. The spirit, if it lasts only from Black Friday (the Friday after Thanksgiving) until New Year's Day (or, as some would have it, for 12 days beginning with December 25th), is indeed a misguided spirit. Many believe that Christmas is not in fact the actual birth date of our Savior, although opinions differ as to what that date should be. Since shepherds were tending to their flock in the fields, some have surmised the season was spring. Yet, others conclude it was the fall season.

The actual date is of secondary importance. What is important is that we celebrate His birth (and in turn our ultimate salvation) throughout the year and throughout our lives. Yes, Christmas day is more than a one day celebration. The Spirit of God's day should be in our lives every day. When the last present under the Christmas is opened and the evening tide befalls your holiday remember the true spirit of Christmas, its Christ our Lord.

God gave us His Son so we might enjoy Christ's Day forever and ever. God's gift to us of His Son dwarfs all other gifts – under the tree or elsewhere. **Today, as you reflect on Christ's Day, don't stop there; carry the Spirit of Christ with you every day of the year. Every day is Christ's Day not only on December 25, but for all eternity.**

## ACTS OF GOD | DECEMBER 26

*"For whoever finds me finds life and receives favor from the Lord. But whoever fails to find me harms himself; and who hate me love death." Proverbs 8: 35 & 36*

---

It was the day after Christmas and a tourist from Britain named Jack Davidson was looking forward to some sunbathing that morning on a beach on the island of Phuket in Thailand. He happened to notice a group of Western tourists staring curiously out to sea. There in the distance, approximately one mile from the shore was a wall of white water. Within seconds, he noticed the yachts and fishing boats being tossed like tiny toys as the white water barreled to shore. Suddenly, the white water rushed with such force that Davidson started to run, but it was too late. He was caught up in its force and submerged under a vehicle, pinned and struggling to survive. A moment later he gasped for air and was freed from the jaws of death. As he climbed to safety, others were being swept away.

People of all faiths asked: "Why us? Why here? Why now? Do you find yourself asking the same questions all, most or some of the time? Do you wonder sometimes if you've somehow been singled out?

If you are Hindu, you would say this was a destructive act of one of your gods. If Buddhist, you would attribute this to karma. If you are Muslim, you would believe that all that happens is in Allah's control.

The Christian also looks to his or her faith to make sense of this. Remember Job was tested, too. Some, as with Job, will see this as a test of their faith. You may wonder where God is amidst all of this. God sent His Son Jesus to be with us (Immanuel means God with us). God was with us. Whether celebrating the birth of a new child, an anniversary, wedding or other occasion, God is with us. When tragedy strikes – earthquakes, tsunamis, volcanic eruptions, tidal waves, fire, whatever the devastation – God is with us. We live in a fractured world. It's not perfect. But God is in control. God will right all wrongs someday soon.

In the meantime, we must not lose faith in the One who love us most. What a way to show love, huh? Take a deep breath (I know – it's easy to say) and try to gain perspective. These so-called "acts of God" (an unfortunate term, if ever there was one) are NOT from God. **Acts of God are all about His love for us. It is not about tsunamis, earthquakes natural disasters or any mayhem. That is contrary to God's character or nature. He never ever operates in catastrophe.** There is another force, an insidious one that is ever present. God will eventually conquer that foe and make all things right again. Where love, care and hope abounds, that is God with us. He is with us not only now but in the future to come. That is truly acts of God.

# LOW LIVES | DECEMBER 27

*"He will reply, 'I tell you the truth, whatever you did not do for one of the least of these, you did not do for me.'" Matthew 25: 45*

---

There are only 363 more days until next Christmas. I realize it's a long way off, and you may be breathing a sigh of relief that it's over. The holidays can take its toll on us. Some family forgo their tradition of feasting and instead volunteer serving food at the local rescue mission, other give the abundance of their bounty to the nearest food bank, or even joining a holiday service in our county jail, bringing Christmas cheer to those rejected by society, much as Jesus would have done.

Our nation has just experienced what is by most accounts, the deepest recession since the great depression of 1929-39. There is an old saying that when the other guy is unemployed, it is a recession. When you are unemployed, it's a depression. Well, for the better part of several years, it's been a depression for roughly ten or so percent of our nation, and that says nothing about those who were underemployed or who'd given up on finding a job and, therefore, were not counted. It also excludes those who were employed but lost their houses, nevertheless.

The outward manifestations of need are the street beggar and the homeless person. Their needs last more than a Christmas day. The needs right now of so many less-conspicuous neighbors should be ever more on our minds and in our hearts. The truth is that, in many—perhaps most – ways, they are very much like you and me. We are all in need of a Savior to rescue us from the mess we refer to as humankind. We are, each of us, "one of the least of these" to whom Jesus refers so mercifully. You and I carry visible and invisible baggage. Some of us hide our inadequacies quite well while others project them blatantly. All of us suffer the "love me" syndrome. We want to be loved, nurtured and cared for. We long for acceptance and belonging. Some of us have never heard His calling. We are too busy caring for our own needs. Do not forget those who are crying for love. There are many who have never heard of the Good News that there is One who loves them unconditionally, regardless of their circumstances.

As you contemplate a new year, think of the "least of these" -- the broken, the addicted, the poor, the hungry, the condemned, the rejected, the low lives. In many ways, they're not much different from you and me. Think about it, we are all in need of a Savior, and the Spirit of Christmas is not for a day.

**The Author of Love commends us to serve the less fortunate with the same Spirit He evidences His love for us. That character of care and service is what His heavenly kingdom is all about.**

## A CHEERFUL GIVER | DECEMBER 28

*"Each man should give what he has decided in his heart to give, not reluctantly or under compulsion. For God loves a cheerful giver." II Corinthians 9: 7*

---

I was talking to my friend after the Christmas holidays and asked him how his Christmas had gone. He said that, as far as he was concerned, it could not end fast enough. He told me that he'd spent Christmas day with his close friends and their three boys. He brought for all. Each of the boys ended up with five presents. When they'd finished opening their gifts, each said in a slightly different way: "Is that all? Are you sure there aren't any more to open?

My friend asked what has happened to the spirit of Christmas. Its focus seems to be on presents – that is, on things – to the exclusion of the spirit of giving. My friend has come to dread Christmas. The notion of having to fight mall crowds in order to purchase presents that are neither needed nor appreciated is upsetting to him.

For decades, there has been a strong movement to put Christ back into Christmas (not nearly as strong as a countervailing movement to capitalize even more on the opportunity to make registers ring). Those of you who know your Bible know that there is no need to put Christ back into Christmas: he wasn't there in the first place. The scriptural celebration of Christ's birth is the Feast of Tabernacles, in the Fall. Christmas is derived from the midwinter solstice, when the sun god (NOT God's son ) is re-born to being a new year.

The fact is that there is an art to giving. All too often, the gift chosen is such that the amount spent is approximately equal to the amount that one's counterpart spent. Sometimes, this is done so as not to embarrass the one whose birthday or other celebration came first. However, too often it is done just for the sake of keeping even. If the giving of the gift is nothing more than a chore, a social necessity, then you have likely missed the point.

A cheerful giver is one who puts a considerable amount of thought into the item(s) selected and focuses less on the amount spent. Giving is very relational. Are you uncertain on how to be a cheerful giver? Focus on God. Learn from Him. He is the Author of Cheerful Giving. He gave without reservation. He gave His all through His Son. It would behoove you to know the Author of Giving. When you do, nothing in this world would matter.

**God is the ultimate cheerful giver. Let Him teach you how to give... cheerfully.**

## HASTENING HIS COMING | DECEMBER 29

*"Looking for and hastening the coming of the day of God." 2 Peter 3: 12*

---

Even Adam and Eve, who have passed away nearly 6,000 years ago, did not witness Jesus' coming. They are asleep along with many other saints who await Jesus' second coming. How close is God's return? John the revelator says it's soon. When we look at the definition of soon the dictionary tell us; in the near future, promptly, early, readily. Even Jesus says He doesn't know when He will return. He confesses only His Father knows. "No one knows about that day or hour, not even the angels in heaven, nor the Son, but only the Father. As it was in the days of Noah, so it will be at the coming of the Son of Man. For in the days before the flood, people were eating and drinking, marrying and giving in marriage, up to the day Noah entered the ark." (Matthew 24: 36-38). Jesus gives us a huge clue in Matthew 24: 14, "And this gospel of the kingdom will be preached in the whole world as a testimony to all nations, and then the end will come."

Which gospel is Jesus talking about? Gospel means "Good News." Paul in 1 Corinthians 15: 1-8, 11 says the gospel He is preaching is the gospel whereby you are saved. Christ died for our sins; He was buried, raised on the third day and appeared to His disciples and more than 500 other people saw Him before He returned to be with His Father in heaven.

The gospel also was given in the Old Testament. Isaiah 7: 14 tells about the virgin will be with child and shall call Him Immanuel, which means God with us. (See also Isaiah 53: 1-12). The congruency of the gospel is also found in the books of Matthew, Mark, Luke and John. Are we to spread the Good News of salvation to all the peoples of the world? Yes. God wants us to have a part in the saving of humankind.

When precisely will Christ return? This year will mark the 150th anniversary of our church. We were founded on the belief of God's soon return. That's why we are called Adventist. Many are beginning to feel wary and disillusioned. Are you? Only the Father knows His son's return. We have waited many lifetimes, but one thing is for sure: God's word is true. He has never failed in His promise. He is coming again soon. As Jesus trusted in His Father when He was here on earth, we are to do likewise. Until then, what matters is that we live a Christ-like life and share that life with others. Whether we see Jesus' return in our lifetime or in the lifetime to come, all the wait will be worth it when we are united with our loved ones, especially our Redeemer.

**We have a part in hastening the coming of the day of God. How you ask? By sharing the Good News of His saving grace! What are you waiting for? Start by receiving His Spirit in your heart so you can love and forgive your relative, neighbor or foe. I am eagerly waiting His coming.**

## **A PLACE CALLED PARADISE** | DECEMBER 30

*"Then he said, 'Jesus, remember me when you come into your kingdom.' Jesus answered him, 'I tell you the truth, today you will be with me in paradise.'" Luke 23: 42 & 43*

---

There were two criminals who were crucified with Jesus on the day He was hanged on the cross. One criminal taunted Jesus: "Aren't you the Christ? Save yourself and us!" But the other criminal rebuked the first: "Don't you fear God," he asked, "since you are under the same sentence? We are punished justly, for we are getting what our deeds deserve. But this man has done nothing wrong." Luke 23: 39-41.

These two men hanging on the cross with Jesus, one on the left, the other on the right, looked at Jesus with differing perspectives and faiths. The first man was presumptuous. He all but demanded that, if Jesus were truly God, he should save Himself as well as this presumptuous one. Though those were to be his final moments on earth, he continued to doubt Christ. He knew that Jesus was an innocent man, but what he saw first and foremost was a potential ticket to freedom – a reprieve so to speak. He was a true criminal.

The second criminal recognized Jesus as the Son of God. Moreover, he felt humbled to be in His presence. What better place to spend his last minutes on earth than with his Savior. He beseeched Jesus to remember him. Jesus assured him he would join Him in paradise today. Which "criminal" are you when it comes to recognizing God as your Savior? Are you the first one who constantly needs assurances and immediate gratification in order to believe? Or do you see Jesus as your Savior no matter what your fate is in life?

We, of course, do not know when we shall gasp our final breath, when we shall give up our "spirit". However, we can know of our salvation right now, much as the second criminal on the cross was assured of his salvation. If you do not believe that, then you are like the first criminal, waiting for Christ to perform some "magic". The fact is that there is nothing more He needs to do to demonstrate His love. You too can know you will be with God in paradise today. **"Today," means your salvation is sealed the moment you accept Christ as your Lord and Savior. This is not a once saved always saved adage. This is about a belief system secured in your trust of God no matter what comes or what may. Won't you receive Him right now? You have nothing to lose but everything to gain. It's like the commitment of saying "I Do" on your wedding day.**

**The Author of Love gave His only Son so that you might join Him in paradise TODAY. Paradise is God. Claim your salvation in God right now like the thief on the cross did.**

## **JESUS CHRIST** | DECEMBER 31

*"He which testifies these things says, 'Surely I come quickly." Amen. Even so, come, Lord Jesus. The grace of our Lord Jesus Christ be with you all. Amen." Revelation 22: 20 & 21 (KJV)*

We've come to the last day of the year and the end of this year's devotional. It is difficult to say good-bye. A New Year approaches. The cycle begins anew. What has your past year been like? Are you ready for another dose of resolutions? Will your new list be better than last year's? Were you able to adhere to last year's list? Can you say you know God a little better than a year ago? It's time to ask you are you anticipating His return?

As I have explained, this devotional was a response to my late mother's desire to portray God in a clearer light than that to which we have been accustomed. This devotional book has been in the making for over ten years. During those years, I have seen the best of times and the worst of times in my life. It's been a bitter-sweet time for me. The sweet time was having finished this book.

The worst time, without question, was my mother's passing on April 21, 2007. She never saw the finished product. I genuinely wish you could have known her. It would be folly to attempt to capture her essence in a single day's devotional. But as I talk about her, it is compelling clear to me that she was Jesus Christ. I know. . .you are thinking that either I have a very big head or I am committing blasphemy. Allow me, to explain.

There was no one I ever respected more or honored and revered than her. She embodied the Spirit of God. I did not know this growing up because I took her for granted. After all, she was my mother. However, as I reflect back on the years she was with me, I can now comprehend how God loves me. She was NOT a God, she was, however, the personification of Godliness. She was a humble and benevolent woman, after God's own heart. You may think I am giving praise and glory that are due only to God. My mother was Jesus Christ on earth. She lived the Godly life of Christ. She was the vessel God used to express His Spirit of love. God knew the right mother to send in my life because I did not know God except through her. I needed a Savior who would love me regardless of my sexual orientation. God showed me His love and acceptance through my mother. I have experienced His love from countless others. Your Salvation will not be because of the scriptures you recited, the faith you have, gender, orientation, caste or commandment keeping. Salvation is because of God's love.

**Where love abounds God is there**. Reflecting back on her life, I wish I had spent more time with her. I miss Jesus. Yes, there is no doubt many others like her exists, and you would do well to get to know them because that is how you will know God. **God's preference is to use people like you and me to reflect His love.** He wants you to be an integral part of the salvation of humankind. You are Jesus Christ too. "Yea I am coming soon, Amen. Come, Lord Jesus. The grace of our Lord be with God's people. Amen."

## LOVE QUOTIENT TEST: HOW DEEP IS YOUR LOVE?

**The following test will reveal, in an imperfect manner, the depth of your personal beliefs and love for your neighbor. This test was designed to test your feelings about certain situations you may encounter in your lifetime and how you would deal with them. There is no right or wrong answers. Answer each question according to your present belief systems. Answer honestly. Don't try to analyze each question. Respond immediately what you feel you would do if you were placed in a similar situation. The scenarios or examples to these questions are hypothetical and made-up. Any similarity you may think in your life is strictly coincidental.**

**Take a blank sheet of paper and jot down your answers. Choose one letter from each question which you believe is the most loving answer. After taking the test and scoring it, there is a key at the end of this book that will reveal the level of love you have in your heart for your neighbor.**

**1. Your husband and his brother were in a successful business together. An audit revealed that your husband was stealing money from the company. When his brother confronted him, an argument ensued and his brother shot and killed your husband. Your brother-in-law was tried and convicted of manslaughter and ultimately sentenced to five years' probation. As the wife of the deceased:**
  - **A, You resent your brother-in law-and his wife. You want him to serve time in prison.**
  - **B. You want vengeance.**
  - **C. You are saddened by the loss of your husband. However, you are willing to forgive them.**
  - **D. You forgive them but will have nothing to do with them in the future.**

**2. You play the lottery and win $328-million dollars.**
  - **A. You give 20% tithe to your church and another 20% to charities and retain the balance.**
  - **B. You give half to the church, 25% to family and friends and retain the balance..**
  - **C. You give it all to help the needy and retain nothing for yourself.**
  - **D. You retain 100% of your after-tax winnings with a mind toward enjoying life.**

**3. As a wife and mother to your 17-year-old daughter, you discover your husband has been molesting her since she was seven and that she is now pregnant with his baby.**
  - **A. You divorce your husband and demand his arrest.**
  - **B. You forgive him but demand his arrest.**
  - **C. You forgive him and try to sustain the marriage. You encourage your daughter to abort the baby.**
  - **D. You forgive yourself, your husband, and comfort your daughter and care for her baby.**

4. **You have been happily married for the past 20 years. You find out that your best friend has been having an affair with your wife. This is the third time you've caught her cheating.**
   A. **You forgive her and your best friend and continue to stay married to her.**
   B. **You file for divorce.**
   C. **You take her back, provided she agrees that both of you go to counseling.**
   D. **You are hurt, humiliated and angry. You tell your best friend's wife about the affair.**

5. **You just heard in the news that your daughter, who has been missing for the past 10 years, was found. She is now 22 years old. She has a six year old daughter from her abductor.**
   A. **You are grateful your daughter was found but angry at her abductor. You want him jailed for life.**
   B. **You forgive her abductor and pray to God for strength to face your ordeal.**
   C. **You want the death penalty for her abductor.**
   D. **You cannot forgive the abductor and hate him for what he did to your daughter.**

6. **You are living in Germany during WWII. Hitler and his soldiers are rounding up all the Jews in your community. There is a Jewish family who have been working for your husband. They ask for your help to protect them and hide them from the Germans. Under the threat of killing one of your children, the Nazis ask for information regarding this particular family.**
   A. **You tell them you are not harboring any Jews in your house.**
   B. **You give up your child to protect the Jewish family.**
   C. **You cannot lie, and you tell the Nazis the whereabouts of the Jewish family.**
   D. **You tell the Nazis where they are, and you ask the Jewish family's forgiveness.**

7. **You are a healthy, robust and outgoing person in the prime of your life. It's been determined that your kidneys match a teenage boy who needs a transplant.**
   A. **You donate a kidney without hesitation.**
   B. **You decline to donate because it would be a hardship for your family.**
   C. **You are totally sympathetic but refuse to donate. You are willing to pay all expenses though.**
   D. **You are fearful of donating because, if something goes wrong, your life would be at stake.**

8. **You are an active member of your church. Once a month your church has potluck. Once a year your church holds a spring clean-up.**
   A. **You are always first to help out for spring clean-up.**
   B. **You are always first in line for potluck and first to leave before clean-up.**
   C. **You are always last in line for potluck and help clean up after potluck.**
   D. **You always attend spring clean-up. You are also last to eat in potluck and help with clean-up.**

9. You meet the girl of your dreams at a party. She is of a different religion. You date her and discover what a lovely character she has. You eventually plan to marry her. Your family and friends disapprove because of her religion.
   A. You break off the relationship to appease family and friends.
   B. You give her an engagement ring and plan the wedding date, regardless of what the family says.
   C. You decide to go to counseling with her and attempt to convince your family to see it your way.
   D. You elope and marry her, regardless of what your family thinks.

10. A. You work for a very successful company as an accountant. You have discovered a system that saves the company millions of dollars. Your boss presents you with a $1,000. reward, which you believe is grossly inadequate. To get revenge with your boss, you start skimming money. After eight years, you are caught stealing over $500,000.
   A. You confess to your boss and promise to make amends.
   B. You deny all charges and rationalize you saved the company millions of dollars.
   C. You accept your guilt and are willing to make restitution.
   D. You are remorseful, confess your mistake and accept your fate.

11. A. You found the man of your dreams. You have been dating him for nearly two years. You decide to marry and set a date. First, you must submit to blood test. His blood test reveals he is HIV- positive. You are negative. He is in the early stage of AIDS.
   A. It doesn't matter to you. You love him and will go ahead with the wedding.
   B. You are both shocked. You both agree it is best to move on with separate lives.
   C. You accept his illness. You show him you care and will be friends but call the wedding off.
   D. You break up with him immediately.

12. Your daughter tells you she has fallen in love with her college professor. He is more than twice her age. They want to get married. He already has a two other wives. He is Muslim; she is Christian. She is white; he is black. She doesn't care about his other wives. She is also pregnant with his child.
   A. You give them your blessings and accept him as your future son-in-law.
   B. You tell her it won't work and recommend she leave him. She can do better.
   C. You counsel your daughter about the hardships she will encounter, including society's backlash.
   D. You let her know that if she marries him, you will disown her.

13. You are the head elder of your church. You received a request for transfer of membership from a single man. His previous church informed you that he is a homosexual.
   A. You deny membership on grounds that he is a homosexual.

**B. You accept him with open arms and personally call him to welcome him to your church.**
**C. You offer him provisional membership. He must practice celibacy as a homosexual man.**
**D. You deny membership, based on the church principles that homosexuality is an abomination.**

**14. You and your wife are drug addicts. Social welfare has deemed you as unfit parents and threatens to place your children in foster care. You get sober but your wife refuses to stop using.**
**A. You advise her to go to a rehabilitation treatment center or you will divorce her.**
**B. You have sympathy for her, make excuses for her and pray for her.**
**C. You call the police in hopes that she will be incarcerated.**
**D. You stay with her, help her get through her addiction, no matter what it takes.**

**15. The news is full of calamities -- earthquakes, tsunamis, murders, bombings and wars to name a few. Some people refer to these as "acts of God." Still others believe in a vengeful God.**
**A. I believe, because of sin, God allows these things to happen as a wake-up call.**
**B. I believe God sent these calamities to punish the gays.**
**C. God has never sent these calamites. God is not the author of calamites or death.**
**D. God destroyed these people so they can be spared a future life of misery. The afterlife is better.**

**16. It is your first date. You believe there is a bright future with your lady friend. You bring her flowers.**
**A. You treat her like a princess. You pick her up at her home and pay for the entire evening.**
**B. You tell your date before picking her up that you prefer to go "Dutch treat".**
**C. You will pay for the entire bill after you check her out and see if she passes your test.**
**D. You will wait to see if she offers to pick up the bill and pay for it.**

**17. Romans 10: 13 says " for everyone who calls on the name of the Lord will be saved." And Acts 4: 12 "salvation is found in no one else, for there is no other name under heaven given to men by which we must be saved.**
**A. I do not believe the only way to have salvation is to know the name of Jesus.**
**B. I believe these verses to say that we can only find salvation through Jesus Christ our Lord.**
**C. I believe there will be people saved from all faiths. Many will not know the name of Jesus.**
**D. Although the verse alludes to salvation through Jesus, we must also have "works by faith."**

**18. Your best friend confides in you that he has contracted syphilis. He asked you not to tell his partner. He plans to tell his partner in his time. However, you know your friend's response pattern. He is a sex addict, and this is the second time he's done this to his partner. You're fearful for his partner's life.**

**A. You respect your friend's wishes and don't say anything to his partner.**

**B. You give your friend 24 hours to tell his partner, if he doesn't tell him, then you will.**

**C. You go behind your best friend's back and tell his partner. You advised him to get tested.**

**D. You contact his partner anonymously through a note, advising him to get treatment.**

**19. You know that your friend is having an affair. However, his wife does not know. Everyone in the community knows of the affair. You feel an obligation to:**

**A. Say nothing. It's none of your business.**

**B. You tell him if he doesn't confess to her, you will tell her.**

**C. You send your friend's wife a signed note telling her of the affair.**

**D. You tell her of the affair.**

**20. You cannot comprehend the early death of your niece and nephew. They died in a car accident. You wonder why God allowed them to perish. They were only 16 and 17 years old.**

**A. You believe it was God's will.**

**B. You blame God for taking them at such an early age.**

**C. You believe God is in charge and knows our fate.**

**D. It was an accident, and God had nothing to do with their deaths. You place your trust in God.**

**21. You have been dating your girlfriend for two years. You decide to get married. After marriage, you plan on having children. After many attempts, it's discovered your wife cannot have children.**

**A. Since you want children to carry your name, you divorce her.**

**B. You talk it over with her and decide to go separate ways.**

**C. Nevertheless, you stay with her and love her even more. You will consider alternatives.**

**D. You share with her your belief that this is God's will, and you separate from her.**

**22. You have a rebellious teenage daughter. She disrespects both of you and talks back. She sneaks out of the house and has gotten into trouble with the law for drugs and theft. She is incorrigible.**

**A. You let her go and do her thing and continue to reprimand her.**

**B. You send her to "boot camp" for treatment for her bad behavior.**

**C. You go to counseling with her.**

**D. You let the judicial system deal with her, and, when she is released, you commit her to treatment.**

23. You are the youngest of three boys in your family. You mother favors the middle child who has never worked. Your elder brother is well off. Your mother has left everything to your middle brother.
    A. You confront your mother and express your resentment toward her.
    B. You tell your elder brother what you discovered and enlist his help to sue the middle brother.
    C. You accept all that your mother has willed. You are saddened by her gesture and forgive her.
    D. You call a meeting with your brothers and try to work out an amicable solution.

24. In the final analysis, my salvation is predicated on:
    A. The name of Jesus Christ, my Lord and Savior.
    B. God's grace.
    C. My belief in God.
    D. Keeping the law of Love and the Sabbath.

25. You have lived a nefarious life. You have cheated, murdered, raped, stolen and lied. You have been considered the most notorious criminal in this country's history. You're on death row. A group of prison ministries has come to minister to your soul. You have been converted and have accepted God.
    A. You believe you are forgiven and have salvation.
    B. You still cannot be saved because of your heinous acts.
    C. You are hoping the governor will grant you clemency because of your change of heart.
    D. You do not believe your past sins can be forgiven. You repent but feel lost.

Answers to your test questions are at the bottom of this Love Depth Key.

Love Depth Key

1. Self-Centered Love: It's all about you. Whatever love behavior you exhibit or demonstrate is motivated by what you'll get out of it. Your motives are governed by what's in it for me. Everything you do and accomplish is for your glory. You're given an inch and you take a mile. You take advantage of anyone who you can dupe. You are first in line at social gatherings. You cheat if you can get away with it. You take advantage of your family, friends, community and government. You are a despicable, conniving, manipulative, deceitful, lying con -- artist and thief. (1-20)

2. Attention Grabbing Love: You do altruistic things to get attention and adulation. You will give to charity to see your name in lights. You give donations, money or pay the bill to absolve yourself of guilt as a trade-off for praise. You give presents that are beyond your means in order to stand out. Everything you do is done for the sake of self-recognition. You seek out those who will uplift you. You will manipulate the system so you stand out. You do not keep appointments well. You come to engagements late. The

**difference between you and self-centered love is how low you can go without being caught. (20-40)**

3. **Mutual Admiration Love: This is a friendship founded "quid pro quo." In other words I'll only do something for you if you do something for me in return. I'm not a giving person. What either of you can benefit from each other you will do. You want your car repaired? you go to your "friend" and you in turn give free concert tickets. This is a barter friendship based upon barter. When the relationship becomes rough and unbearable, you bail out and blame the other person. You're only a friend to the extent it benefits you. You gauge your giving to what they gave you. (40-50)**

4. **Brotherly & Sisterly Love: This is not sibling affection. This is commonality friendship. Buddies who have a lot in common; sports, school, language, culture, family, interests, children, socio-economic status, movies, profession, religion, hobbies, pets, cars, likes and dislikes. You meet for the first time and suddenly discover you have something in common. That commonality can immediately break the ice and a relationship ensues. You hang out together and make plans for dinning, cruises, vacations, exercises or the like. You love the pleasure of your company through a friend. (50-60)**

5. **Extra Mile Love: You go the extra mile. These are considered "good" people to have in your life. You will give money to the beggar without prompting. You will take in total strangers in their house and feed or shelter them. You give more than 10% tithe and offerings. You volunteer in your church or community. You are dependable. You're first to come to church for spring cleaning and last to leave after potluck because you are helper. You can be counted on to say yes when asked to perform a task. You are a doer. (60-70)**

6. **Clanging Cymbal Love: You are the go getters of our home, church or community. You go above and beyond the call. You will fight for justice, love your neighbor and have mercy and do justice. You're in the forefront of equality, freedom, liberty and justice for all. You will give their life up to obtain these idealistic goals. You are considered martyrs and pillars of the community. You are the "Joan of Arc" when it comes to standing up for the right. (70-79)**

7 **Charity Love: This is Agape love, Christ-like love. You know God and exemplify His character. You will show goodness and kindness. You will clothe the naked, feed the hungry, visit the imprisoned, care for the indigent, the orphans, the widows and the undesirables. You will serve the least and unlovable. You forgive and forget. You love unconditionally. You are "a friend that sticketh closer than a brother." You have no greater love than to give-up your life for your neighbor. You are selfless. You are all or nothing. You are giver not taker. You value nothing except the salvation of others. You live to bless others. You will sacrifice all for the good. When you encounter these types of people, you cannot help but be drawn to them. (80 +)**

**KEY VALUES: I have assigned a value for each possible response for each question. For Example: Question #1, the A response has been assigned a value of 3, the B- 1, C- 4 and D-2. Tally your total score and obtain your results from the Love Depth Value Key. Your score will reflect the depth of your love. The author of this test does not claim this test is scientific, accurate or reliable. This test was designed to provoke thinking, reflection, meditation, insight and dialogue on what constitutes the depth of your love.**



**1. A3 B1 C4 D2; 2. A2 B3 C4 D1; 3. A2 B3 C1 D4; 4. A4 B2 C3 D1; 5. A4 B3 C1 D2; 6. A3 B4 C2 D1; 7. A4 B3 C2 D1; 8. A2 B1 C3 D4; 9. A1 B3 C4 D2; 10. A2 B1 C3 D4; 11. A4 B3 C2 D1 12. A4 B2 C3 D1; 13. A3 B4 C1 D2; 14. A2 B1 C3 D4; 15. A2 B1 C4 D3; 16. A4 B3 C1 D2; 17. A3 B2 C4 D1; 18. A1 B3 C4 D3; 19. A1 B3 C2 D4; 20. A2 B1 C3 D4; 21. A1 B2 C4 D3; 22. A1 B2 C4 D3; 23. A1 B2 C4 D3; 24. A2 B3 C4 D1; 25. A4 B2 C1 D3.**

**Regardless of your score, don't take this exercise too seriously. This was for your enlightenment. If you have questions, comments or want to give feedback, you may post it on my website. In your everyday walk with God, you will encounter similar situations from the test as well "Job" like experiences. How you internalize and act on these issues will reveal your relationship and trust in God.**

**In My Personal Walk With God**

- **I have learned and understand God does not hate you. You've heard the line "God loves the sinner but hates the sin." God does love the sinner along with all their faults and imperfections. God loves the whole person. He does not separate or pick and choose which person or behavior He will love. God loves ALL of you. He is an ALL God. (Galatians 3: 26, )**

- **I have learned and understand God is not the author of death. He does not want anyone to perish. If you've witnessed death through natural causes, illnesses or accidents; God did not do that. He is the Author of Life Eternal. Death, illnesses, accident and senseless killings are the results of the cause and effect of our sinful nature, our fracture world and even our universe. God has promised: "Death has been swallowed up in victory, through our Lord Jesus Christ." I Corinthians 16: 54-58. (Genesis 2: 17, 2 Peter 3:9, John 33: 16, John 24:16)**

- **I have learned and understand God never punishes a sinner. You can produce Bible verses in the Bible contrary to what I'm saying. I don't ascribe to that thinking. You ask why? Because God deals with each of us only in love. I would rather have God's "punishment" than man's punishment. We experience punishment when we fail to follow and love Him. (Genesis 3: 9, 21, Hebrews 12: 6)**

- **I have learned and understand God loves everyone; that includes the homosexual, the liar, the thief, the godless, the idolater, the adulterer, the rejects, the** low lives, the sinner, the indigent, the pedophile, the errant priest or pastor, the exhibitionist, the murderer, the loser, the winner, the actress, the actor, the celebrity, the prisoner, the addicts, the saints, the religious, the hypocrite, etc. Did I miss anyone? Did I miss you? And He NEVER ever condemns you or me. (John 3: 16 & 17)

- I have learned and understand God is kind, gracious, merciful, patient, persevering, true and just. (Titus 3: 3-5, Colossians 3: 12, Zechariah 7: 8-10, Ephesians 1: 7 & 8).
- I have learned and understand God will not have a lake of fire that will burn sinners eternally. Our finite minds interpret the book of Revelations as the unsaved along with Satan burning eternally in the lake of fire but God is just and merciful. That is not so. His presence alone is a consuming fire. Thus, annihilation or consumption would be a better concept to understand. We must trust God that His character of love is absolutely true and just. (Romans 6: 23, Romans 6: 37)
- I have learned and understand there will be people in heaven who have never heard the name of Jesus. There will be people in heaven from all walks of faiths, creeds and religions. (Acts 3: 19, Acts 10: 34 & 35)
- I have learned and understand God will forgive any sin no matter how unpardonable or heinous the act may be. That includes the "unpardonable sin." We are forgiven when we accept His forgiveness. (Micah 7: 18 & 19)
- I have learned and understand God does not send natural disasters, earthquakes, suicide bombers, tsunamis, storms, floods, pestilence, famine, drought, calamities, sorrow, "acts of God" or tidal waves. These calamities are the nature of this sinful world. God presently relents but will eventually eradicate ALL evil and never to rise again. (Amos 3:6, Isaiah 45: 5-12, 18, 19, 22, Romans 8: 28)
- I have learned and understand we were created in God's image. With God there is neither male or female. The closer you draw and understand God you will see his nature is nurturing like a mother. (Luke 15:8-10, Hosea 13: 8, Deuteronomy 32:18)

Your understanding and love for God will only be complete when it is reciprocated. "In conclusion, my brothers and sisters in God, I bid you farewell. Aim for perfection, listen to my appeal, be of one mind, live in peace. And the God of love and peace will be with you. Greet one another with a holy kiss. All the saints, send their greetings. May the grace of the Lord Jesus Christ, and the love of God, and the fellowship of the Holy Spirit be with you all. "2 Corinthians 13: 11-14